The Kingdom
of the Scots

The Kingdom
of the Scots .

Government, Church and Society
from the eleventh to the fourteenth century

G. W. S. Barrow

ST. MARTIN'S PRESS · NEW YORK

Printed in Great Britain

Library of Congress Catalog Card Number: 73–82221

First published in the United States of America in 1973

AFFILIATED PUBLISHERS: Macmillan Limited, London
—also at Bombay, Calcutta, Madras and Melbourne

Contents

Maps

The topographical material for all maps is based upon the Ordnance Survey, 1 inch, seventh series, with the permission of the Controller of H.M. Stationery Office, Crown Copyright reserved.

Acknowledgements

All the chapters in this book, with the exception of the first, have been previously published in the form of articles in ten different journals. I am deeply grateful to the publishers and editors of these journals for giving me leave to reprint this material and for the opportunity which has thus been afforded to me of making such corrections and modifications as subsequent scholarly work has shown to be necessary. Chapter 11 first appeared as 'Les familles normandes d'Ecosse' in *Annales de Normandie*, 15ᵉ année (1965); chapter 10 as 'The beginnings of feudalism in Scotland' in *Bulletin of the Institute of Historical Research*, xxix (1956); chapter 6 as 'From Queen Margaret to David I: Benedictines and Tironensians' in *Innes Review*, xi (1960); chapter 7 as 'The cathedral chapter at St. Andrews and the culdees in the twelfth and thirteenth centuries' in *Journal of Ecclesiastical History*, iii (1952); chapter 3 as 'The Scottish Justiciar in the twelfth and thirteenth centuries' in *Juridical Review* pt. 2 (1971); chapter 4 as 'The Anglo-Scottish Border' in *Northern History*, i (1966); chapter 8 as 'The Scottish Clergy in the War of Independence' in *Scottish Historical Review*, xli (1962) and chapter 2 as 'The Scottish judex in the twelfth and thirteenth centuries' in the same journal, xlv (1966); chapter 9 as 'Rural settlement in central and eastern Scotland' in *Scottish Studies*, vi, pt. 2 (1962); chapters 12 and 13 both appeared in *The Stewarts*, x, pt. 2 and xii, pt. 1 respectively (1956, 1962); while chapter 5 was first published in *Transactions of the Royal Historical Society*, 5th ser., iii (1953). In an appreciably different form the substance of chapter 1 has been delivered as the Seton Lecture at University College London, and I am grateful to the Provost and Council of the College for doing me the honour of election as Seton lecturer and thus providing me with the incentive of putting my scattered thoughts on the Scots thane into some sort of order.

Many others, too numerous to catalogue here, have helped directly or indirectly in the making of this book. Perhaps it will not be invidious if I thank the majority of them collectively by paying tribute to the annual Conference of Scottish Medievalists, founded many years ago by my friend Dr. Leslie Macfarlane; for many of the topics and the techniques embodied in this volume have been discussed and advanced at its enjoyable meetings. If this book were to carry a dedication it would most fittingly be offered to Dr. Macfarlane and his fellow-members of the Scottish Medievalists' Conference.

G. W. S. B.

List of Abbreviations

Aberdeen-Banff Coll.	*Collections for a History of the Shires of Aberdeen and Banff* (Spalding Club, 1843).
Aberdeen-Banff Illustrations	*Illustrations of the Topography and Antiquities of the Shires of Aberdeen and Banff* (Spalding Club, 1847–69).
Aberdeen Registrum	*Registrum Episcopatus Aberdonensis* (Spalding and Maitland Clubs, 1845).
Acts Parl. Scot. [*APS*]	*The Acts of the Parliaments of Scotland*, edd. T. Thomson and C. Innes (Edinburgh, 1814–75).
Anderson, *Diplomata*	*Selectus Diplomatum et Numismatum Scotiae Thesaurus* (Half - title: *Diplomata Scotiae*), ed. J. Anderson (Edinburgh, 1739).
Anderson, *Early Sources*	*Early Sources of Scottish History 500 to 1286*, ed. A. O. Anderson (Edinburgh, 1922).
Anderson, *Scottish Annals*	*Scottish Annals from English Chroniclers 500 to 1286*, ed. A. O. Anderson (London, 1908).
Arbroath Liber	*Liber S. Thome de Aberbrothoc* (Bannatyne Club, 1848–56).
Ayrshire Coll.	*Collections of the Ayrshire Archaeological and Natural History Society* (1947–).
Balmerino Liber	*Liber Sancte Marie de Balmorinach* (Abbotsford Club, 1841).
Beauly Chrs.	*The Charters of the Priory of Beauly* (Grampian Club, 1877).

Black, *Surnames*

G. F. Black, *The Surnames of Scotland: their origin, meaning and history* (New York, 1946).

Brechin Registrum

Registrum Episcopatus Brechinensis (Bannatyne Club, 1856).

Cal. Docs. Scot.

Calendar of Documents relating to Scotland, ed. J. Bain (Edinburgh, 1881–8).

Cal. Papal Letters

Calendar of Entries in the Papal Registers relating to Great Britain and Ireland: Papal Letters, edd. W. H. Bliss and others (London, 1893–).

Cal. Papal Petitions

Calendar of Entries in the Papal Registers relating to Great Britain and Ireland: Petitions to the Pope, ed. W. H. Bliss (London, 1896).

Cambuskenneth Registrum

Registrum Monasterii S. Marie de Cambuskenneth (Grampian Club, 1872).

Cawdor Bk.

The Book of the Thanes of Cawdor (Spalding Club, 1859).

Chron. Bower

Joannis de Fordun Scotichronicon cum Supplementis et Continuatione Walteri Boweri, ed. W. Goodall (Edinburgh, 1759).

Chron. Fordun

Johannis de Fordun, Chronica Gentis Scotorum, ed. W. F. Skene (Edinburgh, 1871–2).

Chron. Holyrood

A Scottish Chronicle known as the Chronicle of Holyrood, ed. M. O. Anderson (SHS, 1938).

Chron. Howden

Chronica Magistri Rogeri de Houedene, ed. W. Stubbs (Rolls Series, 4 vols., 1868–71).

Chron. Lanercost

Chronicon de Lanercost (Maitland Club, 1839).

Chron. Man	*The Chronicle of Man and the Sudreys*, edd. P. A. Munch and Rev. Dr. Goss (Manx Society, Douglas, 1874).
Chron. Melrose	*The Chronicle of Melrose* (Facsimile Edition), edd. A. O. Anderson and others (London, 1936).
Chron. Picts-Scots	*Chronicles of the Picts: Chronicles of the Scots*, ed. W. F. Skene (Edinburgh, 1867).
Chron. Stephen	*Chronicles of the reigns of Stephen, Henry II and Richard I*, ed. R. Howlett (Rolls Ser., 4 vols., 1884–9).
Chron. Wyntoun (Laing)	Androw of Wyntoun, *The Orygynale Cronykil of Scotland*, ed. D. Laing (Edinburgh, 1872–9).
Clay, *EYC*	*Early Yorkshire Charters*, ed. C. T. Clay (9 vols., 1935–65).
Coldstream Chartulary	*Chartulary of the Cistercian Priory of Coldstream* (Grampian Club, 1879).
Cooper, *Select Cases*	*Select Scottish Cases of the Thirteenth Century*, ed. Lord Cooper (Edinburgh and London, 1944).
Coupar Angus Chrs.	*Charters of the Abbey of Coupar Angus*, ed. D. E. Easson (SHS, 1947).
Coupar Angus Rental	*Rental Book of the Cistercian Abbey of Cupar Angus* (Grampian Club, 1879–80).
CWAAS Transactions	*Transactions of the Cumberland and Westmorland Antiquarian and Archaeological Society.*
Dowden, *Bishops*	J. Dowden, *The Bishops of Scotland* (Glasgow, 1912).
Dryburgh Liber	*Liber S. Marie de Dryburgh* (Bannatyne Club, 1847).

Dumfriesshire Trans. — *Transactions of the Dumfriesshire and Galloway Natural History and Antiquarian Society* (1862–).

Dunbar, *Scot. Kings* — A. H. Dunbar, *Scottish Kings: A Revised Chronology of Scottish History 1005–1625*, 2nd edition (Edinburgh, 1906).

Dunfermline Court Bk. — *Regality of Dunfermline Court Book 1531–1538*, edd. J. M. Webster and A. A. M. Duncan (Dunfermline, 1953).

Dunfermline Registrum — *Registrum de Dunfermelyn* (Bannatyne Club, 1842).

Dunkeld Rentale [*Dunk. Rent.*] — *Rentale Dunkeldense* (SHS, 1915).

Easson, *Religious Houses* — D. E. Easson, *Medieval Religious Houses Scotland* (London, 1947).

Exchequer Rolls — *The Exchequer Rolls of Scotland*, edd. J. Stuart and others (Edinburgh, 1878–1908).

Family of Rose — *A Genealogical Deduction of the Family of Rose of Kilravock* (Spalding Club, 1848).

Farrer, *EYC* — *Early Yorkshire Charters, etc.*, ed. W. Farrer (3 vols., 1914–16; index by C. T. and E. M. Clay, 1942).

Ferrerius, *Historia* — *Ferrerii Historia Abbatum de Kynlos* (Bannatyne Club, 1839).

Fife Court Bk. — *The Sheriff Court Book of Fife 1515–22*, ed. W. C. Dickinson (SHS, 1928).

Foedera — *Foedera, Conventiones, Litterae et Cuiuscunque Generis Acta Publica*, ed. T. Rymer, Record Commission edition (London, 1816–69).

Fraser, *Douglas* — W. Fraser, *The Douglas Book* (Edinburgh, 1885).

Fraser Facsimiles	*Facsimiles of Scottish Charters and Letters prepared by Sir William Fraser* (Edinburgh, 1903).
Fraser, *Grant*	W. Fraser, *The Chiefs of Grant* (Edinburgh, 1883).
Fraser, *Lennox*	W. Fraser, *The Lennox* (Edinburgh, 1874).
Fraser, *Southesk*	W. Fraser, *History of the Carnegies, Earls of Southesk, and of their Kindred* (Edinburgh, 1867).
Gesta Henrici	*Gesta Regis Henrici Secundi Benedicti Abbatis*, ed. W. Stubbs (Rolls Ser., 2 vols., 1867).
Glasgow Registrum	*Registrum Episcopatus Glasguensis* (Bannatyne and Maitland Clubs, 1843).
Highland Papers	*Highland Papers*, ed. J. R. N. Macphail (SHS, 1914–34).
Hist. Mon. Comm. (Orkney)	*Reports of the Royal Commission on Ancient and Historical Monuments and Constructions of Scotland*, e.g. *Orkney* (Edinburgh, 1909–).
Hist. MSS. Comm.	*Reports of the Royal Commission on Historical Manuscripts* (London, 1870–).
Holyrood Liber	*Liber Cartarum Sancte Crucis* (Bannatyne Club, 1840).
Inchaffray Chrs.	*Charters, Bulls and other Documents relating to the Abbey of Inchaffray* (SHS, 1908).
Inchaffray Liber	*Liber Insule Missarum* (Bannatyne Club, 1847).
Inchcolm Chrs.	*Charters of the Abbey of Inchcolm*, edd. D. E. Easson and A. Macdonald (SHS, 1938).
Innes Review	*The Innes Review* (1950–).

Retours   *Inquisitionum ad Capellam Domini
                               Regis Retornatarum, quae in publi-
                               cis archivis Scotiae adhuc servantur,
                               Abbreviatio*, ed. T. Thomson
                               (1811–16).

Instrumenta Publica   *Instrumenta Publica sive Processus
                               super Fidelitatibus et Homagiis
                               Scotorum Domino Regi Angliae
                               Factis 1291–96* (Bannatyne Club,
                               1834).

Keith, *Bishops*   R. Keith, *An Historical Catalogue of
                               the Scottish Bishops*, ed. M. Russel
                               (Edinburgh, 1824).

Kelso Liber   *Liber S. Marie de Calchou* (Banna-
                               tyne Club, 1846).

Kinloss Recs.   *Records of the Monastery of Kinloss.*
                               ed. J. Stuart (Edinburgh, 1872),

Laing Chrs.   *Calendar of the Laing Charters 854–
                               1837*, ed. J. Anderson (Edin-
                               burgh, 1899).

Lawrie, *Charters*   *Early Scottish Charters prior to 1153*, ed.
                               A. C. Lawrie (Glasgow, 1905).

Lennox Cartularium   *Cartularium Comitatus de Levenax*
                               (Maitland Club, 1833).

Lindores Chartulary   *Chartulary of the Abbey of Lindores*
                               (SHS, 1903).

Lindores Liber   *Liber Sancte Marie de Lundoris*
                               (Abbotsford Club, 1841).

Macfarlane, *Genealogical Coll.* *Genealogical Collections concerning
                               Families in Scotland made by
                               Walter Macfarlane* (SHS, 1900).

Macfarlane, *Geographical Coll.* *Geographical Collections relating to
                               Scotland made by Walter Mac-
                               farlane* (SHS, 1906–8).

May Recs.   *Records of the Priory of the Isle of
                               May*, ed. J. Stuart (Edinburgh,
                               1868).

Melrose Liber   *Liber Sancte Marie de Melros* (Ban-
  [*Melr. Lib.*]   natyne Club, 1837).

Midlothian Chrs.

Moncreiffs

Moray Registrum

Morton Registrum

Munro Writs

Nat. MSS. Scot.

Newbattle Registrum

North Berwick Carte

Northumberland County History

Old Edinburgh Bk.

Origines Parochiales

Paisley Registrum

Palgrave, Docs. Hist. Scot.

Panmure Registrum

Perth Blackfriars

Charters of the Hospital of Soltre, of Trinity College, Edinburgh, and other Collegiate Churches in Midlothian (Bannatyne Club, 1861).

The Moncreiffs and the Moncreiffes, edd. F. Moncreiff and W. Moncreiffe (Edinburgh, 1929).

Registrum Episcopatus Moraviensis (Bannatyne Club, 1837).

Registrum Honoris de Morton (Bannatyne Club, 1853).

Calendar of Writs of Munro of Foulis 1299–1823, ed. C. T. McInnes (SRS, 1940).

Facsimiles of the National Manuscripts of Scotland (London, 1867–71).

Registrum S. Marie de Neubotle (Bannatyne Club, 1849).

Carte Monialium de Northberwic (Bannatyne Club, 1847).

A History of the County of Northumberland (Northumberland County History Committee, 15 vols., 1893–1940).

The Book of the Old Edinburgh Club (1908–).

Origines Parochiales Scotiae (Bannatyne Club, 1851–5).

Registrum Monasterii de Passelet (Maitland Club, 1832: New Club, 1877).

Documents and Records illustrating the History of Scotland, ed. F. Palgrave (London, 1837).

Registrum de Panmure, ed. J. Stuart (Edinburgh, 1874).

The Blackfriars of Perth, ed. R. Milne (Edinburgh, 1893).

PSAS

Proceedings of the Society of Antiquaries of Scotland (1851–).

Raine, *North Durham*

Appendix to J. Raine, *The History and Antiquities of North Durham* (London, 1852).

Reeves, *Culdees*

W. Reeves, *The Culdees of the British Islands* (Dublin, 1864).

Reg. Brieves

The Register of Brieves, ed. Lord Cooper (Stair Society, 1946).

RRS

Regesta Regum Scottorum, edd. G. W. S. Barrow and others (Edinburgh, vol. i, 1960; vol. ii, 1971; in progress).

Regiam Maj.

Regiam Majestatem and Quoniam Attachiamenta, ed. Lord Cooper (Stair Society, 1947).

Reg. Mag. Sig.

Registrum Magni Sigilli Regum Scotorum, edd. J. M. Thomson and others (Edinburgh, 1882–1914).

Robertson, *Concilia*

Concilia Scotiae (Half Title: *Statuta Ecclesiae Scoticanae*), ed. J. Robertson (Bannatyne Club, 1866).

Rot. Scot.

Rotuli Scotiae in Turri Londinensi et in Domo Capitulari Westmonasteriensi Asservati, edd. D. Macpherson and others (1814–19).

St. Andrews Liber

Liber Cartarum Prioratus Sancti Andree in Scotia (Bannatyne Club, 1841).

Scalacronica

Scalacronica, by Sir Thomas Gray of Heton Knight (Maitland Club, 1836).

Scone Liber

Liber Ecclesie de Scon (Bannatyne and Maitland Clubs, 1843).

SHR

The Scottish Historical Review (1903–28, 1947–).

Scots Peerage

The Scots Peerage, ed. Sir J. Balfour Paul (Edinburgh, 1904–14).

Scott, *Fasti* — *Fasti Ecclesiae Scoticanae*, ed. H. Scott, revised edition (Edinburgh, 1915–).

SHS Misc. — *The Miscellany of the Scottish History Society* (SHS, 1893–).

Spalding Misc. — *Miscellany of the Spalding Club* (Spalding Club, 1841–52).

Stevenson, *Documents* — *Documents Illustrative of the History of Scotland 1286–1306*, ed. J. Stevenson (Edinburgh, 1870).

Stevenson, *Illustrations* — *Illustrations of Scottish History from the Twelfth to the Sixteenth Century*, ed. J. Stevenson (Maitland Club, 1834).

Stones, *Documents* — *Anglo-Scottish Relations, 1174–1328. Some selected documents*, ed. E. L. G. Stones (1965; reprinted photographically with new pagination, 1970).

Symeon of Durham — *Symeonis monachi opera omnia*, ed. T. Arnold (Rolls Ser., 2 vols., 1882–5).

Vet. Mon. — *Vetera Monumenta Hibernorum et Scotorum Historiam Illustrantia*, ed. A. Theiner (Rome, 1864).

VCH — *Victoria History of the Counties of England* (1900–).

Watson, *CPNS* — W. Watson, *The history of the Celtic Place-Names of Scotland* (Edinburgh, 1926).

Watt, *Fasti* — D. E. R. Watt, *Fasti Ecclesiae Scoticanae Medii Aevi ad annum 1638* (Second draft, 1969).

Wigtown Charter Chest — *Charter Chest of the Earldom of Wigtown* (SRS, 1910).

Yester Writs — *Calendar of Writs preserved at Yester House 1166–1503*, edd. C. C. H. Harvey and J. Macleod (SRS, 1930).

Introduction

No book which concentrates on Scottish history in the twelfth and thirteenth centuries may claim any monopoly of the title 'kingdom of the Scots'. The history of that kingdom stretches back for over six centuries before the reign of Malcolm III (1058–93), and an equal span separates us from the death of Robert I in 1329. Today the kingdom of Scotland may be thought of as only a ghost or shadow of its former self. Nevertheless, constitutionally speaking it still exists, subsumed like its sister kingdom of England within the United Kingdom. Its survival is recognised in many different ways, perhaps most strikingly by the second official act performed by each successive British sovereign, the taking of an oath to preserve and maintain the protestant religion and presbyterian church government in Scotland. But for most of those who have ever given the matter a thought the words 'kingdom of the Scots' suggest something remote, even essentially medieval. Such a view would be understandable, even though unjust, for the period in which Scotland took its place as a well-known and well-defined minor kingdom of north-western Europe was the three centuries which began with Robert I's reign (1306–29) and ended with the death of that sixth King James who became the first of England (1625). The constitution of the later medieval kingdom and the pattern of its society were derived in remarkably full measure from developments which took place in Scotland between the end of the eleventh and the start of the fourteenth century. That was in truth a formative period, when Scotland acquired the characteristics which enabled her to enter fully into the comity of medieval Christendom. These characteristics included a monarchy which, even if it retained anomalous features, was nevertheless of a recognisably continental type, a feudal organisation of aristocratic landholding and military service, definitive boundaries not only in the geographical sense but also in the growth of a

constitution and a body of settled law and custom, urban communities which balanced lord's power against burgess right and
traders' privilege, and a church based upon territorial dioceses
and parishes, fortified by many of the religious orders familiar
throughout western Europe.

It is the acquisition of these characteristics that provides the
dominant theme of the essays which make up this book. Although
the monarchy is not examined directly, it appears again and again
as a force in Scottish affairs which could never be ignored,
directing, encouraging, inhibiting, dispensing patronage, occasionally meeting some obstacle of external power or ancient
custom which it could not surmount. Among its instruments of
government inherited from an earlier age the *judex* (chapter 2)
emphasises the customary quality of native law and the provincial
basis of social organisation. The justiciar, by contrast (chapter 3),
was an undoubted borrowing from Anglo-Norman and Angevin
practice adapted to the peculiar structure and special requirements
of Scotland. The relationship of the Scots kings with their powerful
neighbours to the south and their compelling need to establish a
secure boundary form the subject of chapter 4. Again, it is crown
policy which dominates the picture of early Scottish feudalism
provided in chapter 10, where we see successive kings not only
introducing a foreign aristocracy bound to them by military
service but also, significantly, imposing this new-fangled form of
social organisation upon the native aristocracy by a process which
was no less inexorable for being gradual. The broad study of
feudal origins leads on naturally to an examination of the truly or
allegedly Norman families who under David I and his grandsons
rapidly adapted themselves to the Scottish scene (chapter 11), and
then to a detailed survey—by way of example—of one of the
great complexes of feudal estates, in this case that of the Stewarts,
which were created by deliberate royal policy (chapter 12).

If secular developments were influenced by royal initiative this
was certainly no less true of ecclesiastical innovations. Indeed, to
an extent not always acknowledged the medieval church in
Scotland, the *ecclesia Scoticana*, was the creature of the Scots
monarchy. Chapters 5 and 6 lay stress on the importance of
policies pursued by Queen Margaret and her sons Edgar,
Alexander I and David I as a result of which various forms of

Benedictine monachism and colonies of Augustinian canons-regular were brought into Scotland. In this field Scotland proved as sensitive as any part of the British Isles to the newest currents of religious life which made themselves felt in the first half of the twelfth century. Obvious innovation of this kind, which multiplied across southern and eastern Scotland the abbeys and priories whose ruins are familiar to the modern tourist, was paralleled by royal support for the establishment of a diocesan system and by strenuous though unavailing royal efforts to persuade the papacy to recognise St. Andrews as a metropolitan and primatial see. Although this seemingly obvious step was not to be taken until the later fifteenth century, there was in the earlier period a general and rapid advance on the ecclesiastical front. It was inevitable that this should lead to conflict, not just with the old order but among different phases and movements within the new order. One such conflict, prolonged and at times bitter, was centred upon the cathedral establishment at St. Andrews itself (chapter 7). In the end it was resolved in typical medieval fashion (which we should be far from despising nowadays) by a compromise which allowed both sides to claim victory. The organisation of the secular clergy and the peculiar relationship which under the bull *Cum Universi* (1192) the Scottish sees enjoyed with the papacy were to prove of fundamental importance at the close of the thirteenth century, when the very survival of the kingdom of the Scots was challenged by Edward I of England. The part played by the Scots clergy in the ensuing struggle is discussed in chapter 8.

While innovation at the behest of the crown gives this book its main theme, my purpose in bringing these essays together would be frustrated if a second theme, that of continuity and conservatism, were not seen to be interwoven with the first. Scotland was already an 'old' country at the start of the twelfth century, or perhaps we should say that it was an imperfectly amalgamated group of old countries. It is indeed the still obscure amalgam of elements, Pictish, Brittonic, Scottish, Anglian and Frankish, which gives the study of earlier medieval Scotland its special attraction and fascination. Some attempt to explore this mixture of elements is made in chapters 1 and 9. No apology is made for the amount of space which the first chapter in particular devotes to evidence drawn from Anglo-Saxon and early medieval England.

The prior existence of something like a common anatomy of British society for which this chapter argues would be of crucial significance in our understanding of Scotland before feudalism. English parallels and comparisons may not be so much in evidence in chapter 9, but even here the underlying thesis is of a common interaction between geographical and social factors in the rural settlement of peoples who, however inured to pastoralism, have come to regard agriculture, the growing of yearly crops, as the dominant partner of their economic system. Continuity and conservatism are certainly prominent in the survey of the highlands with which the book concludes (chapter 13), yet we are never quite out of sight of royal authority and royal initiative. Historically speaking, the highlands were not different in kind from the rest of the kingdom of Scotland, and the ablest kings of the period, David I, William I, the two Alexanders of the thirteenth century and Robert the Bruce, all grasped the essential truth that Scottish royal government would be ineffectual if it failed to embrace the highlands.

PART I GOVERNMENT

1   Pre-feudal Scotland: shires and thanes

The historian who searches the record of later medieval Scotland for traces of those earlier, darker centuries stretching back before the days of King David I (1124–53) will soon find himself pondering two unsolved but connected problems, the shire and the thane. I shall make no attempt at the outset to demonstrate the link which seems to have existed between shire and thane: my hope is that this will become evident as the argument proceeds. If this hope be modest enough, it must be confessed that beyond it lies the larger and bolder hope that a solution to both problems may be found. It should go without saying that there will be little originality in the solution put forward in this chapter. A hundred years ago (1872) that exasperatingly over-learned yet remarkably perceptive scholar E. W. Robertson argued for a necessary connexion between shire and thanage in Scotland and showed that the shire was as much a phenomenon of south as of north Britain.[1] If I have found Robertson full of insights into *minutiae*, the broadest and most stimulating inspiration I have received has come from F. W. Maitland's *Domesday Book and Beyond* (1897).[2] Had I never read and re-read Maitland I would never have asked a number of questions which seem all the more insistent in the light of the Scottish evidence. What follows also owes much to the writings of the late Sir Frank Stenton, and especially to his essay (1910) on manorial structure in the northern Danelaw,[3] which remains the classic exposition of the English soke and soke-man. From a different standpoint, Rachel Reid's paper on

[1] E. William Robertson, *Historical Essays* (Edinburgh, 1872), 117–28.
[2] My references are to the Fontana Library edition (1960).
[3] F. M. Stenton, *Types of Manorial Structure in the Northern Danelaw, Oxford Studies in Social and Legal History*, ed. P. Vinogradoff, ii (1910), 3–96 [henceforth Stenton, *Northern Danelaw*].

'Barony and Thanage' (1920)[4] brought together the Scottish and English evidence in a novel way which illuminated both. Lastly, in this initial round of acknowledgements, I would include the late J. E. A. Jolliffe, whose detailed studies of pre-feudal Northumbria (1926)[5] and Kent (1933)[6]—avowedly following a trail which Maitland had begun to blaze—first opened my eyes to what still seems the possibility of attaining to the truth in the matter of shire and thane.

Four of these five writers may be quoted here to give the argument which follows a useful starting point. 'Frequent reference,' wrote Robertson, 'is made to the shire over all that part of Scotland which may be described as stretching from the Tweed to Inverness, and it is easily identified with the thanage.'[7]

> When we find [Maitland is thinking chiefly of south-western England] a land of scattered steads and of isolated hamlets, there the Germanic conquerors have spared or have been unable to subdue the Britons or have adapted their own arrangements to the exterior framework that was provided by Celtic or Roman agriculture. Very often, in the west and south-west of Britain, German kings took to themselves integral estates, the boundaries and agrarian arrangements whereof had been drawn by Romans, or rather by Celts.[8]

Next, we have Stenton's description of the soke, which I have taken not from the essay already mentioned but from the lucid summing up in his famous Raleigh Lecture on *The Danes in England*.

> Everywhere from mid Northamptonshire to northern Yorkshire there had arisen a characteristic type of estate, known as the soke, in which scattered groups of peasants owed suit of court, rent, and often labour service at a manorial centre.[9]

[4] R. R. Reid, 'Barony and thanage', *EHR*, xxxv (1920), 161–99.

[5] J. E. A. Jolliffe, 'Northumbrian Institutions', *EHR*, xli (1926), 1–42.

[6] J. E. A. Jolliffe, *Pre-Feudal England: the Jutes* (Oxford, 1933; reprinted London, 1962) [henceforth Jolliffe, *Jutes*].

[7] Robertson, *Hist. Essays*, 127.

[8] F. W. Maitland, *Domesday Book and beyond*, 266–7, 410; cf. also p. 377.

[9] F. M. Stenton, *The Danes in England* (1957: reprinted from *Proceedings of the British Academy*, xiii, 1928), 16.

Finally, let some remarks of Jolliffe join these seemingly unconnected threads together:

Rents and services were owed to the king, and for the reception of such dues provinces, shires, commotes, 'lay into' royal centres which were the seats of reeves. They were king's towns, *villae regales.*
. . . *Scir* and commote are not reproduced in detail in Kent . . . but in broad outline Northumbria, Wales and Kent agree. The Northumbrians called these large administrations scirs, and the Kentings had something like them and called them lathes. Some difficulty has always been felt about this word lathe; but, in fact, it is rare rather than obscure. Actually, *lathe* is the exact synonym of soke, and is used with precisely the same inflexions of meaning as the more familiar word.[10]

It seems best to approach the history of the Scottish shire by looking first at the English evidence. This in turn leads us at once to the phenomenon of soke. We might do worse than illustrate this with the example of Tottenham in Middlesex. Tottenham was something of a rarity for the south of England in the Norman age—part of a lordship of the first rank which had been held by an Englishman for ten years after the Conquest and then without a break by his widow and her daughter until 1131. We might therefore expect to find rather less social dislocation or tenurial re-organisation here than in other secular estates, more of the continuity often remarked in estates held by the church. The Domesday of Middlesex is disappointingly laconic, and on pre-Conquest Tottenham it is positively taciturn: 'In the time of King Edward Earl Waltheof held this manor. It was valued at £26.'[11] When, twenty years later, his widow Countess Judith was lady of the manor, there were 30 *villani*, 12 bordiers, 17 cottars, two 'free men' (*francigene*) and four slaves.[12] Domesday Book hardly prepares us for facts which we learn from a variety of later records. The full description of the manor was 'Tottenham and

---

[10] Jolliffe, *Jutes*, 40.   [11] *VCH, Middlesex*, i, 129, no. 96.
[12] Ibid. I have preferred 'free men' to 'Frenchmen' as a translation of *francigene* because of the existence before 1114 of Alfwin Kybbel and Ailward, for whom see below.

Tottenhamshire'.[13] Before 1114 it had been held by an English-man, Alfwin Kybbel, with sake and soke, and Alfwin had another Englishman, Ailward, under him (subsessor).[14] Ailward had certain obligations which a new mesne lord in the period 1114–24, Roger archdeacon of Middlesex,[15] was not allowed to increase. Moreover, the archdeacon must pay two kinds of rent and provide hospitality for the lord's steward and the Bishop of London. Both he and his sub-tenant must do suit to the lord's court, Archdeacon Roger whenever bidden, Ailward willy-nilly.[16] Far into the twelfth century a remarkable series of English personal names—Alfwin, Ailward, Edward (Ailward's son) the reeve, Aldred, Aldwin, Uhtred of London and others— testifies to a native continuity among the prominent men of the manor.[17] It seems that Tottenhamshire would have differed in size rather than in structure from nearby Walthamshire in Essex, otherwise called the 'half-hundred' of Waltham, with its many villani, its half-dozen sokemen, and its score or so of rent-paying tenants (censarii).[18]

Tottenham and Waltham preserve in the eleventh and twelfth centuries traces of a system of what may be called 'extensive' royal lordship, which would once have been general across a great tract of south-eastern England, from Kent to the Fen Country, from East Anglia to Northamptonshire. What sustained this lordship was 'soke', that is to say, goods and services rendered at, and directed from, particular centres, often at some distance from their dependencies. Upon this widely ramified system there

[13] Chron. Guisborough, 369 (referring to 1306).

[14] Lawrie, Charters, no. 53.

[15] Cf. J. LeNeve, Fasti Ecclesiae Anglicanae, 1066–1300, i (St. Paul's, London, compiled by Diana E. Greenway, 1968), 14–15. Roger was possibly not archdeacon later than 1121.

[16] Lawrie, Charters, no. 53. Cf. J. M. Kemble, Codex Diplomaticus Aevi Saxonici (1839–48), no. DCCCXCVII: and threo motlaethu ungeboden on xii monthum.

[17] Lawrie, Charters, no. 53; RRS, i, nos. 6, 9, 13, 34.

[18] VCH, Essex, i, 446. The name Walthamshire (Walthamscire, Walttamssir) occurs in the address of two 'chancery hand' writs of c. 1115, one of Queen Maud (D. & C. Durham, 1. 3. Ebor., no. 13 = RRAN, ii, no. 1108), the other of Henry I (D. & C. Durham, 2. 1. Reg., no. 3 = RRAN, ii, no. 1109). Compare the name Upshire, Place-Names of Essex (EPNS, 1935), 31. It appears from the address of the queen's writ that Walthamshire was an entity which had ministri, 'officers'; and since it evidently included Epping and Nazeing it may be taken to be equivalent to the 'half-hundred' of Waltham.

came to be superimposed, or re-imposed, a hundredal organisation of royal government. Amongst it all, and over a lengthy period reaching back for centuries before the Norman Conquest, there had grown up a manorial system of agrarian exploitation, whose progress was more rapid and inexorable in some regions than in others.[19] And then this whole complex situation was screened from posterity by the catastrophe of 1066. It is hardly surprising that historians have been slow to grasp the character or acknowledge the extent of what seems to have been the oldest system of political and agrarian organisation in Britain of which we possess historical, as distinct from purely archaeological, evidence. I need not dwell on the details of soke in south-eastern England, for they have been analysed and summarised for us by Jolliffe and by Professor R. H. C. Davis,[20] following up the pioneer work of Maitland, Round and others. In west Suffolk, Davis found precisely those features of mixed agrarian and political lordship which had struck Jolliffe as being common, however surprisingly, to the lathes and gavelkinders of Kent and Hastings and to the shires and free tenants of Northumberland.

It seems clear [writes Davis] that the word 'soke' as used by the Domesday Commissioners meant far more than jurisdiction. The fairest translation of it would be the phrase that we have already met, 'customs which the aforesaid land owes to the king' and which the king may, or may not, have given away to some lay or ecclesiastical lord. Sokemen *rendered* soke. . . . We believe that in East Anglia (as opposed to Lincolnshire and the northern Danelaw), socage land is not a Danish but a pre-Danish institution. It is a relic of a period when the land was divided into districts covering several villages, which were administered from a common centre and provided the King with his 'feorm' or food-rents.[21]

---

[19] T. H. Aston, 'The origins of the manor in England', *TRHistS*, 5th ser., viii (1958), 59–83.

[20] R. H. C. Davis (ed.), *The Kalendar of Abbot Samson of Bury St. Edmunds and related documents* (Royal Historical Soc., Camden 3rd Series, lxxxiv, 1954). Cf. also idem, 'East Anglia and the Danelaw', *TRHistS*, 5th ser., v (1955), 23–39, esp. 33–4.

[21] Davis, *Kalendar of Abbot Samson*, pp. xl, xlvi–xlvii.

Although we need not dwell on the details and minute variations, it will be helpful to enumerate briefly the goods and services which the sokeman, 'whosesoever man he was', rendered to the hundred bailiff or to the king's sheriff, or to the lord who stood in place of the king. The following list has special reference to the eleventh and twelfth centuries and to west Suffolk, Cambridgeshire, and, to a limited extent, Hertfordshire and Middlesex.[22] It is, however, clear from Jolliffe's work on Kent that a closely similar list would emerge from the record of gavelkind tenants within a lathe of that county.[23]

The sokeman paid a flat-rate tax of 32d.—two *orae*—for a quarter-hide, called in Suffolk (as in many other shires) 'hidage'[24] and equivalent to the Kentish *gafol*. He did carting or carrying duties (*avera, averagium*) involving the possession of horses, or else he paid money in lieu. He performed bodyguard ('inward') for the king whenever he was in the county, a duty which may have included maintaining and palisading the royal residence. Our Tottenham example suggests that we might add compulsory hospitality at this point. He provided oats as 'foddercorn' for the king's horses,[25] and at the proper season he went to mow the king's meadow. Here and there in Cambridgeshire (Davis says nothing of it in Suffolk) he performed 'heward', evidently distinct from 'inward',[26] and perhaps connected with the duty, elsewhere plentifully recorded, of 'hewing' hedges or hays, if so doubtless in

---

[22] For Cambridgeshire cf. *VCH, Cambridge*, i, 347–50; for Hertfordshire, cf. *VCH, Herts.*, i, 266–74. For Middlesex, cf. *inter alia* Lawrie, *Charters*, no. 53. It is difficult to understand why the Introduction to the Middlesex Domesday (*VCH, Middlesex*, i, 90) says that the absence of sokemen frees the study of Domesday Middlesex from the complexities found in other shires when the survey itself (ibid., 126) shows sokemen at Greenford and Ickenham.

[23] Jolliffe, *Jutes*, 32–9.

[24] Davis, *Kalendar of Abbot Samson*, pp. xxxvii–xl; N. Neilson, *Customary Rents*, Oxford Studies in Social and Legal History, ed. Vinogradoff, ii, 116–19.

[25] Davis, *Kalendar of Abbot Samson*, p. xxxvi. Cf. the important place taken by *prebenda* among Scottish royal revenues (*RRS*, i, 33), although in Scotland *prebenda* seems at least in part to have been for human consumption.

[26] *Inquisitio Comitatus Cantabrigiensis*, ed. N. E. S. A. Hamilton (Royal Society of Literature, 1876) [henceforth Hamilton, *ICC*], 40: the sokemen of Hinxton performed eight 'inwards' and three 'hewards'. 'Heward' is referred to elsewhere under Barham (34) and Tadlow (52). 'Inward' (occasionally latinised *custodia*, 59) occurs very frequently. *VCH, Cambridge*, i, 350, n.1, says without further comment that 'heward' 'seems to be merely a variant [of 'inward'] without special significance'.

the specialised sense of 'deer hedges'.[27] He owed suit to the hundred court, which meant attending it in person every three weeks or paying a fine for non-attendance. Lastly, he paid directly to keep the king, his sheriff or his lower reeves in the comfortable station to which they were accustomed, a payment known as 'sheriff's aid'. It will be recalled that Thomas Becket gained some popularity by threatening not to pay another penny of sheriff's aid if Henry II appropriated it to the royal fisc.[28]

Such a system of goods and services due from outlying dependencies to a royal centre, coupled as it should be with a regular pattern of free tenants' grazing rights and an obligation to grind their corn at the king's mill, was already far decayed in the south-east of England on the eve of the Norman Conquest. It must surely have implied, at a more or less remote period of time, some domestic or domanial slavery, or at least pretty thorough-going servitude. But it must also have necessitated a ministerial or serviential horse-owning aristocracy or gentry,[29] among whom, given customs of partible inheritance, a wide variety might easily develop not only in the amount of land held by any one individual but also in the status of the individual within society. It was thus a system ideally suited to a mixed pastoral-agricultural country conquered by a fairly primitive warrior aristocracy—as happened, we may suppose, when the 'Hallstatt' and 'La Tène' Celts, or later when the Anglo-Saxons, or later when the Danes, first came to Britain.

Before leaving southern England, there are two considerations worth bearing in mind, the first concerned with tenurial obligations, the other a matter of rank and status. In the first place, it can hardly escape notice that the east-country sokeman's duties bear a close resemblance to some of the duties listed in the

[27] Neither Bosworth and Toller, *Anglo-Saxon Dictionary*, nor *The Middle English Dictionary*, ed. H. Kurath and others (1956–) lists 'heward'. Neilson, *Customary Rents*, mentions 'haworthsylver' found at Hamilton, Yorkshire, temp. Henry VIII, citing a custumal of Selby Abbey in Dugdale, *Monasticon Anglicanum* (New edn.), iii, 512. For the duty of maintaining deer-hedges cf. *Rectitudines Singularum Personarum*, 1, 2 (F. Liebermann, *Die Gesetze der Angel-Sachsen*, i, 444–5).

[28] W. Stubbs, *Select Charters* (9th edn.), 152.

[29] Jolliffe, 'Northumbrian Institutions', *EHR*, xli, 15, writes of drengage and thegnage as a 'ministerial intrusion', but it seems to me that such a stratum was essential to the management of any demesne organised in the way described.

treatise entitled *Rectitudines Singularum Personarum*, assumed to be of the eleventh century.[30] If few historians have appreciated the resemblance, this may be because the treatise has always been studied as an early essay on manorial organisation, on the human and social economy of the manor or great estate.[31] This has been despite the fact that at the beginning of the treatise there is a statement of 'thegn's law' which expounds the thegn's duties to the king, or as we might say to the state, while later on the treatise explicitly tells us of certain other duties which are owed to the king.[32] The thegn, for example, has to build or maintain the king's deer-hedges and perform bodyguard. He must also fulfil the *trinoda necessitas* of bridge and castle work and military service: royal dues all. The largest area of coincidence occurs among the duties assigned to the *geneat*, the 'honourable companion' or 'retainer'.[33] He disposes of one or more horses, he pays *land gafol*, he leads loads, he builds deer-hedges and deer-stalls (*stabilitates*), he performs bodyguard, he mows meadows. All this, in fact, so closely corresponds to what even the sokeman of the northern Danelaw had to do that Stenton, not surprisingly, wrote 'Most plausible of all, it may be, is the equation of the *geneat* with the *sokeman* of Domesday'.[34] It does not seem to me that the writ of William the Conqueror, which Stenton adduced in explicit contradiction of his suggested equation,[35] must bear the meaning which he assigned to it. The text of the writ has survived in both an Old English and a Latin version, evidently contemporary.[36] It notifies a grant of Freckenham in Suffolk, including its *geneatas and socumen*, and the fact that the Latin version substitutes *rusticis et sochemanis* (especially taken with the fact that Domesday

---

[30] Liebermann, *Gesetze*, i, 444–53; D. C. Douglas and G. W. Greenaway (eds.), *English Historical Documents, 1042–1189* (1953), 813–16.

[31] Cf. Douglas and Greenaway, op. et loc. cit.: 'it may therefore fairly be regarded as a description of agrarian conditions . . . made by one familiar with the management of a great estate.'; or the words in H. R. Loyn, *Anglo-Saxon England and the Norman Conquest* (1962), 189: 'there were other good landlords in the West Country who took anxious care to survey their lands, and it was one of them who went to the enormous trouble to produce that little gem of social history, the *Rectitudines Singularum Personarum.*'

[32] Liebermann, *Gesetze*, i, 446.   [33] Liebermann, *Gesetze*, i, 445.

[34] Stenton, *Northern Danelaw*, 54.   [35] Stenton, *Northern Danelaw*, 54–5.

[36] T. Wharton, *Anglia Sacra*, i (1691), 336; the case recorded ibid., 339 dealt with the same land, 'which was of Freckenham [Suffolk] and lay in Isleham [Cambs.].'

Freckenham had freemen, *villani, bordarii* and slaves)[37] seems to indicate that the writ uses *geneat* not in the distinctly dignified meaning of the *Rectitudines* but in a much more general sense of 'peasant'.[38] The *geneat* of the *Rectitudines*, for his part, is easily recognisable—and has long been recognised[39]—as the *radman* or *radcniht*, the 'riding retainer' of the west midlands and the Welsh Border, who rides as escort and messenger, does some mowing and reaping for the hay and corn harvests, and plays an active part in the process of hunting deer.[40]

The capacity for survival of men of this type is very remarkable. At Langford in south-west Oxfordshire, in the middle years of the thirteenth century, we find,[41] as the holder of more than ten yard-lands of arable, for which he paid 10s. a year, one Robert Aleyn, or Aleynson, labelled 'half-free' (*semiliber*).[42] His heriot was one riding horse with its harness, he had to provide a horse and cart to carry the lord's (previously the king's) corn three days a year, he ploughed one acre a year for *grasurthe*, he did boon work three days a year with all his family, he owed suit every three weeks to the hundred court of Great Faringdon in Berkshire, and for one day in the year, if called upon, must 'ride at his own expense with the king's treasure to the sea'.[43] It is surely a nice question whether we call Robert Aleynson a rather easterly *radman* or a rather westerly sokeman. Unquestionably he was the successor of a line of *geneatas*. In a north-country context, he would have been called a dreng. Two generations earlier, Elstan the dreng of West Auckland in County Durham held half a ploughgate, for which he paid 10s. a year, performed three boonworks in the autumn

---

[37] *VCH, Suffolk*, i, 518.

[38] It may be noted that the latin version of *Rectitudines Singularum Personarum* in the *Quadripartitus* (Liebermann, *Gesetze*, i, 445) renders *geneat* by *villanus*.

[39] Maitland, *Domesday Book and beyond*, 385, 387; F. M. Stenton, *Anglo-Saxon England* (2nd edn, 1947), 479.

[40] Maitland, *Domesday Book and beyond*, 84 and nn. 2 and 10; Stenton, *Anglo-Saxon England*, 478.

[41] B.M., MS. Cott. Nero A xii (Beaulieu Abbey cartulary), fo. 94ᵛ; cf. ibid., fos. 58ᵛ, 57, 60.

[42] Among the occupiers of the soil at Wereham, Norfolk, in the mid-eleventh century were slaves, freedmen and 'half-free', these last being defined by Professor Whitelock as 'men who were obliged to render service to the lord of the manor and who were unable to leave their lord'; D. Whitelock, *Anglo-Saxon Wills* (1930), 92, 206.

[43] B.M., M.S. Cott. Nero A xii, fo. 94ᵛ.

with all his men except for his own household, ploughed and harrowed two acres, rode at his own expense on the bishop's (equivalent to the king's) errands between Tyne and Tees, and provided four oxen for carting wine.[44] We might also compare Robert Aleynson's somewhat grander contemporary, Henry the dreng of Mousen near Bamburgh.[45] Henry held of the king in chief, paid a rent of 30s., and was liable to tallage, cornage, merchet and heriot. To fulfil his obligation of three annual 'waitings' for the king (*repastus domini regis*), he had to plough once a year at the serjeant's bidding with six ploughs, cart corn once every autumn with twelve carts, and reap three days every autumn with twelve men. He must cut logs for the king and carry them to Bamburgh. On top of all this, he owed suit to the king's mill and paid for pasture rights.

The second consideration, relating to rank and status, is closely connected to the first. Anyone who has studied the information about pre-Conquest Cambridgeshire provided by the Domesday jurors[46] cannot fail to be struck by the threefold stratification of the upper or free ranks of Cambridgeshire society in King Edward's day. The first stratum we may call the non-residents —although presumably some were less resident than others. It comprised the king himself, five earls, an archbishop, a bishop, two abbots, an abbess and a handful of individuals some of whom have by-names rather than titles of office—Edeva the beautiful, Robert son of Wimarch, Esgar the staller. These persons were obviously lords and landowners of the highest kind. We are never told that they held 'under' anyone, nor are we ever told, presumably because we do not need to be told, that they were free to leave, sell or grant their land. To one or more of these potentates nearly all the lesser free folk of the country were personally commended.

The second stratum consisted of the king's thegns, not many more than a dozen all told,[47] usually but not invariably referred

[44] *VCH, Durham,* i, 333.   [45] *Book of Fees,* i, 599.

[46] Hamilton, *ICC,* 1–95; cf. also the Introduction to the Cambridgeshire Domesday in *VCH, Cambridge,* i, and the discussion of the Wetherley Hundred of Cambridgeshire in Maitland, *Domesday Book and beyond,* 164–79.

[47] I have counted ten whose names are given; in order of their occurrence in the record they are Thorkell, Ulfwin, Toki, Ulf Fenesce (Fenisc), Horulf, Ulmar of Eton, Eadric Spur, Aluric, Achill and Sexi. Of these, Horulf, Aluric and Sexi are also called 'men' of King Edward, while Achill is also called a 'man' of Earl Harold.

to by name. The record of the Domesday Inquest calls them 'king's thegns', or more precisely 'King Edward's thegns': it does not tell us of anyone else's thegns. In contrast with the great lords, the thegns are now and then said to be free to leave or sell their land, or to owe some socage service.[48] Nevertheless they may be large landowners, holding entire villages or townships,[49] and at least one, Ulf Fenisc, was a considerable landowner even by national standards.[50] The third stratum is composed of sokemen, in large numbers, often between ten and forty to a village. A few are listed by name,[51] of many we are told what socage service they rendered, of virtually all that they were either free or not free to leave or sell or grant without licence. What I would emphasise here is that of the three strata, 1 seems to stand by itself, 2 and 3 to be much closer to each other. Despite the vastly greater numbers of sokemen, the king's thegn and the king's sokeman seem to be pretty much the same sort of animal. We may nevertheless agree that the thegn is by and large freer and wealthier, and may have responsibilities, especially of a military kind, which the sokeman does not have. But some comparability at least seems to be suggested by the jurors' statement that Bourn was held by 'a thegn of King Edward with twenty-two sokemen'.[52] Even some overlapping occurs, for our record will describe the same individual as in one place the 'thegn', in another the 'man' of King Edward.[53] We also see that in the village of Melbourn the king's thegn Eadric Spur held a sizeable estate alongside ten sokemen with appreciably smaller holdings,[54] while in the adjacent village of Meldreth Eadric Spur, surely the same man,

---

[48] E.g., Hamilton, *ICC*, 23–4 (Toki's land found *avera*), 42, 50 (Horulf could grant or sell), 67, 74 (Eadric Spur likewise), 93 (Sexi likewise).

[49] E.g., Thorkell (Kennett), Ulfwin (Silverley, Wilbraham), Aluric (Arrington); and cf. ibid., p. 89 (Bourn).

[50] Ibid., 42, 90–1. For Ulf Fenisc as a pre-Conquest landowner and *antecessor* of Gilbert de Gand in Derbyshire, Nottinghamshire and Huntingdonshire see *VCH, Derby*, i, 351–2, *VCH, Notts.*, i, 248, 279–81, *VCH, Hunts.*, i, 352.

[51] E.g. Hamilton, *ICC*, 1, 5, 12–13, 24, etc. Cf. pp. 17–18, where one Wichinz is variously described as 'a man of Earl Harold' and a sokeman. He has been identified tentatively with Vikingr, a *cniht* of Thurstan, mid-eleventh century (D. Whitelock, *Anglo-Saxon Wills*, 127, 194–5). The identification would have some interest in the light of the discussion below, pp. 38–9, of the comparability of *hiredmen*, drengs and sokemen.

[52] Hamilton, *ICC*, 89.   [53] See above, n. 47.   [54] Hamilton, *ICC*, 67.

appears as one of ten sokemen who were 'under' the abbot of Ely.[55]

It is noteworthy that no class of 'free men' as such appears in Cambridgeshire survey, yet in neighbouring and closely similar East Anglia there are recorded, for Norfolk roughly equal numbers (some five and a half thousand each), for Suffolk eight thousand and one thousand respectively, of 'free men' and sokemen.[56] It has notoriously proved difficult to suggest any satisfactory criteria which would account for this distinction between free men and sokemen.[57] Suit of court will not explain it, nor a man's power of alienating his land without his lord's permission. Perhaps the effective test was whether or not the lord had free tenants under him 'with all custom'—if he did, they would be his sokemen, if he had less than 'all custom' they would be free men.[58] Whatever the truth of this, we should pay heed to shrewd and sensible observations from Maitland and William Farrer.

We may doubt [wrote Maitland] whether the line between the sokeman and the 'free man' is drawn in accordance with any one principle. When we see that in Lincolnshire there is no class of 'free men' but that there were some eleven thousand sokemen, we shall probably be persuaded that the distinction drawn in East Anglia was of no very great importance to the surveyors or the king. It may have been a matter of pure personal rank. . . . Perhaps when the Domesday of East Anglia has been fully explored . . . we shall come to the conclusion that the 'free men' of one district would have been called sokemen in another district.[59]

Farrer, dealing with Domesday Lancashire, pointed out that the free tenants of manors in two hundreds were called 'thegns', in other two 'drengs', in the remaining two 'free men'. 'This apparently puzzling classification,' he tells us, 'was mainly due to the variable names by which the tenants . . . were locally

[55] Hamilton, *ICC*, 108.   [56] Stenton, *Anglo-Saxon England*, 509.
[57] Ibid.
[58] Cf. Hamilton, *ICC*, 132, 139. Freedom did not necessarily imply freedom to sell one's land; cf. ibid., 141, for a free man holding sixty acres without such liberty.
[59] Maitland, *Domesday Book and beyond*, 137–8.

known, or to the variable terms employed by the clerks who made the returns.'[60]

What then becomes of a man's wergild, of the well nigh unbridgeable gulf which, we have been told so often, yawned between the free peasant's 200s. and the thegn's 1,200? I suspect we may have been slightly mesmerised by the tidy arithmetic of the wergild tables, which in any case come to us from tracts, often antiquarian in flavour, composed by ecclesiastics keener to display their legal lore than their knowledge of the real world.[61] A number of Cambridgeshire sokemen were priests,[62] and one Middlesex sokeman was even a canon of St. Paul's[63] (in those days a mark of standing and respectability), yet when it came to wergilds and oaths priests were supposed to be equivalent not to free peasants but to thegns.[64] The Old English laws recognised gradation among the thegnage, and scholars have noted passages in Domesday which suggest that one thegn might be the *senior* or even *seigneur* of others.[65] We may recall the five thegns who in King Edward's time each held one and one-fifth oxgangs, each with a hall, at Normanton on Trent.[66] Their combined estates were worth only 10s., and this seems to have been all they had.[67] We may also bear in mind those other five thegns of Nottinghamshire who in 1066 held between them two oxgangs at Winkburn.[68] It is not to be conceived that these bonnet lairds could have kept up the appearances of a 1,200s. wergild on the strength of a few acres of arable.

Let us turn from East Anglia and the east midlands to look at some Yorkshire estates, beginning with Sheffield (*see* Map 1).[69] Like Tottenham, this estate had once belonged to Earl Waltheof;

[60] *VCH, Lancs.*, i, 286; cf. also the remarks of C. Johnson, *VCH, Norfolk*, i, 28–32.

[61] Dorothy Whitelock, *English Historical Documents, c. 500–1042* (1955), 431–4.

[62] Hamilton, *ICC*, 47 (one priest performed 'inward' for the sheriff), 66, 89 (two priests not free to alienate their land from the church), 108.

[63] *VCH, Middlesex*, i, 126 (Greenford).

[64] Whitelock, *English Historical Documents, c. 500–1042*, 433.

[65] Whitelock, 429; H. Ellis, *A general introduction to Domesday Book* (Record Commission, 1833), i, 51; Maitland, *Domesday Book and beyond*, 182–3.

[66] *Domesday Book*, i, fo. 285, cited in Stenton, *Northern Danelaw*, 58.

[67] Stenton, 58–9. [68] *Domesday Book*, i, fo. 291.

[69] This paragraph and Map 1 are chiefly based on Farrer, *EYC*, iii, 1–24, and J. Hunter, *Hallamshire* (1819), 220–3, 269–93 *passim*.

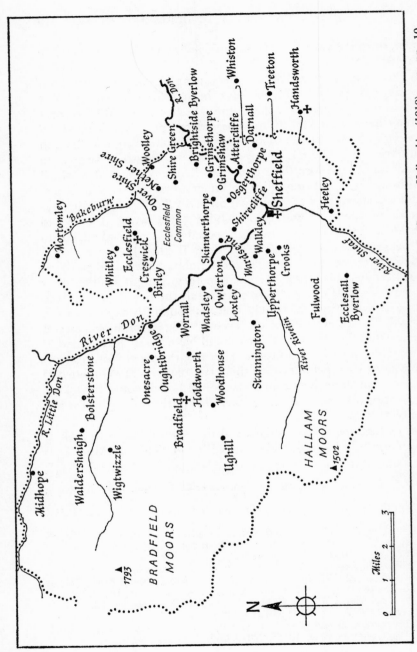

MAP 1. Hallamshire. Names from Farrer, *Early Yorkshire Charters*, iii and J. Hunter, *Hallamshire* (1819), esp. pp. 10, 220–23. It is probable that most of the unnamed sixteen berewicks of Hallam recorded in Domesday Book are represented among the names on this map.

unlike Tottenham, it was a great manor of more than one hall and sixteen berewicks. The chief hall was at Sheffield, but the mother church [*matrix ecclesia*] stood some five miles north at Ecclesfield,[70] a name embodying the late Brittonic or Primitive Welsh word *eglēs*, from Vulgar Latin *eclēsia*.[71] The estate as a whole was known as the soke of Sheffield[72] or the soke of Ecclesfield,[73] but more enduringly by a name which has become world-famous, Hallamshire.[74] At the close of the twelfth century we see the free men of Hallamshire still attending the sokemoot, paying large grassums for 'recognition', paying an annual rent by which they compounded for a variety of older services and customs, and being personally responsible for wood-cutting duties and for assisting at the lord's hunt.[75]

Turning from the West to the East Riding, we cannot but be impressed by the archaic aspect, in the late twelfth century, of those great estates (formerly royal demesne) of Howdenshire and Welton Soke, estates so large that each formed a hundred or wapentake.[76] The freemen of Howdenshire and Welton Soke constituted self-contained political, social and manorial communities bound together by court and custom.[77] They could sell their land to whomsoever they wished, they paid rents which swallowed up all kinds of older services, but they could not free their land from what the documents call 'the *utware* which belongs to the king' or 'whatever pertains to or can be demanded of drengage'.[78] In other words, as the Cambridgeshire Domesday

[70] Farrer, *EYC*, iii, 12–13, no. 1278; cf. ibid., nos. 1266–9.
[71] K. Jackson, *Language and History in Early Britain* (Edinburgh, 1953), 227, 412; K. Cameron, 'Eccles in English Place-Names', in *Christianity in Britain, 300–700*, ed. M. W. Barley and R. P. C. Hanson (Leicester, 1968), 87–92.
[72] Farrer, *EYC*, iii, 11, no. 1276; cf. ibid., no. 1287.
[73] Farrer, 22–3, no. 1295, where grantor and witnesses suggest an act which passed in the lord's court of Hallamshire.
[74] Farrer, 7, no. 1268 (Halumsira); and cf. Hunter, *Hallamshire, passim.*
[75] Farrer, *EYC*, iii, nos. 1273, 1276, 1280, 1286, 1287, 1295.
[76] Farrer, *EYC*, ii, 296–324 *passim*; H. C. Darby and I. S. Maxwell, *The Domesday Geography of Northern England* (1962), 165 (fig. 40).
[77] This is shown generally by the charters printed by Farrer, *EYC*, ii, 312–13, nos. 985, 986, 987, and is well brought out by the addresses of some *acta* of the bishops of Durham 'to all the men of Howdenshire and Weltonsoke, French and English' (ibid., 297, no. 966; 302, nos. 972, 973; 312, no. 985; 324, no. 1000).
[78] Farrer, 308, no. 980; 314, no. 988.

jurors would have put it, 'they could leave freely, but the soke remained' to the estate, i.e. to the king or to the lord who stood in borrowed royal shoes.

It seems to me that we have no warrant for believing that the shire of Howden or the soke of Welton differed in structure or in origins from the sokes of Lincolnshire and Nottinghamshire to which Sir Frank Stenton long ago drew attention, those great tracts of royal demesne, or former royal demesne, which survived as the sokes of Caistor, Kirton in Lindsey, Horncastle, Bolingbroke, Gayton Soke, Greetham or the soke of Newark, to name only seven among many. Indeed, while the earliest instance of a soke given in Stenton's *Anglo-Saxon England* is Southwell beside Newark, his three next examples are either in Yorkshire itself or just beyond its northern border, Howden, Sherburn in Elmet and Darlington.[79] 'The detailed study of Domesday', Stenton has said, 'shows conclusively that sokemen were most numerous upon estates of one particular type, consisting of a central manor with many appurtenant members, often scattered over a wide area.'[80]

The distinguishing mark of the sokeman's tenure in Lincolnshire and Nottinghamshire—as in Cambridgeshire, Suffolk or Kent—was the obligation, regardless of the agrarian arrangements of the village in which he dwelt, to render goods and services to some centre of royal demesne (or delegated royal demesne). The details of these goods and services, as recorded over a period of several centuries, seem especially instructive. There are, for example, primitive traces of military service—the sokeland of Somerby by Grantham 'rendered nothing, but helped in the king's army by land and sea'.[81] There were food-rents. Sokeland at Hickling and Kinoulton in south Nottinghamshire, at the turn of the tenth and eleventh centuries, rendered each year large

---

[79] Stenton, *Anglo-Saxon England*, 487–9. With the bishop of Durham's address to all his men of Weltonsoke, cf. Duke Conan's grant to all his men of Gaytonsoke (Lincolnshire) of their tenures, liberties and customs, *Ancient Charters*, ed. J. H. Round (Pipe Roll Soc., 1888), 54. The manner in which such vernacular names as Weltonsoke and Gaytonsoke are embedded in Latin texts is indicative of their long history.

[80] F. M. Stenton, *The Free Peasantry of the Northern Danelaw* (ed. D. M. Stenton, Oxford, 1969; originally published in *Bulletin de la Société Royale des Lettres de Lund*, 1925–6), p. 9.

[81] Stenton, *Northern Danelaw*, 29; cf. n. 86 below.

measures of malt, grout and wheaten flour, eight hams, sixteen cheeses, two fat cows and (at the beginning of Lent) eight salmon.[82] In 1088 the men of the Nottinghamshire soke of Hodsock dwelling at Blyth did the following services for the lord: ploughing, carrying or carting, making hay, cutting corn, paying merchet and repairing the mill-stank.[83] About 1142, certain peasants (*rustici*) at Revesby, formerly part of the Soke of Bolingbroke, held their land under the lord but not 'upon his own demesne' (*in proprio dominio*). Although they were apparently not free to leave their land without licence, when their lord gave them the opportunity to leave many did so. Of those who remained some performed week-work but others paid only money or food-rents or performed seasonal boons; these Stenton regarded as 'representatives of the sokemen of 1086'.[84] Again, we may compare the free tenants' services at Kirton in Lindsey at the end of the thirteenth century—boon ploughing, riding on errands, cutting and carting timber, repairing the lord's hall, and (for those settled on a tenement known as 'Gressemenlond') guarding prisoners in the local stocks.[85] In the mid-thirteenth century the sokemen of Rothley Soke in Leicestershire had freedom to buy and sell within the soke, observed the custom of partible inheritance, owed suit to the three-weekly court, and had the duty of carting the king's corn from two ploughgates of 'old demesne' to the King's barn in their own carts.[86] In Staffordshire and Derbyshire we find the free 'farmers', *censarii* and (here and there) sokemen, tenants of Burton Abbey, owing suit to wapentake or shire court, performing escort and riding service, ploughing four or five times a year, carting, mowing and reaping, repair of hays or hedges, helping in the lord's hunting arrangements and owing hospitality.[87] Domesday jurors of Worcestershire declared that by a constitution of ancient times the bishop of Worcester was

[82] Stenton, *Northern Danelaw*, 38.   [83] Ibid, 92.
[84] Ibid., 24–7.   [85] *Cal. IPM*, iii, 470–1.
[86] G. T. Clark (ed.), 'Customary of the Manor and Soke of Rothley, in the County of Leicester', *Archaeologia*, xlvii, 89–130, esp. p. 125.
[87] C. G. O. Bridgman (ed.), 'The Burton Abbey Twelfth-Century Surveys', *Collections for a History of Staffordshire, edited by the William Salt Archaeological Society* (1918), 209–300, esp. 240–2. In the earlier of the two surveys (c. 1114–15), Richard son of Godfrey is said to hold 5½ oxgangs of sokemen's land, 3½ for a rent of 10½d. *as a sokeman*, the remainder rent-free *as a radknight* (ibid., 242).

entitled to the renders of sokes and to all customs belonging there (i.e. in the triple hundred of Oswaldslaw) to his own board and to the service of the king and of himself, so that no sheriff can make any claim there, whether in some lawsuit or in any other cause.[88] The bishop of Worcester's triple hundred of Oswaldslaw was surely not radically different from the abbot of Bury St. Edmunds' eight and a half hundreds of west Suffolk.

Estates of the kind we have been considering fell into such a well-understood pattern that from a very early date a simple formula had been devised by which they could be described in landbooks and charters. This formula consisted of a place-name, usually indicating the chief hall, followed by the phrase *cum omnibus appendiciis suis*, 'with all its appendages', or, to use the term favoured by Scots lawyers of a later age, 'with all its pendicles'.[89] We find this formula from the ninth to the twelfth century, used for example in grants of the East Riding estates of Welton and Howden,[90] the North Riding estate of Northallerton,[91] the Durham estates of Bishop Wearmouth (now Sunderland), Darlington, Staindrop and Billingham,[92] the Northumberland estates of Bedlington and Warkworth,[93] the estates of Jedburgh and Melrose in south-eastern Scotland.[94] The formula was also used of more southerly estates, as far apart as Blyth in Nottinghamshire (1088),[95] Walthamshire in Essex (supposedly 1082),[96] the king's manors of Cheddar and Somerton in Somerset and the great Somerset manor and hundred of Taunton and Taunton

[88] Maitland, *Domesday Book and beyond*, 318, n. 3, citing *Domesday Book*, i, fo. 172b.

[89] *Appendicium* is glossed *geburatun* in thirteenth-century copies of what seems to be a genuine charter of the ninth century; *Chronicon Monasterii de Abingdon*, ed. J. Stevenson (Rolls Ser., 1858), ii, 26. For the Scots term 'pendicle' see the *New English Dictionary* (ed. J. Murray and others) and *The Scottish National Dictionary* (ed. W. Grant and D. Murison), s.v.

[90] Farrer, *EYC*, ii, 296, no. 964; 302, no. 974; 304, no. 975.

[91] Ibid., 266, no. 927.

[92] Symeon of Durham, *Opera Omnia* (ed. T. Arnold, Rolls Ser., 1882–5) [henceforth *Symeon of Durham*], i, 211–13; Farrer, *EYC*, ii, nos. 922, 929.

[93] *Symeon of Durham*, i, 201, 208.

[94] *Symeon of Durham*, 52, 197; cf. H. H. E. Craster, 'The Patrimony of St. Cuthbert', *EHR*, lxix (1954), 191–2.

[95] Stenton, *Northern Danelaw*, 92.

[96] H. S. Offler (ed.), *Durham Episcopal Charters, 1071–1152* (Surtees Society, 1968), 16 (a spurious charter composed in the twelfth century).

Deane (1086).[97] So general, indeed universal, was this type of estate that we can hardly doubt that it had been everywhere the normal manifestation of royal or princely lordship, the normal way in which the highest kind of *dominium* had been organised. For the northern half of eastern England we may posit a basically identical system of 'extensive' lordship to that which has left its traces in the south-east as well as in western Wessex and the west midlands. Yorkshire itself provides notable examples of ancient royal demesnes of this type, whose members (in a phrase which goes far back into Old English usage) 'lay to the chief manor'[98] —besides Allertonshire and Howdenshire, we have Driffield, Pocklington, Kilham, Pickering, Aldborough and Gilling.[99] It is worth remarking that six of these—Driffield, Pocklington, Gilling, Allertonshire, Howdenshire and Aldborough—all formed wapentakes or hundreds. In medieval and later times, Aldborough wapentake took its name from Claro on the Great North Road,[100] but in the eleventh century its name was Boroughshire,[101] after the 'old borough', Aldborough, formerly Isurium Brigantum, cantonal capital of the Brigantes. Gilling represents what was evidently in the seventh century a *regio*, to which Bede gives the name in *Getlingum*, 'among the people of Gētla'.[102]

One last diversion will take us to Lancashire. 'This country', Farrer tells us, 'may well be imagined (in 1086) as a huge manor

[97] *Domesday Book*, i, fos. 86, 86b; iv, 162. For the historical topography of Taunton see Joshua Toulmin, *The History of Taunton in the county of Somerset* (revised J. Savage, Taunton, 1822), esp. 44–50.

[98] For this phrase, used of both places and men, cf. Hamilton, *ICC*, 130, 132; *VCH, Lancs.*, i, 289; Jolliffe, *Jutes*, 40, n. 3.

[99] Farrer, *EYC*, i, 335, no. 428; C. T. Clay, *EYC*, iv, *The Honour of Richmond*, pt. 1 (1935), 116. In recent years much important work has been done on the structure of soke- or shire-type estates in Yorkshire and elsewhere by Mr. G. R. J. Jones of the University of Leeds; see, e.g. his papers on 'Early territorial organization in England and Wales' in *Geografiska Annaler*, xliii (1961), and 'Early territorial organization in Northern England and its bearing on the Scandinavian settlement' in *The Fourth Viking Congress* (Aberdeen, 1965). Our understanding of this whole subject will be carried much further forward when Mr. Jones's promised work on agrarian settlement in Yorkshire appears.

[100] A. H. Smith, *Place-Names of the West Riding of Yorkshire* (E. P.-N. Soc., 1961), v, 1.

[101] A. H. Smith, v, 1.

[102] E. Ekwall (*Concise Oxford Dictionary of English Place-Names*, 3rd edn., 1947, 187) accepts this, in contrast to A. H. Smith, *Place-names of the North Riding of Yorkshire* (E. P.-N. Soc., 1928), 288–9; cf. Bede, *Historia Ecclesiastica Gentis Anglorum*, iii, 14, 24 (ed. C. Plummer (2 vols., Oxford, 1896), i, 155, 179–80).

of royal demesne.[103] The free holders, as we have seen, were known indifferently as thegns, drengs or free men. They paid carucate geld at a flat rate of 32d.—two *orae*—per carucate, reckoned as the sixth of a hide.[104] With this we may compare the Suffolk hidage of 32d. per quarter hide, as well as the Kentish land *gafol*. They were responsible for building and repairing the king's halls, and they constructed deer-hedges and deer-stalls (*stabiliture*). They reaped for one day in August, they owed suit to the court of shire or hundred.[105] Here and there, at Childwall and Penwortham for example, we find groups of radmen,[106] as we find them in Cheshire, Staffordshire, Shropshire and elsewhere along the Welsh border.[107] The shires between Ribble and Mersey may have been larger than the shires of Yorkshire but they do not seem different in kind. Hallamshire with its hall at Sheffield and its mother church at Ecclesfield prompts us to look at the 'Eccles' names of Lancashire. They were surely not scattered about the county at random. From the twelfth to the nineteenth century South Lancashire was divided among five hundreds,[108] Salford, West Derby, Leyland, Blackburnshire and Amounderness. Eccles is in Salford Hundred, just west of Salford. Eccleston in West Derby Hundred lies only a few miles east of West Derby, the hundred capital, but in 1086 it formed part of the small hundred of Warrington, afterwards merged with that of West Derby.[109] Eccleston in Leyland Hundred is immediately south-west of Leyland. It was, indeed, the site of the three-weekly hundred or wapentake court in the thirteenth century.[110] Eccleshill in Blackburnshire is not only in Blackburn parish but was immemorially linked to the Celtic-named township of Mellor which occupies a hill on the opposite edge of Blackburn.[111] As for Amounderness Hundred, it has twin Ecclestons, Great and Little, adjacent but in different parishes, the ancient parishes respectively of St. Michael on Wyre and Kirkham.[112] The survival of 'Eccles' names in each of the hundreds of medieval

[103] *VCH, Lancs.*, i, 275.   [104] *VCH, Lancs.*, i, 270–1.
[105] *VCH, Lancs.*, i, 275–6, 285.   [106] *VCH, Lancs.*, i, 284.
[107] *Domesday Book*, i, fos. 263, 263 b, 264, etc.; *VCH, Shropshire*, i, 301; *VCH, Worcs.*, i, 250–1; *VCH, Hereford*, i, 286.
[108] *VCH, Lancs.*, i, 270–1; iii, 1.   [109] *VCH, Lancs.*, i, 270–1; iii, 1.
[110] *VCH, Lancs.*, vi, 155 and n.   [111] *VCH, Lancs.*, vi, 260, 278.
[112] *VCH, Lancs.*, vii, 181ff., 276–9.

Lancashire is paralleled, most interestingly, in Kent, where Eccles is and was in Aylesford parish, while Aylesford itself was the capital of one of the older lathes of Kent, the *locus* of a court by 961[113] and no doubt from much earlier, and still royal demesne in 1086.[114] Other English evidence seems equally suggestive. Eccleston in Cheshire, for example, is two miles south of Chester itself and was in Chester Hundred. The Staffordshire manor of Eccleshall, though it does not seem to have been in any sense the 'capital' of Pirehill Hundred, was nevertheless the centre of an exceptionally large estate with twenty berewicks. It was part of the endowment (probably the early endowment) of the seventh-century church of Saint Chad at Lichfield.[115]

As we turn from the English to the Scottish evidence, we may usefully recapitulate the main points of the argument. From Kent to Northumbria, without a break, some system of 'extensive' royal lordship, based upon a unit known variously as lathe, soke, shire or *manerium cum appendiciis*, had survived long enough for its main features to be traceable in record of the eleventh and twelfth centuries. Associated with the soke or shire, indispensable for its management, was a class of ministerial freemen. Our fore-shortened historical record uses a bewilderingly wide range of terms to describe members of this class: *geneatas*, *hiredmen*,[116] free men, gavelkinders, sokemen, *radmen*, radknights,[117] drengs, thegns. Between thegns and the rest we may allow some real difference of status and responsibilities, yet there was no hard and fast line of demarcation.[118] Otherwise, the terminological distinctions

---

[113] Jolliffe, *Jutes*, 47; F. E. Harmer, *Select English Historical Documents of the ninth and tenth centuries* (1914), 37, 67.

[114] *VCH, Kent*, iii, 208. By 1086 Eccles in Aylesford had passed into the possession of the bishop of Bayeux, ibid., 224–5.

[115] H. C. Darby and I. B. Terrett, *The Domesday Geography of Midland England* (2nd edn, 1971), 168; *VCH, Staffs.*, iv, 42.

[116] Bosworth and Toller, *Anglo-Saxon Dictionary*, s.v. *hired-mann*, give the meaning 'member of a *hired* ['household', 'body of retainers']; *Middle English Dictionary*, s.v. *hired-man*, gives 'member of a king's household', 'vassal, knight or gentleman', and 'household servant'; Liebermann, *Gesetze*, ii (*Wörterbuch*), s.v. *h[ie]redmen* gives 'Haushaltsuntergebene'.

[117] Bosworth and Toller, s.v. *radcniht*, explain as 'a title equivalent to that of a sixhynde man', i.e. a man with a 600s wergild. For the survival of the word 'redknight' into the eighteenth century cf. *VCH, Cumberland*, i, 332.

[118] Thus, in Northumberland holdings listed as thanages in 1212 are called drengages in 1236 (*Book of Fees*, i, 204–5, 598).

were surely due to changing fashions of place and time. In Scottish Northumbria the substantial free population was still being collectively addressed, in the first half of the twelfth century, as 'thegns and drengs', in exactly the same way as their counterparts in English Northumbria.[119] Survivals of this usage may be found well into the thirteenth century, both south and north of the border. Before 1256, Patrick Dreng was co-tenant of one of the two socage estates in the small township of Hethpool just below The Cheviot,[120] while another Patrick Dreng, so styled on his seal, was his slightly earlier contemporary at Renton in Coldinghamshire.[121] Norhamshire and Islandshire (see Map 2) happened to be in Northumberland and England, Berwickshire (see Map 3) and Coldinghamshire (see Map 4) happened to be in Lothian and Scotland; otherwise their polities were identical.[122] We know more about Norham, Holy Island and Coldingham, as shires, simply because they were given to Saint Cuthbert, and church estates remained unaltered over immensely long periods. Berwickshire, on the other hand, was taken back from the church and quickly swallowed up by the much larger sheriffdom of Berwick created in the twelfth century. King Edgar's abortive charter of 1095[123] is a stroke of luck, enabling us to catch a first and last glimpse of the older Berwickshire on the eve of its disappearance. As it was, the name died very hard in popular usage, for Daniel Defoe in the early eighteenth century noted that the district a mile or two round Berwick 'neither in England nor Scotland . . . is called Berwickshire, as being formerly a dependant upon the town of Berwick'.[124] Perhaps it had already suffered diminution even by 1095, for although most of Berwick's *appendicia* lay within a six-mile radius of Berwick itself, they included a group of four estates some twelve to sixteen miles further up the Tweed, one of which, Birgham, never attaining to parochial

[119] Cf. Lawrie, *Charters*, no. 30 and *Coldstream Chartulary*, no. 8 with Raine, *North Durham*, no. 727; and cf. Lawrie, *Charters*, no. 32.

[120] *Northumberland County History*, xi (1922), 267.

[121] Raine, *North Durham*, no. 382.

[122] Norhamshire, Islandshire and Coldinghamshire are fully dealt with in J. Raine's *History of North Durham* (1852).

[123] Lawrie, *Charters*, no. 15 (wrongly stigmatised as spurious; cf. A. A. M. Duncan, 'The earliest Scottish charters', *SHR*, xxxvii (1958), 103–5).

[124] D. Defoe, *A Tour through the whole island of Great Britain*, ed. and abridged P. Roger (Penguin Books, 1971), 563.

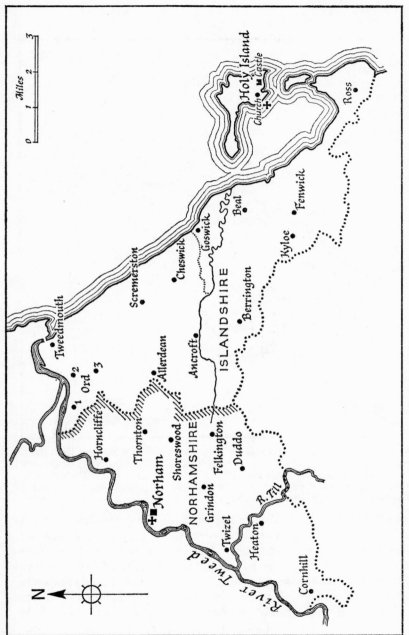

MAP 2. Norhamshire and Islandshire. Based on the map in J. Raine, *History of N. Durham* (1852), p. 2.

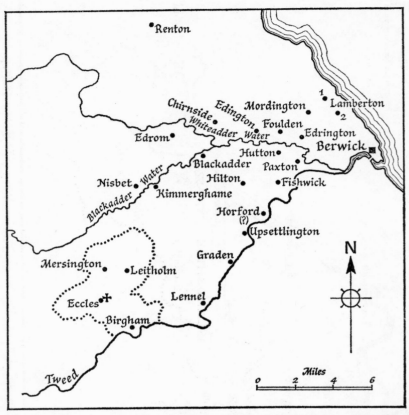

MAP 3. Berwickshire, 1095. Names from King Edgar's charter (*Scot. Hist. Rev.*, xxxvii, 104) together with Eccles and its chapelries Mersington and Leitholm, and also Edington and Nisbet. 'Clilsterhale' (*rectius* 'Dilsterhale'), although in Edgar's charter, is unlocated and therefore omitted. Renton ('Ranynton') is in the charter, perhaps in error.

status, formed one of three chapelries in the large and ancient parish of Saint Cuthbert of Eccles.[125] And if the centre of this old shire had in earlier times been located further west, nearer to Eccles (e.g. at Swinton or Kimmerghame?), it would be easier to explain the otherwise puzzling fact that the name Berwick, denoting an outlying dependency, belonged by 1095 to the shire capital. That sokes might on occasion change their capitals is

[125] Cowan, *Parishes*, 58.

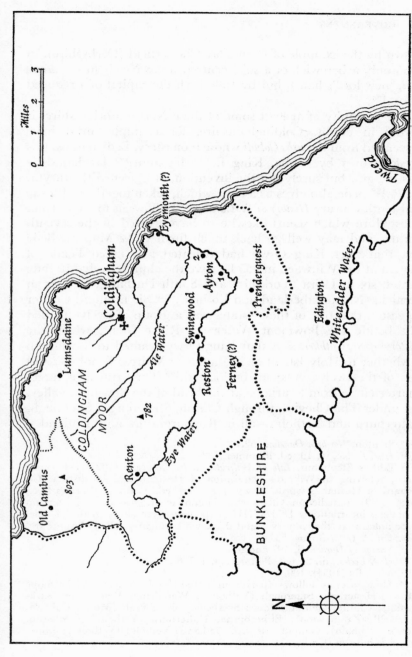

MAP 4. Coldinghamshire, 1095. Names from King Edgar's charter (*Scot. Hist. Rev.* xxxvii, 104), together with Renton (*see* Map 3) Eyemouth has been included as perhaps representing the charter's unidentified 'Crammesmuthe'.

shown by the example of Domesday Chesterfield (Derbyshire), in 1066 only a berewick of a soke centred upon Newbold (= *nēowe bōþl*, 'new lord's hall'), but by 1086 itself the capital of a reduced 'soke'.[126]

The antiquity of at least some of these Northumbrian shires is hardly in doubt. Coldinghamshire, for example, must have descended from the *urbs Coludi* whose monastery, Bede tells us, was presided over by Æbba, King Ecgfrith's aunt.[127] Hexhamshire was the gift, but surely not the invention, of Queen Æthelthryth, *c*. 674.[128] Bede also gives us a clue, which, taken together with the mid-tenth-century *History of St. Cuthbert*,[129] allows us to reconstruct a lost shire which seems likewise to have existed in the seventh century and may well go back much further (*see* Map 5). Bede says that after King Oswy had defeated and killed Penda of Mercia at the Winwaed in 655 he gave the church twelve 10-hide estates, six in Deira (Yorkshire and South Durham), and six in Bernicia (Northumberland and Lothian).[130] Sir Edmund Craster suggested that one of these estates was a group of twelve named vills beside the Bowmont Water (or River Glen), which the *History of St. Cuthbert* says that King Oswy granted to the church —whether to Holy Island or its daughter Melrose is not clear.[131] Ten of the twelve vills can be located.[132] They run in a three-quarter circle from Sourhope at the head of the Bowmont valley, just under The Cheviot, through Clifton, Shereburgh, Staerough, Halterburn and Yetholm—all in Roxburghshire and Scotland—

---

[126] Stenton, *Northern Danelaw*, 52.

[127] *Hist. Eccles.*, iv, 19 (ed. Plummer, i, 243).

[128] Eddius Stephanus, *Life of Wilfrid*, ed. B. Colgrave (1927), 44, *adepta regione*, referring to Wilfred's acquisition of Hexham and its district. Cf. Richard of Hexham's words, *Priory of Hexham*, ed. J. Raine (Surtees Soc., 1864), i, 9: 'praedictam villam cum circumjacente regione circa annum dominicae incarnationis DCLXXIII perpetuam elemosinam dedit.' Daniel Defoe noted that 'the country round this town is vulgarly called Hexamshire' (*Tour through Great Britain*, 537).

[129] *Symeon of Durham*, i, 197 and n.

[130] *Hist. Eccles.*, iii, 24 (ed. Plummer, i, 177–8).

[131] *EHR*, lix (1954), 180.

[132] These are as follows (parish in parentheses): Sugariple, Sourhope (Mow); Hesterhoh, Staerough (Yetholm); Waquirtun, Wackerage (Kirknewton); Cliftun, Clifton (Mow); Scerbedle, Shereburgh (Mow); Colwela, 'Colewell' (Kirknewton); Eltherburna, Halterburn (Yetholm); Scotadun, Shotton (Kilham); Gathan (*var. lect.* Getham), Yetholm (Yetholm); Minethrum, Mindrum (Carham).

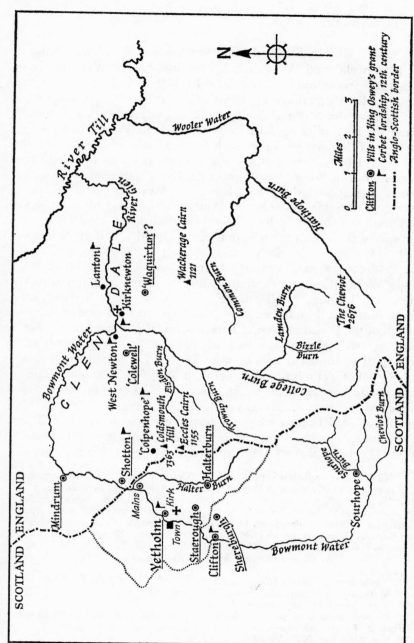

MAP 5. 'Shire of Yetholm': suggested reconstruction. Names from *Symeon of Durham*, i, 197 and n.; *Northumberland County History*, xi.

and, continuing in England with Shotton and Mindrum, finish with 'Colwela' and 'Waquirtun', now lost but certainly in the parish of Kirknewton in Glendale.[133] In the twelfth and thirteenth centuries, long after the Anglo-Scottish border had been established in this area, the Norman family of Corbet appear as proprietors, under the lords of the great barony of Wark on Tweed, of several portions of that barony (and, with the exception of Lanton, only those portions of that barony) which correspond to the English place-names in King Oswy's grant.[134] The *Northumberland County History* was at something of a loss to explain this puzzling and seemingly unfeudal intrusion of Walter Corbet and his relations into lands which should have been held exclusively by de Ros.[135] But surely the explanation is that King David I had granted to Walter Corbet or his father the lordship of Yetholm in Roxburghshire as a knight-service barony, and this automatically made Walter Corbet proprietor, though clearly not tenant-in-chief, of Shotton, 'Colpenhope', 'Colewell' and Newton in Northumberland, and even gave him a sporting chance of being patron of the parish church of Kirknewton.[136] I suggest that these vills 'lay to' Yetholm, and that what we see in the twelfth and thirteenth centuries is an old shire in decay, centred upon the double vill of Yetholm (Town Yetholm and Kirk Yetholm). This shire would have had two parish churches, Kirknewton which (to judge only from its name) was perhaps the younger of the two,[137] and Kirk Yetholm, on whose eastern parish boundary stands a pre-historic tumulus with the unexplained but intriguing name of the Eccles Cairn.[138] The apparent fact that King Oswy's

[133] 'Colwela' is doubtless represented by 'Colewell', now lost, recorded in 1328 as the name of a place in West Newton (*Northumberland County History*, xi, 152). 'Waquirtun', with its unusual first element, is evidently represented in the place-name Wakerich found in 1631 (*Laing Charters*, no. 2090, 499). The Wackerage Cairn, on the march between Kirknewton, Yeavering and Akeld townships, is shown on the nineteenth-century Ordnance Survey 6-inch Map and appears on the O.S. 1 : 25000 Map, Sheet NT 92, Nat. Grid Ref. NT 926277. Cf. A. H. Smith, *English Place-name Elements* (EPNS, 1956), ii, 234, s.v. *wacor.

[134] *Northumberland County History*, xi, 117ff., 128ff., 143ff., 152ff., 182ff.

[135] *Northumberland County History*, xi, 128–9, 143, 182.

[136] *Northumberland County History*, xi, 117ff.

[137] Its dedication is to Saint Gregory the Great, and the site is thought to be ancient. I have not discovered what dedication Yetholm church had.

[138] Nat. Grid Ref. NT 855276.

twelve-vill estate preserved its unity long after it had been lost by the church and even survived the establishment of the Anglo-Scottish border by some two hundred years would point to a shire of great antiquity. At least one of its members, Mindrum, has a name of purely Brittonic character.[139]

It would not be difficult to find evidence in the rest of Teviotdale, Tweeddale and Lothian for a shire system with its characteristic features of fee-farm (Scots, *feu-ferme*) money rents, seasonal ploughing and reaping, wood-cutting and carrying duties, tribute in cattle and pigs and obligatory hospitality (*conveth*, waiting). Here and there we see thanes associated with or attached to shires. Tynninghame in East Lothian was clearly a shire in 1094, even if a reduced one; it had four dependencies and tribute from a fifth, and was held with sake and soke.[140] Neighbouring Haddingtonshire still had its resident thane in the late 1130s;[141] in Bolton (*bōþl tūn*, 'hall settlement'), next to Haddington on the south, we may notice Eaglescarnie, a name evidently containing the 'eccles' element.[142] Robert son of Maccus (1199) got a ploughgate at Lessudden (St. Boswells) for 20s. a year and performing all the services pertaining to that land and which that land used to render, besides (or except?) ploughing and reaping.[143] Edward the monk of Coldingham (c. 1124–36) must send logs to replenish the king's timber-yard at Berwick from a wood in dispute (a 'threipwood') on the edge of Coldinghamshire.[144] The next two kings of Scots carefully excepted from the forest privileges of Coldingham Priory the timber needed for the royal castle of Berwick.[145] As late as 1595, Sir John Skene, Lord Clerk Register, a careful student of the royal antiquities of Scotland, noted in a memorandum that in the event of a royal progress from Holyrood-

[139] E. Ekwall, *Concise Oxford Dictionary of English Place-names* (3rd edn, 1947), 312, derives from W. *mynydd*, 'hill' and *trum*, 'ridge'.

[140] Lawrie, *Charters*, no. 12 (cf. A. A. M. Duncan, *SHR*, xxxvii, 119).

[141] Lawrie, *Charters*, nos. 122, 134, 135.

[142] The earliest recorded form seems to be Egliscarno, 1613 (*RMS, 1609–20*, no. 897; cf. *Retours*, Haddington, no. 217).

[143] *RRS*, ii, no. 422.

[144] Lawrie, *Charters*, no. 174 (for the expression *in calang*, 'in dispute', entering into place-names, cf. Ekwall, *Dictionary*, s.v. Callingwood, Staffs., and note Callange in Ceres, Fife).

[145] *RRS*, ii, no. 46 (William I), which substantially repeats an earlier provision of Malcolm IV (NLS, MS. Adv. 35. 3. 8, fo. 145), omitted in error from *RRS*, i.

house to Falkland Palace the tenants of Musselburghshire (which had not been royal demesne since the eleventh century)[146] were bound to take the king's carriage from Edinburgh to Linlithgow, whence it was to be borne round to Dunfermline by the tenants of Bothkennar and Stirlingshire.[147] Twelfth-century charters speak of the royal kitchen revenues in cows, oxen, hides, woolfells, tallow and fat which were due from south and north of Lammermuir, as well as of the cheese-rents of Tweeddale and venison from Teviotdale.[148]

The whole of larger Lothian, together with Clydesdale and the western counties of southern Scotland would repay a thorough examination for traces of an ancient pattern of shires or cantreds. Attention can here be drawn only in passing to such places as Ecclesmachan (West Lothian), with its possible thanage of Bangour,[149] the royal shire of Cadzow, with its dependency of Machanshire,[150] Carluke with its former church of Eglismalesoch,[151] and the formerly royal estates of Renfrew and Mearns.[152] In these last two we may perhaps see two former 'shires', the one possessing the ancient church of Paisley (Passeleth, from a Cumbric equivalent of Old Welsh *bassalec*, Latin *basilica*, a church)[153] the other possessing Eaglesham, formerly Egglesham,[154] to be compared with the English Ecclestons. It is clear that in the south-west generally the word 'shire' was not in common use. Nevertheless, there is evidence in the twelfth and thirteenth century of the survival of traces of an older system of units of royal demesne in which tribute was brought to centres of kingly power. This seems to be shown in the infeftments made by the twelfth-century kings, where Renfrew, Strathgryfe, Cunningham, North Kyle, Douglasdale and Annandale are surely to be compared

---

[146] *Dunfermline Court Book*, 18ff.
[147] *Miscellany I* (ed. I. D. Willock, Stair Soc., 1971), 146.
[148] *RRS*, i, 36 and no. 131; *RRS*, ii, nos. 62, 315.
[149] Ibid., no. 496.
[150] *Exchequer Rolls*, i, 40, 46 (1287–90); *OPS*, i, 106–8.
[151] J. M. Mackinlay, *Influence of the Pre-Reformation Church on Scottish Place-Names* (1904), 71; Watson, *CPNS*, 196.
[152] *RRS*, i, no. 184.
[153] Watson, *CPNS*, 194; and cf. the name Bassaleg (in Graig), Monmouthshire.
[154] *RRS*, i, no. 184.

with Welsh cantreds and commotes similarly granted out as units to incoming 'Normans'.[155]

The lordship of Callendar and the shire of Stirling are of interest in themselves and will form a useful introduction to a survey of shires and thanes north of Forth. Callendar, in the Latin guise of Calat(e)ria, was important enough to be mentioned in Ailred of Rievaulx's account of William the Conqueror's progress to Abernethy in 1072.[156] This reference would be understandable if the English king had actually lodged there for a night or two. The lordship was royal demesne, the land stretching back from the Forth between the Rivers Carron and Avon, perhaps including Bothkennar[157] which, as we have seen, was singled out by Sir John Skene in his memorandum of 1595. From Callendar's saltpans on the Forth and from its woodland and arable, the twelfth-century kings endowed and enriched their new religious foundations of Holyrood, Newbattle, Dunfermline and Cambuskenneth.[158] The lordship gave the king 'pleas and profits', and the rights of the King's landholding 'bonders' (*bondi*) needed protection.[159] In 1154 one Nes of Callendar (*Kaletirium*), accused of treason to the young King Malcolm IV, was killed in judicial combat.[160] Nes was perhaps the local thane; thanes of Callendar certainly emerge, however briefly, in record of the earlier thirteenth century.[161] The last thane, Malcolm son of Duncan, who gave some of his land to the knights of the Temple, was bought out by King Alexander II in 1234,[162] and his successors

---

[155] On this see the classic study of J. G. Edwards, 'The Normans and the Welsh March', *Proceedings of the British Academy*, xlii (1956), 155–7.

[156] *Chron. Stephen*, iii, 186; cf. *RRS*, i, 8, 40 and Watson, *CPNS*, 105–6.

[157] The early history of Bothkennar (now included in Grangemouth) is obscure, but it seems to have been royal demesne (*Cal. Docs. Scot.*, ii, nos. 522, 533, 545) and *Exchequer Rolls*, i, *passim*. The church seems to have been granted to the Cistercian nuns of Eccles in Berwickshire by David Bernham bishop of St. Andrews (Cowan, *Parishes*, 21), and it may originally have ranked as a chapel dependent on Falkirk church which belonged to the see of St. Andrews. Some of the land of Bothkennar was still royal demesne as late as 1450 (*Holyrood Liber*, no. 123), but most had already been acquired by Holyrood Abbey.

[158] Cf. Lawrie, *Charters*, and *RRS*, i and ii, references in indices s.v. Callendar.

[159] *RRS*, i, nos. 109, 135.   [160] *RRS*, i, 8.   [161] *RRS*, i, 46.

[162] *Holyrood Liber*, no. 65; SRO, MS. Cartae Variae of the Society of Antiquaries of Scotland, 119–20, a charter given by a Master of the Knights of the Temple in England named Robert of Stamford, known to have held that office in 1235 (Dugdale, *Mon. Angl.* (New), vi, II, p. 8).

held what was left of the thanage as a knight-service barony. The parish church of this large 'shire' (for so we may surely call it), its *matrix ecclesia*, which had dependent chapels before 1165,[163] was Egglesbrec[h] ('speckled Eccles'), a name long since superseded by Falkirk (*fage cirice*, 'multi-coloured church').[164] Its owner, the bishop of St. Andrews, made it over to the royal abbey of Holyrood before 1166.[165]

The original shire of Stirling seems to bear the same relation to the later sheriffdom as old Berwickshire bore to later Berwickshire (or for that matter old Haddingtonshire and Linlithgowshire to the later counties of East and West Lothian). That is to say, an ancient shire became the basis or nucleus of a much larger royal sheriffdom. King Alexander I died at Stirling in 1124.[166] He had founded a new chapel for the doubtless equally new castle of Stirling, endowing it with the teinds of his demesnes in the 'soke of Stirling'.[167] Within the soke, better known as the shire of Stirling, but not on the king's immediate demesne,[168] were tenants classified as 'hiredmen' (*hurdmanni*), bonders (*bondi*) and gresmen (*gresmanni*). If these two last be equated with the bonders and gresmen whom we find in Northumberland, Durham, Yorkshire and Lindsey,[169] the 'hiredmen'—'honourable retainers',

[163] *Holyrood Liber*, Appendix I, no. 1, 169.

[164] The name is discussed at length by W. F. H. Nicolaisen, *Scottish Studies*, xiii, pt. I (1969), 47–59. He takes the twelfth-century forms to represent a Gaelic name (modern Gaelic, *an Eaglais Bhreac*), but (54) allows 'a reasonable possibility of an earlier Cumbric name'. See also *Names of Towns and Cities in Britain*, ed. W. F. H. Nicolaisen (1970), 93.

[165] *Holyrood Liber*, Appendix II, no. 4; the church had already been confirmed as a possession of Holyrood Abbey by Pope Alexander III in a privilege of 1164 (ibid., Appendix I, no. 1).

[166] Anderson, *Early Sources*, ii, 167.

[167] Lawrie, *Charters*, no. 182 = *Dunfermline Reg.*, no. 4.

[168] Lawrie, *Charters*, no. 182; cf. the Revesby provision noted in Stenton, *Northern Danelaw*, 25. For the 'shire' of Stirling, cf. Lawrie, *Charters*, no. 143 = *Dunfermline Reg.*, no. 7; *RRS*, i, 40.

[169] Bonders (*bondi*) are found generally in twelfth- and thirteenth-century record for the northernmost counties of England (cf. Jolliffe, *EHR*, xli, 1–42 *passim*), and at Conisbrough in 1327 (*Cal. IPM*, vii, 57). Gresmen are recorded in fourteenth-century Yorkshire, ibid. and Neilson, *Customary Rents*, 174. For Lincolnshire note the name Gressemenlond at Kirton-in-Lindsey, 1304–6, *Cal. IPM*, iii, 470–1. Note on Maps 6 and 9 the names Grassmainston and Grassmiston, standing for an original *gresmannestun*, *gresmennestun* respectively; and for the crofts of the gresmen of Airthrey near Stirling see *Dunfermline Registrum*, no. 116 (p. 133).

'honourable servants', would be a fair enough translation[170]—
were surely equivalent to the drengs or sokemen familiar throughout Northumbria and eastern England. Their successors would
seem to have been the king's serjeants thickly settled around
Stirling as late as the thirteenth century.[171] The castle chapel and
the kirk of the Haly Rude (the parish church of the rising new
burgh) passed to Dunfermline Abbey,[172] and much of the little
information we possess we owe to the quarrels (of a kind very
familiar to the historian of this period) which the Benedictine
monks of Dunfermline engaged in with the Augustinian canons of
the no less royal abbey of Cambuskenneth. The *matrix ecclesia* of
Stirlingshire was the ancient church of St. Ninians, otherwise
known as Eccles (Eggles, Egglis, Egles),[173] located a mile and a
half from the castle, at the *kirketun* or Kirkton.[174] Its parochial
territory, including a number of dependent chapels which
afterwards became churches in their own right, stretched from
Cambusbarron and Cornton in the north to Dunipace and
Larbert in the south and to the boundary of Airth and Bothkennar in the east.[175]

Many shires are recorded in Scotia proper, Scotland north of
Forth (e.g., Maps 6–13). As far as we can see, they tended to be
smaller than the shires of Northumbria, although even there we
might note Kirkbyshire and Mashamshire[176] in the North Riding
as instances of shires which cannot have been very large. The
relatively small average size of a Scotian shire might have been
due to the process of subdivision, of which there is evidence in
southern Britain.[177] On the other hand, it might have been due to
the usual conservatism of Scotia, and we may note Jolliffe's
remark anent the Kentish lathes, that they 'grow smaller as we
go backward in time'.[178] The chief consideration to be borne in

[170] See n. 116 above.   [171] *Dunfermline Reg.*, no. 215.
[172] *Dunfermline Reg.*, no. 2; Cowan, *Parishes*, 187–8.
[173] *Dunfermline Reg.*, 124 (Kirkton). For the spelling forms see *Cambuskenneth Reg.* and *Dunfermline Reg.*, references in indices.
[174] This form occurs before 1174, *RRS*, ii, no. 130.
[175] *Dunfermline Reg.*, no. 215; *Cambuskenneth Reg.*, nos. 25 (p. 44) and 117.
[176] A. H. Smith, *English Place-name Elements*, ii, 110; also *Place-Names of the
North Riding*, 230 ('Mashamshire conterminous with Masham parish'); *Place-
Names of the West Riding*, v, 78.
[177] E.g. Stenton, *Northern Danelaw*, 52, 84–6.
[178] Jolliffe, *Jutes*, 46.

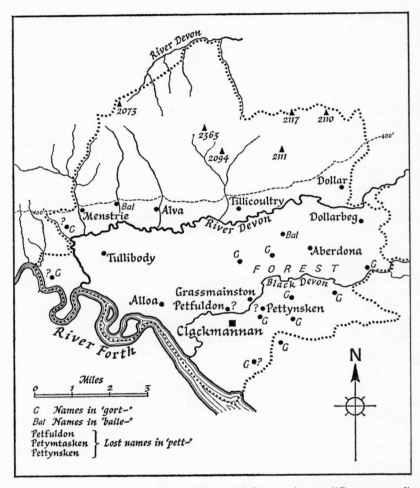

MAP 6. Clackmannanshire. Lost names, and Grassmainston ('Gresmanston')
from *Exchequer Rolls*, i, 572–3.

mind, as it seems to me, when we examine shires, thanages and
thanes in Scotland north of Forth is that we are dealing with a
relatively poor and sparsely populated country. It is fair to make
the same kind of comparison between the north and south of
Britain in this matter as may be made, with more plentiful and
less ambiguous evidence, in respect of the introduction of feudal

military tenures and organisation during the twelfth and thirteenth centuries.[179] It may be useful to look first at the duties, tenure and privileges of the Scotian thane, and to see whether this seems to put him on much the same footing as one common type of English thegn, the chief embodiment of the ministerial element in the population of shire, soke or lathe. The question of origins and chronology will be left to the last.

Where feudal barons were planted in Scotia in the twelfth and thirteenth centuries, sometimes replacing thanes, they were granted the jurisdiction of sake, soke, toll, team, infangthief, pit and gallows.[180] It is a fair assumption that the thane used to exercise this basic civil and criminal jurisdiction on the king's behalf, doubtless with the help of the hereditary *judex* or dempster and of the hereditary dewar or relic-keeper.[181] Wherever thanes and not lairds (*domini*) were placed over the peasant population it was their duty to see that teind was paid promptly to the church.[182] A defaulting thane paid eight cows to the king, a defaulting peasant one cow and one sheep, a provision reminiscent of chapters 59 and 60 of the eleventh-century Northumbrian Priest's Law.[183] Just as the earls had the duty of calling up and leading the 'common' or 'Scottish' army of their earldoms, so also it seems to have been the thane who organised this military service at shire level.[184] The shire was the unit for assessing and rendering the king's forinsec service—military service, cain and conveth—precisely as in English Northumbria it was the unit for rendering forinsec service, cornage and waiting.[185] The phrase 'forinsec service as much as belongs to the third part of a vill in Coupland', from a Cumberland document of *c.* 1203,[186] can be exactly paralleled in numerous Scottish documents, e.g. 'as much

[179] Below, pp. 293, 295.
[180] *RRS*, ii, 50; to instances there given add *Holyrood Liber*, no. 65, land granted in feu-ferme, formerly held by a thane, carrying with it pit and gallows, soke and sake, etc.
[181] Below, pp. 69–82; W. C. Dickinson, 'The Toschederach', *Juridical Review*, liii (1941), 85–109.
[182] *RRS*, ii, no. 281 (1187 × 89).
[183] D. Whitelock, *English Historical Documents, c.* 500–1042, 438; Liebermann, *Gesetze*, i, 384.
[184] *RRS*, ii, 57.
[185] For the English evidence, cf. Jolliffe, *EHR*, xli, 10ff., 30.
[186] *St. Bees Reg.*, Appendix, no. XXVIII, 544.

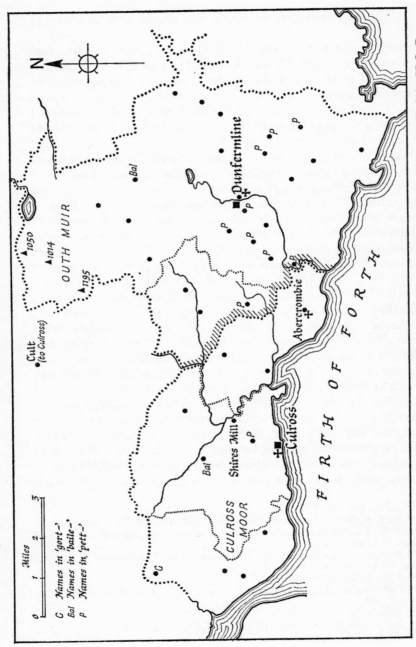

MAP 7. Shire of Culross and suggested 'shire' of Dunfermline. For Culross cf. *PSAS*, lx (1927), 70, 87-8 (=SRO, Reg. Ho. Supp. Charters, *sub dat.* 1217). Dunfermline names from *Dunfermline Registrum*.

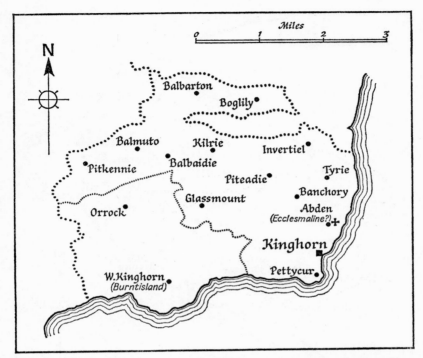

MAP 8. Shire of Kinghorn. Names chiefly from *Exchequer Rolls*, i, 564. For the (arch)bishop of St. Andrews' 'palace' at Abden, in ruins in 1484, cf. SRO, NRA (Scot.)/0153/6. Abden, for *abthania, abdaine*, may be the site of the lost Ecclesmaline for which see *Inchcolm Chrs.*, 103–4.

forinsec service as belongs to a half-ploughgate in Kellieshire',[187] 'as much service in aids and other forinsec service as belongs to a Scottish half-ploughgate in Crail-shire'.[188] These happen to be taken from royal charters, but private conveyances of land almost invariably stipulated for the burden of forinsec service to be met in one way or another, usually with the formula 'as much forinsec service of the lord king as belongs—to so much land, to that land, to a named vill'. One example must suffice among many. Blebo was a small shire west of St. Andrews from which the bishop of St. Andrews drew revenue. A feu-charter of 1263 required the recipient of land in Blebo to pay a quitrent to the donor (or

[187] *RRS*, ii, no. 286.   [188] *RRS*, ii, no. 469.

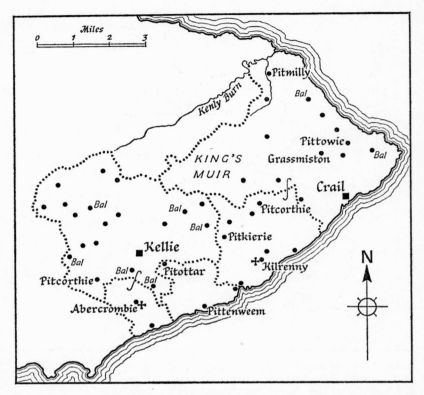

MAP 9. Shires of Crail and Kellie. Most of the names are to be found in Lawrie, *Charters* and *RRS*, i and ii.

vendor), an annual ferme to the superior or heritor (*heres*), and in addition 'as much aid of the lord king and of the bishop as belongs to the third of a davoch (a 'Scottish ploughgate') and the provision of one man's food in the lord king's army'.[189]

We find the thanages or thanedoms of Scotland rendering the same mixture of goods and services as seems to characterise the tenure of thegns, drengs and sokemen in northern England. As late as Robert I's reign Sir Hugh of Ross, afterwards Earl of Ross, got the thanage of Glendowachy, just across the Deveron from Banff, for the service of providing from each davoch of the

[189] NLS, MS. Adv. 34.6.24, pp. 248–9; for Blebo-shire, cf. *RRS*, ii, no. 28.

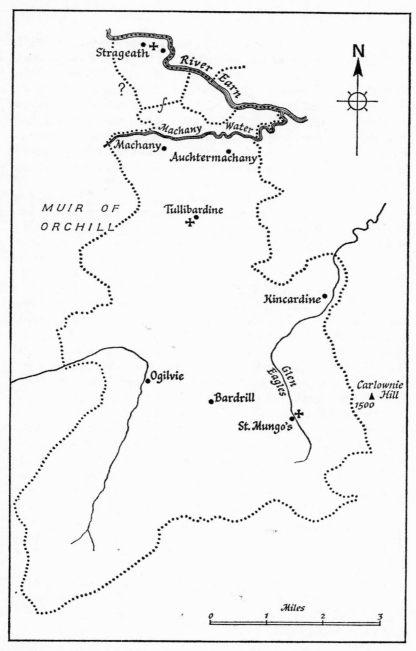

MAP 10. 'Catherlauenach.' Cf. *Inchaffray Liber*, p. xxix; Watson, *CPNS*, 223.

thanage eight horses for carting once a year.[190] We are easily reminded of Henry of Mousen who had to provide twelve carts for his drengage, and of the carting services of sokemen in West Suffolk, Cambridgeshire, Leicestershire and Lindsey. Beside the carting duties of the tenants of Musselburghshire, Bothkennar, Stirlingshire and Dunfermline already mentioned, we may note that some tenements in the shire of Culross were burdened with a service called 'areage and carriage' in the sixteenth century.[191] 'Areage' is a form of *averagium*, the word used in the eleventh and twelfth centuries for carting or carrying service.[192]

The rent owed to the king from Bangour, the chief estate in Ecclesmachan, West Lothian, had been (before 1205) four chalders of oatmeal, four merks of silver, eight pigs and eight shillings.[193] This is reminiscent of mixed money and food-rents found in England in connexion with sokeland or thegnage holdings. For example, Earl Cospatric of Dunbar took Bewick and Eglingham in north Northumberland from the abbot of S. Albans, in the early twelfth century, on the following terms. Cospatric was to hold 'in fee-farm, (in or and?) thegn's law, in sake and soke, toll, team and infangthief' for £4 yearly and a further payment of 20s. or, should money run short, seven oxen worth 3s. each.[194] The association of fee-farm tenure with thegnage and drengage in northern England has long been recognised.[195] In Scotland feu-ferme tenure came to be regarded as the peculiar hallmark of thanage. The historian John of Fordoun tried to account for this by attributing to King Malcolm II (d. 1034) a deliberate policy of granting out to his most highly-favoured subjects—knights, thanes and noblemen—landed estates to be held at rent in perpetuity, yet never so freely but that some fixed annual render remained to the king.[196] It seems that neither in England nor in Scotland was thanage—or for that matter dren-

[190] *RMS*, i, Appendix I, no. 5.   [191] *PSAS*, lx (1927), 79, 83.

[192] John Skene, *De verborum significatione* (Edinburgh, 1597), s.v. Arage. 'Average signifies service quhilk the tennent aucht to his maister, be horse or cariage of horse.'

[193] *RRS*, ii, no. 496.

[194] *Historiae Dunelmensis Scriptores Tres*, ed. J. Raine (Surtees Soc., 1839), p. lv (Appendix, note to no. 38). This document has been printed in a number of different works.

[195] E.g. *VCH, Durham*, i, 314 and no. 3; Jolliffe, *EHR*, xli, 26.

[196] *Chron. Fordun*, i, 186.

gage—ever a true tenure. The terms expressed a ministerial or serviential relationship. Only gradually and imperfectly was the position of thegns and drengs sorted out into the familiar categories of knight-service, serjeanty and free socage.

Where the shires were royal it was the thane's duty to supervise the king's residence, if one existed, and to provide the king with lodging. The duty may be seen as a specific instance of the more general, indeed universal, obligation of hospitality or entertainment denoted by the Gaelic term *conveth* or its English equivalent 'waiting'. In northern Scotland at least two and probably three royal thanages had the word *conveth* permanently applied to them as a place-name—Conveth, now in, but formerly equivalent to, Laurencekirk (Mearns), Conveth or Conevache, now Inverkeithny (Banffshire) and Conveth, now Convinth west of Inverness.[197] With these instances of local specialisation we should compare the south-western names Sorn, Sornfalla, etc., with much the same meaning.[198] Waiting is not to be thought of as in every case having the literal sense of 'hospitality'. We have seen that the varied agricultural and ministerial duties of Henry of Mousen could be summed up as *repastus domini regis*, the lord king's feast or waiting.[199] Similarly, where we see waiting (or its apparent equivalent *frith(elagium)* or *frithalos*) figuring largely in the Exchequer Rolls of the thirteenth century, we find that the waiting 'of one night' or 'of four nights' takes the form of sizeable renders of cattle, swine, cheese, malt, barley meal, foddercorn and poultry.[200]

Ailred of Rievaulx says that William the Conqueror marched to Abernethy by way of Calatria, a shire-thanage. Two centuries later, in 1296, Edward the would-be Conqueror advanced as far as Elgin in Moray.[201] On Tuesday, 23 July, he spent the night under canvas in the Enzie, the wooded country between Cullen and Fochabers. When enough boats had been collected to ferry the king and his army across the Spey, Edward lodged the next

[197] Watson, *CPNS*, 220; *Exchequer Rolls*, i, 548; *Aberdeen-Banff Coll.*, 652; *Moray Reg.*, no. 21; *Cawdor Bk.*, 88.
[198] W. C. Dickinson, 'Surdit de Sergaunt', *SHR*, xxxix (1960), 174 and nn. Watson, on the other hand, explains the Ayrshire Sorn by Gaelic *sorn*, 'kiln' (*CPNS*, 200).
[199] *Book of Fees*, i, 599 (above, p. 16).
[200] Dickinson, op. et loc. cit.; *Exchequer Rolls*, i, 4, 6, 12, 16, 20–1.
[201] Stevenson, *Documents*, ii, 29.

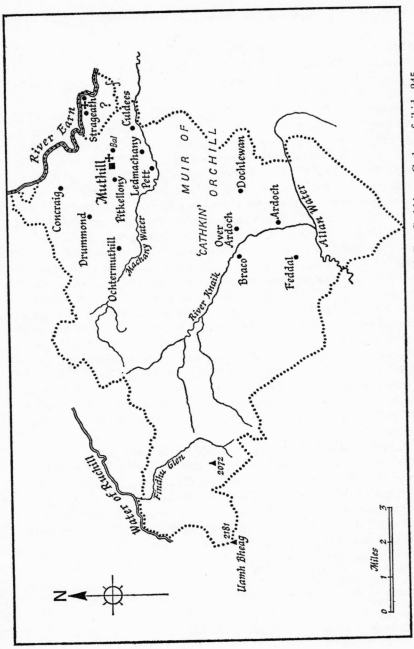

MAP 11. 'Cathermothel.' Cf. *Lindores Chartulary*, nos. 24, 25, 28. For Cathkin or Cotken cf. ibid., 245.

night at the 'manor of Rathenech' on the west bank.[202] Rathenech, now lost, was a royal thanedom. In King William the Lion's time one Yothre mac Gilhys held it of the Crown, providing a serjeant's service in the army and enjoying a net for his fishing in the Spey.[203] Yothre's son Ewen, his grandson Angus and his great-grandson Ewen were each in turn thanes of Rathenech. In 1264 Thane Ewen delivered up his large granary there to the king's clerk of liverance.[204] The king's hall at Rathenech was rebuilt in that year with a roof of double boards and walls of planks;[205] presumably this was King Edward's lodging in the summer of 1296. On 30 July, just after Edward had turned south from Elgin, William of Rathenech came to him at Rothes, solemnly renounced his share in the Franco-Scottish Treaty of 1295, and gave in his homage;[206] to be followed not long afterwards by Angus of Rathenech.[207]

Yothre's net in the Spey may be traced back to David I's time as the 'revenue of fish' (*rectitudo piscium*) due to the king's thane at Fochabers.[208] It shows us that the thane had privileges or rewards as well as duties. At Kinmylies west of Inverness the king's thanes were accustomed to hold one fishery in the River Ness.[209] In the thanages of Angus and Mearns, and no doubt in many other areas, lands assigned to the church rendered the basic tributes of cain and conveth (equivalent to cornage and waiting in northern England) to the king's thanes. These burdens may have included a payment in return for pasture rights like the English pannage.[210] At St. Cyrus in Mearns William I expressly granted the tenants of the estate held there by St. Andrews Cathedral Priory common pasture along with his thane and other men.[211] We know that at

---

[202] Stevenson, ii, 29, where for 'en la mor sur la rivere de Spe' read (as in *Instrumenta Publica*, 179) 'en Lennoy sur . . .', i.e. the Enzie; and for 'Rapenache maynor' read 'Rathenache maynor'.

[203] *APS*, i, 101.

[204] *Exchequer Rolls*, i, 10, where for 'Kathenes' read 'Rathenes', i.e. Rathenech.

[205] *Exchequer Rolls*, i, 14 (where the lost name appears as 'Kathenes' and 'Rothenet').

[206] *Instrumenta Publica*, 109–10 and 158; *Cal. Docs. Scot.*, ii, 209.

[207] *Cal. Docs. Scot.* ii, 211; *Instrumenta Publica*, 164.

[208] Lawrie, *Charters*, no. 255.

[209] *Moray Reg.*, no. 34 (reading *piscariam* for *piscarii* in line 7 of p. 27).

[210] Neilson, *Customary Rents*, 68ff.; *Spalding Misc.*, v. 209.

[211] *RRS*, ii, no. 352.

this time the priory paid cain and conveth to the thane, for shortly afterwards the new lord who had replaced the thane remitted this burden.[212] Walter of Berkeley, to whom King William had granted Inverkeilor farther down the coast, in Angus, released the parish church of St. Mo-Chonoc and its parson from the *grescan* ('grazing cain') which used to be paid to the thanes of Inverkeilor.[213] Next door to Inverkeilor is Inverlunan, now Lunan, and at the close of the twelfth century a lay proprietor there, Neil Mac Ywar, surely the thane, similarly released the local parson from all the cain and conveth which used to be paid from the ancient church lands of Inverlunan.[214] At Laurencekirk, then called Conveth, the thane not only possessed some unspecified right in the church lands but apparently the patronage of the parish church as well.[215] At Arbuthnott in the twelfth century the 'due cain' was said by a witness in 1206 to have been paid from the *kirketun* to thirteen successive thanes prior to *c*. 1189.[216]

English historians have notoriously found it hard to decide to what extent the thegn or the dreng was a free man, noting in particular his liability to heriot, to tallage at the lord's will and, here and there, to merchet.[217] There is a similar ambiguity in the Scottish evidence. If we could accept a phrase from a charter of William I,[218] which unfortunately is not authentic as it stands, the king's thanes were included among the *nativi*, neyfs, men who were tied to the estate of their birth. The phrase should not be dismissed lightly, for a genuine document of *c*. 1230 proves that some clergy in Scotia were classed as *nativi*.[219] A more substantial ground for doubting whether the Scots thane enjoyed a status which the feudal lawyers would have judged to be completely free is the evident weakness of the thane's tenurial position. Had it been as strong as that enjoyed by feudal knights and barons it is hard to see how the kings of the twelfth and thirteenth centuries could have granted so many thanages to their new feudal vassals or brought about such radical changes in thanage holdings.

A further feature of Scottish thanages or shires should be

[212] *St. Andrews Liber*, 238.   [213] *Arbroath Liber*, i, no. 56.
[214] *RRS*, ii, no. 590.   [215] *RRS*, ii, nos. 344, 345.
[216] *Spalding Misc.*, v, 211.
[217] F. W. Maitland, 'Northumbrian Tenures', *EHR*, v, 628; Neilson, *Customary Rents*, 89; Rachel Reid, *EHR*, xxxv, 173; Jolliffe, *EHR*, xli, 15–19, 24.
[218] *RRS*, ii, no. 251.   [219] *Moray Reg.*, 83–4.

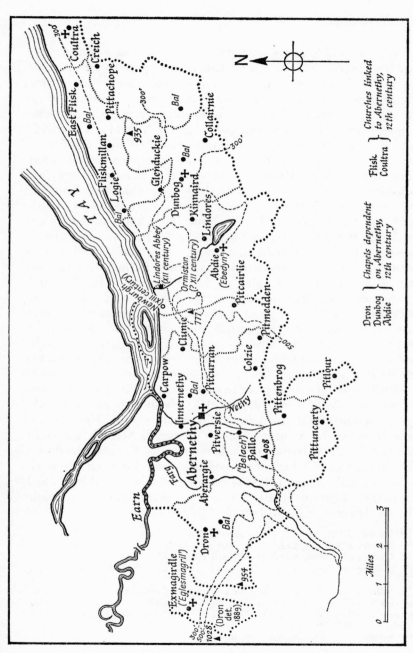

MAP 12. Conjectural 'shire' of Abernethy: suggested reconstruction. Names from various sources, but cf. esp. *Arbroath Liber*, i, no. 35 and *Lindores Chartulary*, *passim*.

noticed, one which offers scope for a more searching comparison with the English evidence than can be attempted here. A geographically definable stretch of permanent common pasture seems to have been an essential, probably a very primitive, characteristic of the lathe, soke and shire in England, and exactly the same seems to have been true of Scotland (*see* Maps 4, 7, 9–11). Thus with Shildon Moor (Corbridge, Northumberland)[220] and the Shiremoor of Tynemouth(shire)[221] we may compare Coldingham Moor, the Borough Muir of Linlithgow, Slamannan Muir (for Callendar), Sheriffmuir (for some shire of Dunblane or Lecropt, and perhaps equivalent to 'shire moor'), Culross Moor, Outh Muir (for Dunfermline), King's Muir (for Crail), and perhaps Hardmuir (for Auldearn and Brodie?).[222] The Muir of Orchill, otherwise Cotken (Gaelic, *Coitcheann*, 'common'), which immemorially no man cultivated, seems to have formed the common grazing for a vanished shire of Cathermothel (Muthill) and perhaps for a vanished shire of Catherlavenache (Carlownie or Blackford) as well.[223] A great deal more work needs to be done before this aspect of the Scottish shire or thanage is set in a clearer light, and in this connexion Dr. Adams's recently published list of Scottish commonties is likely to prove invaluable.[224] Just as a 'king's down'[225] or 'king's muir', a 'shire moor' or 'sheriffmuir', seems to have been an essential ingredient in the composition of a lathe or shire, so also we may note as apparently equally fundamental the king's mill or shire mill. Here again, there is scope for a large piece of research. Stenton noted in Lincolnshire the existence of mills reserved to the chief lord of a soke, in respect of which some payment was due even although the actual milling might be carried out at a mill owned by a local landlord.[226] There is Scottish evidence which might be set beside this. At Tranent, e.g., Robert de Quincy allowed the canons of

[220] Jolliffe, *EHR*, xli, 12, citing *Northumberland County History*, x, 57.
[221] Jolliffe, *EHR*, viii, 212.   [222] *Cawdor Bk.*, 267.
[223] *Lindores Chartulary*, no. 28; see Maps 10 and 11.
[224] *Directory of Scottish Commonties*, ed. I. H. Adams (Scottish Record Soc., 1971).
[225] Jolliffe, *Jutes*, 49–51. With these common and royal pastures in Kent we may compare Tilney Smeeth, in West Norfolk, which was anciently common pasture for seven villages of the Norfolk Fenland (F. Blomefield, *History of Norfolk*, ix (1808), 79–80).
[226] Stenton, *Northern Danelaw*, 36, n. 3.

Holyrood to have one-third of their teind corn ground wherever they pleased, while the remaining two-thirds was to be ground at Robert's own mills at Tranent or Longniddry.[227] But if those mills were too busy to deal with all the canons' corn in one operation they must take their corn to the mill which was known as the 'sheriff's mill'.[228] This mill has long since disappeared, but the Shires Mill of the shire of Culross is still on the modern map, and 'king's mills' (not all of which were necessarily ancient shire mills) are by no means uncommon throughout Scotland. Ednam Mill in Roxburghshire is still working, the lineal successor of an ancient royal mill whose rights were carefully protected when the Tironensian abbey of Kelso was established in the twelfth century.[229]

Although we can hardly prove that the whole of Scotia was once divided into shires,[230] the shire obviously determined the pattern of lordship and land distribution over some long period prior to the twelfth century. Most of the shires that we know about were in the east and the low country, not in the west or the Highlands. This may be due to the fact that fertile and populous land will tend to generate and hand down a greater volume of historical documentation. On the other hand, we must, for the present at least, bear in mind the possibility of a rather different system having once prevailed in the far west and the islands. In the record which has survived, the term shire is occasionally combined in an English word-order, as in *Carel sira*,[231] Crailshire, *Dunde syra*,[232] Dundee-shire. More often the order, although formally Latin, as *sira de Chellin*,[233] the shire of Kellie, *schira de Foregrund*,[234] the shire of Forgan, may represent a basically Celtic vernacular word-order, of the same type as produced the familiar 'burn of —', 'mill of —', 'mains of —' place-names which Professor Nicolaisen has examined so thoroughly.[235] Occasionally we

[227] *Holyrood Liber*, no. 62.
[228] *Holyrood Liber*, no. 62: 'molendinum quod uocatur shireuis milne'.
[229] *RRS*, ii, no. 188.
[230] Cf. Jolliffe's remark, 'we should have gone far to fill Northumbria with shires', *EHR*, xli, 15.
[231] *Laing Chrs.*, no. 2; cf. *RRS*, ii, no. 469; *but: sira de Cherel*, Lawrie, *Charters*, no. 207; *schira de Karel*, *RRS*, ii, no. 29.
[232] *St. Andrews Liber*, 224; *but: sira de Dunde*, ibid., 59.
[233] Lawrie, *Charters*, no. 207.   [234] *RRS*, ii, nos. 123, 174.
[235] W. F. H. Nicolaisen, *Scottish Studies*, iii, pt. 1 (1959), 92–102; iv, pt. 2 (1960), 194–205; ix, Pt. 2 (1965), 175–82.

have a clearly Celtic order, as in Skirdu[r]stan,[236] the shire of St. Drostan of Aberlour, or, further up the valley of the Spey, Skeir Alloway,[237] the shire of Alvie in Badenoch. It might be objected that in these last two instances, or even elsewhere, our word 'shire' means no more than 'ecclesiastical parish'; after all, the ordinary Scottish Gaelic words for parish are *sgir* or *sgireachd*.[238] For two reasons, the objection can hardly be sustained. In the first place, several Scottish shires seem to have been either less or more than one single parish or took their names from non-ecclesiastical sites. Kinninmonthshire, for example, seems to have been less than the parish of Ceres, while the shires of Blebo and Ardross, even if they could be shown to have been coterminous with the parishes of Kemback and Kilconquhar respectively, retained conspicuously distinct names. Stirlingshire and Callendar, on the other hand, whatever may have been their original form, came to embrace more than one ecclesiastical parish each.[239]

The second reason is the overwhelming improbability that the word 'shire', well established throughout northern England and southern Scotland to denote an estate of the type we have been examining, could have been introduced north of the Forth solely in this narrower and distinct meaning. For introduced the word must certainly have been. It is an Old English loan-word firmly embedded, by the twelfth century, in a Celtic-speaking country. It is natural to ask whether what was borrowed was not just the word but also the thing which it denoted. And if we ask that, shall we not also ask whether 'thane', another Old English loan-word embedded in Celtic society, was borrowed in the same way, not only as a word but also as an institution or office? An answer to these questions lies at the heart of our problem. The matter is not merely philological, for in Scotia as farther south thane and shire go together. Shires needed thanes. In Scotland individual thanes

---

[236] Macfarlane, *Geographical Coll.*, i, 230 (Skirdustan).

[237] Macfarlane, ii, 525 (Skeir-Alloway), 574 (Skeir Alvie).

[238] W. Shaw, *A Gaelic and English Dictionary* (1780), s.vv. *sgire, sgireachd*; H. C. Dieckhoff, *A pronouncing dictionary of Scottish Gaelic* (1932), s.v. *sgir*; J. L. Campbell and D. Thomson, *Edward Lhuyd in the Scottish Highlands, 1699–1700* (1963), 193.

[239] We may note a tendency for dependent parts of larger shires to acquire the qualification 'shire' for themselves; e.g. Herbertshire, in Dunipace (Stirling), presumably named after one of its thirteenth-century lords named Herbert de Morham; and Machanshire, a dependency of Cadzow (Lanark).

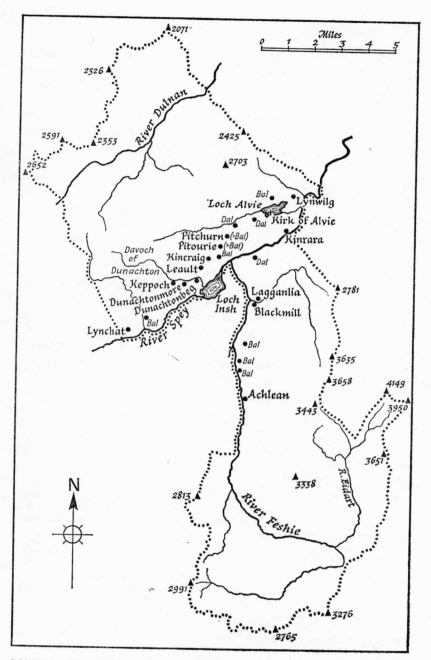

MAP 13. Shire of Alvie (Skeiralloway). Cf. Macfarlane, *Geographical Coll.*, ii, 573–4 and I. F. Grant, *Everyday life on an old Highland Farm* (1924).

are not found unattached. Where twelfth and thirteenth-century record uses 'shire', occasionally (it seems) *prepositura*,[240] record of the fourteenth century and later uses *thanagium*,[241] a thanage or thanedom.

The Scandinavians may be safely discounted as the originators in Britain of soke or shire or thanage.[242] Even if we could suppose that the sokemen of Lindsey and Nottinghamshire as a class were Scandinavian in origin, it is inconceivable that between the late ninth and mid-eleventh century the Scandinavians could have transplanted the soke and sokemen to south-eastern England, including Kent, to English and Scottish Northumbria, and to Scotland beyond the Forth, to say nothing of the west midlands and the Welsh Border country. This is not to say, of course, that in the eleventh century many of the sokemen of the northern Danelaw were not of Danish descent. The evidence of their Scandinavian ancestry seems overwhelmingly strong.[243] But here we are concerned with the soke as a social institution, with sokemen as a class. It seems clear that when the Danes settled in England sokes, with their ministerial stratum of thegns and sokemen, were already there, and were in fact the normal manifestation of royal demesne, into enjoyment of which the Danish newcomers were naturally ready to enter.

The Anglo-Saxons might seem more attractive candidates for

[240] E.g. *Moray Reg.*, no. 34. King David I's *prepositus*, Swene, commanded to help the prior of Dunfermline, 1124X1128 (Lawrie, *Charters*, no. 85), was perhaps the king's thane in the shire of Dunfermline or some neighbouring shire. The word *provincia* seems also to have been used for 'shire': besides the *castrensis provincia* of Stirling (ibid., no. 209) and the *provincia* of Elgin (*RRS*, i, no. 175) we may note other passages suggesting an equation of *provincia* with 'shire', *RRS*, ii, 137, 161; below, p. 200, n. 34.

[241] The word *thanagium* (*teinagium*, *thainagium*) seems to have come into use before 1203 (*Scone Liber*, no. 55), certainly before the end of Alexander II's reign (ibid., no. 65). Its use from the later thirteenth century onward is too general to need exemplification.

[242] For an opposite view, cf. Stenton, *Anglo-Saxon England*, 511–12: 'it cannot be an accident that a social organization to which there is no parallel elsewhere in England occurs in the one part of the country in which the regular development of native institutions had been interrupted by foreign settlement.' In *Northern Danelaw*, 91, Stenton had taken a more cautious view; and we may recall Maitland's dictum 'but in truth we must be careful how we use our Dane', *Domesday Book and beyond*, 176.

[243] Cf. F. M. Stenton, *The Free Peasantry of the Northern Danelaw*, and also the essays in *Mediaeval Scandinavia* (Odense), ii (1969), 163–207, especially the remarks of Professor Kenneth Cameron, ibid., 176–9.

the honour of inventing the soke or shire. Not only are those words both English, but it has been generally, though by no means universally agreed that at least in south-eastern Britain the Germanic peoples began their colonisation with something like a clean slate. Jolliffe's views on this matter unfortunately seem slightly ambiguous, but in his book on Kent (1933) and still more in his essay a year later on the 'Era of the Folk' he seems to have come down emphatically in support of the Germanic or Teutonic quality of the lathe or shire as a mark of primitive folk freedom.[244] Yet even he allowed for the influence of what he called (perhaps rather strangely) 'Celtic community'[245] and for the intermingling in Northumbria of Anglian and Celtic elements. The pre-Anglian (for convenience, they may be called the 'Brittonic') characteristics of Northumbrian institutions, revealing similarity or identity with Welsh institutions at many points, have long been recognised.[246] Until Davis's work on East Anglia had complemented Jolliffe's work on Kent and Northumbria, this connexion had not been thought to contain serious implications for the early character of much of southern and midland England. Now, however, it is surely time to see how the lines converge. On the one hand, the shires of Northumbria are the counterpart of the cantreds and commotes of Wales. On the other hand, they are also the counterpart of the lathes of Kent, the sokes and half-vanished 'shires' of west Wessex, East Anglia and the region of the Five Boroughs. Most English historians have of course ignored the Scottish evidence, or have not thought it more than marginally relevant.[247] In a work devoted to the history of the medieval Scottish kingdom it is of central importance, but it also seems to have much relevance to a general reconsideration of the English material.

In searching for origins and some acceptable framework of

---

[244] Jolliffe, *Jutes*, pp. viii, 30, 39; *Oxford Essays presented to H. E. Salter* (1934), 1–32.

[245] *EHR*, xli, 42.

[246] *EHR*, xii, 40–2. The subject has been usefully surveyed by W. Rees, 'Survivals of Ancient Celtic Custom in Medieval England', in *Angles and Britons*, ed. H. Lewis (Cardiff, 1963), 148–68.

[247] Since Jolliffe, *EHR*, xli, 30–1 and nn., went out of his way to touch briefly on the evidence for Lothian, it was especially unfortunate that he placed Kirkcaldy and Fothrif south of the Forth and referred twice to Erskine's (instead of Lawrie's) *Early Scottish Charters*.

chronology it is natural to look for evidence of the antiquity of the Scots thanage or shire. Of the sixty to seventy thanages in Scotia of which some record survives, a not inconsiderable number were located at places which have Brittonic or at least P-Celtic names. These names can hardly have arisen after the use of Gaelic had become widespread in eastern Scotland. In other words, they should be earlier than the ninth century. Many of them in fact are likely to be very much older than this, for they refer to major natural features, especially confluences. Strowan, in Strathearn, if it has the same meaning and origin as Struan in Atholl,[248] may possibly be in this class. Much the commonest, however, are the 'aber' names. It is agreed that *aber* was a distinctively P-Celtic form which belonged to whatever P-Celtic language was spoken by the Picts, and was of course shared by them with the Cumbric-speaking population of southern and south-western Scotland.[249] In this class we have,[250] as the names of former thanages and/or shires, Aberchalder (now Cawdor),[251] possibly 'Aberkarf' if we may regard this as an alternative to Cromdale,[252] Aberlour, Aberchirder, Aberdeen, Arbuthnott, Aberluthnot (Marykirk), Kinnaber, Aberlemno, Arbroath and (possibly) Inverbervie, formerly [H]aberbervi.[253] Kinninmonth in

248 Watson, *CPNS*, 350 says we may suspect Welsh influence in the name Struan (or Strowan) in Atholl; he does not discuss Strowan (or Struan) in Strathearn, shown to be a thanage in *Inchaffray Charters*, nos. 15, 19: *PSAS*, lxxxvii, 61.

249 Watson, *CPNS*, 458ff.; cf. K. Jackson in *The Problem of the Picts*, ed. F. T. Wainwright (1955), 148–9. The southernmost aber- name to survive in Scotland is Aberlosk in Eskdalemuir, Dumfriesshire, but formerly St. Mungo in the same county was Abermelc (Lawrie, *Charters*, no. 50). It is extraordinary that no trace of aber- names has been found in north-west England between Solway and Dee.

250 Unless otherwise stated, names of thanages are derived from W. F. Skene's list in *Chron. Fordun*, ii, 416–7 and his fuller account in *Celtic Scotland*, iii, 247–78. I know of no list of Scottish shires.

251 *Moray Reg.*, no. 40, where Abbircaledouer in the bailiary of Nairn is evidently Cawdor and not one of the Inverness-shire Aberchalders.

252 Ferrerius, *Historia*, pp. xix–xxi (1336), where Aberkarf must refer to a place in the neighbourhood of Cromdale, presumably at the confluence of a burn with the Spey. Cromdale itself is a partly Brittonic name (Watson, *CPNS*, 419); for its thane in 1367 cf. *Moray Reg.*, no. 286.

253 Inverbervie is not on Skene's list and cannot be shown to have been a thanage. The barony belonged to Earl David of Huntingdon and it seems likely that it was an estate of the same type as other Kincardineshire estates with which barons were infeft in the twelfth century, e.g. Arbuthnott, Conveth and St. Cyrus.

east Fife has a hybrid or rather a Gaelicised name, whose last element stands for a Pictish equivalent of Welsh *mynydd*, 'hill'.[254] Nearby Blebo, like Blelack in Cromar, Aberdeenshire, was formerly Bladebolg, literally 'bag of meal', identical with Blatobulgium in the *Antonine Itinerary*, which is agreed to be Birrens in Dumfriesshire.[255] The fact that thanages were located at places with ancient names does not in itself mean that thanages were also ancient, yet it is hardly what we should expect if the thanage system were a relatively recent borrowing.

Turning from the names given to entire thanages or shires to those given to the *appendicia* or component members which made up the shires, we cannot help noticing how often names containing the Pictish element *pett*, a 'portion' or 'share', appear attached to touns or vills which formed *appendicia* (*see* Maps 6–9, 11, 12).[256] Where, for example, shires or other royal estates figure on the early Exchequer Rolls, their component vills paying Crown rents commonly have *pett*-names,[257] and the same is true of episcopal rentals from Aberdeen and Dunkeld.[258] The very meaning of *pett*, a portion of something larger, seems peculiarly well suited to a shire consisting in *manerium cum appendiciis*. Moreover, we may see that in Scotia the ploughgate and the davoch (sometimes treated as identical)[259] bore some relation to the shire, in the sense that a shire seems to have been expected to contain a known total of ploughgates or davochs. It is therefore worth noting that in a number of instances the names of ploughgates and davochs were names in *pett-*. We may cite, for example, Pitteuchar in Kinglassie, West Fife (in the shire of Goatmilk).[260] Rather oddly, three ploughgates in Moulin, Perthshire, are found in the late twelfth century with four place-names attached to them, three

[254] Watson, *CPNS*, 402.

[255] *St. Andrews Liber*, 123, 190; Watson, *CPNS*, 411; *Roman and Native in North Britain*, ed. I. A. Richmond (1958), 146. Cf. Blelock in Auchtergaven, Perthshire, Blabolg in the fourteenth century (*RMS*, i, Appendix II, no. 1134).

[256] For particularly useful discussions of this much-discussed element cf. Watson, *CPNS*, 407–14; K. Jackson, *Problem of the Picts*, 146–8; W. F. H. Nicolaisen in *Dundee and District*, ed. S. J. Jones (British Association, 1968), 146–8; K. Jackson, *The Gaelic Notes in the Book of Deer* (1972), 114–16.

[257] *Exchequer Rolls*, i, 9, 39, 446, 548 (bis), 560, 564 (bis), 566, 572 (bis), 573.

[258] *Dunkeld Rentale*, references in index to Pitcairn, Pitleoch, Pitpointie, Pittendynie and others. *Aberdeen Registrum*, i, 55–6, 58, 251, 370.

[259] Below, p. 267.   [260] Below, p. 278.

being *pett*-names and the other a name in *baile*-.[261] Petcarene, now Tullochcurran, was the name of a davoch of Strathardle,[262] itself one of the four royal *maneria* (= 'shires') of Gowrie.[263] A spurious charter in the Register of Deeds stipulated for the service of two davochs from the lands of Lauriston and 'Pettennes' (= Pethannot?) in St. Cyrus, Mearns.[264] Although the charter itself cannot be authentic, the implied rating of 'Pettennes' at one davoch may have genuinely early authority. It might be argued that a shire system could have been superimposed on a country which already had *pett*- names, but even so it is worth remarking how conveniently these names seem to fit into the shires. Sometimes, as in the case of Pitlour (now in Strathmiglo, Fife, but formerly in Abernethy detached, Perthshire), they might carry anomalous county boundaries with them (*see* Map 12).[265] As the use of Gaelic spread, the incidence of *baile*- names for *appendicia* would naturally increase. Here and there we know, and in many cases we may suspect, that *pett*- names were changed into *baile*-names.[266] In English-speaking districts *appendicia* would tend to be given names in -*tūn*; this would agree well with an old land-book gloss which equates *geburatūn* with *appendicium*.[267]

In view of what has been said of the 'Eccles' names in England and southern Scotland, the place-names in Scotia containing this element seem to possess a special interest. The word **eglēs* was taken from Vulgar Latin *eclēsia* at an early period, when what Professor Jackson has called Primitive Welsh and Primitive Cumbric were forming themselves into distinct dialects, and when Christianity was still in a relatively early stage of its establishment among the P-Celtic speaking peoples of this island.[268] Where the word occurs in England it has been taken to belong to the P-Celtic

[261] *RRS*, ii, no. 321.

[262] *Moray Reg.*, no. 79; *Coupar Angus Chrs.*, i, no. 38.

[263] *RRS*, i, no. 243 (p. 264).

[264] *SRO*, Register of Deeds, viii, fo. 220r; cf. *Lindores Chartulary*, no. 8 and p. 238.

[265] *RRS*, ii, no. 339; H. Shennan, *Boundaries of Counties and Parishes in Scotland* (1892), 256.

[266] E.g. Pitlochry, modern Gaelic Baile Chloichrigh, and to other instances given by Watson, *CPNS*, 407, we may add two farm names from the 'shire' of Alvie in Badenoch, Pitourie now Ballourie and Pitchurn now Balchurn, for which cf. I. F. Grant, *Everyday Life on an old Highland Farm, 1769–1782* (1924), 158, 167; Macfarlane, *Geographical Coll.*, ii, 574. *See* Map 13.

[267] Above, n. 89.   [268] Above, n. 71.

stratum of our linguistic history, and the same view has been held, but extremely cautiously, of a number of its occurrences in the south of Scotland.[269] The problem, as noted by Professor Cameron, is how to interpret the Scottish 'Eccles' names in general, most of which are found north of the Forth. In the formation of ecclesiastical place-names, the usual Gaelic word for 'church' was *cell*, in the dative case *cill*.[270] This produced the well-known 'Kil-' names (e.g. Kilmacolm, Kilmarnock, Kilwinning) which are to be found almost everywhere in Scotland north of Forth and also fairly numerously in the south-west.[271] Their distribution, however, shows vastly greater numbers in the western isles and along the western seaboard and as the map is followed eastward the reduction in numbers is very marked. It is true that up and down the eastern side of Scotland such names are by no means unknown. In Fife, for instance, we have Kilrenny, Kilmany, Kilmaron, Kilconquhar and Kilgourie; in Perthshire Kirkmichael was formerly Kylmichel;[272] in Aberdeenshire there are Kennethmont and, near Fyvie, a lost 'Kilmaclome';[273] in Moray Kilmalemnock.[274] Nevertheless, such names remain a comparative rarity anywhere east of the Perthshire glens and the braes of Angus, Mar and Moray. The distribution of Scottish 'Eccles' names (whose total is very much smaller than that of 'Kil-' names) shows an almost exactly opposite pattern (*see* Map 14). 'Eccles' names surviving in medieval or seventeenth-century record, or to the present day, are largely confined to southern Scotland (except for the extreme south-west, Ayrshire, Wigtown and Kirkcudbright) and, north of the Forth–Clyde line, to the eastern counties of the country.[275] Indeed, with possible though doubtful exceptions

[269] K. Cameron, 'Eccles in English Place-names', in *Christianity in Britain, 400–700*, 90–1.

[270] Watson, *CPNS*, *passim*; J. M. Mackinlay, *Influence of the Pre-Reformation Church on Scottish Place-names*, 74–120.

[271] Watson, *CPNS*, chapters VI and VII shows that names in *cill-* occur rather more frequently in Ayrshire and Renfrewshire than in Dumfriesshire, Kirkcudbright and Wigtownshire.

[272] *Dunfermline Reg.*, no. 227.

[273] Kennethmont < Kelalcmund, *RRS*, ii, no. 295; Kilmaclome occurs in 1266 (*Exchequer Rolls*, i, 21).

[274] Watson, *CPNS*, 327–8.

[275] This statement is derived chiefly from obvious sources such as *RMS*, *Retours*, Macfarlane, *Geographical Coll.*, and Mackinlay, op. cit., 65ff.

MAP 14. 'Eccles' names in eastern Scotland. Two names not shown are Eccles (in Penpont) and the parish of Ecclefechan, both in Dumfriesshire. Chief sources are *Retours*, *Reg. Mag. Sig.*, Mackinlay, *Pre-Reformation Church and Scottish Place-names*, Cowan, *Parishes*, and Watson, *CPNS*.

in the Lennox and Easter Ross,[276] they seem to be confined to the area from mid-Aberdeenshire to Fife and east Perthshire. Anyone proposing to classify these names as Gaelic would therefore have to overcome the serious objection that Gaelic-speaking Scots, or Picts who had borrowed Gaelic, would not have been likely to use the Old Irish *eclais* (Gaelic, *eaglais*) in eastern Scotland when the overwhelmingly general usage in the west had been to use *cill*, especially since it is clear from surviving names that names in *cill-* could be formed in the east just as well as in the west. To suppose such a radical change in name-forming habits as the Gaelic speakers moved eastward, or as Gaelic began to replace Pictish in the east, seems to fly in the face of probability. For the 'Eccles' names occur in just those areas where P-Celtic names have succeeded in surviving in largest numbers, where in fact we have the 'test elements' such as *aber, pett, pol, pert*, etc.[277] If it be the case that 'Eccles' names do not occur north of Monymusk in central Aberdeenshire, this would provide interesting confirmation of Bede's belief that Christianity reached the Pictish people in two instalments, an early (fifth-century?) instalment reaching the Picts 'on this side of the mountains', and a second instalment, in the sixth century and later, reaching those 'beyond the mountains'.[278]

Whatever date we give for the origin of the primitive shire, we can hardly suppose that it was invented by the church. The church adapted itself to the existing social system. If 'Eccles' names seem to occur in association with shires more frequently than could be dismissed as coincidence—and this seems to be true of England and southern Scotland—the reasonable inference would surely be that many of the earliest churches were deliberately

---

[276] Shanacles in Kilmaronock, Dunbartonshire is Schennaglische in *Retours*, Dumbarton, and this is no doubt a straightforwardly Gaelic name, *sean eaglais*, 'old kirk', and not a true 'eccles' name. More problematical, however, is Eglas or Egleis, recorded in *Retours*, Ross and Cromarty, for the lands of Kirkfairburn in Urray, Ross.

[277] See *Problem of the Picts*, 147, 150, for maps showing the distribution of some of these elements. The argument put forward here does not seem to be weakened by the fact that a majority of surviving 'pett-' names are hybrid Pictish/Gaelic; indeed, it may be suggested that many 'eccles' names are likely to be of some hybrid type (cf. W. F. H. Nicolaisen, in *Dundee and district* (1968), 148).

[278] *Hist. Eccles*, iii, 4 (ed. Plummer, i, 133).

founded shire by shire, and often placed close to the shire centre, as in Hallamshire, Salfordshire or Blackburnshire. Thus, if we find that most of the 'Eccles' names of Scotia are distributed shire by shire (there are certainly exceptions), it would be possible to argue that shires were already there when the first missionaries came. And in this connexion, it is worth remarking how many Scottish 'Eccles' names are no longer capable of location on the modern map, or no longer referred to actual places of worship even at the time, some centuries ago, when they were recorded in legal documents (*see* Map 14). A class of names which shows such a strikingly high proportion of lost names and lost places may be thought to be an old class, unless there are strong reasons to the contrary.

It is time to see what conclusion, however tentative, we have reached as a result of several distinct lines of argument. The words 'thane' and 'shire' seem to have come into Scotland north of the Forth to denote respectively a ministerial tenant and a subdivision of royal demesne already existing and already shared with England and Wales. The adoption of these Old English words may be seen as part of that unmeasured but persistent Anglian influence among the Picts whose earliest recorded beginnings go back to King Oswald's time, and which may go back to King Æthelfrith's or even before. But of course it is not suggested that the borrowing of these actual words took place at such an early date as that, in the sixth or seventh centuries. If it could be accepted (following Professor Henry Loyn's work)[279] that *þeg(e)n*, in the sense of a landed retainer of the king, enjoying an estate and privileges yet carrying out governmental, judicial, and even agrarian responsibilities, did not gain a wide currency in England until the ninth century, perhaps the later ninth century at that, then we could scarcely date the importation of the word into Scots usage much before the tenth century. Nevertheless, its adoption must surely have been due to a real English influence, which has left other traces in such things as personal names and place-names (e.g., the Fife hybrid place-name Ballebotle, now Babbet and the Fife hybrid personal name Gillecuthbert).[280] In

---

[279] H. R. Loyn, 'Gesiths and Thegns in Anglo-Saxon England from the seventh to the tenth century', *EHR*, lxx (1955), 529–49.

[280] *North Berwick Carte*, no. 4 (cf. *St. Andrews Liber*, 137, 180).

the same way, we should probably ascribe the adoption of the Gaelic word *toisech* to mean 'thane', of which there is much less abundant yet nonetheless firm evidence,[281] to an unmeasured yet persistent Scottish influence among the Picts which may go back to the early sixth century and must have gathered momentum steadily from the seventh century onwards. Until work has been done on the Old English word *scir* to match what Loyn has done for *þeg(e)n* we are left guessing in the dark as to the likely period for its adoption into Scottish usage.

Other questions will remain. For example, if shires and thanes in some form or other already existed in Scotland before those terms came to be used, by what terms were they previously known? Here it can only be suggested, as a possible field for future investigation, that some word cognate with, or ancestral to, Old Irish *cathir*, 'city' (secondarily, 'monastery'),[282] or Primitive Welsh *caer*, 'fortified centre',[283] might have lain behind the historical 'shire' in Scotland. This might explain such names as Cathermothel and Catherlauenache (Carlownie), for which no satisfactory explanation has ever been forthcoming.[284] It might also explain such 'shire' place-names as Kirkcaldy (otherwise tautologously explained as 'fort of hard-fort')[285] and perhaps Crail (Carel, Karel, etc.).[286] We should also notice the use of the word *cathir* in the legendary narrative which prefaces the Gaelic *notitiae* in the Book of Deer.[287] When, according to this narrative, Columba and Drostan came to Buchan, the local mormaer offered them the *cathir* of Aberdour as a site for a monastery, but finding that Aberdour did not suit them they would not be

---

[281] W. J. Watson, *The Place-names of Ross and Cromarty* (Inverness, 1904), 114; Skene, *Celtic Scotland*, iii, 270, 272–4. Cf. Jackson, *Gaelic Notes in the Book of Deer*, 112–14.

[282] *Dictionary of the Irish Language* (Royal Irish Adademy, 1913–), s.v. A. Graham, 'Archaeological Gleanings from Dark Age Records', *PSAS*, lxxxv, 64–91 (see esp. 66, 68), is not helpful.

[283] A. H. Smith, *English Place-name Elements*, i, 76, s.v. *cair*.

[284] Watson's explanation (*CPNS*, 223) that Cathermothel refers to the Roman camp at Ardoch, some five miles from Muthil, is unconvincing; and of Catherlauenache he merely says that it means 'elm-fort' without locating the fort in question. He says that both names 'came to be used as names of districts', but perhaps they had always been so used.

[285] *CPNS*, 371.

[286] *CPNS*, 369, where, however, the name is not explained.

[287] Jackson, *Gaelic Notes in the Book of Deer*, 30 (translated, 33).

satisfied until they had exchanged it for 'the other *cathir*' of Deer. Professor Jackson, the latest editor of these texts, takes *cathir* in this passage to bear its normal later Irish meaning of 'monastery'.[288] The story, however, contains no suggestion that the two saints had time to found any monastery at Aberdour (nor is there the slightest evidence that a monastery ever existed at that place), while *cathir* is used of Deer before the monastery had been founded. The story, indeed, reads very awkwardly if one insists on translating *cathir* by 'monastery'. We might also imagine some word such as *cathir* behind the *magna civitas* employed by the writer of the Chronicle of the Kings of Scotland, *sub annis* 971–95, to describe Brechin.[289] It is not in the least unlikely that Cathermothel (= Muthil parish), Catherlauenache (= Strageath, afterwards Blackford parish), Aberdour, Deer and Brechin had formed ancient and distinct portions of royal or princely demesne; and it may be remarked in passing that all of them save Blackford still contain place-names in *pett-* today,[290] while Brechin and Deer once contained more *pett-* names than they do now.[291]

Another Latin word which may have been used by early writers to convey the sense of 'shire' in its meaning of 'royal centre plus district or *appendicia*' is *urbs*, as found in certain contexts in Bede's *Ecclesiastical History* and Eddius's *Life of Wilfrid*. In these writings we find such names as *urbs Giudi* (? Inveresk, i.e. Musselburghshire), *Coludi urbs* (Coldinghamshire), *urbs Bebbae* (Bamburghshire).[292] The royal *urbs* called *Inbroninis* (*In Bromis?*)[293] where Wilfrid was incarcerated might have been a lost shire located by the River Breamish (*Bromic*),[294] perhaps in the neighbourhood of Hedgeley or Beanley which was comital demesne in the twelfth century.[295] The seventh-century *urbs regis* of Dunbar

---

[288] Jackson, 30.   [289] *Chron. Picts-Scots*, 10.

[290] Pett, Pitkellony (Muthil); Pitnacalder (Aberdour); Pitfour, Pitfoskie (Deer); Pitforthie, Pittendriech (Brechin).

[291] For Deer, cf. Jackson, op. cit., 41, where Pett mec Garnait is likely to have been close to Deer. Brechin had a lost Pitpollok occurring frequently in *Brechin Reg.* (references in index).

[292] *Hist. Eccles.*, i, 12; iv, 19, 25; iii, 6, 16 (ed. Plummer, i, 25; 243, 262; and 138, 158–9).

[293] Eddius Stephanus, *Life of Wilfrid*, ed. Colgrave, 72.

[294] *Symeon of Durham*, i, 199.

[295] *Northumberland County History*, xiv, 399.

(*Dynbaer*)[296] in East Lothian was almost certainly a shire-centre in the eleventh and twelfth centuries. In these and similar instances the primary reference of the word *urbs* was no doubt to the fortified centre itself. But if the pattern of north British royal lordship suggested in the preceding pages is close to the truth such centres would have been integrally linked to the districts dependent on them, and it would make little difference whether we regard *urbs* as signifying the centre by itself or the centre and its district taken together. For the district as distinct from, or as subsuming, the centre, Bede and his contemporaries have the words *regio* and *provincia*, but it has always been recognised that Bede used these words in a variety of senses.[297] It is however worth noting that in his account of Aedan's life as bishop among the Northumbrians (634–51), Bede says that he used to travel about the kingdom preaching 'per cuncta et urbana et rustica loca'.[298] We can scarcely translate this as 'in cities and in rural areas', but it would surely make good sense to take it as meaning that Aedan preached not only at the shire centres but also in the berewicks or *appendicia* 'lying to' those centres.

One Celtic word which is an obvious candidate as the forerunner of thane in Scotland is Primitive Welsh *maer*, agreed to be a borrowing of Latin *maior*.[299] The word is of course familiar in medieval and later Scottish usage as mair (*marus*), the title of various petty officials concerned with collecting taxes or carrying out the necessary routine of the courts, e.g. executing summonses and poinding, putting rebels to the horn and giving sasine to one party in a land suit.[300] Officials of this comparatively subordinate kind were quite distinct from thanes, but Professor W. Croft Dickinson showed long ago that the Scottish mair had once been a more dignified officer with higher responsibilities, and he draws our attention to the interesting fact that Wyntoun, in a passage

---

[296] *Life of Wilfrid*, 76. Dunbar became the chief place of the comital dynasty of Cospatric (afterwards earls of Dunbar or March). We may note that the Anonymous Life of St. Cuthbert refers to a *regio* called Ahse (Aehse, Echse) midway between Hexham and Carlisle (*Two Lives of Saint Cuthbert*, ed. B. Colgrave (1940), 116), possibly represented by Haltwhistle, Hakatwisel in 1178 (*RRS*, ii, no. 197).

[297] Stenton, *Anglo-Saxon England*, 18, 290–2.

[298] *Hist. Eccles.*, iii, 5 (ed. Plummer, i, 135).

[299] Jackson, *Language and History in Early Britain*, 354.

[300] *Fife Court Bk.*, pp. lxiv–lxv.

dealing with William the Conqueror, uses 'mair' apparently as equivalent to 'thane'.[301] A class of senior mairs, to which the borrowed term *þegn* came to be applied between the tenth and the twelfth century, would have had a natural place in a hierarchy whose upper ranks are known to have contained, under the king, a small number of mormaers. We may now accept that mormaer meant 'great *maer*',[302] and we know that these important officers held power and authority over the principal provinces of Scotia. Thus the gradation mormaer: maer would have been formally equivalent to earl: thane, but appropriate to the period before the English terms had been fully adopted. If the term *maer* survived more stubbornly in south-western Scotland, under Cumbric influence, this might help to account for the fact that the term 'thane' never seems to have secured a foothold in that region.[303]

[301] *Fife Court Bk.*, p. lxii, no. 3 (*Chron. Wyntoun* (Laing), ii, 158).
[302] Jackson, *Gaelic Notes in the Book of Deer*, 103-9.
[303] Cf. *RRS*, i, p. 45 and no. 242.

2 The *judex*

We have little evidence of judicial arrangements or of judicial officers in Scotland before the twelfth century. Notoriously the fact that record of sufficient quantity and reliability becomes available only from the twelfth century means, in this instance as in others, that what appears for the first time in this century may have been developing over a long period. It has long been recognised that the *judex* represented a survival from pre-twelfth-century Scotland, that he formed a part of the older, Celtic order of society. It has also long been known that gradually the *judex*, under his more familiar title of 'dempster', sank from a prominent to a subordinate, eventually to an insignificant, position. This chapter reviews the evidence for the existence and functions of the *judex* from *c.* 1100 to *c.* 1300.

The *judex* deserves more attention than he has yet received from legal historians, and more than can be given him here. Among other things, there should be more study of the comparative position of the Scottish *judex* and his counterparts in other parts of the British Isles which had, or appear to have had, a related judicial system—the *breitheam* of Ireland, the deemster of Man, the lawman of the Isles and Scandinavian England, and certain of the *judices* and doomsmen occurring in English record of the eleventh and twelfth centuries. There is space here only for three contributions to a fuller study: (1) an account of the various types of activity which surviving record allows us to attribute to the *judex*; (2) a provisional list (which could no doubt be augmented from more exhaustive research) of *judices* mentioned in this record (appendix A); and (3) two unpublished documents which throw light on one important aspect of the *judex*'s duties in the reign of William the Lion (appendix B). It will, I think, emerge even from this brief study that the *judex* was not merely a survival, but a somewhat remarkable survival, from Celtic

Scotland. A long series of personal names can be established, running from the reign of David I to that of Robert I, among which names of an archaic or vernacular type show a notable predominance. The conservatism of which this is evidence suggests nothing less than the tenacious survival of an ancient judicial caste.

A brieve of David I in favour of Dunfermline abbey permitted the abbey's tenants at Newburn to be impleaded only in the abbey's court, but stipulated that the king's *judex* of that province should be present in the court 'in order that lawsuits and judgements should be prosecuted and given justly'.[1] Three *judices*, two of whom were evidently attached to the province of Fife and Fothrif, took part in the famous trial of the dispute anent the marches of Kirkness, *c.* 1128.[2] Two of these three *judices*, Earl Constantine of Fife and Maldoueni son of Macbeth, deferred to the seniority and greater wisdom of their colleague, Dufgal son of Mocche, noted for his skill in the law (*juris peritia*).[3] The so-called *Assise Regis Willelmi* contain four chapters which mention *judices*, and there seems nothing to suggest that these particular chapters are not authentic products of William I's reign.[4] Chapter X refers to earls, barons and *judices* of Scotia formally approving an assize of no great importance. Chapter XXVI, drawn up at Montrose, decreed that whenever the king entered any province the *judices* (the plural is noteworthy) of that province must attend him by the first night after his arrival and must not leave the court before the king's departure save with his permission. If any of them did so, he would forfeit eight cows to the king. The *judices* of Galloway approved certain criminal law provisions at Dumfries (chapter XXII), and in chapter XXIII they are shown giving a ruling in the *curia regis* at Lanark (on 1 May in an unknown year between 1175 and 1200) anent the levying of the king's cain throughout Galloway.

These texts show clearly that *judices* were normally attached to a province and that there could be more than one *judex* of a province at any one time. More generally they suggest that the *judex* had an important part to play in the administration of law and justice, including justice dispensed in the *curia regis*. This is borne out by an examination of the list given below in appendix

---

[1] Lawrie, *Charters*, no. 105.   [2] Lawrie, *Charters*, no. 80.
[3] Lawrie, *Charters*, 67.   [4] *Acts Parl. Scot.*, i, 374, 378–9.

A, which not only shows *judices* explicitly attached to the provinces of Caithness, Buchan, Mearns, Angus, Gowrie, Fife, Strathearn, Lennox and Nithsdale (Strathnith), but also includes a number of *judices* to whom the title *regis* is applied.

In extant record *judices* are mentioned most commonly in the testing clauses of charters and similar legal documents. Here their functions cannot be distinguished from those of other witnesses, but two points may be noted. The first is that probably the large majority of these formally attested *acta*, at least for the greater part of the period we are reviewing, were issued at the session of some court, either royal or private. The frequency with which *judices* appear as charter witnesses is some evidence that they were carrying out one duty expected of them by David I. Secondly we should notice that the decline in the standing of the *judex* can already be discerned before the end of our period in the charters and their witness-lists. In the twelfth century the *judex*'s name regularly appears high up in the witness-list; towards the end of the thirteenth century it is usual to find his name in a distinctly subordinate position. What is more, there is an interesting variation in the class of legal document to which a *judex* was named as witness. Thus *judices* seldom witnessed ecclesiastical *acta*, and with one notable exception they are rarely found witnessing royal acts after the reign of David I. The exception is Brice, evidently the king's *judex* of Angus, who attested fairly regularly the *acta* of King William I whenever these were issued in the region between Mearns and Gowrie.[5] This fact recalls chapter XXVI of the *Assise Willelmi*. It is tempting to suppose that Brice himself had some hand in the promulgation of this particular assize, and was almost the only royal *judex* who faithfully observed its provisions. Most of the *acta* witnessed by *judices* were issued by earls or lesser lay subjects. Even here, however, there is evidence of declining status. Nothing is more striking than the frequency with which acts of Earl Gilbert of Strathearn (1198 x 1208) were witnessed by Constantine, *judex* of Strathearn,[6] but it is uncommon to find acts of Earl Gilbert's successors witnessed by subsequent *judices*. Far more private legal documents have survived from the thirteenth century than from the twelfth, but instead of becoming

[5] *RRS*, ii, nos. 343, 454, 466, 497, 590.
[6] *Inchaffray Chrs.*, nos. 3–5, 9, 11–17, 19, 25.

easier to discover *judices* in these later records it seems actually to become harder.

In the documents studied for the purposes of this article there is evidence of *judices* taking part in the making of an extent,[7] witnessing a decision in the justiciar's court anent replegiation in a case of cattle stealing,[8] serving on an inquest anent forinsec service,[9] being sworn, diligently examined and interrogated at an ecclesiastical inquiry into common pasture rights,[10] attending the head court of a barony,[11] placing a seal to a legal document at the granter's instance,[12] and attending the justiciar's court.[13] All these examples relate to Scotland north of Forth. In the reign of Alexander I, when his brother David was ruling Cumbria and Teviotdale, the Cumbrian *judices* Leising and Oggo in company with three other local notables swore that certain lands were the property of the church of Glasgow.[14]

Overwhelmingly the commonest activity of the *judex*, as far as surviving records go, was the formal perambulation of marches, to determine the lawful boundaries of estates. With this process frequently went the act of *traditio*, putting a person in sasine of the land whose marches had been publicly and lawfully determined by perambulation. If we include one instance where the *judex* is explicitly said to have taken part in an act of *traditio* at the command of the king,[15] we have record of ten occurrences of perambulations in which *judices* took part, even if only as witnesses.[16] This probably does not mean that perambulation was in fact the legal activity in which *judices* most commonly joined, but merely that of all their activities this was the one likely to be recorded in documents worth preserving.

The two documents printed below in appendix B from the unpublished Arbroath abbey cartulary (British Museum, MS. Add. 33254) give evidence of *judices* taking part in perambulations which supplements that already known from other sources. No. I

[7] *Moray Registrum*, app., Carte Originales, no. 19.
[8] *Arbroath Liber*, i, no. 231.   [9] *Arbroath Liber*, no. 250.
[10] National Library of Scotland [NLS], MS. Adv. 34.6.24, p. 217.
[11] *HMC 7th Rep.*, App., p. 705.   [12] *St. Andrews Liber*, 349.
[13] *St. Andrews Liber*, 347; *Laing Chrs.*, no. 8.   [14] Lawrie, *Charters*, no. 50.
[15] *Coupar Angus Rental*, i, 325 (no. 14).
[16] *Coupar Angus Rental*, i, 325 (no. 14); *Arbroath Liber*, i, nos. 227, 228, 229, 366; British Museum [B.M.], MS. Add. 33245, fos. 160, 162–3; *Dunfermline Registrum*, no. 196; Lawrie, *Charters*, no. 80.

names Brice, the king's *judex*, and Bozli, *judex* of Mearns, as participants in a perambulation of land held by Geoffrey de Melville in what is now Fordoun parish. The letter probably belongs to the period 1199–1214, and the perambulation referred to evidently took place between 1172 and 1199. No. II is a testimonial declaration by Brice the *judex regis* himself. It thus has a unique distinction, for no other document issued by a *judex* in his judicial capacity is known to survive from this period. Brice's declaration relates to an important perambulation of land in Mearns which has long been known from a document in the printed Arbroath cartulary.[17] The perambulation was carried out on the king's orders under the direction of Earl Gilbert of Strathearn and Bishop Matthew of Aberdeen, acting as royal justiciars. Brice the *judex* was present with them at the king's command so that the dispute might be settled by good men who should perambulate the land in question according to the assize and custom of the realm.[18] Brice was not the only *judex* present, for the list of jurors and perambulators given in his declaration (a fuller list than that given in the published cartulary) shows that among them was Duncan the *judex*, while his colleague Boli Mac Gillerachcah may perhaps have been the same as Bozli the *judex* of Mearns addressed in no. I. It may have been in the capacity of senior *judex* present that Brice had the duty of proffering the reliquary or shrine on which the perambulators took their oath to act justly without fear or favour. One may compare a perambulation for 8 January 1493, in which the disputants were to abide by 'al and quhatsumevir marchis and devisis of propyr and commone pastur assygnit marchit and devidit be the saidis assisowris of perambulacione or the mar part of thame sworne tharto apone Sanct Marnoys ferteris in presens of the Kyngis justice'.[19] Here the role of the *judex* seems to come very close to

---

[17] *Arbroath Liber*, i, no. 89; another text appears in B.M., MS. Add. 33245, fo. 145.

[18] This reinforces the evidence noted by the editors of the *Acts of the Parliaments of Scotland* (vol. i, 53) implying the existence of an enactment of King David I anent perambulation whose text has now been lost.

[19] *Arbroath Liber*, ii, 227. Here 'ferteris' corresponds to the *scrinarium* of Brice's letter (see below, p. 81). Since Saint Marnan or Marnoch had a local cult in the district to which the case cited from *Arbroath Liber*, ii refers, the implication is that in every district some locally venerated shrine or reliquary was available, which could be used for the purpose of legal oath-taking.

that of the toschederach, and it is worth noting that the geographical distribution of these officials seems to have coincided almost exactly.[20]

These two documents reinforce the impression that the *judex* remained a key figure in the administration of the law north of the Forth well into the thirteenth century.

Appendix A

List of judices *occurring in record of the twelfth and thirteenth centuries*

This list is arranged under provinces, running roughly north to south. Where the province name is given without brackets, the *judex* is explicitly attached to that province in at least one of the sources. Where the province appears in brackets, the context of the source is such as to suggest attachment to that province. Where a *judex* is given any title other than *judex* in the source, this is noted in italic type after the source; and whenever the *judex* is styled 'king's *judex*' this fact is noted. Dates are those of the documents constituting the source.

[20] Cf. W. C. Dickinson, 'The *Toschederach*', *Jurid. Rev.*, liii (1941), 85–109. Professor Dickinson outlined the geographical distribution on p. 103, but his statement that the office of toschederach did not occur in Galloway must be modified in the light of his own evidence (art. cit., 86) that it was known in Nithsdale.

Caithness

GILMAKALI   1225 × 1242
Moray Reg., no. 259.

(Moray)

FERGUS   1295, 1309
Moray Reg., app., Cart. Orig., nos. 19, 20.
dictus Demster.

Buchan

FARHARD   1211 × 1233

(PHERHARCHD')   1251
Abdn. Reg., i, 15; *Arb. Lib.*, i, no. 227.

(Buchan)

MATADIN   1131–2
ESC, no. 97 and p. 338.
brithem.
Probably an act issued by a mormaer of Buchan and his wife, the daughter of an earl of Fife. It is not certain whether it concerns property in Buchan or

Fife, and a Fife context must therefore be considered possible.

CRISTINUS   1300
Arb. Lib., i, no. 231.
See also Duncan, below, under (Angus and Mearns).

(Mar)

BROCCHIN   1150 × 1199
(BROCIN, BROKIN)
ESC, nos. 107, 223; *A.B. Coll.*, 546–7; B.M., MS. Add 33245, fo. 128.
The Brocin who witnesses *ESC*, no. 107 (*c.* 1173; Lawrie's date is much too early) and no. 223 (*c.* 1150) is not called a *judex*. Nevertheless, it seems not improbable that he is to be identified with Brocchin the *judex* who witnesses *A.B. Coll.*, 546–7. The remaining reference is to an important agreement relating to Angus, witnessed by several great magnates and clergy, and by three *judices*, including Brokin. Its date-limits are 1189 × 1198. Again identity is not proved, but seems possible. On the other hand we may be dealing with a father and son of the same name, each holding office in north-east Scotland. While Mar seems the most likely context, a Buchan or even an Angus context cannot be wholly ruled out.

KINETH   1187 × 1207
(KINET, KINEF)
B.M., Harley Chrs., 83. C. 24; *Lind. Cart.*, nos. 5, 81.

Mearns

BOZLI   1199 × 1214
B.M., M.S. Add. 33245, fo. 160.
Possibly the same as the juror who appears (ibid., fo. 163) as Boli Mac Gillerachcah (Gille Fhearchair?). Possibly also Bozli is to be identified with Beolin, entered below under (Angus and Mearns).

(Mearns)

DUNCAN   1198–9
B.M., MS. Add. 33245, fo. 163; cf. *Arb. Lib.*, i, no. 89.

Angus

KERALD   1228, 1244
                    1214 × 1251
Arb. Lib., i, no. 229 and nos. 133, 227, 228, 306; *Brech. Reg.*, ii, Cart. Orig., no. 1; NLS, MS. Adv. 34.6.24, p. 376.
Son of Malcolm, below; brother of Adam, below. *Judex* of Angus in 1228; king's *judex* in period 1225 × 1239.
It is probable that Careston, Angus, takes its name from this Kerald. The Dempsters of Careston were a well-known late-medieval family, from whom

the Dempsters of Dunnichen were descended.

(Angus and Mearns)

BRICE 1189 × 1221
Arb. Lib., i, nos. 34, 62, 74 *ter*, 89, 126, 206, 215; B.M., M.S. Add. 24276, fo. 53; *PSAS*, lxxxvii, 60–1; *Brech. Reg.*, i, no. 2; B.M., MS. Add. 33245, fos. 128, 160, 162–3; *Fraser Facsimiles*, no. 11.
Brice normally appears as the king's *judex*, and is not styled *judex* of Angus in any surviving record. But his activity was clearly focused on Angus, or, at its widest extent, on an area reaching from Mearns to Gowrie. *Brech. Reg.*, i, no. 2, shows him holding land at 'Kerdan' (Cardean, in Airlie, Angus, and Meigle, Perthshire) and 'Breckyn' (probably Braikie, in Kinnell, Angus).

BEOLIN 1214 × 1224
(BELDIN)
Brech. Reg., ii, Cart. Orig., no. 1; NLS, MS. Adv. 1.15.18, no. 27.
In NLS, MS. Adv. 15.1.18, no. 27, he appears as Beldin *judex* of 'Ferne' (Fern, Angus?), presumably indicating his place of residence rather than his place of jurisdiction. It is worth noting that Fern is adjacent to

Careston, for which see under Kerald, above.

MALCOLM (*c.* 1220?)
NLS, MS. Adv. 34.6.24, p. 376.
Father of Kerald, above.

ADAM 1219, 1228
Arb. Lib., i, nos. 228, 229.
Brother of Kerald, above. King's *judex* in 1228.

THOMAS 1251
Arb. Lib., i, no. 227.
This document deals with Arbroath abbey property in Tarves, Formartine. See also Thomas Squier, under (Fife and Fothrif).

DUNCAN (1248) 1250 × 1289
Brech. Reg., i, no. 3; *Arb. Lib.*, i, nos. 247, 250, 366; cf. ibid., Cart. Orig., no. VI; Fraser, *Douglas*, iii, nos. 4, 6; *Lind. Cart.*, no. 124.
Lind. Cart., no. 124, which dates 1286 × 1289, refers to Kelly, in Tarves, Formartine, but it is not certain that the charter was issued in Aberdeenshire. The identity of the Duncan *judex* who witnessed this charter with the Duncan *judex* (called king's *judex*) appearing in the remaining references must be regarded as doubtful. Gilbert earl of Angus granted to Duncan, the king's *judex*, the whole land of

'Petmulin' (cf. 'Petmowy' in the barony of Kirriemuir, 1510 [Fraser, *Douglas*, iii, 195], now Pitmuies, in Kirkden) between 1262 and 1285 (ibid., 4, no. 4). Ibid., 5–6, no. 6 is dated 1272. Christian daughter of Kerald the *judex* (see above) conceded land at 'Abernaftathar,' Angus to Duncan the *judex* (NLS, MS. Adv. 34.6.24, p. 377.

ANDREW   1296, 1304, 1306
Cal. Docs. Scot., ii, p. 203 and nos. 730, 816; Palgrave, *Docs. Hist. Scot.*, 306.
le Jugeor, le Jugger, le Demsterre.

KERALD   *c.* 1304–7?
C.A. Chrs., nos. 74, 77.
These documents relate to land in Blairgowrie and Rattray parish, Gowrie, but the name Kerald suggests a relationship to the earlier Kerald.

(Atholl)

MALISE   *c.* 1198
NLS, MS. Adv. 15.1.18, no. 60.

EWAYN   1264
St. A. Lib., 349.

Gowrie or Perth

MACBETH   1189 × 1197
Scone Liber, no. 21; *C.A. Rent.*, i, 325; B.M., MS. Add. 33245, fo. 128. Conceivably, this is the Macbeth who served as sheriff of Scone in this same period, for whom cf. *Arb. Lib.*, i, no. 35; *PSAS*, lxxxvii, 61.

WILLIAM DE FORDALE 1266
(FORDALL)   *c.* 1284–90
Scottish Record Office [SRO], J. Maitland Thomson Photos, no. 12; cf. *Laing Chrs.*, no. 8; *HMC, 7th Rep.*, App., 705. The first reference is to a document relating to Cultmalundie, in Tibbermore, Perthshire. Possibly William de Fordale took his name from Fordel, in Arngask, rather than Fordell in Dalgety.
King's *judex* of Perth (*c.* 1284–90).

(Gowrie)

DUNCAN   *c.* 1225(?)
C.A. Chrs., no. 37.

ARTHUR   1288 × 1306
C.A. Rent., ii, 289.

KERALD   *c.* 1304–7?
C.A. Chrs., nos. 74, 77.
See above, under (Angus and Mearns).

Fife

MACUNGAL   1160–2
St. A. Lib., 128.

MALCOLM   1165 × 1171
St. A. Lib., 247.

(Fife and Fothrif)

DUFGAL son of MOCCHE
c. 1128
ESC, no. 80.

MELDOINNETH son of MACHE-
DATH c. 1128 × c. 1136
(MALDOUENI, MALDOUENI
MACOCBETH, MALEDOUN
son of MACBEAD)
ESC, nos. 68, 74, 80, 97.

HENRY c. 1170–80
St. Andrews Liber, 254–5.

MALCOLM 1200 × 1238
St. A. Lib., 329; NLS, MS. Adv.
15.1.18, no. 20; B.M., Loans
29, no. 355.

THOMAS SCUTIFER c. 1250
(THOMAS DICTUS 1260, 1266
SQUIER, THOMAS
SQUIER)
St. A. Lib., 347; *Laing Chrs.*, no.
8; NLS, MS. Adv. 34.6.24,
p. 217. Described as king's
judex.

JOHN DE POTYN 1260
St. A. Lib., 346.
The reference is to a session of
the justiciar's court held at
Perth, but relating to land in
Fife. John de Potyn (his name
doubtless from Pottie, in Dron)
is described as *judex* for that
day.

WALTER 1260
St. A. Lib., 346.
See preceding note.

RICHARD DE FODY c. 1290–5
Laing Chrs., no. 15.
Surname doubtless from Foo-
die, in Dairsie.

ROGER KAYR c. 1330(?)
Balmerino Liber, 37–8; NLS,
MS. Adv. 34.6.24, p. 486.
King's *judex*.

(Fothrif or Gowrie)

BRIDIN POTANACH
1227 × 1231
(BRIDUS PORTANAHE)
Dunf. Reg., no. 196; SRO, J.
Maitland Thomson Transcripts,
5.
Bridin is called king's *judex*.
The first reference relates to
Dunduff, in Dunfermline, the
second to Moncreiffe, in Dunbarney. Potanach is perhaps
formed adjectivally from Potin,
i.e. Pottie, in Dron.

(Fothrif)

ANGUS 1204 × 1230
Dunf. Reg., no. 145.
This charter relates to Cleish,
Kinross-shire.

Strathearn

CONSTANTINE c. 1189 × 1208

Inchaff. Chrs., nos. 3–5, 9, 11–17, 19, 25; *Arb. Lib.*, i, no. 35.
Constantine probably had sons named Gillecrist and Gilbert; cf. *Inchaff. Chrs.*, no. 39; *Lind. Cart.*, no. 29.

ADAM son of Abraham
c. 1284–90
HMC 7th Rep., App., 705.

(Strathearn)

MACBETH   1221–4
Inchaff. Chrs., nos. 46, 47, 52.
Perhaps identical with Macbeth Mór, who witnessed *Inchaff. Chrs.*, nos. 51, 56.

GILLEFELAN   *c.* 1272
(GILLEFOLAN)
Inchaff. Chrs., no. 103; SRO, J. Maitland Thomson Photos, no. 12. The references relate to Pitlandy, in Fowlis Wester, and Cultmalundie, in Tibbermore.

HALDAN   1295, 1296
(HALDANY)   *c.* 1290
Camb. Reg., no. 7; *Moray Reg.*, 467–9; *Cal. Docs. Scot.*, ii, p. 200.

de Emester, for *Demester*.

(Menteith)

DUNCAN   *c.* 1275
NLS, MS. Adv. 34.6.24, p. 377.
Granted Lanrick in Menteith by Earl Walter Stewart.

Dᴋs

Lennox

GILLECRIST   *c.* 1208–34
(CRISTINUS)
Fraser Facsimiles, no. 36; *Pais. Reg.*, 174–5, 178.
Dead before 1234.
A Lennox man named as excommunicate in a document of 1294 (*Pais. Reg.*, 203), Gillecolm son of Dovenald Macbref, may give the names of a son and grandson of a Lennox *judex*.

(Lennox)

GILBERT   1204 × 1241
Kelso Liber, no. 222.

(Carrick)

GILMUR   1260
SHR, xxxiv, 48–9.

(Desnes, or East Galloway)

MACMARES   1162 × 1175
Holy. Lib., no. 23.

NEUM (NEUIN?) *c.* 1185 × 1228
MACANARGUS
Holy. Lib., no. 70.

Strathnith

GILLECRIST   Late xii cent.
(KILLECRIST)
Kel. Lib., no. 347; *Holy. Lib.*, no. 55; SRO, Yule Collection, III, no. 1.

(Strathnith)

GILLID   1214 × 1229
Melr. Lib., i, no. 199.

Cumbria

LEYSING   *c.* 1100–30
(LESING, LEISING)
ESC, nos. 20, 50, 153.

OGGO   *c.* 1100–30
(OGGA, OGGU)
ESC, nos. 20, 50, 153.

Scotia (?)

CONSTANTINE   *c.* 1128
earl of Fife
ESC, no. 80.
Called *magnus judex in Scotia.*
But see below, p. 105.

Appendix B

I

Letter of Gilbert earl of Strathearn anent a perambulation in
Mearns (1199 × 1214).
British Museum, MS. Add. 33245, fo. 160[r-v].[1]

Rubric: Gilberti comitis de Strathern testimoniales littere super
justa perambulacione Galfridi de Malavilla et terre illius quam
tunc temporis habuit Robertus filius Warnebaldi.

Gilbertus Comes de Strathern Bricio Judici domini Regis, Bozli[2]
Judici Mernis, Morahe Mac enprior et omnibus aliis viventibus
presens scriptum visuris vel audituris qui ad perambulacionem
terre Galfridi de Malevilla et terre illius quam modo tenet
Robertus filius Warnebald' fuerunt, salutem et amicicias.
Noveritis me et Matheum Episcopum de Aberden et Bricium
Judicem domini Regis et Morahe[3] Macenprior et multos alios
quorum quidam vivunt quidam defuncti sunt interfuisse ex
precepto domini Regis ad perambulacionem terre Galfridi de
Malevilla et terre illius quam prenominatus Robertus filius
Warnebald' tenet in presenti, et nos terras illas juste et legitime
pro posse nostro in divisis legitimis earundem perambulasse in
tantum quod nos qui infueramus ex parte domini Regis et

---

[1] Punctuation and the use of u, v, i and j have been modernised.
[2] So in MS., with a line of suspension or contraction over the name. Note
Boli among the jurors in no. II.
[3] The MS. transposes *et* and *Morahe.*

sepenominatus Galfridus in unum tunc temporis convenimus. Unde michi vestri amico est consilium salubre ne divisas predictarum terrarum a tam probis et sapientibus hominibus perambulatas in aliquo transmutetis. Valete.

II

Letter of Brice *judex regis* anent a perambulation in Mearns (11 November 1221).
British Museum, MS. Add. 33245, fos. 162^{v}–163^{r}.

Rubric: Balfeith terrarum perambulationis littere, inter Unfridum de Barklay et Valterum filium Sibaldi.

Noverint omnes hoc scriptum visuri vel audituri quod ego Bricius Judex domini Regis, volens testimonium perhibere fidele de hiis que veraciter novi, coram Deo et sanctis eius protestor quod cum quondam esset controversia inter Unfridum de Berkelay et Valterum filium Sibaldi[4] super divisis terrarum eiusdem Unfridi quas dedit ei dominus Rex Willelmus pro humagio et servicio suo et terrarum eiusdem Valteri et earundem pertinen*tiis*, ex precepto domini Regis Willelmi convenerunt super terras eorum Matheus Episcopus Aberdonen*sis* et Gilbertus Comes de Strathern' tunc Justiciarii domini Regis. Et ego Bricius Judex domini Regis unacum eis affui ex precepto domini Regis ad litem inter predictos milites dirimendam per bonos viros qui perambularent terras eorum secundum assisam et consuetudinem Regni. Ita scilicet quod ambulacio facta fuit illo die a bonis viris et qui bene sciebant divisas terrarum predictorum militum et qui, accepto scrinario a manu mea, juraverunt quod neque propter aliquod donum neque propter timorem Unfridi de Berkel' qui tunc fuit vicecomes obmitterent, quin juste et per rectas divisas perambularent terras predictas. Facta ergo fuit perambulacio per has divisas, scilicet a mosso usque ad nemus et de nemore usque ad fontem et de fonte usque ad profundum vadum, et de vado usque ad Feach, et deinde versus orientem, ita quod dimiserunt Belfeach[5] a dextris, et ita descenderunt usque ad Bervyn'.[6] Hii autem fuerunt perambulatores qui juraverunt: Anegus Mac

[4] Fo. 163r. [5] Balfeith, in Fordoun. [6] The Bervie Water.

Dunecan', Malbride Macleod et Dufscolok de Fetherhessach et Murah et Malmore Mac Gillemichel et Gillecrist Mac Flafarh'[7] et Cormac de Nug, Boli Mac Gillerachcah,[8] Dunecanus judex, Gillepatric Macprior, Malisius Machormandi, Gillecrist Macblei et Kennach' Macblei. Et hoc protestatus sum apud Forfar die Sancti Martini eodem anno postquam domina Regina Johanna primo intravit in Scociam, coram domino nostro Rege Allexandro et coram domino Willelmo de Boscho Cancellario domini Regis, et domino *Thoma* clerico, Johanne de Makhesuel senescaldo domini Regis, et domino Hervico de Kynros, et domino Johanne de Haya, et domino Roberto de Inverkelid*er* Vicecomite de Mernis,[9] Ada senescaldo domini Abbatis de Aberbr*othoc*, et multis aliis. Et ad huius rei maiorem securitatem faciendam inposterum huic scripto sigillum meum apposui.

[7] In *Arbroath Liber*, i, no. 89, the charter of Humphrey de Berkeley, this name appears as Gillecrist mac Fadwerth'. The best version is given in the copy of this charter in B.M. MS. Add. 33245, fo. 145ᵛ, Gillecrist mac Fladwerthah. It is the Gaelic personal name Flaithbertach (Flaherty).

[8] With Boli compare Bozli above, no. 1. Gillerachcah may be for Gille Fhearchair, 'servant of (Saint) Ferchar'. Watson, *CPNS*, 304, suggested that there might have been 'a saint named Ferchar who does not appear in the Calendars'. Glenfarquhar (in Fordoun), part of Humphrey de Berkeley's fief, and the name of this juror's father, may be evidence of a small local cult of a saint named Ferchar in Mearns.

[9] This document helps to eke out our sketchy evidence for the succession of sheriffs of Mearns. It shows Humphrey de Berkeley holding this office approximately between 1172 and 1199. John de Hastings was sheriff of Mearns in the period 1165 × 1178 (*Spalding Misc.*, v, 209). The next certainly attested sheriffs were Robert of Inverkeilor and Philip de Melville, probably in that order. Philip de Melville occurs as sheriff in *Arbroath Liber*, i, nos. 124, 125, of uncertain date but earlier than ibid., no. 126, a royal confirmation not later than 1225. Robert of Inverkeilor was sheriff at the date of this document, 1221, and witnessed ibid., no. 127, of uncertain date. It has been held, on the strength of *Brechin Registrum*, ii, no. 1, that Robert the Steward was yet another sheriff of Mearns about this time. But in view of the fact that a witness to two contemporary charters towards the end of William the Lion's reign (*Arbroath Liber*, i, nos. 72, 74) was Robert the Steward of Inverkeilor, it seems certain that Robert of Inverkeilor and Robert the Steward were one and the same.

3   The justiciar

1   Terminology

In this chapter the word 'justiciar' is preferred to the two other words, 'justice' and 'justiciary', which are sometimes used in an identical, or in much the same, sense. It is made clear in the articles devoted to these three words by the *New English Dictionary*[1] and the *Dictionary of the Older Scottish Tongue*[2] that long-standing Scottish usage supports the choice of 'justiciar'. The word denoted the highest officer under the Crown responsible, in the thirteenth and fourteenth centuries, for the administration of justice and also in some degree, at least in the earlier part of this period, for overseeing royal government generally, as it was exercised in the various provinces of Scotland. It is true that 'justice' represents more exactly the earlier, twelfth-century, preference for the abstract noun *justitia* to denote the administrator as well as the justice he administered. But towards the end of the twelfth century *justitia*, as applied to the man, began to yield place to *justitiarius*, and this word, perhaps by way of its French derivative, had given rise, before the close of the fourteenth century, to a Scots vernacular word approximating to the modern 'justiciar'. 'Justiciary', on the other hand, was in the earliest period of its use confined to the office (*justitiaria*), a usage preserved in the modern expression, the High Court of Justiciary. It has been used for the officer (*justitiarius*) chiefly in comparatively modern times, and usually by historians, not by lawyers or administrators. Accordingly, 'justiciary' will mean here exclusively the justiciar's office, or the

[1] *A New English Dictionary on Historical Principles etc.*, edd. J. A. H. Murray and others, vol. v (Oxford, 1901), s.vv. 'Justice', III; 'Justiciar'; 'Justiciary'[1] and 'Justiciary'.[2]

[2] *A Dictionary of the Older Scottish Tongue*, edd. W. A. Craigie, A. J. Aitken and others, vol. iii (no date), s.vv. 'Justice', II; 'Justiciar', 'Justiciary'; cf. also 'Justery'.

activity of administering law and justice. As a rule, 'justiciar' will be used for the officer who forms the subject-matter of this chapter, although where special circumstances warrant it the word 'justice' may also be employed in the same sense.

This is not the place to discuss the origins or early history of the justiciar and his office in Europe as a whole.[3] It will suffice here to state that the *justitia*, later *justitiarius*, meaning the principal administrative and judicial officer of the Crown, came to Scotland from Norman England, almost certainly in the reign of David I (1124–53). A comparison of surviving originals and early copies of twelfth-century texts with those of the thirteenth century will show how the clerks regularly used the abstract form, *justitia*, in the reigns of David I, Malcolm IV and the earlier years of William I, and how they came to prefer, and eventually employ almost exclusively, the form *justitiarius* denoting a personal agent.[4] Later copyists, however, frequently ignored this distinction, and some modern editors have helped to blur the terminological development. It is, for example, impossible to use Sir Archibald Lawrie's edition of the charters of David I and his son Earl Henry[5] as evidence for clerical usage in the twelfth century. In his collection, the address of nos. 111, 137, 171, 220 and 255 includes *justitiariis*, although the originals have *just'* or *justit'* (*justic'*). Enough originals survive in which the word is written out in full to show that the abbreviations should be extended to *justitiis*.[6] Likewise, Dr. D. E. Easson, on his own admission,

---

[3] See F. West, *The Justiciarship in England, 1066–1232* (Cambridge, 1966); C. H. Haskins, *Norman Institutions* (1918, republished 1960), esp. pp. 85–103; E. Jamison, 'Judex Tarentinus' in *Proceedings of the British Academy*, liii (1967), 289–344.

[4] See, for *justitia*, Lawrie, *Charters*, nos. 90, 106, 124, 126; *RRS*, i, nos. 29, 30, 31, 39, 40 (David I); ibid., nos. 119, 120, 127, 128, 184, 192, 196, 198, 201, 220, 223, 255, 256, 258 (p. 273), (Malcolm IV); *RRS*, ii, nos. 39, 46, 62, 67, 80 (William I). For *justiciarius*, see, e.g., *Nat. MSS. Scot.*, i, pl. XLVIII (= MacPhail, *Pluscardyn*, facsimile facing p. 70); *Chron. Melrose*, p. 90; Raine, *North Durham*, no. 378. In documents written in French, however, the form *justice* (*justise*) may be found throughout the thirteenth century. See, *e.g. Nat. MSS. Scot.*, i, pl. LXI (Scone, 28 March, 1270), where the earl of Buchan appears as *justice descoce* (equivalent to *justiciarius Scocie*), and Hugh Barclay as *justice de Loenesse* (equivalent to *justiciarius Laudonie*).

[5] Lawrie, *Charters*, *passim* between nos. 90 and 266.

[6] Lawrie, *Charters*, nos. 90, 145, 236. Moreover, no surviving original royal act prior to 1200 justifies the reading *justitiariis*.

altered a manuscript *justicia mea* to *justiciarius meus*, in a royal confirmation for Coupar Angus abbey.[7]

Adjectives denoting or implying gradation among justiciars are decidedly uncommon within the period under review. In texts of official provenance, indeed, they are extremely rare. Malcolm IV refers to his *supprema justicia*,[8] but the term occurs only once. The chronicler Roger Howden, writing of events of 1199, styles Earl Patrick I of Dunbar *summus justiciarius totius regni Scotie*.[9] The fourteenth-century chronicler John Fordun, almost certainly retailing a lost thirteenth-century source, says that in 1255 Alan Durward was appointed *summus justiciarius* for seven years.[10] Elsewhere he describes Durward (in 1249) as *totius tunc Scociae justiciarius* (or, in another MS., simply *regni justiciarius*).[11] It would be unsafe to rely on these passages from chroniclers, even if they are contemporary, for the exact title given to particular justiciars, but, as we shall see, there is independent evidence to suggest that superior and subordinate justiciars might function together. It is noteworthy that neither in official texts nor in chroniclers or other unofficial sources do we find the term *capitalis justitiarius*, known in England from Henry I's time.[12] Nor, less surprisingly, is there any trace of the corresponding term *magister justitiarius* employed in the Norman kingdom of Sicily.[13]

2 The background

Our picture of Scottish law and justice in the twelfth and thirteenth centuries is largely derived from the work of two

---

[7] *Coupar Angus Chrs.*, i, no. 25 (p. 53).   [8] *RRS*, i, no. 220 (1162 × 65).

[9] *Chronica Magistri Rogeri de Houedene* (ed. W. Stubbs, Rolls Series, 1871), iv, p. 98.

[10] *Chron. Bower*, ii, 90; *Chron. Fordun*, i, 297.

[11] *Chron. Fordun*, p. 293; *Chron. Bower*, ii, 80. Since the Melrose chronicle is one of Fordun's sources for this period, it is surely significant that *sub anno* 1251 that chronicle refers to Durward as *dominum Alanum hostiarium Scocie et etiam tunc iusticiarium*, a phrase which although it conveys a markedly different impression from Fordun is sufficient to explain his own phrases (*Chron. Melrose*, 110). Note also the term *magnus justiciarius* as an alternative in one of the Scotichronicon MSS. for *justiciarius Scotiae, sub anno* 1231 (*Chron. Bower*, ii, 59, n.).

[12] F. West, *Justiciarship in England*, pp. 22–3. Professor West cites no instance of *justitiarius* earlier than the middle of Henry I's reign and does not discuss the usage of *justitia* and *justitiarius*.

[13] For this title see the article by the late Miss Evelyn Jamison, cited above, n. 3.

scholars of the last generation, the late Lord Cooper of Culross and Professor William Croft Dickinson.[14] Between them they succeeded in establishing what may fairly be called the received opinion. Put briefly, the opinion is that the period down to Robert I's reign formed the first of three historical phases in the development of Scots jurisprudence and legal administration. This phase, beginning with crude borrowing at a primitive level in the 'Anglo-Norman Age' (c. 1124–c. 1214), was later character-ised by the overwhelming predominance of canon law and ecclesiastical tribunals (c. 1214–c. 1270), and subsequently by a late flowering of specifically 'Scottish' law, chiefly on an English model, which was blighted before it could bear fruit by the onset of the wars of independence. The reign of Robert I saw a brave but inadequate attempt to restore the law as it had been before 1296, but this attempt, instead of forming a true restoration, marked the prelude to the second phase, the 'Dark Age' of Scottish legal history.

Lord Cooper's conclusions, which in any case related solely to the evidence of the civil, as distinct from the criminal, law, underwent some modification between 1944, when he published his *Select Scottish Cases of the thirteenth century*, and 1946 when his edition of the *Register of Brieves* was brought out by the Stair Society. In his introduction to the earlier book he wrote:

If at this period there was any substantial volume of major contested litigations between lay litigants before lay tribunals, it is distinctly odd that so little trace should have been left in the private and family charter collections which still survive in considerable numbers. Further, the church was busily engaged during the thirteenth century in acquiring additional possessions by gift or otherwise, and the records frequently provide evidence of earlier transmissions of the lands while they were still held in lay hands. Once again, however, we hear of little

---

[14] See especially T. M. Cooper, *Select Scottish Cases of the thirteenth century* (Edinburgh and London, 1944); *Register of Brieves* (Stair Soc., 1946); *The Dark Age of Scottish Legal History, 1350–1650* (David Murray Lecture, Glasgow, 1952); W. C. Dickinson, *Fife Court bk.*, *Carnwath Court bk.*, and 'The Administration of Justice in Medieval Scotland', *Aberdeen University Review*, xxxiv (1951–2), 338–51.

or nothing in such records regarding earlier litigations except with reference to perambulations.

If therefore the complete records had survived, it seems justifiable to hazard the conjecture that they would have shown very much what the present collection indicates, *viz.*, that until the later years of the thirteenth century important civil controversies, when not settled by agreement or arbitration, were usually left to the decision of the skilled and ubiquitous ecclesiastical lawyers, who in Scotland found ample scope for their activities owing to the absence of a fully organised judicial system and a legal profession to work it.[15]

On the judges and lawyers actually at work in Scotland, he concluded:

It follows that to a large extent the same class of persons was administering justice in both Scotland and England, but in Scotland they were acting under Papal authority and administering Canon Law while in England they were acting under Royal authority and administering common law. This substantial identity, or at least similarity, in personnel between civil judges, ecclesiastical judges, and arbitrators may explain why Scottish litigants latterly made so little difficulty about submitting questions to ecclesiastical tribunals.[16]

Before *Select Scottish Cases* had actually appeared in print, Lord Cooper had had his attention drawn to the unpublished lists of styles in the Ayr and Bute manuscripts. This discovery induced him to modify his views somewhat, and in a postscript which reads rather awkwardly after what had gone before he wrote:

The assortment of remedies available to the Scottish litigant before the justiciar or the sheriff in or about 1300 was far richer and more varied than other sources of information would lead us to expect. . . . If these conclusions are well founded, they confirm the conjecture already expressed as a result of the examination of the legislation of 1318 that the disappointing picture of the work of the lay tribunals to be derived from the

[15] Cooper, *Select Cases*, p. xxvi.　　[16] *Select Cases*, p. xlv.

reported cases is attributable mainly to the loss of the records and not to the non-existence of suitable material to place on record.[17]

Editing the *Register of Brieves* gave Lord Cooper the opportunity to sum up with what we may take to be his considered and mature judgement:

> The conclusion to which the accumulating evidence points is that during the later years of the thirteenth century and early years of the fourteenth, Scotland had made considerable progress towards erecting on Norman foundations and in the English style her own distinctive conception of the Temple of Themis.[18]

The view which has come to hold the field subsequently seems rather nearer to Lord Cooper's earlier, unqualified estimate of the primitive nature of substantive secular law and of the inadequacy of judicial machinery. Mr. H. G. Richardson, for example, in a review of *Select Scottish Cases*, wrote:

> The outline history to be found in the introduction indicates how relatively backward the judicial organisation in Scotland was as compared with that in England. A comparison with contemporary Ireland might suggest too that, however repugnant an English over-lordship might be, it would had it become effective have brought immense benefits to the sister kingdom. In Scotland, as in Ireland, the trouble was that the English kings never accomplished the task to which they had set their hands, and few calamities are so disastrous as an imperfect conquest and a long reluctance to admit failure. As it was, Scotland drew from England the chief materials for a legal system which, though lagging far behind, attained in the thirteenth century a standard that contrasts favourably with the conditions under which justice was administered in Scotland in the following centuries.[19]

[17] *Select Cases*, pp. lxv–lxvi.   [18] *Reg. Brieves*, p. 3.
[19] *English Historical Review*, lx (1945), p. 425.

More recently, Professor Peter Stein seems to have put the pessimistic view even more strongly:

For the early period, then, we must rely largely on the evidence provided by the chartularies of cathedrals and monastic houses and, to a lesser degree, the muniments of noble families. Litigation in the lower secular courts is bound to be under-represented in such sources. Yet, *allowing for the accidents of survival in the records*, it is clear that before about 1270, all important civil disputes were settled either by arbitration or in ecclesiastical tribunals, and not in the secular courts. The reason would appear to be that only in tribunals composed of churchmen could a litigant expect to find educated men capable of dealing with matters of complexity. Royal justice was just not sufficiently competent and active, so litigants sought ecclesiastical justice instead.[20]

The impression left by all these views is that the substantive law of thirteenth-century Scotland was primitive and jejune, while the machinery for its administration was inadequate even although there was so little to administer. To judge how true this impression is would carry us far beyond the proper scope of a chapter dealing with the justiciar. Since, however, the justiciar, if he was anything at all, was presumably a key figure in the legal administration thus disparaged, an estimate of his functions and effectiveness will be relevant to any conclusions we may wish to draw on the larger questions of medieval Scots law. At least there is evidence that contemporaries did not always regard Scottish law and justice as negligible. Apart from references to the 'approved laws and customs of the realm' and the like,[21] it is clear

[20] P. Stein, 'Roman Law in Scotland', in *Ius Romanum Medii Aevi*, Pars V, 136 (Milan, 1968), p. 23 (my italics).

[21] See, e.g. (1) the Scoto-Norwegian Treaty of Perth (2 July, 1266) which three times uses the phrase 'laws and customs of the realm of Scotland', once in the form 'iuxta leges et consuetudines regni Scocie approbatas' (*APS*, i, 420), with which we may compare the almost exactly contemporary *Dictum of Kenilworth* (31 October, 1266): 'contra jura approbata et leges ac regni consuetudines diu obtentas' (Stubbs, *Select Charters*, 9th edn (1913), 408). Other instances are (2) *Arbroath Liber*, i, no. [229], referring to a perambulation 'secundum legalem assisam Regis David usitatam et probatam in regno Scocie usque ad illum diem' (1228); (3) the bull of Innocent IV (1251), cited below,

that the church authorities, far from being complacent, as they might have been if Roman Law and ecclesiastical tribunals had monopolised the scene, showed alarm, dismay and even anger over what they regarded as encroachments on their liberties by the secular courts. Thus, in the years 1205–7 Pope Innocent III wrote four separate letters dealing with a serious dispute between St. Andrews cathedral priory and Saer de Quinci, lord of Leuchars, anent the patronage of Leuchars church.[22] Notwithstanding the charter of Ness son of William, who had granted his church of Leuchars to St. Andrews, a grant duly confirmed by William king of Scots 'as is the custom of that realm', Ness's grandson Saer de Quinci had ignored the priory's possession and presented his kinsman Simon de Quinci to the living. Worse still, Saer had taken the dispute, and another concerning Lathrisk church, to the *curia regis* of Scotland, 'contrary to justice and to the custom of the Scottish church'. In the final letter of a series in which his indignation has mounted steadily, the pope explains that Saer refuses to litigate save *coram rege*. The prior of St. Andrews, thus most unfairly compelled to appear before the king and submit to his examination, was terrified by the king's threats into accepting an unlawful compromise which gravely injured the church. That the king's court seems to have had the last word, at least for the time being, is suggested by the presence in the St. Andrews cartulary of a royal confirmation of an agreement between the parties dating to *c.* 1210–11, at some date so thoroughly erased from the vellum as to be now almost wholly illegible.[23]

It seems that King Alexander II could take as firm a line as his father. In 1225 he prohibited further hearing before papal judges-delegate of the case The Bishop and Chapter of Moray *versus* Robert Hode and his wife Maud.[24] The dispute concerned

n. 28, referring to 'custom in accordance with the law of the realm'; (4) *Arbroath Liber*, i, no. 247 (1255), the terms of a charter to be kept 'secundum jus, legem et assysam terre'; (5) Stones, *Documents*, no. 11 (6 November, 1258), letter of Henry III referring to the Scottish king's council governing 'secundum leges et bonas consuetudines illius regni hactenus usitatas'; and (6) the Treaty of Birgham (1290), which twice mentions 'the laws and customs of the realm [of Scotland]' (Stevenson, *Documents*, i, no. 108, p. 169).

[22] *St. Andrews Liber*, pp. 350–2.   [23] *RRS*, ii, no. 491.
[24] *Moray Registrum*, pp. 459–61.

the *manerium*[25] of Lhanbryde, near Elgin, which the king asserted
to be his own barony, and therefore not amenable to ecclesiastical
jurisdiction. As a barony it was to be dealt with in the royal
court.[26] The record of that court's decision, drawn up in the form
of a chirograph, was sealed reciprocally by the bishop and
chapter of Moray and by the king himself and Robert Hode. It
was, incidentally, witnessed by, among others, William Comyn
(earl) of Buchan, who at the time was justiciar of Scotia.

Two important letters of 1250 and 1251 are even more
significant pointers in the same direction. The earlier,[27] addressed
to the young King Alexander III by the bishops of Scotland after
a session of the council at Edinburgh, protested that something
hitherto unheard of in the realm had been introduced by the
king's councillors, namely, that ecclesiastical persons might be
dispossessed of their property and even of churches granted to
them in alms tenure without the intervention of the prelates
acting in a judicial capacity. The council at this period was still
largely controlled by Alan Durward and his friends, but it is not
clear whether it was they, or their rivals the Comyns, who were
the object of this protest. The second letter evidently arose from
the same political crisis, and is much longer and wider in scope.[28]
It is addressed by Pope Innocent IV to three English bishops,
who are commanded to act at once to remedy a serious situation
which has emerged in Scotland through the improper or illegal
actions of the 'new councillors' (*novi aulici*) who are presuming to
control the boy-king. Out of the ten major grievances listed, the
seven which are relevant here amounted to an allegation that
there had been a concerted attack on ecclesiastical jurisdiction in
Scotland. It was said that sentences of spiritual penalty had been
revoked in the king's name, that lawsuits anent eleemosynary
lands had been brought before lay tribunals, that these tribunals,
giving ear to perjured evidence, had pronounced unjust judgements and enforced them by dispossession (*spoliatio*), that it had
been proclaimed in the king's name that patronage cases should

[25] Here, evidently, in its 'English' sense of 'landed estate', not merely in its
usual later 'Scottish' sense of 'residence' or 'manor house'.

[26] 'Illustri Rege Alexandro prohibente et asserente predictum manerium
suam esse baroniam et ideo de ipso in curia Regia et non ecclesiastica debet
litigari.'

[27] Robertson, *Concilia*, ii, 241–42.   [28] *Concilia*, 242–6.

be dealt with in secular courts, that the taking of oaths and pledging of faith should not be enforced by ecclesiastical penalties, that the magnates had forbidden the laity to submit to money fines imposed by the bishops and, finally, that the magnates had used royal brieves of prohibition (*edicta prohibitoria*) to stop ecclesiastics prosecuting (presumably in church courts) for non-payment of teinds. Again, it is not clear whether the *gravamina* expounded in Pope Innocent's letter were directed against the Durward or Comyn faction, but for our purposes the identity of the accused is immaterial. It is sufficient to recognise that in the opinion of the church the secular rulers of mid-thirteenth-century Scotland were prepared to oppose ecclesiastical with secular jurisdiction and possessed some at least of the necessary machinery with which to do it: secular tribunals before which property cases could be brought, and brieves of prohibition staying proceedings before the church courts.[29]

It is, of course, undeniable that in the first half of the thirteenth century Scotland witnessed the widespread use of Roman Law (especially in the shape of Canon Law), while ordinary lay subjects of the Crown had recourse frequently and easily to tribunals which were either completely ecclesiastical in nature and personnel, or at least a mixture of the ecclesiastical and the secular. The position seems rather to have been that, as compared with England in the same period, the various types of court available to Scottish litigants (including, therefore, the papal *curia*) enjoyed much freer competition, and ecclesiastics may have been able to have cognisance of a much wider range of legal business than their English counterparts. While this would produce a very different situation in the two countries, it would not amount to saying that 'royal justice (in Scotland) was just not sufficiently competent and active'. By 1267 the king of Scots was invoking a papal privilege in his favour, that lawsuits should not be taken outwith the realm, to stop a case brought against Kelso Abbey.[30]

At the beginning of this century Miss Mary Bateson published, in a *Miscellany* volume of the Scottish History Society, a Norman-

[29] An exemplar of a brieve of prohibition is given in the Ayr MS. cap. lxiii (Robertson, *Concilia*, ii, 238–9; *Reg. Brieves*, pp. 46, 55). Cf. renunciations of brieves of prohibition by litigants, *Inchcolm Chrs.*, nos. 21 (1252), 25 (1263).
[30] *Kelso Liber*, no. 396.

French treatise which she entitled 'The Scottish King's Household'.[31] Although its date has not been satisfactorily established, there are some grounds for assigning it to *c.* 1292 and for supposing that it was written for the benefit of the new king John Balliol and of those who were to advise him on the government of his kingdom.[32] At all events, the treatise appears to be well-informed and authoritative. In an important passage on the justiciars (*justices*), the treatise states that the magnates ought to appoint suitable men, apart from those who hold office heritably, 'such as shall have the skill and ability to administer law and justice both to poor and to rich, and to uphold and supervise the king's rights in all points pertaining to the crown, so that no complaint shall be presented to the king save only those which cannot be redressed without the king's personal intervention'.[33] The treatise clearly envisages an active role for the royal justiciars not only in criminal but also in civil jurisdiction.

The letters of 1250–1 might be dismissed as an excess of clerical nervousness, and the treatise of (?) 1292 as both unofficial and idealistic. But if, independently of such evidence, we find that throughout the long period from David I to Robert I there was in fact a continuous history of royal justiciars, if we find them holding courts, dealing with crime and with civil causes, attending, significantly, sessions of ecclesiastical or quasi-ecclesiastical tribunals, frequently present with the king and organised in such a way that most of the kingdom of Scotland could feel the impress of their activity, then we may be more inclined to mitigate the

[31] *SHS Miscellany*, ii, 3–43.

[32] This is suggested chiefly because the treatise (1) is earlier than 1309 (ibid., p. 4); (2) evidently belongs to a period where there has been a hiatus in royal government, either a prolonged minority or more probably an interregnum; (3) recommends (chap. 12) the appointment of a treasurer, said to be the successor of the clerk of the wardrobe. Whereas Alexander III had had a clerk of the wardrobe in 1268 (*Dunfermline Reg.*, no. 87), King John is the only king of Scots prior to the fifteenth century known to have had a treasurer (Master Alpin of Strathearn, for whom see *Holyrood Liber*, no. 91; *The register of John de Halton, bishop of Carlisle, A.D. 1292–1324*, ed. T. F. Tout and W. N. Thompson (Canterbury and York Society, 1913), i, 34; he was bishop of Dunblane 1296–*c.* 1301); (4) recommends (chap. 9) that the king should have as almoner a knight or brother of the Temple. It is known that Alexander III during his minority (1255) had as almoner one Brother Richard of the order of Knights of the Temple (Stones, *Documents*, p. 31), but the practice obviously cannot have survived the suppression of the order *c.* 1309.

[33] *SHS Misc.*, ii, 36.

harshness of the judgements passed in recent years upon the inadequacy of Scottish royal justice in the twelfth and thirteenth centuries.

3 The justiciar's court

In the twelfth century, as is well known, courts were reluctant to announce or identify themselves in written record. Cases are much more often said to have been heard or determined *coram rege* or in the presence of a multitude of barons (or good men) than in a fixed institution neatly labelled 'the court of such and such a county (or honour)' or 'the court of Baron So-and-so'. To find no reference to a 'court of justiciary' in the Scotland of Malcolm IV or William I is not to say that no such court existed. Under King Malcolm, for example, the ownership of Newbattle in Midlothian was, at the king's command, adjudged by judicial process (*ordine judiciario*) in the presence of his justiciar.[34] At the beginning of King William's reign Robert Brus of Annandale's property and liberties were established in an important charter in which the king stipulated that reserved crown pleas should be dealt with and impleaded before the king's justiciars within the sheriffdom (of Roxburgh?).[35] In another important charter of about the same date it was provided that if an aggrieved man failed to get justice from the abbot of Holyrood the king's sheriff and justiciar were to do him justice.[36] Whether this implies appeal in two stages, i.e., first to the sheriff's court, which failing, to the justiciar's court, or, as seems altogether more probable, recourse by the aggrieved litigant or pursuer to a court held in the sheriffdom, convened by the sheriff and presided over by the justiciar, it seems clear that some sort of justiciar's court is envisaged. An agreement dating between 1189 and 1195, in which the two parties pledged their faith in the hands respectively of the king's chancellor

[34] *Newbattle Registrum*, no. 3.
[35] *RRS*, ii, no. 80. It seems probable that *comitatus* in this charter is to be understood in the sense of 'court of a *vicecomitatus* or sheriffdom', as in *Dryburgh Liber*, no. 223 (p. 163), dating to 1200, and *Midlothian Chrs., Soutra Registrum*, no. 44 (1271), referring to Lanark and Roxburgh respectively. See also R. E. Latham, *Revised Medieval Latin Word List* (1965), s.v. *comes*. *Comitatus* in this sense of 'county' (= 'shire') court had, of course, been normal English usage since the late eleventh century.
[36] *RRS*, ii, no. 39.

and Earl Duncan of Fife (justiciar of Scotia), and to the record of which both the chancellor and earl fixed their seals, looks as though it may have been sanctioned and promulgated in the justiciar's court.[37] Neither the king's name nor his presence was mentioned (although they so often were in similar documents of this period), yet the agreement obviously had the solemn force of law, and was witnessed by a mixed group of lay and ecclesiastical magnates as well as by three *judices regis*, royal dempsters. We shall see shortly that the formula for a valid session of the justiciar's court in the thirteenth century seems to have been justiciar(s) + magnates (usually + certain officials or minor dignitaries). In a comparable record probably belonging to the period 1182–*c.* 1188, when Walter Olifard I was justiciar [of Lothian], Liulf son of Elgi and his five sons made a formal quitclaim of property in the court of the prior of Coldingham: 'and since we will that (the quitclaim) be firm, we have confirmed it in faith by an oath in the hand of Walter Olifard the king's justiciar that it shall be kept perpetually without fraud or subsequent challenge.'[38] Even if in this case the justiciar and the local sheriff (who both witness the deed) were present at Coldingham, the justiciar's role can hardly have been that of a subordinate member of the priory court. Since Coldingham is close to Berwick, it may be that the ceremony of oath-swearing took place at a session of the justiciar's court held at the capital of the sheriffdom. We must, however, note that a century later justiciar and sheriff are found attending the court of the prior of Coldingham.[39]

The justiciar's court emerges more clearly from the evidence of the thirteenth century, although even in this later period the clerks seem reluctant to use such convenient phrases as *curia justiciarie* or *iter justiciarie*. The earliest exchequer rolls (which, of course, survive only in later copies) cover the years 1264–6 and 1288–90.[40] They make frequent use of the phrase *lucra justiciarii* and occasionally speak of *officium justiciarii*. Strictly translated, these should mean 'profits of the justiciar' and 'office of the justiciar' respectively; but it is probable that *justiciarii* is to be taken as a misrendering of *justiciarie*, 'of justiciary', the word which occasionally occurs in the copied rolls[41] and is used in the earliest original rolls to survive, dating from the fourteenth century.[42]

However interpreted, the phrases point to some jurisdiction exercised by the justiciar, even if not explicitly to any 'justiciar's court'. To a considerable extent (especially in southern Scotland) this jurisdiction seems to have been organised on a basis of sheriffdoms, but there are interesting signs of a more primitive arrangement based upon the ancient provinces and districts.[43] The rolls give no indication of whence the *lucra justiciarii* were derived. Most of the few cases explicitly mentioned seem to be criminal, although a case of debt appears on the sheriff of Fife's account in 1264–6.[44] The 'Laws of Malcolm Mackenneth' which, though surviving only in MSS. of the fourteenth century and later, seem to contain genuinely early material, give the justiciar's fee for each day of his ayre as 100s.[45] None of the rather patchy evidence from the exchequer rolls is incompatible with the statement in the treatise of (?) 1292, already referred to, that 'the justiciars shall have their sessions of their justice-ayre (*eire de justice*) twice a year, once in the season of grass and once in the season of winter'.[46] Surviving record gives some slight support to this seasonal pattern, for it reveals two groups of transactions involving the justiciars, one having dates running from about the end of April to early August, the other running from about Michaelmas to January. Evidence of this kind, although somewhat difficult to interpret, seems more reliable than the rules laid down in the so-called *Assise Regis Willelmi*. Chapter XXV,[47] e.g., providing for the two head courts of the justiciar to be held annually at Edinburgh and Peebles, can hardly be supported by any actual contemporary documents of the twelfth or thirteenth centuries.

In the later fourteenth century, the evidence becomes much more precise and explicit, and the exchequer rolls refer to accounts from sessions of the *iter justiciarie*.[48] The clerks' terminology has become more stereotyped and their proceedings more businesslike.

---

[41] *Exch. Rolls*, 27.   [42] *Exch. Rolls*, 557, 558.
[43] *Exch. Rolls*, 4, 9, 13, 18.   [44] *Exch. Rolls*, 32.   [45] *APS*, i, 709.
[46] *SHS Misc.*, ii, 36–7.   [47] *APS*, i, 379.
[48] E.g., *Exch. Rolls*, i, 543, 546, 561, 563, 570, 590.

Thus, in 1366, we have the record (still preserved in the muni-ments of the Dean and Chapter of Durham) of 'the court of the justice-ayre held at Melrose on Monday, the sixth day of the month of July, A.D. 1366'.[49] The act was witnessed by, among others, the justiciar of Lothian (Sir Robert Erskine) and Adam Forester, clerk of the rolls, and it was sealed with a seal bearing the significant legend + S[IGILLUM] OFFICII IUSTICI-ARIE LAUDONIE. A few years later (23 January, 1372) we have the important statement of William earl of Douglas, lord of Liddesdale and justiciar besouth Forth: 'Whereas according to the custom of our elders, the justice-ayre of the sheriffdom of Berwick used to be held at Berwick', now, owing to the English occupation, it has to be held in another place.[50] The earl's 'elders' may have been no further back in time than his parents' or grandparents' generation, but it is more likely that he was appealing to really 'ancient' custom, the good old days of peace before the death of King Alexander III.

From about the middle of the thirteenth century we begin to have evidence of a more self-conscious justiciar's court whose acts were recorded by clerks aware of the necessity for a more formal phraseology than was usual in the reigns of William I and Alexander II. On 25 April, 1235, the earl of Lennox and Gilbert son of Samuel made an agreement at Blackhall (in Paisley) at a court which is merely described as 'before Walter son of Alan, the Stewart, justiciar of Scotia (and a number of other notables named and unnamed)'.[51] The subject of the agreement was land in the Lennox. The holding of the session at Blackhall was doubtless due to the fact that this was the Stewart's principal seat. The earldom of Lennox would normally rank as one of the earl-doms of Scotia. Historically, however, the Lennox, although Gaelic-speaking in the twelfth and thirteenth centuries, formed part of Strathclyde; it remained in the bishopric of Glasgow; and in the guise of the sheriffdom of Dumbarton it was assigned to the justiciary of Lothian by the 1260s.[52]

Despite the informality of the language and the geographical discrepancy, there need not be any doubt that this was a session of the justiciar's court. But fifteen years later we have what seems

[49] Raine, *North Durham*, no. 326.   [50] *North Durham*, no. 147.
[51] *Paisley Registrum*, 170–71.   [52] *Exch. Rolls*, i, 27.

to be the first of a number of documents which show advance into a more formal stage of development. On 12 November, 1250, Godfrey son of Thomas of Tynedale issued a quitclaim and surrender of land for default of service 'in a full court of lords (*in plena curia dominorum*) at Forfar, before the justiciar of Scotia, Sir Alan Durward, William of Brechin and Robert Mowat then sheriff'.[53] On 2 July, 1253, 'in a full court' and before Alexander Comyn earl of Buchan justiciar of Scotia, in the presence of the bishop of Brechin, William earl of Mar the king's chamberlain and very many others, clergy and laity, gathered upon 'Cole-dunes' in Kingoldrum, Sir Thomas of Rattray on behalf of his wife Christina reached agreement (*amicabilis et finalis concordia*) with Arbroath abbey anent the marches of 'Glencaveryn'.[54] The document recording this agreement is replete with phrases or echoes of notarial Latin.[55] On 13 October, 1260, 'in the court of justiciary at Perth (*ad placita justiciarie apud Perth*), before Sir Freskin Murray, Sir David of Lochore and Sir John Cameron performing the office of the earl of Buchan, justiciar of Scotia', one Falletauch appeared in person to quitclaim his right in the land of Drumcarro to the attorney of the prior of St. Andrews.[56] No fewer than twenty-four witnesses are named, including two men described as *judices* and a third who is otherwise known to have been a *judex*.[57] On 4 October, 1266, 'before a full court of Fife and Fothrif', on the muir of Pitcorthie (in Carnbee, Fife), in the presence of Adam earl of Carrick acting in place of Alexander Comyn earl of Buchan, justiciar of Scotia, Richard Siward made a final concord with Richard Chamberlain and his wife Jean.[58]

[53] *Yester Writs*, no. 15. [54] *Arbroath Liber*, i, no. [294].

[55] E.g. the use of the word *actor* to describe Sir Thomas's role as proctor for his wife who was pursuer in the case; and the phrases *sine litis strepitu; laboribus, expensis et indempnitatibus recompensacionem facere volentes; per aliquorum malivolorum consilium vel per pravam suggestionem; vexare vel impetere vel questionem aliquam movere.*

[56] *St. Andrews Liber*, 346–47. The phrase *placita justiciar[ie]* also occurs in an undated inquest of *c.* 1260 (*Cal. Docs. Scot.*, iv, 385, the original now being SRO, RH5/19).

[57] John de Potyn and Walter are styled *judices*; the last witness, Thomas Squier, is known to have been a king's *judex* in the 1260s (above, p. 78).

[58] *Laing Chrs.*, no. 8. The original chirograph, endorsed 'Contra Dominum Ricardum Sywarth', is Edinburgh University Library, *Laing Chrs.*, Box 1, no. 19. Some of the place-names have been incorrectly transcribed in the printed *Calendar*, e.g. Giblotistun', Belighiston', Craghinhac', Stinchandemir'.

The deed was witnessed by, among others, Sir Ralph Lascelles sheriff of Fife, Thomas Squire the king's dempster, and William of Fordell, who is also known to have acted as a dempster in this period.[59] On 18 May, 1276, 'in a full court at Edinburgh before Sir Hugh Barclay then justiciar of Lothian and many responsible men (*in plena curia apud Castrum Puellarum coram multis probis hominibus*)', John of Pencaitland resigned his right in the land of Pencaitland.[60] This followed upon a visit to the land by certain knights *missi a domino rege* to have an extent carried out by the faithful men of the neighbourhood, presumably acting in response to a brieve of extent.[61] Because John of Pencaitland's seal was neither old nor well-known, the justiciar and Sir Simon Fraser (sheriff of Peebles?) set their seals to the deed. On 30 April, 1281, 'in a full court of the justiciar (or "of justiciary"?), on the muir of Nigg (Kincardineshire), before the bishop of Aberdeen, Alexander Comyn earl of Buchan justiciar of Scotia, Sir Reginald Cheyne the father and many other knights and responsible men', a dispute was heard and settled between Arbroath abbey and two Kincardineshire landowners.[62] The cartulary copy of the court's decision carried the significant note, perhaps from an endorsement of the 'original', *et hoc exprimitur in rotulis justiciarii* (for *justiciarie*?) *de Kinkardyn*. This must mean that records of the sessions of justiciary in this sheriffdom were preserved on rolls, and we may reasonably infer that the same practice was followed in most, if not all, sheriffdoms.[63] On 5 December, 1284, 'in a full court' at Glasgow before Sir William de Soules, then justiciar of Lothian, and other magnates, an agreement was made between Paisley abbey and John of Auldhouse.[64] The deed was witnessed by the justiciar and many other notables; and even though among the many seals placed for corroboration on the half of the

[59] Above, p. 77.

[60] Fraser, *Facsimiles*, no. 65. The last-named witness was Ralph de Eyclyn, and it may be noted that Sir Ralph Heclin witnessed *Paisley Registrum*, 65–6, cited below, n. 64. Ralph d'Eghlyn [i.e. of Echline in Dalmeny, West Lothian], of Haddington, was a tenant in chief of the Crown in the Sheriffdom of Edinburgh (= Lothian) in 1296 (*Instrumenta Publica*, 137, 140).

[61] Cf. H. McKechnie, *Judicial process upon brieves, 1219–1532* (David Murray Lecture, Glasgow, 1956), 10–11.

[62] *Arbroath Liber*, i, no. [230].

[63] Perambulations of 1236 and 1253 were entered on the rolls of the king's chapel or of the lord king (*Arbroath Liber*, i, nos. [227] and [294]).

[64] *Paisley Registrum*, 65–6.

chirograph to be retained by the abbey was the seal of the officiality of Glasgow, i.e. of the bishop's Official, nevertheless it is perfectly clear that this was a secular court held before the justiciar of Lothian 'in the season of winter'. Finally, in February 1300, at Castleside in Aberdeen, before John Comyn earl of Buchan, justiciar of Scotia, 'holding the pleas of his office', a case of cattle stealing was dealt with by a court including the bishop and sheriff of Aberdeen and a number of other notables.[65]

Although these nine illustrations have been drawn from what is often called the 'charter evidence', it must be emphasised that the documents themselves are not charters. They are carefully dated narrations of court proceedings and decisions, some of them very close in character to the English final concords familiar from the records of the court of Common Pleas and from the eyre rolls. If they lack the precise phrasing and stereotyped formulae of Roman law and notarial practice such as we find in the fairly abundant surviving record of ecclesiastical tribunals, they represent nevertheless a considerable advance towards formality and standardisation when compared with the twelfth century. Few as they are (and it would be hard to find an equal number of documents from the same period which illustrate sessions of the same type), they show the court of justiciary in action, particularly in civil causes. They help to put some of the flesh of reality on to the rather bare bones of the Ayr and Bute formularies which give us little more than the wording of several brieves pleadable before the justiciar.

4   The geographical division of the justiciarship

In the introductions to the first two volumes of the *Regesta Regum Scottorum*[66] the evidence not only for the emergence and earliest development of the justiciar's office, but also for the geographical division of the justiciars' activity, was presented in detail. For the twelfth century, therefore, this section will do little more than summarise arguments already set forth at length. Edward I's *Ordinance for the land of Scotland* (1305) provided for four pairs of justiciars, one pair for Lothian, another for Galloway, and two for 'the lands beyond the Scottish Sea' (i.e. Scotia), one for south

[65] *Arbroath Liber*, i, no. [231].   [66] *RRS*, i, 49–50; ii, 43–7.

of the Mounth, the other for north of the Mounth.[67] Although this represents a significant elaboration of the earlier pattern, it is not a complete departure from the arrangement recommended by the treatise of (?) 1292, which declared that there should be in Scotland three justiciars, a justiciar of Lothian, a justiciar of 'beyond the Scottish Sea' and a justiciar of Galloway. This recommendation entirely fits what we know to have been the situation from 1258 to 1290. How much further back the three-fold division can be taken is not easy to say, but I have argued elsewhere that even if this system underwent modification between 1200 and 1258 it had already been effectively achieved in the last two decades of the twelfth century.[68]

Setting aside for the moment the question of Galloway, we may argue for the existence of a justiciar of Lothian, in fact at least, though not in name, from the time of Malcolm IV. We may, indeed, assign the office to David Olifard in the opening years of William I. It is possible that King David I had already introduced a justiciar for Lothian, that part of his kingdom which was closest in its general character to Anglo-Norman England, from which he took so many of his institutional innovations. Certainly, from about the late 1130s King David's charters and brieves began to include justiciars among their addressees,[69] and this practice, which was obviously not fortuitous, was followed by his son Earl Henry, who enjoyed the position of king-designate.[70] Thirty-two of David I's and seven of his son's surviving acts relating to Scotland include justiciars in their address, sometimes between earls and barons, more often immediately after barons and before sheriffs.[71] The evidence does not allow us to say that justiciars were regionally based before 1153, but at least it is clear that the office must have existed and highly probable that it was exercised continuously and not just occasionally or casually. Under Malcolm IV we have explicit mention of a justiciar of Scotia and of a justiciar of Fife.[72] While it is possible that both offices were in fact held by the same man (the earl of Fife), it was

---

[67] APS, i, 120.   [68] RRS, ii, 44–6.
[69] Lawrie, Charters, nos. 90, 106, 111, 122, etc.
[70] Lawrie, Charters, nos. 124, 129, 135, 137, 147, etc.
[71] These may be found in Lawrie, Charters between no. 90 and no. 266, passim; and in RRS, i, between no. 29 and no. 44 passim.
[72] RRS, i, nos. 223, 214.

only the former which survived. But the fact that a mid-twelfth-century brieve could be addressed to a 'justiciar of Fife', ought to be considered along with the exchequer roll evidence from the period 1264–6 which shows justiciary profits accruing in various ancient districts as well as in sheriffdoms, and perhaps even along with the record of the justiciar's 'full court of Fife and Fothrif' held in 1266.[73] 'Fife and Fothrif' seems to refer to the ancient district or province rather than to the newer sheriffdom.

David Olifard, who lost Sawtry in Huntingdonshire during the troubles of King Stephen's reign, was shown favour by his god-father King David and was granted by Malcolm IV the land between the North and South Calder Water in the nether ward of Clydesdale which became the great medieval lordship of Bothwell.[74] Although he was a frequent witness to the acts of King Malcolm, it is only in two charters belonging to 1165 that his name occurs sufficiently high in the witness lists to suggest that he occupied a position of outstanding importance.[75] His placing in the witness-lists of the acts of King William before 1170 is con-sistently high. In ten surviving acts he is styled 'justiciar'.[76] In one document, recording a session of the *curia regis* held at Stirling in 1167, dealing with a dispute over the church at Edrom in Berwickshire, the only two laymen named are Earl Waltheof of Dunbar and David Olifard.[77] There is no proof that David Olifard was in fact justiciar of Lothian, but it seems reasonable to surmise that he was. Between *c.* 1170 and *c.* 1178 a number of royal acts relating to Scotland south of the Forth are witnessed by Robert Avenel, Richard Cumin, Robert de Quinci, and Geoffrey de Melville, all styled 'justiciar'.[78] Whether they were acting in succession and enjoyed only brief terms of office, or whether in this period there were two or more justiciars simultaneously, it again seems reasonable to assign to them the justiciarship of Lothian. From *c.* 1178 we find David Olifard's son Walter Olifard

[73] *Exch. Rolls*, i, 4, 9, 13, 18; *Laing Chrs.*, no. 8; 'plena curia de Fif et de Fothref'.
[74] Below, p. 289.   [75] *RRS*, i, nos. 261, 262.
[76] *RRS*, ii, between nos. 14 and 108 *passim*.
[77] Raine, *North Durham*, no. 642. Unfortunately, the fact that the royal confirmation of this (ibid., nos. 40, 41 = *RRS*, ii, no. 105) was dated at Perth led the editors of *APS* (i, 65) to locate the session of the *curia regis* at Perth, and this has misled later scholars.
[78] *RRS*, ii, 43.

I, serving as justiciar, and his term seems to have run through to the later 1180s.[79] Walter Olifard is styled justiciar in only eight royal acts,[80] but it is surely significant that in other acts of this period where he is not given the title his name nevertheless occurs high among the laymen, even occasionally taking precedence of the hereditary Stewart.[81] Walter Olifard's name drops out of royal acts after c. 1188 and almost immediately we notice that the name of William of Lindsay (lord of Crawford) begins to appear at or near the top of the list of laymen's names in the testing clauses.[82] One royal charter probably issued in April, 1189, happens to give us a glimpse of an exceptionally well-attended royal council, with an unusually large clerical element.[83] The witnesses begin with three bishops, six abbots, two priors and the king's chancellor. First among the laymen come no fewer than five earls. Of the remaining five laymen, all barons of the first rank, William Lindsay appears second, yielding place only to Robert de Quinci, a senior baron who had already served as justiciar. In three further royal acts of slightly later date (1189–95), one of them the 'foundation charter' of Glasgow Fair, William Lindsay appears prominently with Earl Duncan of Fife and Roland son of Uhtred lord of Galloway.[84] Here it is probable that we see the three justiciars of the Scottish kingdom acting together at sessions of the king's council. Although William Lindsay is styled 'justiciar' in only five royal acts,[85] his place in the line of justiciars of Lothian *de facto* if not by title seems assured. It may be, however, that for at least part of his term, from 1195, he shared office with Earl Patrick of Dunbar, for the earl appears as 'justiciar' in a charter which almost certainly belongs to July 1195,[86] and, as we have already noticed, he was said to be *summus justiciarius* in 1199.[87] Although there are an appreciable

[79] *RRS*, ii, 43.   [80] *RRS*, nos. 162, 195, 197, 199, 200, 233, 237, 248.
[81] *RRS*, nos. 204, 205, 210, 213, 215, 220, 221, 223, 236, 261. In no. 236 the two laymen who witness between the earls and Walter Olifard, Nicholas de Treilin and Peter de Ros, were respectively nephew and son-in-law, and co-heirs, of the great Yorkshire baron Walter Espec, founder of Rievaulx. They were evidently taking a founder's interest in the affairs of Melrose Abbey, Rievaulx's daughter house, and would naturally be accorded precedence by courtesy; cf. *Rievaulx Chartulary* (Surtees Soc., 1889), 3, 21. I have to thank Mr. William Scott for this information.
[82] *RRS*, ii, nos. 284, 287, 293, 295, 313.   [83] *RRS*, no. 284.
[84] *RRS*, nos. 299, 308, 368.   [85] *RRS*, nos. 316, 317, 365, 400, 406.
[86] *RRS*, n. 381.   [87] Above, p. 85 and n. 9.

number of acts in this decade to which William Lindsay is not named as witness, he is still being given his title or at least accorded a high precedence as late as December 1196, and perhaps as late as 1198.[88]

Earl Patrick's term seems to have continued until 1205 or after,[89] but by 1208 we find David Lindsay I (son of William Lindsay) holding office simultaneously with Gervase Avenel (son of Robert Avenel).[90] It is evidently to this period that we should assign a formal exchange by Hugh le Breton, vassal of Earl David of Huntingdon, of land in Conington, Huntingdonshire, for land in the Garioch.[91] In the presence of King William, Hugh solemnly swore to observe the terms of the exchange 'in the hand of David of Lindsay then justiciar of the king of Scots'. The title given to Lindsay by the clerk who wrote this private charter was possibly not official, but it is in line with other evidence that a regional justiciar might be referred to simply as 'justiciar of the king' in documents of non-royal provenance.[92] A witness to Hugh le Breton's exchange who was actually placed before David Lindsay was Walter Olifard II, apparently not only Lindsay's successor but the first man to be called 'justiciar of Lothian' in a formal document (28 August, 1219).[93] From this time onwards the justiciarship of Lothian is clearly traceable, and the succession of men who held the office can be established with a fair degree of precision. But even if in the period from c. 1165 to 1219 we do not find a justiciar of Lothian eo nomine, we may take it as reasonably certain that some ten individual magnates, all substantial barons and including three pairs of fathers and sons, served the Crown in this capacity.

Tracing the early history of the justiciarship of Scotia, Scotland benorth Forth, seems to be at least as plain sailing as elucidating the beginnings of the justiciarship of Lothian. We have seen that King Malcolm IV addressed one surviving brieve (concerning Perth) to a justiciar of Scotia. It does not seem possible to

---

[88] *RRS*, ii, nos. 405, 406, 407.　　[89] *RRS*, no. 460.
[90] *RRS*, nos. 481, 483.　　[91] *Lindores Chartulary*, no. 129.
[92] E.g. Raine, *North Durham*, no. 388; *Coupar Angus Rental*, i, 340–1 (no. 60); *Glasgow Registrum*, i, no. 127.
[93] *Newbattle Registrum*, no. 121. In record of 1229 an English clerk styles Walter Olifard 'justiciar of Scotland', surely an exception proving the rule (*Cal. Docs. Scot.*, i, no. 1041).

establish the identity of this officer. The guess may be hazarded
—since King David's brieves and charters are addressed to
'justiciars' in the plural—that there was a justiciar for Scotia even
before 1153. If so, the strongest candidate for the post would be
the earl of Fife, Duncan I, to whom King David, after his son's
death in 1152, assigned the important task of escorting his young
grandson round the districts of Scotia to show him to the people
as heir to the throne.[94] In 1128 Earl Constantine of Fife had been
styled 'great *judex* in Scotia',[95] a title which would normally
connect him with the ancient order of *judices* (Old Irish, *brithe-
main*), between whom and the incoming Anglo-Norman justiciars
one can trace no true organic link.[96] Nevertheless, it might be
natural or even essential for the Crown to give the newer office to
the premier earl who already held some sort of superior dempster-
ship; or it might even be the case that the scribe responsible for
the unique record of 1128 genuinely confused *justicia* with *judex*.[97]
All this is speculation. The ground becomes firmer only when we
reach the second quinquennium of King William's reign. In royal
charters from *c.* 1172 Earl Duncan II of Fife, who had succeeded
his father in 1154 and who lived on until the first half of 1204 (by
then surely an old man), begins to appear with the title of
justiciar.[98] He is so styled in forty-five of William I's acts,[99] in
two (admittedly copies, not originals) appearing as justiciar of
Scotia.[100] That on occasion in this long period of office the earl
of Fife had at least two fellow-justiciars seems clear from a royal
charter of 1187–95 witnessed by Earl Gilbert of Strathearn as
justiciar (surprisingly taking precedence of the earl of Fife)[101] and
by reputable record of 1199–1214 and 1221 proving that not only
the earl of Strathearn but also Matthew bishop of Aberdeen
(1172–99) acted as royal justiciars in Scotia at different times in
the last two decades of the twelfth century.[102] Common sense as

---

[94] *RRS*, i, 5–6.   [95] Lawrie, *Charters*, no. 80.   [96] Above, p. 80.

[97] The Latin of this document is 'literary', indeed flowery, in character.

[98] *RRS*, ii, no. 134. Note that ibid., no. 38 (anent Dunfermline, 1165 ×
1171), is addressed 'to Earl Duncan and (the king's) justices and sheriffs of
Fife and Fothrif'.

[99] *RRS*, between no. 134 and no. 429, *passim*.   [100] *RRS*, nos. 275, 388.

[101] *RRS*, no. 337. It is conceivable that the copyist has made a mistake here,
but we are certainly not entitled to assume this, and the texts in the Dunfermline cartulary are of high quality.

[102] Above, pp. 80–2.

much as any positive evidence would suggest that ill health might now and then have incapacitated Earl Duncan and created the need for deputies; but we cannot help noticing the frequency with which Earl Gilbert witnesses royal acts of the period 1180–1200 in company with Earl Duncan, their two names, indeed, often appearing next to each other in the lists of attestations.[103] Earl Duncan's successor as justiciar was not his son Malcolm but a leading member of the family of Cumin (Comyn) in Scotland, William Cumin, who was to become, through his wife Marjorie, earl of Buchan some two years before King William's death. Twelve of William I's acts were witnessed by William Cumin as justiciar, and in five he appears as justiciar 'of Scotia' or 'of the Scots'.[104] His career is even better attested in Alexander II's reign, when the full title 'justiciar of Scotia' seems to have become the rule.[105] A year or so before William Cumin's death in 1233 he had been succeeded in the justiciarship by the hereditary Stewart, Walter son of Alan II.[106] From that point on, as is shown in the table published below as an appendix to this chapter, a continuous succession of holders of the office may be traced with some precision. In view of what has already been said of hereditary tendencies among the justiciars of Lothian, it seems worth drawing attention to the fact that both Earl William's son Alexander and his grandson John held office as justiciar of Scotia between 1251 and 1300, the former for as long as thirty-six years. No thirteenth-century earl of Fife ever held this office, although the Fife family seems to have enjoyed almost a monopoly of it in the twelfth century.

It is much harder to trace the early development of the justiciarship of Galloway, which barely outlived the thirteenth

[103] *RRS*, ii, nos. 137–421, *passim*.

[104] *RRS*, nos. 465, 472, 475, 485*, 489*, 490, 492*, 493, 497, 502*, 522, 523* (* denotes use of regional title).

[105] E.g. Raine, *North Durham*, no. 63; *Moray Registrum*, nos. 25, 32 and p. 459.

[106] *Chron. Bower*, ii, 59, says that King Alexander II, having spent Christmas (1230) at Elgin, on his return, at St. Andrews 'a little before the Purification of the B.V.M.' (February 2), appointed Walter son of Alan, the Stewart, to be justiciar of Scotia (or in one late MS., *magnus justiciarius*). Probably this should be referred to 1231–2, as in *Chron. Wyntoun*, v, 88–9; *Chron. Wyntoun* (Laing), ii, 241–2. A date of appointment of 2 February, 1232, would square with the surviving record evidence, despite *Balmerino Liber*, no. 1, evidently a bad copy (cf. Anderson, *Diplomata*, pl. XXXIV). I am grateful to Mr. William Scott for helping to elucidate this point.

century.[107] In three royal acts of *c.* 1190–1200 the lord of Galloway, Roland (*alias* Lachlan) son of Uhtred, was styled 'justiciar',[108] and as such appears in company with Earl Duncan and William Lindsay. One of the acts is a brieve seeking to enforce the king's 'assize of Galloway'.[109] A provision anent the levying of royal tribute (*cain*) from Galloway was made in the *curia regis* at Lanark by the king's *judices* of Galloway before Roland son of Uhtred and other *probi homines*.[110] It seems probable, therefore, that Roland was in effect, if not by title, justiciar of Galloway. I have not found any certain evidence of a justiciar of Galloway during the long period between Roland's death in 1200 and 1258, when John Comyn of Badenoch held the office. It is possible that John's powerful uncle Walter Comyn, earl of Menteith, acted as justiciar of Galloway after the suppression of the Gallovidian revolt of 1235, but this suggestion rests only on the fact that the king placed Earl Walter in charge of Galloway after the revolt and on the English complaint of 1244 that he had built a castle in Galloway.[111] Even John Comyn's term of office is hard to trace clearly. Justiciar in 1258,[112] and apparently at a time when Colban was earl of Fife (therefore between 1266 and *c.* 1272),[113] he is last heard of in office in 1275, when he took part in King Alexander III's punitive expedition to the Isle of Man.[114] Yet there was evidently a break in Comyn's term, for in 1264 the office was held by Aymer of Maxwell,[115] and the Exchequer Rolls seem to afford

---

[107] *APS*, i, 120. No fourteenth- or fifteenth-century justiciars of Galloway are indexed in the first two volumes of *RMS*, although there is mention of several justiciars of special areas or regalities, e.g. Annandale and Man, Bute and Arran, etc.

[108] *RRS*, ii, nos. 309, 401, 406.   [109] *RRS*, ii, no. 406.   [110] *APS*, i, 378.

[111] Anderson, *Early Sources*, ii, 497; Anderson, *Scottish Annals*, 353. The fact that the criminal provision of 1245 expressly exempted Galloway from the justiciar of Lothian's sphere of activity in one particular respect suggests that there was no justiciar of Galloway at that date (*APS*, i, 403).

[112] J. G. Edwards, *Littere Wallie* (Cardiff, 1940), p. 184 (no. 317).

[113] Fraser, *Facsimiles*, no. 58, witnessed, it seems, by 'K' earl of Fife, evidently Colban. But it is hard to reconcile this charter, purporting to be issued by the disgraced Countess Isabel of Menteith and her second husband Sir John Russell, driven furth of Scotland in 1259, with the dates of Colban's tenure of the earldom, and for the present the document must be disregarded.

[114] *Chron. Stephen*, iii, 570.

[115] *Melrose Liber*, no. 310. Aymer of Maxwell was sheriff of Dumfries in the period 1264–6 (*Exch. Rolls*, i, 16, 22).

a glimpse of Maxwell's tenure as justiciar of Galloway.[116] They show, moreover, that the justiciarships of the two regions, Galloway and Lothian, were quite distinct.[117] In the 1280s and 1290s we find Sir William Sinclair acting as justiciar of Galloway.[118]

Even if the gaps in the evidence for Galloway represent actual gaps in the tenure of a regional justiciarship for the extreme south-west, we can hardly question the reality of a continuous justiciarship for both northern and southern halves of the Scottish kingdom. It seems to be borne out by an examination of the addresses of judicial and executive brieves issued by the writing-offices of Malcolm IV and William I. Brieves, after all, were mainly ephemeral and their survival has been patchy and fortuitous. What remains of this class of record is almost certainly only a minute fraction of the original output of the king's chapel. Yet some eight extant brieves of King Malcolm and seventeen of King William are addressed to justiciars and sheriffs (with or without 'officers' and 'bailies').[119] It would surely be a mistake to ignore the plain inference to be drawn from these business-like, matter-of-fact documents: the justiciary had a continuous existence, and there was normally more than one justiciar at a time.

The cumulative effect of evidence drawn from the long period between the reign of David I and the close of the thirteenth century is impressive. It points clearly to a twofold geographical division of the justiciarship obtaining over most of the period, and to a threefold division established for at least the later twelfth and the second half of the thirteenth centuries. The division adopted was rooted in the ancient, almost immemorial divisions of the kingdom. Scotia, the country to the north of Clyde and Forth, although it had many sub-divisions of its own, clearly also had a unity as compared with the land to the south. It was the old essential kingdom of the Scots, and its justiciar might be expected to establish his precedence—by the thirteenth century if not by

[116] *Exch. Rolls*, 17, account of Maxwell (styled only sheriff of Dumfries), dealing with the profits of justiciary of Galloway.

[117] *Exch. Rolls*, 17.

[118] *Exch. Rolls*, 36–7; *Instrumenta Publica*, 15 (1291).

[119] *RRS*, i, nos. 106, 111, 192, 200, 201, 214, 223, 258 (Malcolm IV); ibid., ii, nos. 38, 44, 70, 87, 95, 113, 131, 156, 177, 178 (cp. 179), 182, 189, 207, 259, 294, 354, 507 (William I).

the twelfth—as the senior or superior justiciar, *summus justitiarius* or *magnus justitiarius* in the phrases of Fordun's chronicle. Lothian, in justiciary terms, seems to have comprised the sheriffdoms of Ayr, Dumbarton, Lanark, Stirling, Linlithgow, Edinburgh, Haddington, Dumfries, Peebles, Selkirk, Roxburgh and Berwick.[120] Galloway was apparently coterminous with the lordship containing the sheriffdom of Wigtown and the districts later brought together as the Stewartry of Kirkcudbright.[121] This regional division of the justiciarship was not paralleled in contemporary England, where the 'local' justiciarships of the earlier twelfth century, associated with counties, seem to have been discontinued by Henry II before 1166,[122] and where county-based justices scarcely re-emerged until the later fourteenth century, in the shape of the justices of the peace.[123] The closest parallel with the Scottish scheme to be found in the English king's territories was probably the arrangement made for Wales after the Edwardian conquest (1278–84).[124] The justiciar of Chester with responsibilities for North Wales, his successor the justiciar for North Wales established in 1284, and the justiciar for West Wales established in 1278, must in some respects at least have resembled the Scottish king's regional justiciars of Galloway, Lothian and Scotia.

5   The scope of the justiciar's activity

We have already seen that in the thirteenth century the justiciars held courts with competence in civil as well as criminal causes.

[120] *Exch. Rolls*, i, 27.

[121] *Exch. Rolls*, i, 36–7, 39. It is probable that 'Galloway' embraced a larger area in the twelfth century.

[122] D. M. Stenton, *English Justice between the Norman Conquest and the Great Charter, 1066–1215* (1965), 65–71; cf. also H. A. Cronne, 'The office of Local Justiciar under the Norman Kings', *University of Birmingham Historical Journal*, vi (1958), 18–38.

[123] See the excerpts from 34 Edward III, c. 1 in S. B. Chrimes and A. L. Brown, *Select Documents of English Constitutional History, 1307–1485* (1961), 82–3; and cf. B. H. Putnam, *Proceedings before the Justices of the Peace in the fourteenth and fifteenth centuries* (1938). I have disregarded such unusual arrangements as were made in favour of Count John of Mortain early in Richard I's reign (cf. A. L. Poole, *From Domesday Book to Magna Carta* (2nd edn., 1955), 348). For a brief period in 1190 Hugh du Puiset bishop of Durham held the justiciarship of England north of Humber (ibid., 351–2).

[124] F. M. Powicke, *The Thirteenth Century* (1953), 435–6; cf. W. H. Waters, *The Edwardian Settlement of North Wales* (1934).

It is probable that they were already holding such courts in the twelfth century, although the evidence for the period before 1214 is much less clear. Most of our information about the work actually carried out by the justiciars has to do not with sessions of the court of justiciary but with their presence in the *curia regis* (in its judicial capacity) and at meetings of king's council and parliament, with their witnessing innumerable brieves and charters issuing from the *capella regis* (the royal writing-office), with their attendance at and participation in courts of various kinds held by the prelates, magnates and papal judges-delegate, with their execution (usually in response to a royal precept) of perambulations, extents and other, miscellaneous, commissions.

It will be convenient, although not entirely satisfactory, to review the evidence for the justiciar's activities under the two headings of crime and civil causes. One disadvantage of this analysis is that it takes no account of the justiciar's role as an officer with general responsibilities in the field of royal government. The likelihood that from time to time the justiciar might exercise such a role emerges from an examination of certain episodes in the thirteenth century, especially during the years of political stress from 1244 to 1260. Comparison with contemporary English practice would suggest that in the twelfth century also the justiciar might be assigned tasks and responsibilities wider than an oversight of the administration of justice.

(i) *The justiciar and crime*

At the beginning of his reign, in a charter granting liberties to a subject, William I stipulated that the reserved *regalia*, i.e. the *causae* of treasure trove, murder, premeditated assault, rape, arson and plunder, should be impleaded before his justiciars in a particular sheriffdom.[125] From this time onward it is not difficult to trace the association of the royal justiciars with the pursuit, apprehension, trial and punishment of criminals. Certainly, the exchequer rolls of the later thirteenth century take their criminal jurisdiction for granted,[126] while the 'Laws of Malcolm Mackenneth' not only deal with the disposal of chattels of men fined, 'sold' or condemned to death before the justiciar, but also pre-

---

[125] *RRS*, ii, no. 80.　　　[126] *Exch. Rolls*, i, 4, 17, 31, 34, 36.

scribe scales of forfeiture to be imposed by the justiciar north and south of Forth (eight cows and £10 respectively) which seem to go back at least to the twelfth century if not even earlier, and were associated with serious law-breaking.[127] The reservation of four of the *regalia* listed in King William's charter forms a chapter to itself in the *Assise Regis Willelmi* (said to belong to 1180), which makes no reference to the justiciar.[128] Nor, more surprisingly, do justiciars figure in the almost certainly genuine and contemporary 'assize' of 1197, dealing with the suppression of violent criminals and plunderers.[129] This assize seems to have been modelled upon Hubert Walter's *Edictum Regium* of 1195.[130] Despite this silence, the justiciar's complex role in police work, military campaigns and the enforcement of legislation by the imposition of heavy penalties is shown clearly enough in the scanty evidence which chance has preserved. A royal brieve for Melrose Abbey enforcing the 'assize of Galloway' against thieves was witnessed by two justiciars (1195-8).[131] Persistent refusal either to pay teind or to compel its payment by inferiors in the dioceses of Glasgow, Moray and (by implication) St. Andrews was punishable in the last resort by the justiciar.[132] One of the four great men charged by King William in 1211 with the task of crushing Guthred MacWilliam's revolt was said to have been the 'earl of Buchan', probably a proleptic reference to William Cumin, justiciar of Scotia, who may have become earl as early as 1212.[133] Eighteen years later, after further revolts, Earl William, still justiciar, was put in charge of Moray by King Alexander II and furnished with a great force of foot soldiers.[134]

The beginnings of the well-known dittay (indictment) procedure in Scotland cannot be traced back reliably before the provision

[127] *APS*, i, 711; cf. *RRS*, i, 65-6; ii, no. 281.
[128] *APS*, i, 374-5 (chap. XII).
[129] *APS*, i, 377 (chap. XX). I am grateful to Professor A. A. M. Duncan for pointing out to me that the passage interpolated into this chapter 'in Moravia vel alibi' rests on late MS. tradition and almost certainly represents a misrendering of an uncommon form of *murdrum*, 'murder'.
[130] Stubbs, *Select Charters* (9th edn.), 257-8.   [131] *RRS*, ii, no. 406.
[132] *RRS*, i, 65-6.   [133] *Chron. Bower*, i, 532; *RRS*, ii, 63.
[134] *Chron. Bower*, ii, 58. One may note also the justiciar of Lothian's military responsibilities in 1264(?) and 1286 (*Exch. Rolls*, i, 17, 47), and the justiciar of Scotia's military role in 1263-4 (ibid., 18, where Invery is probably to be identified with Inverie in Knoydart; cf. E. Beveridge, *The Abers and Invers of Scotland* (1923), 76-7. See also *Chron. Fordun*, 301).

Eκs

of February, 1245, which apparently related only to Lothian, Galloway being explicitly exempted and Scotia ignored.[135] It may be that a parallel provision, now lost, was made about the same time for Scotia. Certainly, by 1266, the dittay procedure was normal in Aberdeenshire, for the sheriff was allowed £32 on his account for that year because of the poverty of four men who were to provide a pledge to thole their trial 'on a certain dittay to be produced before the justiciar'.[136] The procedure seems to have been borrowed direct from English legislation dating back as far as Henry II's Assize of Clarendon of 1166.[137] Under the 1245 provision the justiciar of Lothian was to make a careful and secret inquiry into evil-doers and their harbourers 'by the oath of three or four responsible and faithful men, together with the oath of the steward of each toun in the various sheriffdoms'. All known suspects since Christmas, 1243, were to be arrested and brought before the justiciar to thole trial 'by a faithful jury' (*per fidele visnetum*). Those convicted in the justiciary court of felonies which were Crown pleas ('murder, robbery and suchlike') would forfeit their chattels to the Crown. The chattels of thieves, however, and those convicted of manslaughter and other lesser felonies, would remain with the lords of the lands in which the men concerned were found to possess them. Offenders guilty of crimes less heinous than those reserved to the Crown could evidently be tried by the justiciar, but must be handed back to their lords for sentence (*justitia*). The justiciar's role was central in the 1245 provision. The justiciars of Scotia and Lothian figured prominently in two other assizes of King Alexander II. The first, promulgated at a Stirling council of October 1230,[138] dealt with replegiation in criminal cases; the second, also produced at a Stirling council (19 May, 1248), concerned the quality of the oaths supporting testimony which might threaten loss of life, limb, land or grazing.[139] It was because the two justiciars of Scotia appointed after Walter the Stewart's death in 1241 (Philip

---

[135] *APS*, i, 403 (chap. XIV).   [136] *Exch. Rolls*, i, 34.

[137] Stubbs, *Select Charters* (9th edn.), 170–3. For recent studies of the texts of this assize and their authenticity, see H. G. Richardson and G. O. Sayles, *The Governance of mediaeval England from the Conquest to Magna Carta* (Edinburgh, 1963), 438–49, and J. C. Holt, 'The Assizes of Henry II: the evidence of the texts', in *The Study of Medieval Records: essays in honour of Kathleen Major* (Oxford, 1971).

[138] *APS*, i, 399 (chap. IV).   [139] *APS*, 404 (chap. XV).

de Melville and Robert Mowat)[140] acted so feebly to repress a feud raised by the Comyns against the Bissets that in 1244 Alexander II replaced them by the royal doorward—Alan Durward—who vigorously maintained law and order until supplanted by the Comyns seven years later.[141] When, in September, 1289, the young earl of Fife was ambushed and murdered near Brechin, we are told by Bower's chronicle that it was Andrew Murray who pursued the murderers as far south as Covington in Clydesdale.[142] Bower implies that this was because Murray had been appointed guardian in place of the earl, but there is no other evidence for this and there would scarcely have been time to make the substitution before raising the hue and cry. It is in every way probable that Murray's part in the business was due to his being justiciar of Scotia in succession to the earl of Buchan, for we know that he held this office by c. 1293.[143] Finally, we may note that it was a case involving the crime of cattle stealing which was heard before the justiciar of Scotia at Aberdeen early in 1300.[144]

(ii) *The justiciar and civil causes*

It is unnecessary to rehearse here the evidence given above, in eight separate illustrations covering the period 1235–84, of the justiciary court's settlement of disputes between subject and subject. As far as we can judge, this activity was taken at least as much for granted as the corresponding work of ecclesiastical or mixed tribunals. But it will be useful to supplement this small though significant body of evidence by looking at examples of both older and newer forms of action in civil causes, and considering how closely the justiciars were connected with their implementation.

[140] *Chron. Melrose*, 88, records the death of Walter son of Alan, the younger, early among the events of 1241. Robert Mowat appears simply as sheriff of Forfar on 25 January, 1241, but as justiciar by 18 April (*Coupar Angus Chrs.*, i, nos. 45, 46) and 'justiciar of Scotia' by 28 April (*Coupar Angus Rental*, i, 339, no. 53, where for *Richardo* read *Roberto*). On 29 and 31 October, at Forfar, both Philip de Melville and Robert Mowat appear as joint justiciars of Scotia (*Glasgow Registrum*, i, no. 179; *Perth Blackfriars*, 1, no. 1), while Melville appears singly on 11 January, 1242, apparently accorded a relatively subordinate precedence (*Glasgow Reg.*, no. 183). According to *Chron. Bower*, ii, 75, the justiciars were replaced by Alan Durward in 1244, evidently before 7 June (*Perth Blackfriars*, 4, no. 5).   [141] *Chron. Melrose*, 88.
[142] *Chron. Melrose*, 148.   [143] *Family of Rose*, 29.   [144] *Arbroath Liber*, i, no. [231].

Throughout the period under review the justiciar can be seen taking a prominent part in the archaic process of perambulation. In conservative Scotland, slow to adopt any of the rich variety of solutions to property disputes which became open to English landowners and litigants from the reign of Henry II, perambulation, as a fully 'legal' and not merely as an administrative process, flourished until the later thirteenth century, and survived for much longer.[145] To some extent it was a substitute for the petty assizes, grand assizes and final concords familiar in the courts of Angevin England. That already, in the twelfth century, Scots litigants might be tempted to make use of the final concord in its English form even for lands within the Scottish kingdom is shown by the remarkable fine levied at Westminster on 29 October, 1198, between William de Brus (Bruce), lord of Annandale, and his knightly tenant Adam of Carlisle (Carlyle), anent eight ploughgates in Lockerbie.[146] Such desperate remedies can scarcely have been welcomed by the Scottish crown, but despite the obvious advantages of the final concord the Scottish courts seem to have stopped just short of its full adoption.[147] It was common for an agreement (*conventio, concordia, amicabilis compositio*) to be reached in, or at all events solemnised by, a court, but there are no signs of any move towards the crucial English developments of the secure tripartite chirograph or of the fictitious lawsuit enabling a fine merely to provide a firm title. Similarly, although a high proportion of the Scottish landowning class must have been familiar with the advantages of the petty assizes, Scotland was surprisingly slow to adopt any version of the actions of novel dissasine and mortancestor. Some scepticism has been shown with regard to the apparent introduction of the novel dissasine into Scotland at the Stirling council of October 1230.[148] Lord Cooper,

[145] *APS*, i, 707 (c. 8). See also *Arbroath Liber*, ii, 227 (1493); and cf. *Laing Chrs.*, no. 1647, for the importance of detailed marches in feu charters as late as 1612.

[146] *Feet of Fines, 10 Richard I* (Pipe Roll Soc., vol. XXIV, 1900), pp. 53–4 (no. 79); calendared in *Cal. Docs. Scot.*, i, no. 2666. This fine was filed under 'Northumberland', possibly because William de Brus was a tenant-in-chief at Harterness and Hartlepool, then in that county.

[147] The term *finalis concordia* is not uncommon in thirteenth-century Scottish record, and is used, e.g. in *Laing Chrs.*, no. 8, cited above, p. 11, n. 54, in *Arbroath Liber*, i, no. [294], cited above, p. 10, n. 50, and in *Holyrood Liber*, no. 71 (1228). Cf. also SRO, GD 254/1.

[148] *APS*, i, 400 (chap. VII). Cf. Cooper, *Select Cases*, pp. xlii–xliii.

accepting the suggestion that the action did not come into Scotland before *c*. 1270, wrote that 'so far as the charter records of the thirteenth century are concerned, the rest is silence but for a single writ of novel disseisin issued by Edward I in 1291'.[149]

Unquestionably, the absence of evidence from the 'charter records' is striking, although we might fairly ask how much reference we would have to early English novel disseisins if we had only the 'charter records' to draw upon. One precious survival among the Durham cathedral archives (apparently over-looked by Lord Cooper), while not proving the authenticity of the assize of 1230, shows that it could well be accepted as genuine.[150] Mariota of Chirnside and her son Patrick, son of Richard, had pursued the prior of Coldingham in the court of Walter Olifard (II) justiciar of Lothian, anent one ploughgate at Renton (in Coldinghamshire) 'by the lord king's brieve of recognition'. Olifard was justiciar from *c*. 1215 till his death in 1242. The action referred to cannot have been by a brieve of right, which would not have involved a *recognitio* nor brought the case before the justiciar. It is more likely to have been a brieve of dissasine or of mortancestor, and since a widow would hardly bring a mortancestor in respect of her late husband's land, even when her son was also a pursuer, the former seems more probable. Mariota of Chirnside *versus* the prior of Coldingham should be compared with a contemporary case noticed and commented on by Lord Cooper: Mariota, Samuel's daughter *versus* the bishop of Glasgow.[151] Here the pursuer, incidentally another widow, had claimed right in the estate of Stobo, Peeblesshire, in the sheriff court of Traquair (= Peebles), 'by a royal brieve' (*per litteras regias*). The date must be between 1233 and 1258, probably *c*. 1250.[152] The action can scarcely have been on a brieve of right, as Lord Cooper supposed, for the pursuer (evidently one of the two daughters and co-heirs of a man called Samuel) was claiming the land against the bishop, not invoking royal assistance to force the bishop to do right to her. The brieve referred to is more likely

---

[149] Ibid., p. xliii.   [150] Raine, *North Durham*, no. 378.

[151] *Glasgow Registrum*, i, nos. 130, 131; Cooper, *Select Cases*, 40–1.

[152] At its date, William Bondington was bishop of Glasgow (1233–58), and Gilbert Fraser was sheriff of Peebles or Traquair. Fraser was sheriff in August, 1241 (*Newbattle Registrum*, no. 121), and his next known successor, Aymer of Maxwell, is found in office in 1262 (*APS*, i, 100).

to have been either of mortancestor or of general inquest (i.e. succession).[153] A document of *c.* 1248–55, though less specific, also shows a pursuer proceeding against a defender (his cousin) 'by the lord king's brieve [*litteras*]' in a case concerning two oxgangs in Nether Ayton, Berwickshire.[154] If the novel dissasine was introduced into Scotland in 1230, it would be natural for the companion procedure of mortancestor to be brought in at the same time. In any case, 1270 is appreciably too late for the first appearance in Scotland of brieves of dissasine, for in an interesting letter of 20 February, 1262, addressed to the constable of Berwick, Hugh Barclay, justiciar of Lothian, states that John of Reston had pledged his land before the justiciar *vis-à-vis* the king 'for two pairs of the lord king's brieves of dissasine'.[155] Later in the same year, we have the record of an inquest held at Peebles in response to the king's brieve (6 November, 1262) to ascertain whether one Robert Cruik was deforcing the king's burgesses of peat, whins, and common grazing in Waddenshope.[156] Moreover, at a council at Stirling on 17 December, 1253, Emma of Smeaton claimed her father's land against Dunfermline abbey *per litteras regias de morte antecessoris*, and we may note that the justiciar of Scotia and the former substitute justiciar of Lothian were both present.[157]

In Scotland north of Forth and in Lothian, there is abundant surviving record to illustrate the justiciar's prominent role in the processes of perambulation and measurement, and in the closely related 'executive' or 'administrative' act of *traditio*, handing over or putting in sasine, which often followed upon a solemn perambulation. Thus, in Scotia, Earl Duncan is found measuring land in Rattray, handing over a marsh in Blairgowrie and perambulating Invererne in Moray.[158] Between 1172 and 1199

---

[153] *Reg. Brieves*, 41 (chap. xxii).   [154] Fraser, *Keir*, 197–8, no. 1.
[155] J. Raine, *The Priory of Coldingham* (Surtees Soc., 1841), p. 1.
[156] *APS*, i, 100–1.
[157] *APS*, i, 425–6; *Dunfermline Registrum*, nos. 82, 83, 110. Note also *Melrose Liber*, ii, Appendix, no. 13, a brieve of Alexander III, Berwick, 13 April, 1268 (*anno regni nostri xix*) to the sheriff of Traquair (Simon Fraser) and others, commanding him to go to . . . the land of the abbot and convent of Melrose beside the Gala Water to discover whether . . . are deforcing (*occupant*) the abbot and convent of their land by diverting the stream to a new course. The sheriff is to take a verdict on the question by the oath of *probi viri* and retour it under his seal as soon as possible 'along with this brieve'.
[158] *RRS*, ii, nos. 222, 420, 543.

the earl of Strathearn and the bishop of Aberdeen, acting as royal justiciars and on the king's orders, carried out a perambulation of Balfeith in Mearns and also of land in Fordoun parish in respect of which we still have a letter of the earl addressed to his fellow perambulators.[159] In 1224 the marches of Clayquhat and Drimmie (Coupar Angus Abbey *versus* Scone Abbey) were sworn to and perambulated at the king's command by the justiciar, William Cumin earl of Buchan.[160] In 1236 a dispute between Arbroath Abbey and Earl William's widow, the Countess Marjorie, anent land in Tarves, Aberdeenshire, was settled, partly by means of perambulation, in the presence of Walter Stewart, the earl's successor in the justiciarship.[161] The decision of his court was evidently entered in 'the lord king's roll', perhaps a centrally kept record or else to be compared with the justiciary roll for Kincardineshire already mentioned in connection with a similar case of 1281.[162] In 1246, Alan Durward, as justiciar of Scotia, ordered the sheriff of Perth to hold an inquest, involving perambulation, into the marches of Wester Feddal (in Ardoch).[163] In 1254 the king commanded by brieve (*per literas suas preceptorias*) that Alexander Comyn earl of Buchan, justiciar of Scotia, should cause the marches of Conon and Tulloes in Angus to be justly perambulated by responsible and faithful men according to justice and the assize of the land.[164] The task was duly performed and the result recorded in a document sealed by the justiciar. Similar instances may be found for Lothian. Land in Edinburgh was handed over to Pain the goldsmith at the king's command by William of Lindsay, presumably when he was justiciar, c. 1189–98.[165] In June 1233, Walter Olifard, justiciar of Lothian, along with the abbot of Melrose and the king's chamberlain, handed over certain land to the former thane of Callendar in compensation for other land which he had surrendered to the king.[166] On 1 December, 1245, Olifard's successor in office, David Lindsay II, took charge of the Scots contribution to an Anglo-Scottish perambulation designed to draw the marches correctly between the prior of Kirkham's lands at Carham in Northumberland and

[159] Above, pp. 80–2.
[160] *Coupar Angus Chrs.*, i, no. 34.
[161] *Arbroath Liber*, i, no. [227].
[162] See above, p. 99.
[163] *Lindores Chartulary*, no. 23.
[164] *Arbroath Liber*, i, no. [366].
[165] *RRS*, ii, no. 570.
[166] Fraser, *Facsimiles*, no. 43.

the knight's fee of Hadden in Roxburghshire.[167] The matter was delicate, for the line to be agreed upon was not only a boundary between two estates but also the frontier between two kingdoms. One of the few extant brieves of King John Balliol commanded Geoffrey de Moubray, justiciar of Lothian, to restore sasine to a dispossessed party (1294).[168] It is tempting, though quite speculative, to see in the well-known perambulation of Clerkington in East Lothian, c. 1141, after Archdeacon Thorald had made a formal agreement with King David I, an early instance of a justiciar's perambulation, for the task was carried out by nine named notables, the list being headed by William of Graham, followed by Durandus (= Thorald) the sheriff.[169]

The justiciar's presence in tribunals other than his own or the *curia regis* before the king is well-enough evidenced to suggest that it was not merely casual. Even during the period when it may be agreed that ecclesiastical jurisdiction in Scotland was being pushed to its widest limits, i.e. during the reign of Alexander II, it seems to have been royal policy to maintain some secular observation or supervision in cases dealt with by ecclesiastical or mixed tribunals. It can hardly be an accident that in 1239 the justiciar of Scotia was a prominent witness to the decision of a tribunal under the papal legate Cardinal Otto, anent the patronage of the church of Fithkil (Leslie).[170] When in 1223 Walter Olifard the younger was present at a judges-delegate court at Musselburgh his role was not merely passive.[171] He attended with a household which included three of his knights, three sergeands, a royal clerk and his own clerk; and he intervened to the extent of seeing that the sum of money promised by one party to the other would be duly handed over. The same justiciar may be seen playing the same role, as pledge for due payment, in a case

[167] Stones, *Documents*, no. 8; C. M. Fraser, *Ancient petitions relating to Northumberland* (Surtees Soc., 1966), 43–4.

[168] Fraser, *Facsimiles*, no. 77.

[169] Lawrie, *Charters*, nos. 134, 135. William of Graham, who here takes precedence of the sheriff and other notables, witnesses ibid., no. 72, next after the king's son. He was conceivably justiciar of (or at least in) Lothian under David I.

[170] *Inchcolm Chrs.*, no. 18.

[171] *Glasgow Registrum*, nos. 126, 127. The former document is a declaration anent the case issued by Walter Olifard as justiciar.

of 1232, where the court concerned cannot be certainly identified.[172]

It would require the laborious and minute examination of scores and hundreds of private charters to establish the full extent of the justiciar's association with legally enforceable undertakings entered into by the king's free subjects. A major difficulty in the intepretation of the evidence lies in the fact that a private charter will not normally state whether it has been drawn up and promulgated in a lord's court or in the justiciary court or in the court of a sheriffdom. It is extremely rare to find a legal deed explicitly giving such information, such as the tack of Poniel granted to William lord of Douglas by Henry of Lambden abbot of Kelso (Glasgow, 3 February 1270) which was given *in plena curie justiciar[ie]*.[173] Many surviving private deeds carry the attestation of the justiciar, usually in first place or at least very prominently. Thus, Walter Olifard the elder, probably when he was justiciar of Lothian between *c.* 1178 and *c.* 1188, was first witness (and his successor William Lindsay was second witness) to a deed by which Richard de Melville confirmed the agreement made between Geoffrey (II?) de Melville and his mother Maud Malherbe anent Tartraven (West Lothian).[174] The agreement may have been made in the justiciar's court or in de Melville's court, but the record does not tell us. Again, William Cumin, 'justiciar of the king' (i.e. justiciar of Scotia, *c.* 1205–12), witnessed in first place a charter of John Giffard of Powgavie for the monks of Coupar Angus.[175] We do not know whether this charter passed in the court of justiciary or sheriffdom, or in some private court. The same is true of the important marriage contract of 6 April, 1259, between Hugh of Abernethy and William lord of Douglas.[176] Alexander Comyn earl of Buchan heads the list of witnesses to the indenture. He is not given the title of justiciar of Scotia but it is most improbable that he was not then holding the office. Sir William de Soules 'then justiciar of Lothian' witnessed first a frank marriage grant by Henry Graham to Adam son of John Swinburne.[177] All that we can be reasonably

---

[172] Raine, *North Durham*, no. 132. [173] *Kelso Liber*, no. 202.
[174] Fraser, *Melvilles*, iii, 2–3 (no. 4).
[175] *Coupar Angus Rental*, i, 340–1 (no. 60). [176] Fraser, *Facsimiles*, no. 57.
[177] Bodleian Library, MS. Dodsworth 49, fo. 4.

sure of is that the attestation of the justiciars in these instances (which could be multiplied many times over) was not likely to have been an act of mere politeness. We have already seen that in the thirteenth century the justiciar of Lothian and the sheriff of Berwick might attend sessions of the court of the prior of Coldingham.[178]

One primitive but persistent ceremony to which reference is not uncommonly found in the period under review was the pledging of faith (to enforce agreements, etc.) by swearing an oath in the hand of some independent (usually prominent) authority. In the earlier part of our period faith was often sworn in the hand of an important ecclesiastical dignitary, but it is noteworthy that the justiciar also was enlisted to fill this role. Thus, in an agreement (already mentioned) of 1189–95, probably reached before the justiciar of Scotia, one party, a layman named Neil MacIver, pledged his faith in the hand of the justiciar, while the other party, a clergyman, pledged his in the hand of the king's chancellor, Hugh of Roxburgh.[179] We have also seen that in a case before the prior of Coldingham's court in the 1180s one party pledged his faith in the hand of Walter Olifard the king's justiciar.[180] David Lindsay I is also found acting in this capacity in the early thirteenth century.[181] On occasion, a litigant who pledged his faith in the hand of an independent, or supposedly independent, authority might also submit himself in the future to the jurisdiction of that authority.[182] But it is interesting to notice that when on 27 November, 1286, the abbot of Arbroath and Ingram de Balliol, lord of Redcastle, reached agreement probably before the Guardians of Scotland, they proffered their faith in the hand of the bishop of St. Andrews but submitted themselves for the future to the jurisdiction of the justiciar of Scotia, whoever he should be.[183] A role comparable to witnessing the charters of private subjects and receiving their solemnly proffered faith was the placing of the justiciar's seal to private deeds or to records of

---

[178] Above, p. 95, n. 39.   [179] *RRS*, ii, no. 590.
[180] Raine, *North Durham*, no. 388.   [181] *Lindores Chartulary*, no. 129.
[182] *Inchcolm Chrs.*, no. 19 (1240). One may note that William of Brechin, a witness to this agreement reached in an ecclesiastical tribunal, also witnessed *Yester Writs*, no. 15 (1250), evidently a case dealt with before the justiciar. It is also to be noted that the king's seal was affixed to the document recording the agreement of 1240 (*Inchcolm Chrs.*, no. 19).
[183] *Arbroath Liber*, i, no. [293].

agreements made in court.[184] This practice may have been a principal factor in the establishment of a special official seal of justiciary, although the development seems to have been surprisingly long in coming.

The justiciar might also be concerned in the holding of inquests of various kinds, e.g. for the service of an heir (1262)[185] or to discover if a purchaser of heritable freehold had come by his property lawfully (1259),[186] or how a freeholder had acquired and lost sasine of certain land (1260).[187] An inquest was held, probably in 1259 or 1260,[188] to determine whether Thomas, son of Somerled of Darleith, had had sasine of Darleith (in Cardross) before the death of Maldoven earl of Lennox. The jurors returned their verdict 'before the Chamberlain [Aymer of Maxwell?] at Dumbarton in a full court when he was holding the justiciary session (*placita justiciar[ie]*)'.[189]

In general, however, the task of carrying out inquests seems to have fallen on the sheriff or even upon lesser officers. It is probably significant that in 1259 we find the justiciars of Lothian commanded to hold an inquest not of first instance but to confirm that an earlier inquest had been carried out 'faithfully'.[190]

6 The justiciars

At the beginning of this chapter it was asserted that the office of justiciar was imported into the twelfth-century Scottish kingdom from Norman England. Although it seems impossible to doubt the truth of this assertion, much that has been said of the Scottish justiciar in the intervening pages, far from demonstrating a continuing parallelism with English practice, has shown how divergently the office developed once it had become acclimatised north of the Border. To put the matter briefly, in England the justiciar was first overtaken by the creation of the courts of

[184] Cf. among many possible instances *Kelso Liber*, nos. 190, 192.
[185] *APS*, i, 101.   [186] *APS*, i, 99.   [187] *Cal. Docs. Scot.*, i, no. 2193.
[188] *Cal. Docs. Scot.*, iv, 385 (the original is SRO, RH5/19). The retour was made to an unnamed chamberlain (Aymer of Maxwell or William earl of Mar?). The persons named would be compatible with a date of c. 1259– c. 1270, but one may particularly compare *APS*, i, 102, an inquest at Dumbarton in 1263 sealed by Aymer of Maxwell's attorney.
[189] The original reads *placita justiciar'*. The extension *justiciarie* seems justified and preferable to Bain's *justiciaria*.
[190] *APS*, i, 98–9.

common law and then transformed by the emergence of a whole
class of professional lawyers who, though they might remain
technically clerical, became to all intents and purposes laymen as
the thirteenth century advanced. In this section of the chapter we
shall see the greatest single contrast between the English justiciars,
'professionalised' into justices of King's Bench and Common
Pleas and barons of Exchequer, and the Scottish justiciars who
on the eve of the first war of independence (1296) remained
substantially identical in function and rank with their predecessors
of the mid-twelfth century. Perhaps the fundamental conservatism
of Scottish society was nowhere more astonishingly evinced than
in the history of this indispensable prop of royal government,
which began as an exotic innovation yet within a few generations
took on the protective colouring of a thoroughly native species.
In the century from Richard I to Edward I English justices were
numerous, professionally trained, clerks rather than laymen,
middle class rather than noble in origin, recruited for their talent
rather than because of a claim derived from their parents. In the
same century, from the reign of William the Lion to the inauguration
of Robert I, Scottish justices were few, without legal training,
laymen rather than clergy, noblemen rather than of middle rank,
and enjoying office by something akin to hereditary succession.

Down to the end of William the Lion's reign we know of no
justiciar (save for Matthew bishop of Aberdeen) who was not a
lay baron of the first rank. The standing of the earls of Fife,
Dunbar and Strathearn, the three foremost earls of Scotland,
requires no comment. David Olifard and his son and grandson,
Walter I and Walter II, were lords not only of Smailholm and
other estates in Berwickshire but, most conspicuously, of Bothwell
—after the Stewart's lordship of Renfrew, the greatest secular
lordship in Lanarkshire to be held by a subject superior. The
Olifard 'claim' to the justiciarship did not lapse in 1242. Walter
the younger's heir was Walter Murray (*de Moravia*), already lord
of Bothwell by 1253, very probably justiciar of Lothian by 1255,
certainly so two years later.[191]

[191] *Midlothian Chrs.*, *Soutra Registrum*, no. 44, implies that Walter Murray was
the immediate successor either of Walter Olifard II (d. 1242) or of David
Olifard, Walter's son. Cf. *Origines Parochiales*, i, 55; *Glasgow Registrum*, i, no.
203; Stones, *Documents*, no. 10; and J. Hodgson, *History of Northumberland*, III,
i, 12–3.

Richard Cumin, Geoffrey de Melville (a considerable land-
owner in West and Mid Lothian), Robert de Quinci (lord of
Tranent and *jure uxoris* of Leuchars and much other land in Fife),
Robert Avenel (lord of Abercorn and Eskdale) and William of
Lindsay (lord of Crawford), all fit easily into the same pattern.
Richard Cumin's son William was to become justiciar of Scotia
and eventually, by a judicious marriage, earl of Buchan. Robert
Avenel's son Gervase served for a time as justiciar of Lothian
jointly with David Lindsay I, son of William Lindsay. The picture
is not sharply changed as we move further into the thirteenth
century. No further Avenels appear, and it was doubtless coincidence that in the later 1240s the substitute justiciar of Lothian
was David Graham,[192] kinsman of Henry Graham of Dalkeith
who had succeeded to the Avenel inheritance, *jure uxoris*, on the
death of Roger Avenel in 1243.[193] In any case, David Graham
was of baronial rank, and belonged to a family which, in the
person of William Graham, may possibly have provided the first
of all justiciars of Lothian.[194] David Lindsay's son of the same
name served as justiciar of Lothian from *c.* 1242 to *c.* 1251.[195]
David Lindsay II's successor, Thomas de Normanville, whose
brother was lord of Maxton in Roxburghshire and whose family
held the lordship of Stamfordham in Northumberland,[196]
resembled David Graham in being of a baronial family although
not a tenant-in-chief himself. The evidence for the family relationships of Hugh of Berkeley (Barclay), who enjoyed a long (though
briefly interrupted) term as justiciar of Lothian after Walter
Murray had been driven from office in 1258, is not plentiful.
Nevertheless, it would be surprising if Hugh did not belong to the
baronial family of Berkeley or Barclay established in Scotland
since 1165. He and his brother Walter (who bore a Christian
name favoured by the main Scottish family of Barclay), were
apparently the sons of Roger Barclay of Forgandenny,[197] and

[192] *APS*, i, 404 (1248).   [193] *Scots Peerage*, vi, 194, 200.
[194] See above, p. 118, n. 169.
[195] Lindsay was still justiciar on the eve of Alexander II's death on Kerrera,
off Oban, in July, 1249 (*RMS*, ii, no. 3136), and there is no reason to suppose
that he did not continue in office until the *coup* of 1251.
[196] *Melrose Liber*, nos. 249, 251; *Northumberland County History*, xii, 305;
Cal. Docs. Scot., i, no. 2672. For the Norman origins of the family, see L. Loyd,
Origins of Some Norman Families (Harleian Society, 1951), 73–4.
[197] *Lindores Chartulary*, nos. 68, 69.

both were named as confederates in the Scots-Welsh 'treaty' of 1258.[198]

Hugh Barclay's successor, William de Soules, was hereditary Butler and lord of Liddesdale, but he may have owed his appointment to the justiciarship more to a family claim through his mother, Annora de Normanville, Thomas's cousin.[199] De Soules's successor, Geoffrey de Moubray, was lord of Dalmeny and Inverkeithing.

The line of justiciars benorth Forth after William Cumin's death includes the hereditary Stewart (Walter son of Alan II), Alan Durward (aspirant to the earldoms of Atholl and Mar), Alexander Comyn earl of Buchan (Earl William's son), and at the end of the century John Comyn earl of Buchan, son and heir of Earl Alexander. Between these last two earls came Andrew Murray of Petty, younger son of Walter Murray of Bothwell, formerly justiciar of Lothian.[200] Indeed, the only possible exceptions to the rule of magnatial status were Stephen Fleming, briefly justiciar of Lothian in the early 1260s, and Robert Mowat (de Monte Alto) and Philip de Melville, who shared the justiciarship of Scotia for three years from 1241 to 1244. That this last pair proved insufficient to stand up to the Comyns may demonstrate that they were comparatively minor landholders, but both their families were baronial and there had been at least one Melville justiciar before 1200. As for Stephen Fleming, nothing seems to be known of his background. He may have been the sole exception to prove the rule; but at least his surname is not incompatible with knightly or minor baronial status.[201] Nor does the case of Galloway contradict this impression of the overwhelmingly aristocratic quality of the justiciarship. There, Roland son of Uhtred (himself lord of Galloway), John Comyn of Badenoch, chief of his name. Aymer of Maxwell and William Sinclair of Roslin all conform to the pattern already seen else-

[198] *Littere Wallie*, 184.

[199] Cf. T. McMichael, 'The feudal family of de Soulis', *Dumfriesshire Trans.*, 3rd ser., xxvi, 170–74; *Northumberland County History*, xii, 300.

[200] *Scots Peerage*, ii, 124–5.

[201] Michael Fleming, son of Jordan Fleming, was sheriff of Edinburgh 1198 × 1214 (*RRS*, ii, no. 560), while William Fleming witnessed seven acts of William I, *c*. 1195–9 (ibid., between no. 376 and no. 408). See also *Scots Peerage*, viii, 520.

where. The eventual capture and retention of the office of Lord Justice-General of Scotland by the chief of the family of Campbell had, as it seems, respectably ancient precedent.[202] Although we know of no contemporary comment on the point, it looks as though a man needed to be an earl or lord of a barony or at least to be of noble birth and family if he was to be able to wield the justiciar's authority effectually in the conservative society of twelfth- and thirteenth-century Scotland.

7 Terms of appointment, substitutes and subordinate staff

The formulary styles given in the Ayr MS. include three examples of royal letters of appointment of justiciars (chapters VIII–X).[203] The first announces the appointment of a justiciar of Lothian, who is to perform everything which pertains to the office of justiciary by right and the custom of the realm. The justiciar is to have power to choose a suitable man to act in his stead whenever he himself may be absent for good reason. The king's lieges are commanded to obey and assist the justiciar or his substitute in all that touches his office. The second letter provides for the appointment of a special justiciar (or special justiciars) to determine a lawsuit originated by a royal 'brieve of sasine (dissasine?)'. The last letter announces the appointment of two persons (or either of them), in place of the justiciar of Lothian, to hold the justiciary court (*placita justiciarie*) at a particular place.

Jejune as they are, these letters suggest a number of points of interest. First, the terms of appointment of a principal justiciar were apparently left as vague and general as possible, pointing to duties which might range widely and were probably well known through long usage. Secondly, the justiciar's office might be performed by a deputy, and this deputy might be appointed either by the justiciar himself or by the king directly. Thirdly, the office, at least when performed by deputies, might be held jointly. Fourthly, a justiciar (or at least a deputy-justiciar) might be appointed to deal with a particular case.

The first three of these features seem to be entirely in accord with the evidence from the thirteenth century. Even the fourth feature seems to be exemplified in an actual case from 1259.[204]

[202] *Scots Peerage*, i, 337. [203] *Reg. Brieves*, 36–7. [204] *APS*, i, 99.

We can obtain a little more information on terms of appointment from the treatise of (?) 1292 on the Scottish king's household. The author of the treatise classifies justiciars as *foraynz ministres*, 'exterior officers', officers, that is, whose place and duties lay outwith the king's court proper and certainly outwith the royal household.[205] He says that they ought to be chosen by the magnates, but this surprising recommendation is surely to be taken along with other internal evidence as indicating a period when there had been some break in the continuity of the monarchy, as was conspicuously true of the years 1286–92. We may be sure that normally the appointment of the justiciar lay with the king himself; and the unusually frequent changes in the personnel of the office between 1251 and 1262 reflected the difficulties of a fairly prolonged royal minority. The scope of the justiciars' duties, as summarised in the treatise, deserves to be quoted in full:

(The justices) shall know how, and be able, to provide law and justice to poor as well as rich, and to preserve and control the rights of the king in all matters which pertain to his crown. They shall do this in such a way that no plaints should be presented to the king save only those which, because the justices and sheriffs have failed to deal with them, cannot be remedied without the presence of the king himself. And there shall be in Scotland three justices, that is to say a justice of Lothian, a justice of (Scotland) north of Forth, and a justice of Galloway. They shall hold their sessions of the justice-ayre twice a year, once at the season of grass and a second time at the season of winter (corn); and they shall appoint coroners for whom they are wont to be responsible. And the justices ought to enquire on their ayre into the conduct and administration of the sheriffs and sergeands of fee and challenge them at the bar and present their misdemeanours to the king personally, and at other times when they have defaulted.[206]

It is worth emphasising that the terms of reference outlined for the justiciars in the first paragraph amount to a general commission to provide justice in civil pleas and to exercise supervision

[205] *SHS Misc.*, ii, 36.   [206] *SHS Misc.*, ii, 36–7.

over pleas of the crown. However much the Scottish justiciar may have fallen short of the English justices of assize and common law courts in skill, competence and availability, he was expected to stand in the same buffer position as they did between the crown's subjects and the highest source of secular justice, whether this was king in council or king in council in parliament.

The justiciar's responsibility for appointing coroners does not seem to be vouched for elsewhere, but may well go back to early times. When, c. 1166, King William's Annandale charter (already mentioned)[207] provided that prosecutions of crown pleas within the Annandale liberty should be made by a man of that fief chosen by the king, who would bring them before the king's justiciars, the officer in question seems to have been a sort of coroner. For what it is worth, one of the *Assise Regis Willelmi* (chapter XXX) refers to prosecution by sergeants, coroners or toschederachs.[208] The provision for justiciars to exercise a corrective jurisdiction over defaulting sheriffs is not well illustrated in surviving record, but its authenticity is confirmed by the twelfth-century regulations anent teind. These laid it down that if a sheriff failed to bring a defaulter to justice or withheld teind himself the justiciar was to exact from him the king's full forfeiture.[209]

The earliest recorded instance of a substitute justiciar is found towards the end of Alexander II's reign (19 May, 1248), when David Graham acted in place of David Lindsay II (*tunc loco justitiarii Laudonie*).[210] There may have been some political motive behind this substitution at which we can only guess, for in the next few years Lindsay emerges as an opponent of the Comyns while David Graham, although a protégé of the anti-Comyn earl of Dunbar, appears as a Comyn supporter.[211] On the other hand there could have been wholly non-political reasons for the deputisation. There is no suggestion of politics underlying a number of later instances where clerks, knights, sheriffs and magnates acted as the justiciars' substitutes. In 1259 Andrew the clerk was appointed deputy of the justiciar of Scotia to carry out a special inquest;[212] in 1260 Sir Freskin Murray, Sir David

[207] *RRS*, ii, no. 80 (above, p. 122, n. 121).   [208] *APS*, i, 380.
[209] *RRS*, ii, nos. 179, 281, 507.   [210] *APS*, i, 404.
[211] *Scots Peerage*, vi, 200–1; *Cal. Docs. Scto.*, i, no. 2013.   [212] *APS*, i, 99.

Lochore (sheriff of Perth) and Sir John Cameron (afterwards sheriff of Perth) were 'performing the office' (*gerentes vices*) of the justiciar of Scotia;[213] the earl of Carrick acted in place of the same justiciar in 1266.[214] Another case from 1260 is more obscure. In May, the justiciar of Scotia and the king's bailies of Carrick were commanded to hold an inquest anent the land of Auchensoul (in Barr, Ayrshire),[215] and in the following September the retour was actually made by Stephen Fleming, styling himself 'bailie of Carrick'.[216] The documents, apart from suggesting that Fleming was here in effect the justiciar's deputy, raise some puzzling questions. For the justiciar of Scotia to act in his official capacity outwith the boundaries of Scotia (other than as a principal royal councillor) was anomalous when set beside most of the other evidence we have for geographical division.[217] But the decade 1250–60 was one of political turmoil when custom and precedent might well be overridden. Two justiciars in this period, Alan Durward and Alexander Comyn earl of Buchan, were powerful and ambitious noblemen even judged by the magnatial standards which, as we have seen, were expected for Scottish justiciars.[218] It may be that both men sought to exploit the office politically and to convert into a positive superiority a seniority which had doubtless been inherent in the position of justiciar of Scotia since its earliest days. And indeed, some consciousness of the special dignity of the office may already have been present in the mind of Earl Alexander's father Earl William, for in at least two of his own private charters he styles himself *Willelmus Cumin comes de Buchan justiciarius Scotie*.[219] The suggestion that in the 1250s some

---

[213] *St. Andrews Liber*, 346.   [214] *Laing Chrs.*, no. 8.
[215] *Cal. Docs. Scot.*, i, no. 2193.   [216] *Cal. Docs. Scot.*, i, no. 2674.
[217] Some Lennox cases provide a noteworthy exception (e.g. *Paisley Reg.*, 170–1; *APS*, i, 99), showing that although the sheriffdom of Dumbarton was assigned to the justiciary of Lothian in the 1260s (above, p. 97) the justiciar of Scotia might have cognisance of cases arising in this sheriffdom. But the great majority of cases for which there is evidence between 1167 and 1300 support the view that the justiciar of Scotia dealt with cases arising in Scotland benorth Forth while the justiciar of Lothian dealt with cases arising in Scotland besouth Forth (other than Galloway in the periods when this further division applied, or may have applied).
[218] Cf. D. E. R. Watt, 'The Minority of Alexander III', *Transactions of the Royal Historical Society*, 5th Ser., xxi (1971), 1–23.
[219] *St. Andrews Liber*, 250, 252. A comparable enhancement of dignity in the justiciarship of Lothian may be seen in Alexander II's confirmation in 1242

deliberate steps were taken to exalt the justiciarship of 'Scotia' into a justiciarship of 'Scotland' would not only be intelligible in terms of the contemporary tendency to apply the term 'Scotia' to the whole Scottish kingdom; it would also seem to be supported by the striking fact that Stephen Fleming, who in September 1260 was merely the king's 'bailie of Carrick', had actually been joint justiciar of Lothian in the previous November[220] and was to serve as justiciar again in the early 1260s.[221]

If, however, we take the period under review as a whole, the practice of appointing deputies cannot be said to have been common. It seems to have been rather more usual to have joint justiciars, or at least more than one justiciar at a time. We have seen that the bishop of Aberdeen and the earl of Strathearn (1172–99) acted together as justiciars at a time when the earl of Fife was evidently justiciar of Scotia.[222] A little later, David Lindsay I and Gervase Avenel shared the justiciarship of Lothian.[223] On the death of Walter Stewart II in 1241 the king appointed two men, Philip de Melville and Robert Mowat, to succeed him. They are found acting both jointly[224] and, on occasion, severally.[225] The experiment (if such it may be called) was a failure; we hear of only two more joint justiciars for Scotia before 1305. In the case of Lothian, it seems that only in 1259 did a pair of justiciars serve together between c. 1210 and 1305.

Twelfth-century record is laconic even with respect to the justiciars themselves, so it is hardly surprising to find it silent on the subject of a justiciar's subordinate staff. It is not until we reach the justiciarship of Walter Olifard the younger in Lothian (c. 1215–42) that we find clear references to a justiciar's clerk. A document of 1231, drawn up in the curia regis at Roxburgh, was witnessed by Walter Olifard, justiciar of Lothian, and (at the end)

the year of Walter Olifard II's death) of Walter's endowment of the chapel of 'Osbernystun' beside Bothwell. The royal charter gives Walter the title of justiciar of Lothian (Glasgow Registrum, no. 182). For an English parallel a century earlier, cf. the style adopted by Geoffrey de Mandeville 'Galfridus dei gratia comes Essexi et Justiciarius Londonie' (J. H. Round, The Commune of London (1899), 118).

[220] Cal. Docs. Scot., i, no. 2162.   [221] Exch. Rolls, i, 17.
[222] SHR, xlv, 25–6 (above, p. 81).   [223] RRS, ii, nos. 481, 483.
[224] Glasgow Registrum, no. 179.
[225] Glasgow Registrum, no. 183, Coupar Angus Chrs., i, no. 46; Coupar Angus Rental, i, 339 (no. 53).

by David the clerk of Sir Walter Olifard.[226] By itself this might not point to any official position, but the likelihood that it does is strengthened by the appearance of David the clerk along with a royal clerk as witness to an official pronouncement of Walter Olifard in 1223,[227] and by his description as 'Master David clerk of the justiciar' and even as 'David clerk of justiciary' in two closely contemporary, though undated, documents of this period.[228] Most significant of all, we have a record of an international boundary perambulation (1 December, 1245) in which the Scottish commissioners' names begin with David Lindsay justiciar of Lothian and continue with David Graham (shortly to be Lindsay's lieutenant) and David the clerk, who takes precedence of the local sheriff.[229] Master David may be regarded as the first known clerk of justiciary in Scottish history. Of his thirteenth-century successors we may note Hugh the clerk at the time when Hugh Barclay was holding office.[230] One Robert, clerk of the lord justiciar of Scotia, appears in record of 6 December, 1238;[231] and the same justiciar's *ad hoc* deputy in 1259, Andrew the clerk, was very probably one of Robert's successors.[232] The exchequer rolls of 1264–6 also mentioned a justiciar's sergeand,[233] and this office may perhaps be carried back to 1223, when we have record of three of Walter Olifard's sergeands.[234] One, admittedly, is described as the baker, but the first two, Osbert the Great and Osbert the Scot, were possibly men who served Olifard in his justiciar's duties.[235]

8 The justiciar's political importance

Down to the death of Alexander II in 1249 the justiciars regularly witnessed a high proportion of those royal acts which have survived. Before *c.* 1200 it is not always obvious that a charter or a brieve carries the justiciar's attestation, because of the twelfth-century clerks' unhappy reluctance to assign titles to their

---

[226] Raine, *North Durham*, no. 126.   [227] *Glasgow Registrum*, no. 126.
[228] *Midlothian Chrs., Soutra Registrum*, nos. 12, 17.
[229] *Cal. Docs. Scot.*, i, no. 1699.   [230] *Exch. Rolls*, i, 26.
[231] *Moray Registrum*, no. 107.   [232] *APS*, i, 99.   [233] *Exch. Rolls*, i, 4.
[234] *Glasgow Registrum*, no. 126.
[235] Osbert the Great is found witnessing a charter of Walter Olifard's son David (ibid., no. 120).

lay witnesses, save in the case of earls. But a careful scrutiny of witness-lists will show that even in that earlier period the justiciar's attestation carried weight, and his name, with or without title attached, commonly occurs high up in the testing clauses. In the period after 1249, the output of the king's chapel underwent some changes, both in volume and in character, yet there are still plenty of extant royal acts to which justiciars were named as witnesses. Throughout our period as a whole it is clear that the witnessing of a royal act by a justiciar may mean no more than that he happened to be present at court on the day the charter or brieve was issued, or that he had at least been consulted and was so directly concerned that his name could not be omitted. In the large majority of cases we may safely infer the justiciar's actual presence. Apart from these run-of-the-mill documents which would tend to be produced as part of the court's daily business, there survive a number of acts which were evidently drawn up or approved or promulgated on some more solemn occasion—a session of the *curia regis* in its judicial capacity, a specially well attended council, a *colloquium* or parliament. It is rare for the documentary record of occasions of this type not to demonstrate the importance which seems to have been attached to the justiciar's presence.

A handful of examples (disproportionately few for William I's reign) will be sufficient illustration. Thus, in 1167 David Olifard was one of the only two laymen named as attending an important session of the *curia regis* at Stirling.[236] Earl Duncan of Fife, we are told, spoke first in King William's *plenier parlement* in 1173.[237] Admittedly, he was the premier earl, but he was also, as we have seen, justiciar of Scotia. William Lindsay, probably as justiciar of Lothian, attended the council of April 1189, which saw the election of Roger of Leicester to the see of St. Andrews.[238] The form of an extant record dating 30 March, 1226, suggests a great council at Stirling with the justiciar of Lothian taking precedence of the other laymen present.[239] On 13 October, 1230, and 3 February, 1231, there were evidently major council sessions at

[236] *RRS*, ii, 193 ('Comment').
[237] *Chronicle of the War between the English and the Scots in 1173–1174*, by Jordan Fantosme (ed. F. Michel, Surtees Soc., 1840), 14, l. 288.
[238] *RRS*, ii, no. 284.
[239] *Arbroath Liber*, i, no. 171; *Moray Registrum*, no. 29. Only the earls, the Stewart and the Lord of Galloway, come before the justiciar.

Stirling and Clackmannan respectively, duly attended by the justiciars of Scotia and Lothian.[240] At the end of March 1231, the latter (but not, significantly, the former) was present at a judicial session of the *curia regis* at Roxburgh.[241] The two justiciars witnessed a royal charter given at a *colloquium* at Liston in Lothian on 8 April, 1236.[242] We find the justiciar of Scotia referred to in connection with a *plenum colloquium* at Holyrood in 1255.[243] The justiciar of Lothian attended a parliament held in Roxburgh castle in May 1266.[244] Both justiciars figured prominently at the Candlemas parliament of 1284 (Scone, 5 February).[245] The justiciar of Lothian was present at a *colloquium domini regis* held at Holyrood on 25 January, 1285.[246] The justiciars of Lothian and Galloway (William de Soules and William Sinclair) were named in the long list of magnates present at the parliament of Birgham in March 1290, as was Sir Andrew Murray (of Petty) who was probably justiciar of Scotia.[247] It is, however, puzzling that whereas de Soules's name is placed very high on the list (of the laymen below earl's rank only Bruce of Annandale and Murray of Bothwell precede him), the other two names come relatively low down. Andrew Murray was also present at the Candlemas parliament of 1293 (Scone, 10–18 February),[248] the year when we have the best evidence of his being justiciar of Scotia.[249]

Much the same impression is conveyed by a study of the major 'state papers' of the period, especially the treaties and other international agreements, and also the unusual political provisions of the kind which marked the disturbed years 1250–60 and 1290–2. The 'Treaty of Falaise' (1174) is scarcely in point here, for it was a formal submission under duress, not a pact made between free agents. Even so, we may note that among the Scots magnates required to be (in reality, to provide) hostages under the treaty were Earl Duncan of Fife, Richard Cumin and Walter Olifard the elder.[250] The fifteen nobles on the Scottish side who proffered solemn oaths in warranty of the Treaty of York (1237) were headed by the earls of Fife and Menteith, immediately

[240] *APS*, i, 399; *Balmerino Liber*, no. 1.　[241] Raine, *North Durham*, no. 126.
[242] *Nat. MSS. Scot.*, i, pl. xlix.　[243] *APS*, i, 426.
[244] *Kelso Liber*, no. 190.　[245] *APS*, i, 424.　[246] *SHR*, xlv, 37, n. 5.
[247] *APS*, i, 441 = Stevenson, *Documents*, i, no. 92.
[248] *Glasgow Registrum*, i, no. 239.　[249] *Family of Rose*, 29.
[250] *Scone Liber*, no. 1 (p. 3).

followed by Walter the Stewart and Walter Olifard who, although not so styled, were in fact the two justiciars.[251] The two corresponding justiciars in 1244 (Alan Durward and David Lindsay II) were among the four magnates who swore an oath on the king's soul for the observance of the Treaty of Newcastle.[252] When the government of the young Alexander III was changed in September 1255, under pressure from Henry III of England, the list of new men appointed to the young king's council and to the government of the realm began with two bishops, four earls, the Stewart and the lord of Annandale.[253] The next two names were those of Alan Durward and Walter Murray of Bothwell. Durward (though not so described) was in fact the new justiciar of Scotia, entering upon his second term of office. It is highly probable that Murray of Bothwell was the new justiciar of Lothian; his placing in the list would suggest as much and we know that he held the office two years later.[254] Correspondingly, the names of the ejected justiciars (the earl of Buchan and Thomas de Normanville) figure in the list of those magnates formally removed from the king's council.[255] When, two years later, the tables were turned and the Comyns were again in power the treaty which they and their supporters made with the prince of Wales (March 1258) gave prominence to the names of the justiciars of Scotia (once again the earl of Buchan) and of Galloway (his kinsman, John Comyn of Badenoch).[256] Hugh Barclay (along with his brother Walter) also appears, perhaps not yet appointed to the justiciarship of Lothian which he was to hold by the following autumn.[257] It may have proved unexpectedly difficult to dislodge Walter Murray from office, although in the spring of 1258 Murray, along with his colleague Alan Durward, was hoping for a safe temporary retreat in one of the English border castles.[258] It is also noteworthy that justiciars might serve as envoys or at any rate be appointed from the ranks of men who had had ambassadorial experience. Walter Olifard II, while justiciar of Lothian, was one of the Scots plenipotentiaries who

[251] Scone, *Documents*, no. 7 (p. 25).   [252] *Cal. Docs. Scot.*, i, no. 1654.
[253] Stones, *Documents*, no. 10 (p. 30).   [254] Above, p. 122, n. 191.
[255] Stones, *Documents*, no. 10 (p. 31). For Thomas de Normanville as justiciar of Lothian in the period 1251 × 1253, see *Melrose Liber*, i, no. 322.
[256] *Littere Wallie*, 184.   [257] *Scone Liber*, no. 108.
[258] *Cal. Docs. Scot.*, i, no. 2121.

prepared the Treaty of York in 1237.[259] Thomas de Normanville was one of the two Scottish envoys sent to Henry III's court at the time of the English king's acute embarrassment in May 1258.[260] William de Soules was King Alexander's envoy at the English court both before and after his appointment to the justiciarship.[261] His successor, Geoffrey de Moubray, some years before he became justiciar, was one of the three Scots who travelled to Gascony in the summer of 1286 on the little-known but obviously important mission to King Edward I to ask for his help in the crisis into which King Alexander's sudden death had plunged his kingdom.[262] Sir Adam of Gordon, joint-justiciar of Lothian in 1305, had acted as envoy for the Scots guardians in 1301.[263] He had also served as a warden of the East March,[264] and this recalls the fact that over a century earlier Sir Adam's distant kinsman Earl Patrick I of Dunbar had been justiciar (of Lothian?) and warden of Berwick, in one or both of which capacities he had taken charge of the Scottish share in rebuilding the vitally important border bridge at Berwick when it had been washed away in a spate.[265]

9 Conclusion

Professor West begins his book on the justiciarship in England by saying that 'the justiciar has had no historian'.[266] He is concerned only with the English justiciar and for that unique dignitary and his office he has now supplied the want. Unhappily, it remains true that the Scottish justiciar also has had no historian. We can scarcely deny a common ancestry for the justiciars in both countries, a common stock of administrative concepts from which strong kings might draw a sturdy and fecund progeny. But common ancestry was not to lead to common upbringing. The Scottish justiciarship developed, at a remarkably early period, in ways which differed profoundly from the paths taken not only by the English justiciar *par excellence*, the king's *alter ego*, who forms

[259] *Cal. Docs. Scot.*, i, no. 1317.   [260] *Cal. Docs. Scot.*, i, nos. 2126–7.
[261] *Cal. Docs. Scot.*, ii, nos. 104, 272. De Soules had succeeded to the justiciarship by 1279 (*Melrose Liber*, i, no. 347).
[262] *Chron. Bower*, ii, 138.   [263] *Cal. Docs. Scot.*, ii, no. 1244.
[264] *Cal. Docs. Scot.*, no. 1169.
[265] *Chron. Howden*, iv, 98 (see *RRS*, ii, 44–5).
[266] F. West, *The Justiciarship in England*, p. ix.

the subject of Professor West's study, but also by the *justitiae* or *justitiarii*, the justices of King's Bench, Common Pleas and assize (to say nothing of the justices of the peace) whose office and functions may all be traced to an original notion of the man who at the highest level under the king exercises law and justice in the king's name. In England the justiciarship may be said to have reached the end of its useful life by 1232, and the doubtful experiment of reviving it in 1258 lasted only a few years before the office vanished for good in 1265. But long before this unique justiciarship decayed and disappeared the English Crown had developed, with much trial and some error, a system of royal judges which proved competent to cope with the legal and judicial side of the old justiciar's activity, even after this had been greatly expanded. Scotland saw no such separation between a great justiciar who could be the king's other self and a cadre of professionals whose duty it was to direct the king's courts in Westminster Hall and, at more or less regular intervals, to take the king's court to the provinces. The former had never been needed and the latter could only have arisen in response to a vastly more complex and elaborate network of courts than thirteenth-century Scotland either required or could afford. The Scottish justiciar doubtless had much less professional skill than the English common law justice but he retained a wider competence, political and governmental as well as judicial. For his legal work he must have had to rely on the learning and experience of trained lawyers, for whose existence in Scotland from the closing decades of the twelfth century the documentary evidence is sufficient proof.[267] But the events of Alexander III's minority, when the justiciarships were clearly among the essential prizes of

[267] Here we may note Lord Cooper's remarks (*Select Cases*, 11): 'The Earl [Patrick of Dunbar, 1182–1232], who was obviously in the hands of skilled advisers, certainly taught both his adversaries and the Lateran authorities a lesson in the efficacy of obstructive tactics.' In this connexion, we should note the appearance of certain *magistri* in Scottish records of the later twelfth century, some at least of whom may have been lawyers with Scottish clients. A Master Angerius figures prominently in Coldingham Priory record and witnessed, e.g. a charter of Earl Patrick himself, in company with the well-recorded Master Richard of Coldingham (Raine, *North Durham*, no. 116). He was perhaps the 'Master Angerus of Durham' who witnessed with 'Master Angerus of Beverley' a deed of *c.* 1170–80 connected with Durham cathedral church (*A Medieval Miscellany for Doris Mary Stenton*, edd. P. M. Barnes and C. F Slade, Pipe Roll Soc., New Series, vol. xxxvi (1962), p. 210). Angerus of

power sought by each rival faction, are a reminder that the office stayed unspecialised, a crucially important channel through which to exercise royal authority and dispense royal favour and patronage.

This chapter, by setting forth the evidence for the justiciar's activity in a variety of fields, judicial and legal, administrative and political, has tried to present some idea of the justiciarship as a principal institution within the framework of Scottish royal government. A study of the office as it was actually exercised in a period so formative for the historical Scottish kingdom ought at least to put us on our guard against hasty condemnations of the native secular legal machinery. It is not self-evident that the institutions at the disposal of the Scottish state for administering justice during the period from David I to John Balliol were inadequate for the purposes for which they were designed. The highly developed apparatus of Angevin justice, with its substantial corpus of common law, its multiplicity of courts and its proliferation of writs and other remedies, no doubt suited the peculiar character of England. That country had known a long tradition of centralised monarchical government and had learned to combine with it an extensive delegation of royal authority. In the same way, it may be accepted that the peculiar character of Scotland demanded a more respectful regard for provincial differences and entrenched feudal power. In that climate, the rather old-fashioned 'baronial' justiciarships, firmly based upon the ancient geographical divisions of the kingdom and held by noblemen powerful in their own right, may have been especially appropriate and therefore more effective than a wholesale and artificial importation of alien institutions, such as seemed for a time to succeed in Angevin Ireland but in the end signally failed to provide that country with a workable and unitary legal system.

Beverley was perhaps the Master Angerius judged suitable by Pope Alexander III in 1171 to act as compurgator for the archbishop of York along with a Master Vacarius (*Materials for the history of Thomas Becket archbishop of Canterbury* edd. J. C. Robertson and J. B. Sheppard, Rolls Series (1875–85), vii, 500). It has been supposed that this Master Vacarius was the famous Lombard jurist prevented by King Stephen from teaching Roman Law in England (*The Liber Pauperum of Vacarius*, ed. F. de Zulueta, Selden Soc., vol. xliii (1927), pp. xix–xxi). It seems in any case probable that these particular *magistri* were men with legal skill. These are fairly frequent references to *iurisperiti* in thirteenth-century Scottish record; note, e.g. the expression in a pronouncement of 1293: 'habito prius super hoc iuris peritorum consilio' (*Glasgow Registrum*, no. 238).

TABLE OF JUSTICIARS, c. 1165–1306

	Scotia	Lothian	
1165(1154?)–1205	Duncan II earl of Fife (d. 1204)	David Olifard	c. 1165–c. 1170
		Robert Avenel Richard Cumin Robert de Quinci Geoffrey de Melville	c. 1170 × c. 1178
1172 × 1199	{ Matthew bishop of Aberdeen (d. 1199) { Gilbert earl of Strathearn (d. 1223)	Walter Olifard I	c. 1178–c. 1188
		William Lindsay	c. 1189–c. 1198
		Patrick earl of Dunbar (d. 1232)	c. 1195–c. 1205
c. 1205–c. 1232	William Cumin (Comyn) earl of Buchan (d. 1233)	David Lindsay I and Gervase Avenel (d. 1219)	c. 1208(–c. 1215?)
1232–1241	Walter II son of Alan, the Stewart (d. 1241)	Walter Olifard II (d. 1242) David Lindsay II	c. 1215–1242 c. 1242–9(1251?)
1241–1244	Philip de Melville and Robert Mowat (de Monte Alto)	(David Graham, deputy)	1248
1244–1251	Alan Durward (Hostiarius) (d. 1275)		
(× ?)1253	Philip of Meldrum or Fedarg and Michael Mowat*		1253
1253–1255	Alexander Comyn earl of Buchan (d. 1289)	Thomas de Normanville	c. 1251–c. 1253 (1255?)
1255–1257	Alan Durward	Walter Murray of Bothwell Hugh Barclay	1257(1255?–1257) 1258

* I am grateful to Dr. D. E. R. Watt for the reference to SRO, GD 254/1 where these names (not dealt with in the text) occur.

TABLE OF JUSTICIARS, *c.* 1165–1306—*continued*

Scotia   Lothian

(Scotia dates)	Scotia	Lothian	(Lothian dates)
1258–1289	Alexander Comyn earl of Buchan	Thomas de Normanville and Stephen Fleming	1259
		Stephen Fleming	(*c.* 1260–1262?)
c. 1293(1289?)– 1296(?)	Andrew Murray of Petty d. *c.* 1299	Hugh Barclay	*c.* 1262–*c.* 1279
1300 (–1304?)	John Comyn earl of Buchan (d. 1308)	William de Soules (d. 1292/3)	*c.* 1279–*c.* 1292/3
1305–1306	Robert Keith and William Inge (south of the Mounth)	Geoffrey de Moubray (d. 1300)	1294–1296(?)
	Reginald Cheyne and John de Vaux (north of the Mounth)	Adam of Gordon and John de Lisle	1305–1306

Galloway

c. 1185–1200	Roland son of Uhtred lord of Galloway (d. 1200)
1258 (and after?)	John Comyn of Badenoch (d. × 1279)
1264	Aymer of Maxwell
(1266 × 1272?) 1275	} John Comyn of Badenoch
1287 (or earlier?)– 1291 (or later?)	William Sinclair
1305–1306	Roger Kirkpatrick and Walter Burghdon

4   The Anglo-Scottish border

On any showing, two crucial dates in the later history of the Border were 1603, when it ceased to divide two states with different sovereigns and ruling dynasties, and 1707, when it ceased to divide two independent kingdoms. This is not to say that since 1707 the Border has become extinct. It remains for some purposes a national frontier, it still has an administrative validity, it is still a legal and linguistic divide, above all, much more powerfully, it still enshrines and perpetuates a multitude of emotions whose roots lie far back in our history. But if one seeks the period in which the Border was at the height of its effectiveness, when it existed with all its faculties unimpaired, that period was medieval. For good or ill, the Border was one of the major creations and institutions of medieval Britain, and it behoves a medievalist to explain it.

Historians not only agree that the Border was a medieval institution, they point to the very men whose handiwork it was: King Henry III of England and his brother-in-law King Alexander II of Scotland. One authoritative English work speaks of 'the establishment of the existing Border in 1237',[1] another says that 'the Border itself was not finally confirmed as a frontier until 1249, and even then an area remained debatable between the two countries'.[2] According to the most up-to-date account from the Scottish side, 'a definite border line was not drawn until the middle of the thirteenth century'; 'the treaty of York (1237) finally fixed the Border on the Tweed–Solway line'.[3] Thus it is implied, first that the Border has remained since 1237 substantially

---

[1] Sir Maurice Powicke, *The Thirteenth Century*, p. 574. Elsewhere, however, Sir Maurice pointed out that 'the settlement of 1237 maintained the borders between England and Scotland as they had been established in the days of Henry II and John'; ibid., p. 587.

[2] J. C. Holt, *The Northerners* (1961), p. 209.

[3] W. C. Dickinson, *Scotland from the earliest times to 1603* (1961), pp. 70, 81.

uncontroversial and unaltered; secondly, that before 1237 the Tweed–Solway line, if it formed the Border at all, was only one of a number of lines prevailing from time to time. Prior to 1237, disagreement and fluidity; since 1237, agreement and rigidity: such is the essence of the received opinion. With the Border since 1237 this chapter is not chiefly concerned. Not that the changes or 'adjustments' made in the line of the frontier during the later middle ages can be dismissed as trivial. They involved the loss to Scotland on the east of Berwick, which down to 1296 had been the chief town and seaport of the kingdom, and on the west of the parish of Kirkandrews, a few thousand acres largely composed of intractable bog. More important than this, perhaps, was the fact that on the east these alterations accompanied a change in the essential character of the Border, which having been conceived of as a line practically devoid of military significance, took on a strongly defensive aspect, in keeping with the chronic warfare of the fourteenth, fifteenth and sixteenth centuries. As a result of this militarisation of the Border, the town of Roxburgh, which like Berwick had been one of the principal Scottish burghs before 1296, disappeared, even though its site remained in Scotland. Because of Scottish military weakness, the total abandonment of Roxburgh was preferable to maintaining a town and castle which could all too easily fall into English hands.

This chapter will confine itself to the Border before 1237, touching incidentally on the proposition that the York treaty of that year was a true landmark in Border evolution. Of this earlier period, fluidity, as has been said, is thought to have been the keynote. This does not mean vagueness, but variation among several possible choices. Supporters of the vagueness theory can be found, but to my mind their thesis does not carry much conviction. The notion that there was ever a sizeable tract of territory (as distinct from small pieces of no man's or debateable land) where the English and Scottish kingdoms as it were shaded off into each other is based either upon an entirely false belief that precise boundaries are a modern invention or else upon a naively charitable estimate of our early kings, whose greed for land and power was in fact determined solely by the extent of their own and their neighbours' military resources. Our forebears were seldom able to express themselves with absolute precision in written

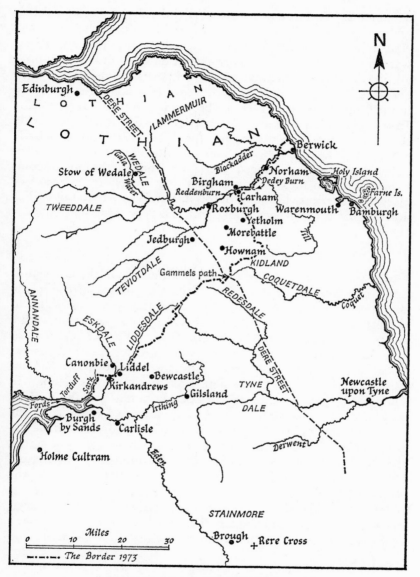

MAP 15. The Anglo-Scottish Border.

documents. We must not ascribe to them a vagueness which is really our own failure to extract precision from the evidence. The men of that age had no maps, but they had dikes and watercourses, cairns and crosses carved on great oak trees: above all, they had the testimony of living witnesses handed down from generation to generation. It is therefore as a march, a boundary in the fullest sense, that I see the Border in the period before 1237. In the later middle ages it was occasionally the practice to divide the Border into three sections, the West March, the Middle March and the East March. This not altogether happy arrangement never quite replaced an older and more fundamental twofold division into West and East. Not merely for the sake of clarity, but because history requires it, I shall adhere to this earlier and simpler division, beginning with the West March.

1   The West March

One consequence of the decline of Northumbria in the late eighth and ninth centuries was that the British kingdom of Strathclyde or Cumbria recovered much of its ancient power and began to expand southward from the Clyde valley into the basins of the rivers which flow into the head of the Solway Firth: Nith, Annan, Esk, Liddel, Irthing and Eden. At its greatest extent, this re-invigorated Cumbrian kingdom stretched between two famous boundary marks, the Clach nam Breatann ('Britons' Stone') in Glen Falloch, above the head of Loch Lomond, and the Rere or Rey Cross at the western edge of Stainmore Common in the North Riding of Yorkshire. It is a striking illustration of the persistence of ancient boundaries that of these two landmarks, the Clach nam Breatann is only three miles north of the march between the sheriffdoms of Perth and Dumbarton,[4] while the Rere Cross, or what remains of it, is but a short distance from the point where Yorkshire meets Westmorland. Neither, however, marks *the* Border, for an explanation of which we must turn to the eclipse and extinction of the Cumbrian kingdom in the tenth and

---

[4] Measured from Inverarnan. The Clach nam Breatann is on the shoulder of Cruachan Cruinn, and since there is the Allt Criche ('March Burn') running into Falloch opposite this hill, it may be surmised that the county march formerly followed this line.

eleven centuries.[5] In 945 Edmund, the king of Wessex who inherited the general overlordship of the English peoples built up by Edward the Elder and Athelstan, overran Strathclyde and committed it to the king of Scots, Malcolm I, on some condition of vassalage. The Britons threw off Scottish overlordship in the following generation and kept their independence until about 1018, when the last of their kings, Owein son of Dyfnal, died. From 1018 to 1092, with the possible exception of a few years before 1055, the former kingdom of Cumbria was under Scottish rule. Its separate identity survived the end of its political independence for many centuries. It found expression in many different ways, of which the most striking and persistent was the great extent and special position of the diocese of Glasgow, whose cathedral was the cult-centre of Cumbria's patron saint, Kentigern or Mungo. Before 1133 the diocese included most of Cumberland and Westmorland, and as late as 1267 John of Cheam, the Surrey man who strangely and uncomfortably occupied the chair of Saint Kentigern, lodged a preposterous yet historical claim that his diocese of Glasgow should reach to the Rere Cross on Stainmore.[6] The separatism of Cumbria died very hard, and the rivalry between Glasgow and Edinburgh, often remarked by observers of the Scottish scene, is no modern phenomenon. It has an unbroken history reaching back into the centuries when a fierce Scottish nationalism north of the Forth was challenged by an equally fierce British nationalism in the valley of the Clyde.

The Scottish kings who ruled Cumbria from 1018 to 1092 may have imported a small Scottish aristocracy. They also had to accommodate members of the old House of Bamburgh, the Eadwulfings, who regarded Northumbria as their hereditary right and disliked being ousted from it by Danes and Normans. In the 1050s the district of Carlisle seems to have been held by one member of this English family, Cospatric, Uhtred's son,[7] and

---

[5] For a study of this kingdom and its relations with Scotland and England, see D. P. Kirby, 'Strathclyde and Cumbria: a survey of historical development to 1092', in *CWAAS Transactions*, lxii, New Series (1962), pp. 77–94, especially pp. 85–8.

[6] *Chron. Lanercost*, 65.

[7] If the famous charter of Cospatric is genuine; cf. F. E. Harmer, *Anglo-Saxon Writs* (1952), pp. 419–24.

FKS

thirty years later it was certainly held by a nephew of this Cospatric, one Dalfin, whose father, somewhat confusingly, also had
the name Cospatric.[8] In the 1090s, however, King William Rufus
resumed, from a position of vastly greater strength, the imperialist
policy of the great West Saxon kings, Athelstan, Edmund and
Edgar. The old Cumbrian kingdom formed a salient thrusting far
into English territory, so that the king of Scots might lodge in his
own land at Brough-under-Stainmore and be within two days'
ride of York. Accordingly, in 1092, Rufus crossed the Pennines,
took possession of Carlisle, drove out Dalfin son of Cospatric, and
brought into the district foreign knights to garrison the castle he
built at Carlisle and (what was still more noteworthy) foreign
peasants to till the soil of the surrounding countryside.[9] A little
later, he put, first Duncan, then his half-brother Edgar, on the
Scottish throne as client kings.[10] The chief of the Normans
established at Carlisle as a consequence of Rufus's act of aggression
was Ranulf Meschin of Bricquessart, nephew of Hugh of
Avranches earl of Chester. The contemporary sources which
narrate Rufus's annexation do not say what were the northern
limits of the annexed territory; it is only a late authority which
states somewhat vaguely that Ranulf's land extended between the
Rere Cross and Solway.[11] But a Scottish charter issued probably
in 1124, about the time that Ranulf lost his fief, shows that this
fief, explicitly called Cumberland, was bordered by the territory
of Annandale.[12] After 1133, the boundary between Cumberland
and Annandale coincided with the boundary between the new
diocese of Carlisle and the old diocese of Glasgow, now effectively
deprived of its southernmost territory. The feudal records of
Annandale and the diocesan records of Glasgow and Carlisle give
a consistent picture of this boundary in the later twelfth and
thirteenth centuries. Since it is perfectly clear that Carlisle was
an English, Glasgow a Scottish diocese, it follows that the boundary between the two, where it can be ascertained, was also the
Border between England and Scotland.

[8] Anderson, *Early Sources*, ii, 37. Kirby (art. cit., 93) thinks it more likely
that the Cospatric of the charter was Dalfin's father, Cospatric son of Maldred.
[9] Anglo-Saxon Chronicle, *sub anno* 1092 (in the Everyman translation by
G. N. Garmonsway, p. 227).
[10] A. A. M. Duncan, 'The Earliest Scottish Charters', xxxvii, 125–35.
[11] *Cal. Docs. Scot.*, ii, no. 64 (*c.* 1275).   [12] Lawrie, *Charters*, no. 54.

During the second half of the twelfth century Robert Brus, lord of Annandale, granted to Holm Cultram abbey, on the southern shore of the Solway Firth, the tidal fishery of Torduff, on the opposite shore.[13] Early in the next century the grant was confirmed by William Brus, who declared the southern boundary of this fishery and of the adjacent fishery of Rainpatrick to be the midstream line of the River Esk;[14] and rather later this was explicitly described by his son as 'the midstream line of the river which divides my land (i.e. Annandale) from Cumberland'.[15] Today, the Border leaves the main channel of the Esk at a point three miles east of Torduff, and follows the tiny River Sark to the western end of the Scots Dike, where it turns east to rejoin the Esk just south of Canonbie. The Border at this point was fixed in 1552, by an arrangement which assigned the parish of Kirk-andrews-on-Esk to England and the adjacent parish of Canonbie to Scotland. Before 1552, these parishes constituted most of the 'Bateable' or 'Debateable' Land, Kirkandrews being known as the 'English Bateable Land', Canonbie as the 'Scots Bateable Land'.[16] In the thirteenth century, and presumably in the twelfth century also, both these parishes, Kirkandrews and Canonbie, belonged to the deanery of Eskdale in the diocese of Glasgow.[17] It may therefore be inferred that during most of that period the Border followed the River Esk from its mouth up to its confluence with the Liddel Water and then turned eastward, as it does today, up the Kershope Burn to reach the first high ground of the Cheviots. But was this the border fixed by William Rufus? One of our best guides to this part of the Border, as to so much Cumberland history, is James Wilson, and in a note which he added to his article on twelfth-century Cumberland in the Victoria History of that county he showed that Rufus's frontier could not have simply followed Esk and Liddel to the Kershope Burn.[18] Canon Wilson did not have space to develop his argument, but it may be

[13] F. Grainger and W. G. Collingwood, *The Register and Records of Holm Cultram* (*CWAAS*, Record Series, 1929), 34.
[14] *Melrose Liber*, Appendix, no. 3; British Museum, MS. Harl. 3891, fo. 83.
[15] *Melrose Liber*, Appendix, no. 7.
[16] W. Mackay Mackenzie, 'The Debateable Land', *SHR*, xxx, 109-25, especially p. 125.
[17] SHS, *Miscellany*, v, 95; *Glasgow Registrum*, no. 114 (A.D. 1220).
[18] *VCH, Cumberland*, i, 335.

stated briefly thus. When Ranulf Meschin was given Cumberland he established two Border baronies, Burgh-on-Sands to guard the main route into Scotland across the fords of Solway, and Liddel, further east, to guard the lesser route into Eskdale. The barony of Liddel, granted to a Fleming named Turgis Brundis, had passed by the middle of the twelfth century to Turgis of Rosedale, presumably his descendant. Turgis of Rosedale founded the house of Augustinian Canons of Liddel—which soon became known as Canonbie—as a cell of Jedburgh priory, and he and other members of his family made additional grants to Jedburgh of the parish church of Kirkandrews on Esk and of land between the two rivers Esk and Liddel at their confluence.[19] It is an inescapable inference that the barony of Liddel included land on the north side of both rivers, and it is a reasonable assumption that it embraced the modern parishes of Kirkandrews and Canonbie. Since it is inconceivable that a barony founded as a result of Rufus's annexation would have been half in England and half in Scotland, we are bound to infer that for the Normans, as for the modern tourist or eloping couple, England was left behind not at the Esk but at the Sark. How was it, then, that the Border had moved south to the Esk by the thirteenth century? Canon Wilson did not venture an explanation, and it may be rash to suggest that that part of the territory of Liddel which had become linked with Jedburgh, either by ownership or by parochial patronage, came to be regarded as ecclesiastically subject to Glasgow and consequently politically part of Scotland. This would have been authorised by the settlement of 1157–8 (shortly to be mentioned), and it may be pointed out in this connexion that the diocese of Carlisle was vacant from 1157 to 1203.

If we ask why Rufus chose to stop short at the Solway and leave Annandale and most of Eskdale and Liddesdale in Scottish hands, the answer must surely be that it was a matter of strategy. The key to Norman warfare was the castle. Far from having any concept of a continuous frontier line, such as the Roman Wall, the Normans were content to erect a number of strongly-sited, self-sufficient castles to dominate the main routes of communication. It mattered little, therefore, if the enemy made casual and temporary penetrations far into their territory, so long as their

[19] *RRS*, ii, no. 62.

castles held firm. As Rufus saw it, the new castle of Carlisle of 1092, paralleling the New Castle upon Tyne of 1080, constituted the essence of the Border. The fact that Solway and Esk became the actual Border line was an accident of Norman strategy.

Accident or not, the Solway boundary was not accepted by the Scots. In 1136 King David I took possession of Carlisle, and under an agreement made with King Stephen at Durham in February restored the Border to the Rere Cross on Stainmore. For the next twenty-one years, the West March resumed the line which it had followed in the eleventh century. The Scottish king made no effort to suppress the see of Carlisle, but it seems that he regarded Cumberland and Westmorland as an integral part of his realm, unlike the earldom of Northumberland of which he also took possession about the same time. Indeed, there are signs that even in the 1120s neither David of Scotland nor his brother King Alexander I accepted the anglicisation of Cumberland. Around 1122, before his accession, David caused an inquest to be held by a local jury into the endowments of the see of Glasgow, partly to support his action in detaching Teviotdale from the bishopric of Durham.[20] The jury was not led to find any endowments of Glasgow in what is now Cumberland, but one of the jurors was a Cumberland magnate, Gille son of Bued, lord of Bewcastle and of Gilsland (which has preserved his name). One of the witnesses to David's charter of Annandale for Robert Brus, almost certainly given at Scone on the occasion of David's accession in 1124, was Hervey son of Warin.[21] Perhaps it is only a coincidence, but if so a remarkable one, that a Hervey son of Morin(us) was lord of Dalston by Carlisle, a witness to Ranulf Meschin's foundation charter to Wetheral Priory, about 1100,[22] and a tenant of the Honour of Richmond before 1130. King Alexander I's foundation charter to Scone Priory, between 1115 and 1120, was witnessed by a magnate named Forn, who was almost certainly Forn son of Sigulf, ancestor of the barons of Greystoke, and grandfather of a

---

[20] Lawrie, *Charters*, no. 50.
[21] Lawrie, *Charters*, no. 54 (the original is B.M., Cotton Charters, no. xviii, 45, not, as Lawrie wrongly states, in the Duchy of Lancaster archives).
[22] *Wetheral Register*, no. 1 and note on p. 6; Cumberland Assize Roll, 6–7 Edward I (P.R.O., J.I.1/133, m. 29) (*Hervicus filius Maurini*, lord of Dalston); *EYC*, iv, 11 (no. 9).

half-brother of Alexander's queen, Sibyl.[23] In this period, the lord of Allerdale was Waltheof son of Cospatric, brother of that Dalfin whom Rufus had driven from Carlisle in 1092.[24] Cumberland had lords whose title to their land went back well before the Norman annexation, or who associated themselves with Scottish rulers after the annexation. David I's action in 1136 merely brought back under Scottish rule landowners and peasants who can hardly have had time to accept the Solway as the fixed and immemorial border between the northern and southern kingdoms.

Twenty-one years later, in the summer of 1157, this situation was dramatically and, as it proved, permanently reversed. Henry II, twenty-four years old and on the threshold of the most vigorous period of his reign, compelled the king of Scots, Malcolm IV, a youth of fifteen, to surrender Carlisle, Cumberland and Westmorland. In the winter following, lest there should be any doubt what the surrender implied, King Henry came to Carlisle in person and summoned King Malcolm to meet him there. The English king had just visited Newcastle and Wark on Tweed, and was obviously Border-conscious. It was made plain to the young king of Scots that the Border of which Henry was conscious now began at the Solway. It is true that Malcolm's next two successors protested again and again at the injustice of this action, until by the Treaty of York of 1237 Alexander II, by abandoning his claim to the two north-western counties, implicitly accepted the Solway–Esk Border. But if we must look for a date at which the West March assumed what is substantially its present line it is surely 1157 rather than 1237, and for 1157 there had been a precedent in 1092.

2 The East March

Just as on the west the line of the Border is determined by Solway and Esk, so on the east it is determined by the River Tweed. There is the soundest of geographical reasons why this river, which enters the sea nearly sixty miles north of the Solway Firth, should be chosen in preference to the Tyne, whose mouth is almost due east of the Solway. The Cheviot Hills, beginning on the west

[23] *Complete Peerage*, xi, Appendix D, p. 108 and n. (h).
[24] *Wetheral Register*, 5, n.

only a few miles above Canonbie, terminate on the east at a point very close to the Tweed and only fifteen miles from the sea. In consequence, much the greater part of the Tweed is cut off from more southerly river-systems by a large tract of hilly country relatively unattractive to human settlement and lacking good communications. Only for fifteen miles or so does the Border follow the centre line of a valley with a natural unity, whereas if it took the line of Irthing and Tyne it would be making an artificial division of this kind for over sixty miles.

But if the geographical reasons seem compelling enough, the historical reasons are far from self-evident. It is agreed that before and after the Roman occupation of Britain, and indeed for several centuries after the arrival of the English at Bamburgh, the region between Tyne and Forth formed a cultural and, more often than not, a political unity: first, as the tribal territory of the Votadini; afterwards as the province of Bernicia. Of this, the history of the Northumbrian kingdom in its heyday offers the clearest illustration. In Bede's time the Firth of Forth formed the chief element in the border between Angles and Picts. Mr. Peter Hunter Blair has drawn attention to the seventh- and eighth-century activities of a dynasty of Anglian ealdormen, probably based on Edinburgh, whose frontier with the Celtic world lay in that natural border zone where the Rivers Carron and Avon enter the Forth, a zone which retained its Celtic name of Calatria far into the twelfth century.[25] Battle after battle was fought here long before a curious repetition of history made it the scene of Stirling Bridge, Falkirk and Bannockburn. Perhaps the greatest of these engagements took place in 711, when the Picts were defeated 'between Avon and Carron' by the English under Ealdorman Berhtfrith. Eastward and southward from this debateable land lay an unbroken stretch of Anglian territory. Nothing shows this more clearly than the position of Anglian monasteries such as Tynningehame and Coldingham, and above all the earliest endowments of Lindisfarne, which included Abercorn west of Edinburgh and Melrose on the middle Tweed. The present Border can have meant nothing, even in a local sense, when King Oswy granted Lindisfarne twelve estates along the upper

[25] P. Hunter Blair, 'The Bernicians and their northern frontier', in *Studies in Early British History*, ed. N. Chadwick (1954), p. 170–1; *RRS*, i, 8 and n.

Bowmont Water, including Mindrum and Shotton, now in England, and Sourhope, Halterburn, Clifton, Shereburgh, Staerough and Yetholm, now in Scotland.[26]

With the decline of Northumbria, there came a drastic though unrecorded change. The ninth century saw the rise to power of a warlike and aggressive Scoto-Pictish kingdom north of the Forth. Whatever its internal weaknesses, this kingdom achieved the remarkable feat of preserving its integrity in the face of Scandinavian onslaughts, so that no significant numbers of Norwegians or Danes ever gained a permanent footing between the Moray Firth and the Firth of Forth. The Scoto-Pictish kings thus played a part in North Britain which corresponded to the part played in South Britain by the kings of Wessex. Once the main impetus of Scandinavian invasion and settlement had slackened, it was inevitable that Saxons advancing northward should meet Scots advancing southward. It was simply a question of when, where, and upon what terms.

In the past, historians have given one or other of two different answers to this question, according to nationality.[27] English historians have in general accepted the statement of an anonymous Northumbrian annalist of the early twelfth century that Lothian, that is the land between the River Avon and the River Tweed, was formally ceded to Kenneth, king of Scots, by Edgar, king of the English, probably in 973, and that the cession—like Edmund's earlier cession of Cumbria—was conditional, that is, that King Kenneth, on receiving Lothian, commended himself to King Edgar as his vassal. In these English accounts, the battle of Carham of 1018 is not given any special significance. Scottish historians, on the other hand, have ignored or played down the story of Edgar's cession of Lothian, and have said bluntly that Lothian was won for Scotland at the battle of Carham. Between these irreconcilable accounts comes (again from Northumbria) an apparently reliable statement that Lothian was surrendered to the Scots by the Northumbrian earl, Eadulf Cudel, about 1016. Mrs. Anderson, almost the only recent historian to give due

[26] Above, p. 32–4.
[27] For the following paragraph my main guide has been M. O. Anderson, 'Lothian and the early Scottish kings', *SHR*, xxxix, 98–112. In particular, I find myself convinced by Mrs. Anderson's arguments for dating the battle of Carham in 1018, as against the date 1016 preferred by Sir Frank Stenton.

attention to this statement, accepts as probably true the story of Edgar's cession in 973, and reconciles it with the story of a later cession by explaining that the Scots probably lost all or part of Lothian in 1006, when King Malcolm II's great invasion of Northumberland was repulsed with heavy loss.[28]

The bearing of all this upon the Tweed border-line would be more evident if the origin and extent of Lothian were less of a mystery. The name itself is distressingly obscure. It is not English, and is therefore presumably pre-English, Brittonic; it nevertheless does not occur in sources which, in their present form at least, are earlier than the late eleventh century. It must surely be supposed that throughout the Anglian occupation of Bernicia some trace or memory was preserved of a northern sub-division of former Votadinian territory. It does not follow, and, indeed, seems most unlikely, that the southern boundary of this sub-division was the River Tweed. A more probable boundary would be the stretch of empty moorland known to the English as *Lombormor*, Lammermuir. It is certain that this was recognised as a boundary in the tenth century, and under King Alexander I in the early twelfth century it separated that part of his kingdom in which the royal demesnes were actually in the king's hands from that southern part where they were in the hands of his younger brother, the future David I.[29]

Evidence which is too considerable to be brushed aside shows that long before the supposed 'cession' of Lothian to King Kenneth in 973 the Scots were exerting pressure upon, and indeed almost certainly appropriating for settlement, the territory north of Lammermuir, and it points unmistakably to a Scottish penetration of some sort as far as the River Tweed. One of the few facts known about the reign of Kenneth Mac Alpin (843–58), who united the Scottish and Pictish kingdoms, is that he frequently carried war into Lothian.[30] There is further evidence of Scoto-Pictish military pressure upon the northernmost region of Anglian Northumbria in the reigns of Giric son of Dungal (878–89) and of Constantine son of Aed (900–43).[31] Between 954 and 962 the fortress of Edinburgh was laid waste, and thereafter this key

[28] Ibid., 110–11.   [29] *RRS*, i, 36–7.
[30] Anderson, *Early Sources*, i, 288.   [31] Ibid., 364–6, 406–8, 446.

position remained in Scottish hands.[32] When the British king Rhydderch attacked Culen, king of Scots, in 971, it was in Lothian that he discovered and slew him.[33] The *History of Saint Cuthbert*, which Sir Edmund Craster would date to *c*. 945, describes how in the time of Guthfrith, the Danish Christian king of York (883–94), the Scots 'crossed the Tweed' to devastate St. Cuthbert's Land,[34] a pointless statement if the Tweed still flowed through the middle of territory safely in English hands. The same work implies elsewhere that the river had already come to form a march between St. Cuthbert's Land proper (of whose Englishness there was never any doubt) and regions further north where the saint possessed or claimed numerous estates. For it declared that *Lindisfarnensis terra* extended 'from Tweed to Warenmouth',[35] and if Edromshire and Melrose and other Cuthbertine lands now in Scotland did not require to be marked out in some way from the rest, why say that the land of Holy Island began at the Tweed? The proof of this surely lies in subsequent events. The see of St. Cuthbert, whether at Chester-le-Street or at Durham, never lost its ancient endowments just south of the Tweed, whereas for its estates north of the Tweed it had to fight every inch of the way, often without success. A nice illustration of the difficulties involved may be seen in a property situated in the very middle of the river itself: the valuable fishing near Berwick known as Haliwarestell, i.e., 'the Saint's fishing'. Insofar as this was English, it was confirmed to the monks of Durham by Bishop Ranulf Flambard *c*. 1100, but on the Scottish side it was not till the 1130s that King David forbade his sheriff to meddle with Durham's possession of this profitable stretch of water.[36] Already then, by the 940s the clergy of St. Cuthbert seem to have lost their lands north of the

---

[32] Anderson, *Early Sources*, i, 468. Despite Dr. Anderson's comments there and Mrs. Anderson's in *SHR*, xxxix, 100–3, I think there can be little doubt that the subject of the Scottish Chronicle entry referred to here was Edinburgh, not Carriden or Blackness. Cf. K. Jackson, in *The Anglo-Saxons*, ed. P. Clemoes (1959), pp. 38–41.

[33] Ibid., 476 (where Ybandonia is doubtless for Laudonia, in line with the other versions). Cf. K. Jackson, 'The Britons in southern Scotland', *Antiquity*, xxix, 87.

[34] *Historia de Sancto Cuthberto* in *Symeon of Durham*, i, 213–14; cf. H. H. E. Craster, *EHR*, lxix, 178.

[35] *Symeon of Durham*, i, 199.

[36] Raine, *North Durham*, no. 727; Lawrie, *Charters*, no. 154.

Tweed. The reason for this, surely, was that the region as a whole had been acquired by rulers who, unlike the House of Wessex, had no historic cause to regard themselves as patrons and bene-factors of the saints of Lindisfarne.

What, then, is the significance of Edgar's cession of 973 and of the battle of Carham? King Edgar's action—in the best version which has come down to us—is linked with his promotion of Eadulf 'Evil Child' as earl over the Northumbrians 'from the Tees to Myreforth'. Some scholars have taken Myreforth (Myreford) to mean the Firth of Forth, and have silently swallowed the absurdity of Edgar with one hand granting this wide territory to Earl Eadulf and with the other taking half of it away again to grant to King Kenneth. Myreforth certainly cannot refer to the Forth, and remains unidentified. But since, in the light of what has just been said, it seems most unlikely that the Scots would have been content in 973 with anything less than the larger Lothian reaching to the Tweed, it would seem more probable that Myreforth (if not corrupt) was a well-known ford across the Tweed, and that Earl Eadulf's territory, the rump of ancient Bernicia, corresponded closely to the later earldom of Northumberland. What English annalists recorded as the 'cession' of Lothian was, on this view, the recognition by a power-ful but extremely remote south-country king of a long-standing *fait accompli*. As for the battle of Carham, it does not seem to have had any bearing on the definition of the Border. It merely put the English of Northumbria on the defensive for a generation or so, south of a Border which fundamentally was already defined.

If the Scots, holding Lothian *de jure* from 973, had possessed it *de facto* from a considerably earlier time, would this not make it easier to understand certain Scottish features of Lothian which we must otherwise suppose all took shape in the 120 years between Edgar's cession and the death of Malcolm Canmore? There are, e.g. a number of Gaelic place-names in Lothian, reaching to the lower Tweed and Teviot. There is a fair scattering of Gaelic personal names among early-twelfth-century Lothian landowners. There is the fact that the twelfth-century earls of Fife held a good deal of land in Lothian, especially in East Lothian, and possessed the 'earl's ferry' which plied between Elie and North Berwick. There is the firm establishment across territory hallowed by associations with Cuthbert, Boisil, Baldred and the rest, of the two great Scoto-Pictish churches of St. Andrews and Dunkeld. In marked contrast with the see of Glasgow in respect of its outlying district of Teviotdale, the see of St. Andrews was never challenged even by the strongest bishop of Durham in respect of its outlying district of Lothian and the Merse. The bishop of Dunkeld's possessions, and consequently his diocese, included Cramond and Aberlady on the southern shore of the Firth of Forth, and Bunkle and Preston within a few miles of Berwick. One of the curiosities of modern Midlothian is the way in which that county crosses the watershed of the Moorfoot Hills and penetrates far into Tweeddale down the valley of the Gala Water. The explanation, surely, is that as a result of the Scottish acquisition of Lothian, the bishop of the Scots, i.e. the bishop of St. Andrews, obtained the ancient church of St. Mary of Wedale, which passed into the diocese of St. Andrews and hence into the sheriffdom of Edinburgh.[37] The holiness of this church, with its sanctuary and its fragments of an image of the Virgin, brought, as was believed, all the way from Jerusalem by no less a person than King Arthur, was famous throughout the middle ages,[38] and is recalled in the name of Stow by which the parish is still known and has been known, presumably, since the days of Anglian supremacy.[39] Since there was no sudden conquest of Lothian, nor any general displacement of its English-speaking aristocracy and peasantry, the Scotticisation of the province must have proceeded gradually over a fairly lengthy period. Developments of the kind I have mentioned would be more readily intelligible if we could accept that the Scots held the upper hand in Lothian from the earlier part of the tenth century.

Evidence for the firmness and the antiquity of the Tweed–

[37] For the bishop of St. Andrews' possession of Wedale see *Cal. Papal Letters*, i, 30, 61. It appears that William Malvoisin, bishop of St. Andrews 1202–38, asserted the lordship of his see over Wedale by suppressing or superseding the rights of an hereditary priest. A person bearing the significant Celtic name Gillis ('Jesus's servant') of Wedale seems to have been hereditary priest there in the 1170s (*Melrose Liber*, no. 51, 52, and cf. the marginal comment in the second facsimile appended to the preface, 'et sciendum quod Wedale tunc temporis non fuit episcopi set Gilisii de Wedal cui successit Willelmus episcopus malevicinus quocumque modo').

[38] F. Lot, *Nennius et l'Historia Brittonum* (Paris, 1934), 195, n. 8.

[39] As an element in place-names, Old English *stow* often means a holy or consecrated place, as in Stow on the Wold, St. Mary Stow, etc. Cf. A. H. Smith, *English Place-Name Elements*, pt. ii, 158–61.

Cheviot border becomes plentiful in the twelfth century. The Continuation of Symeon of Durham's *History of the Kings* says that the Tweed divides Lothian (*Loida*) from Northumbria,[40] and the Continuation of the same author's *History of the Church of Durham*, speaking of the building of Norham Castle by Ranulf Flambard in 1121, states that Norham was on the border between the English and Scottish kingdoms.[41] In a contemporary Tironensian work Kelso is said to be on the Tweed, in the province of Lothian 'which on one side touches Albany of the Scots and on the other is joined to the borders of Northumbria.[42] The earliest known charters of the Scottish royal house confirm the Border line, by implication, at many points, for they deal with almost every piece of riparian land on the left bank of the Tweed. Significantly, the first royal charter to deal with land south of the Tweed is David I's grant of Redden to Kelso Abbey, 'as I had it in my own hand'.[43] It is of course at the Redden Burn that the Border takes the critical step of leaving the Tweed and turns south towards the Cheviot Hills. The Redden Burn, famous as a Border trysting-place in the later middle ages, was the scene of a meeting between English and Scottish representatives in 1245. The business of the meeting was to trace the exact line of the Border across Wark Common. The proceedings were reported to Henry III by the sheriff of Northumberland, Hugh de Bolebec of Bywell, in a letter memorable both for its detail and its air of conscious rectitude.

I and the knights of Northumberland met the Justiciar of Lothian, David Lindsay, the earl of Dunbar, and many other Scottish knights at Reddenburn. Six English and six Scottish knights were elected as a jury to make a true perambulation of the march between the two kingdoms, and in particular between the lands of Carham (in England) and Hadden (in Scotland).

The six English knights, with one accord, immediately set off along the rightful and ancient marches between the two kingdoms, but the Scottish knights entirely disagreed and contradicted them. I and the Justiciar of Lothian thereupon

[40] *Symeon of Durham*, ii, 278. [41] *Symeon of Durham*, i, 140.
[42] Migne, *Patrologia Latina*, clxxii, col. 1426.
[43] Lawrie, *Charters*, no. 176.

decided to elect a second jury to reinforce the first. Once again, the English knights agreed on the boundary and the Scots dissented.

Since the Scots had thus obstructed the business, I took it upon myself to empanel a third jury, this time of 24 English knights, who declared the true and ancient marches on oath. But when they started to make a perambulation of this line, the Justiciar and his fellow-Scots forcibly prevented them, and stopped them carrying out the perambulation by threats.[44]

1245 is not the first occasion on which Reddenburn appears as an Anglo-Scottish trysting-place. The chronicler Roger Howden refers to two meetings at Redden between Hugh du Puiset bishop of Durham and King William the Lion of Scotland, the first in 1174 to arrange a truce in time of war,[45] the second in 1181 to hold a conference on the disputed election to the bishopric of St. Andrews.[46] Evidently Redden was one of the accepted places for passing from one country to the other, comparable with Berwick and Norham. The choice of Norham as the scene of many of the crucial sessions of Edward I's court when it deliberated on the Great Cause (the competition for the Scottish Crown) in 1291 and 1292 was surely prompted as much by the traditional role of Norham as an international meeting-place as by the shelter which the bishop's great castle afforded. As early as 1095, King Edgar's charter to Durham, which concerned men on both sides of the Border, had been issued in the churchyard at Norham.[47] In 1164 the archbishop of York, Roger de Pont L'Evêque, eager to exercise his legatine jurisdiction over the Scottish church, attempted to cross into Scotland at Norham, only to be met by officers of King Malcolm IV, who sent him back to England in confusion.[48] There was no bridge at Norham, but there was a river crossing of great antiquity, as is shown by the fact that the earliest recorded name of the place was Ubbanford, 'the ford of Ubba', a name already long obsolete at the end of the tenth century.[49]

[44] Cal. Docs. Scot., i, no. 832; full text best edited in Stones, Documents, no. 8.
[45] Chron. Howden, ii, 56–7.
[46] Gesta Regis Henrici Secundi Benedicti Abbatis (ed. W. Stubbs, Rolls Series), i, p. 281 (where Ravendala is a mistaken form for Revendena).
[47] Lawrie, Charters, no. 15.   [48] Chron. Melrose, 37.
[49] Symeon of Durham, ii, 101.

It is not often that royal or private charters refer to the Border in the twelfth or thirteenth centuries, but when they do it is to the line substantially as we know it today or as it is defined in the important series of Tudor and Stewart surveys. When, in the 1190s, the laird of Hownam granted the sheep-grazing of Raeshaw to Melrose Abbey, he described its southern boundary as running 'from the dike between Raeshaw and Cuthberthope along the entire march between me and Richard de Umfraville as far west as Dere Street'.[50] Though the charter does not say so the march between Richard de Umfraville of Redesdale and William of Hownam was in fact the Border, running now seemingly as it did then. For some reason, the Umfravilles themselves were even more reticent. Before 1195 William de Umfraville granted to the Cistercians of Newminster grazing rights over a large part of the wild territory of Kidland. William described its northern boundary as running from Windy Edge—presumably what is now Windy Rig or Windy Gyle—to the springs of Usway Burn 'as much as belongs to me there'.[51] The line indicated is that of the present Border, but William's caution presumably means that, as we might expect on these lonely wolf-ridden uplands, its exact course was not marked on the ground. Much more explicit references to the Border come from some charters of the early thirteenth century, by which Walter Corbet and Robert of Shotton granted land in Shotton to Kelso Abbey.[52] The land included the sheep-grazing of 'Colpenhope', whose boundaries were carefully described, one of them being 'the burn which divides the kingdoms of England and Scotland'. Colpenhope has now become Coldsmouth, and a study of the charters with the help of a large-scale map shows that the burn referred to was the Halterburn, which did indeed carry the line of the Border down to comparatively modern times. It was, naturally, important to be sure of the Border line whenever legal proceedings were involved. Early in the thirteenth century Earl Patrick of Dunbar, as lord of Birgham, gave the canons of Kirkham Priory, owners of Carham on Tweed, permission to construct a fishing pool in the

[50] *Melrose Liber*, no. 131.
[51] *Chartularium abbathiae de Novo Monasterio* (ed. J. T. Fowler, Surtees Society), 75.
[52] *Kelso Liber*, nos. 361, 363.

river between Birgham and Carham, either at 'Langeford' or between 'Langeford' and 'Netherford'.[53] At a later date, the prior of Kirkham got the sheriff of Northumberland to hold an assize of Novel Disseisin against the earl 'regarding a certain fish-pool between Carham and Bingham within the marches of England', inasmuch as the earl and his men had thrown down this fish-pool and had built another one higher up, running across the mid-stream line of the water of Tweed.[54] The outcome of the dispute is not known, but Earl Patrick could have pleaded that if he had granted the canons licence to make a fish-pool this could not possibly have been in England, and the matter would not have been within the jurisdiction of the sheriff of Northumberland. From our point of view, the interest of the case lies in the insistence upon the *filum aque de Tweda*, the mid-stream line of the river, as forming the precise Border between the two kingdoms.

There is one last piece of evidence which seems to confirm the belief that in the middle decades of the thirteenth century the Border implicitly recognised by the Treaty of York—that is to say our present Border, with the modifications already touched on— was by then an old-established institution. This is the *Laws of the Marches* of 14 April, 1249.[55] It is a well-known document, but it is marked by certain peculiarities whose significance has perhaps been ignored. The *Laws* deal with the procedure to be followed in the case of disputes between the subjects of different kingdoms, and the first odd feature is the framework within which the procedure on the East March is described. Englishmen on the East March are divided into three classes, those dwelling 'between Dedey and the sea', those dwelling 'above Dedey', and those dwelling in Coquetdale and Redesdale. For each class there was a proper place for the formal rebuttal of charges by an accused person. Those 'between Dedey and the sea' answered at Hamis-ford; those 'above Dedey' answered at the Redden Burn; those from Coquetdale and Redesdale answered at Gamelspath. Gamelspath presents no difficulty. It was—and is—that stretch

---

[53] These names seem to be represented today in the names of fishing beats between Carham and Birgham, 'Langstream' and 'Netherstream'. I owe this information to a map of fishings in the Tweed displayed at The Collingwood Arms Hotel, Cornhill on Tweed.

[54] Bodleian Library, MS. Fairfax 7, fo. 76^v.

[55] *Acts Parl. Scot.*, i, 414.

of the Roman road of Dere Street where it crosses the main Cheviot ridge, providing a route into Scotland from both Coquetdale and Redesdale. Reddenburn we have noted already as a trysting-place. Both names wear an old, traditional look, but still more significant in this respect seems to be the mention of Dedey and Hamisford. The reason for distinguishing between those living below Dedey and those above it was that the Dedey Burn (now the Duddo Burn), which flows into the Tweed at Cornhill, was the ancient, probably the immemorial boundary of Norhamshire.[56] From Dedey to the sea was Saint Cuthbert's Land, where men were subject to the bishop of Durham. Above Dedey they were subject to the earl and sheriff of Northumberland. Had the *Laws of the Marches* been devised, or even reformed, in the 1240s, as a consequence of the Treaty of York of 1237, one might have expected them to name Berwick Bridge or Norham as the proper place for formal accusations and declarations of innocence. Instead, the *Laws* required appearance at Hamisford, a name which, we may suspect, was already well on the way to obsolescence in the later middle ages. But it so happens that the continuator of Symeon of Durham's *History of the Kings*, writing in the early twelfth century, states in passing that the point on the River Tweed where Ranulf Flambard built his castle of Norham —'the north ham'—was called 'Et-hamesforda'.[57] The preservation of this name in the Old English locative (*aet Hamesforde*) suggests strongly that even when this work was written the name was of considerable antiquity. Hamisford, then, the ford of the 'north ham' or Norham, was no other than that ancient passage of the River Tweed which in the earliest days of the English had been known as Ubbanford. Rather than credit the commissioners of 1249 with an extraordinary antiquarianism, it would be more reasonable to believe that here as elsewhere they were merely recording traditional border arrangements which dated from long before their own time.

This supposition is reinforced by the second peculiarity of the

[56] J. Raine, *History of North Durham*, p. 15; *Survey of Border Lands*, 1604, ed. R. P. Sanderson (Alnwick, privately printed, 1891), p. 43.

[57] *Symeon of Durham*, ii, 260. Dr. George Neilson made the identification of Hamisford in the Laws of the Marches with Ethamesforda in Symeon, but does not seem to have seen the implications of this for the dating of the Laws. Cf. *Stair Soc. Misc.*, i (1971), 17.

document. Under the *Laws of the Marches*, every person making an accusation against a subject of the other kingdom was required to swear the necessary supporting oaths on his own behalf. Only four persons were exempt from this rule: the kings of England and Scotland and the bishops of Durham and St. Andrews. A standard-bearer or a constable might swear for a king, and the bishop of Durham's oath might be offered by the prior of Holy Island. But the proper person to make oath for the bishop of St. Andrews was the priest of St. Mary of Wedale. It is very hard to believe that in 1249 the bishop of St. Andrews, or for that matter the king of Scotland and his officers, would have thought of nominating for this duty the incumbent of a distant rural parish, however respectable. But if the *Laws* of 1249 represent arrangements originally made far back in the tenth or eleventh centuries, before the development of either a parochial or a diocesan system and at a time when the Stow of Wedale was the object of undoubted, though unexplained veneration, the part played by the priest of Wedale in the *Laws of the Marches*—like the similarly obscure part he played in the *Law of Clan Macduff*[58]—would become, if not less puzzling, at least a little less surprising.

Like many British institutions, the Border may be seen as a compromise, a compromise which in 1237 already had a history of some three centuries. It was too far south for West Saxon kings who would have liked to rule the whole territory governed by their Northumbrian predecessors. It was too far north for Scottish kings who would have liked to fix their eastern limits at Tyne or Tees, more in line with their western limit on Stainmore or Duddon. But Lothian was too remote for West Saxon kings to hold, and the Scottish grip upon this rich and fertile province became too strong to be easily shaken. At the same time, a combination of able bishops and warlike earls in Northumbria made it impossible for the Scots to secure a foothold south of the Tweed. Moreover, Scottish kings who tried to shift the political centre of gravity of their kingdom so far to the south paid a heavy price in failure to control the far north and the Highlands. But even though it was a compromise, the Border played a part in the development of the medieval kingdoms of England and Scotland which it would be a mistake to underestimate. In a

[58] *Chron. Wyntoun* (Laing), ii, 141.

fashion which seems awkward and unhistorical, the Border cut both Bernicia and Cumbria in half; yet the effect was to strengthen the Englishness of Northumberland and Cumberland, whose communities, however independent they might feel and sometimes actually be with regard to a government based upon the south, showed no tendency to become Scottish. For the nascent Scottish kingdom of the eleventh and twelfth centuries, the importance of the Border can hardly be exaggerated. The Solway–Tweed line brought under Scottish rule two tracts of non-Scottish territory, British on the west, English on the east. Quite apart from the immense material resources which these provinces added to the monarchy, their acquisition compelled Scottish kings and their subjects to find some fresh formula in which to express their relationship. It was found in the feudal concept of the *regnum Scottorum* or *regnum Scotie*, the kingdom of the Scots or of Scotland. Unlike *Scotia*, Scotland properly so called, which stopped short at the Forth, the *kingdom* of Scotland reached south to Tweed and Solway, and incorporated territory which until well into the twelfth century was still regarded, racially or geographically, as *Anglia*, England. There can be no question that the establishment of the Border was a principal factor in defining and consolidating the medieval Scottish kingdom.

PART II   CHURCH

5 The royal house and the religious orders

The impetus given by Queen Margaret to the process by which the older Scottish church was transformed into the medieval *Ecclesia Scotticana*, and the prodigality of her youngest son, King David I, to a wide variety of religious orders, were prominent aspects of what was really a family enterprise. The establishment of English and continental monks and canons north of the Border in the late eleventh and early twelfth centuries was in strikingly full measure the exclusive work of the royal house, a work, moreover, which the ruling members of this house seem to have undertaken with a conscious sense of dedication and unity of purpose. From the time of Queen Margaret to the death of King David, with the probable exception of the years from 1094 to 1097 when Donald Bán was leading an anti-foreign reaction, there was complete continuity in the encouragement shown to the foreign religious orders. This chapter will examine the reception by Scottish rulers of the main currents of western monasticism, and discuss in detail some of the significant ways in which they were able to draw upon their connexions outside Scotland in order to reproduce within their own kingdom a pattern, albeit on a small scale, of the religious life which was a feature of contemporary England and France.

When, *c.* 1070, the English Margaret became Malcolm Canmore's queen, there was, as far as we know, nothing in Scotland resembling at all closely the type of monastic or regular life generally familiar in the west. This fact must have struck Margaret forcibly and unfavourably. She was far from being a bigot, and could appreciate religious merit even among the native Scots.[1] But her origins and upbringing meant inevitably that for her the ideal of the Christian life was approached most closely not

[1] *Vita S. Margaretae*, by Thurgot, ed. G. H. Hinde (Surtees Soc., li), p. 247; Lawrie, *Charters*, no. 8.

only by an adherence to the accepted laws of the church as a whole but more especially by the revived and reinvigorated religious life, following the rule of St. Benedict, which was a feature of the English church in the years after the Conquest.

It is natural therefore to find that the first phase in the process of introducing non-Celtic monasticism into Scotland began as soon as Queen Margaret could make her influence felt there, and was connected with two of the leading English centres of the new monastic movement, Durham and Canterbury. The connexion between Durham and the Scottish ruling house certainly dates from Margaret's time, though the establishment of a daughter-house of Durham within the Scottish kingdom, which might have been expected then, was not effected until considerably later. The first attempt, indeed, at a colonisation from Durham[2] was a complete failure. In the seventies of the eleventh century the religious life had been revived with striking success at a number of places in Northumbria by a group of devoted men under the leadership of Aldwin, a monk of Winchcombe, and Thurgot, an Englishman from Lincolnshire, who became successively priors of the newly-refounded monastery of Durham.[3] At this period, Teviotdale, by which we must understand a district wider than the valley of the Teviot merely, and embracing the lower valleys of Tweed, Yarrow, Ettrick and Jed, lay within the ecclesiastical jurisdiction of the bishop of Durham, although politically it was part of the Scottish kingdom. Moreover, the church of St. Cuthbert had a special claim to the site of the saint's abbey at Old Melrose, at that time an uninhabited wilderness. Aldwin and Thurgot (the latter not yet actually a monk) went to Melrose, c. 1075, and began to follow the religious life there in solitude. Thurgot could not then have had Queen Margaret for a patroness, for when he and Aldwin refused to make a declaration of allegiance demanded by King Malcolm they were forced to leave Scottish soil.[4] Later, however, Thurgot became closely associated with Queen Margaret as her spiritual confidant.

[2] This proleptic use of 'Durham' seems justified because Aldwin and Thurgot were associated with Bishop Walcher, and their revival of northern monasticism shortly came to fruition at Durham.

[3] D. Knowles, *Monastic Order in England*, 164–71. Aldwin and Thurgot were priors of Durham 1083–7, 1087–1107.

[4] *Symeon of Durham*, i, 111–12.

In his biography of the queen, Thurgot says that she founded a church at the place where she was married to King Malcolm, that is, at Dunfermline. A letter of David I written probably in 1128,[5] shows that the church of Dunfermline was a daughter-house of Christ Church, Canterbury, and thus must have been the product of the cooperation between Margaret and Lanfranc of which there is clear evidence in a letter of the archbishop, of uncertain date, which has been printed by several authorities.[6] Nearly all the members of the Scottish royal family, with the significant exception of Donald Bán, are named as previous benefactors to Dunfermline in the charter of privileges given by King David, c. 1128,[7] when a new and bigger church was begun, and the priory raised to abbatial status.

The date of the founding of Holy Trinity or Christ Church, Dunfermline, as a daughter-house of Holy Trinity or Christ Church, Canterbury, and the dates of Thurgot's setback at Melrose and his subsequent personal association with Margaret are all uncertain. Probably the Canterbury connexion began first. Certainly it was Canterbury that provided the first religious house of the new type in the Scottish kingdom, and this moreover was in Scotland proper, the country north of the Forth, and not in Scottish Northumbria. It is possible that the Canterbury monks serving Queen Margaret's new church were driven out by Donald Bán;[8] this, if true, might explain why Edgar—the first of Margaret's sons to become king of Scotland—asked Archbishop Anselm to send him monks from Canterbury,[9] though, of course, the Dunfermline convent might have needed replenishing from other and more natural causes.

It was Edgar who effectively resumed the connexion with Durham, naturally enough, since its prior was his mother's former

[5] This letter, from a fifteenth-century copy at Canterbury (Dean and Chapter MSS., *Reg. B*, fo. 305), was printed, with a discussion of its significance, in the *SHR*, xxxi, 18–28.

[6] E.g. Lawrie, *Charters*, no. 9; A. Haddan and W. Stubbs, *Councils and Ecclesiastical Documents*, ii, pp. 155–6.

[7] *Dunfermline Registrum*, no. 1. Also omitted are the names of the two eldest sons of Malcolm and Margaret, Edward (killed 1093) and Edmund (who may have supported Donald Bán; cf. William of Malmesbury, *Gesta Regum* (Rolls Series), ii, 477).

[8] *Symeon of Durham*, ii, 224.

[9] Lawrie, *Charters*, no. 25.

associate, became in this period her biographer, and was doubtless well known to him.[10] About 1098, he gave to St. Cuthbert and the monks of his church the shire of Coldingham, north of Berwick.[11] This grant was followed by others, so that the Durham monks soon possessed in Lothian a large and profitable estate.[12]

Since the time of Andrew of Wyntoun, Edgar has often been called the founder of Coldingham Priory. No less an antiquary than Canon Raine the elder, who perhaps knew more about Coldingham and its priory than any man before or since, stated categorically that 'the Priory of Coldingham was founded by Edgar, King of Scotland, in the year 1097 or 1098, and attached to the Convent of Durham as one of its cells'.[13] Without doubt, this Scottish daughter-house of Durham resulted from the necessity of sending monks from the cathedral priory to take charge of its rather distant Scottish estates. But the emergence of Coldingham as an organised religious house under a prior can hardly date much before 1140. Edward, the 'monk of Coldingham', who in a terse writ of before 1136 was ordered by King David to supply enough logs to make a woodpile for the king at Berwick, and on whose behalf the king commanded the sheriff of Berwick to give him possession of the tithes of a fishing in the Tweed,[14] seems to have been more probably the Durham monk in charge of the estate of Coldingham than a subordinate member of a religious community there. In 1139, however, and again c. 1140–1, King David and his son Earl Henry speak of the monks serving the church of Coldingham,[15] and, c. 1147, appears the name of H., prior of Coldingham, the first in record.[16] Many Scottish endowments were made to Durham Priory during these years, among them the church of St. Mary in Berwick, which

[10] Thurgot was instructed by Queen Margaret to take charge of her children (*Vita*, ed. Hinde, p. 251).

[11] Lawrie, *Charters*, nos. 18 and 19.

[12] Duncan II had earlier given land in Lothian to Durham; Lawrie, *Charters*, no. 12; *SHR*, xxxvii, 119; cf. also *Liber Vitae*, ed. in facsimile by A. Hamilton Thompson (Surtees Soc., cxxxvi), fo. 12v. But whether or not Duncan II intended the monks of St. Cuthbert to establish a cell in Scotland, his grant proved abortive.

[13] *History of North Durham*, p. 374.

[14] Lawrie, *Charters*, nos. 174 and 154. The fishing was named Halwarestelle, which seems to show that it had belonged to St. Cuthbert's Land from earlier times.

[15] Lawrie, *Charters*, nos. 121 and 133.   [16] Lawrie, *Charters*, no. 182.

King David granted in exchange for the church of Melrose, which had belonged to Durham, but which after April 1136 went to the white monks of Rievaulx.[17] In short, Coldingham Priory cannot be assigned to a single founder, though it grew from Edgar's gift.[18]

No doubt, Thurgot, while he was holding the unusual dual office of prior and archdeacon of Durham, was also well known to King Edgar's younger brother Alexander. Under Edgar, Alexander held wide lands in the south of Scotland, and his expectation of the Scottish throne must have been quite apparent, since Edgar never married and had no children. With Thurgot and a number of prominent churchmen, Alexander was present at Durham in 1104, when he had the honour of being the only lay-man to take part in the official examination of St. Cuthbert's body before its translation.[19] It is not surprising that when Alexander succeeded his brother as king of Scots in 1107, he turned to Thurgot for help in the reform of the Scottish church. After negotiations with Henry I and Archbishop Thomas of York, Thurgot was appointed bishop of the Scots (or bishop of St. Andrews), being consecrated in 1109.[20]

The presence of a Benedictine monk and a leader of monastic revival at the head of the Scottish church might have been expected to produce an extension of Benedictine monasticism in the northern kingdom, but this did not come about. It must be remembered that Bishop Thurgot, in any case an old man, found his new position extremely difficult. It is true that Durham's possessions were confirmed, and that the king, and his queen Sibylla (a bastard daughter of Henry I), made benefactions to the Canterbury monks of Dunfermline Priory, as had King Edgar before them.[21] But it is interesting to see that King Alexander's share in the introduction into Scotland of the orders of regular clergy already familiar in England embraced exclusively the canons following a regular, quasi-monastic life, who at this period were already beginning to be distinguished as 'Augustinians'.

[17] Lawrie, *Charters*, no. 99 (probably *c.* 1136).
[18] Lawrie seems to have been the first to make the point that Edgar was not the founder of Coldingham Priory; ibid., p. 251.
[19] *Symeon of Durham*, i, 258.
[20] *Symeon of Durham*, ii, 204; J. Dowden, *Bishops of Scotland*, 1–2.
[21] *Dunfermline Reg.*, no. 1.

The Austin canons took an early and important lead in bringing to the north of England the new currents of religious life which had originated chiefly on the continent. Their success in the north was due very largely to the patronage extended to them by the two successive archbishops of York, Thomas II, who first instituted regular canons in the ancient church of Hexham (1112), and Thurstan, who was the especial patron of the Austin priory of St. Oswald at Nostell in Yorkshire.[22]

Alexander was evidently well aware of these new developments. In the north of England, the great feudatories, and even some of middle rank—Walter de Gand, Walter Espec, Robert de Lacy, Robert Brus of Cleveland, and others—could give a lead in this founding of houses for Austin canons; in Scotland, such a lead must come from the king. The native clergy do not seem to have been at all moved by the advance of the Gregorian reform, and both clergy and magnates tended to be actively hostile to the advent of foreigners in any guise. King Alexander's predilection for the regular canons resulted in the actual establishment of one Augustinian community (Scone), and the projected establishment of three others (Inchcolm,[23] Loch Tay, and St. Andrews). These foundations were all in Scotland north of Forth, and two of them were extremely important. Why King Alexander chose St. Oswald's, Nostell, as his source for obtaining these missionary priests is not known, but the project was doubtless carried out with the help and approval of Archbishop Thurstan, who from the time of his consecration if not earlier was a close friend of the canons of Nostell.[24] Moreover, the first prior of Nostell, Athelulf or Athelwold, was, like Thurstan, a royal chaplain,[25] and a cleric of outstanding ability. Whatever the reason, it was to canons from

---

[22] J. C. Dickinson, *The Origin of the Austin Canons and their introduction into England* (1950), 116, 120. The community which by 1120 had become the Austin priory of St. Oswald had earlier received the support of Archbishop Thomas II (d. 1114); *EYC*, iii, 160.

[23] The authorities for Alexander I being the founder of Inchcolm are John Fordun and Walter Bower (*Chron. Fordun*, i, 227; *Chron. Bower*, i, 286–7). It is clear, however, partly from Fordun, *loc. cit.*, but chiefly from a document printed by Dr. Easson, *Inchcolm Charters*, no. I, that the original endowment was held in trust until canons could be established on Inchcolm, and that this probably did not take place until after the end of David I's reign.

[24] J. Wilson, in *SHR*, vii, 143.

[25] *Annales Monastici* (Rolls Series), ii, 223.

Nostell, under their leader Robert, that the king made over the ancient church of Scone in Gowrie, at the heart of the old Scoto-Pictish kingdom, a site associated from immemorial time with political and religious solemnity.[26] We can hardly over-emphasise the significance of King Alexander's action in bringing to serve its church members of an order of priests who represented the very vanguard of the Gregorian reform and of the new ideas at work in the western church.

It is unfortunate that the date of this mission—for as such it must have been regarded—from Nostell to Scone cannot be fixed with certainty. The early addition to the original text of the Melrose Chronicle which tells us that 'the church of Scone was handed over to canons' was entered at the year 1115.[27] The *Scotichronicon* says that the priory church of Scone was dedicated by Thurgot, bishop of St. Andrews, and he left Scotland for good during 1115.[28] The evidence regarding Nostell seems to show that 1115 is too early by some years for the founding of Scone; the most probable date is nearer 1120.[29] The priory was certainly in being in the period 1122–4, when the king granted to its canons the island at the mouth of Loch Tay where Queen Sibylla had died (1122),[30] the intention being that the canons should build a church there and serve it 'in the habit of religion'. Of this proposed daughter-house of Scone nothing more is known, at least in the twelfth century.[31]

Important as it was, Scone was not the chief ecclesiastical centre of Scotland. To King Alexander must go the credit of making the first moves not only to establish at St. Andrews a bishop consecrated according to the accepted law of the church and amenable to himself, but also to install in the bishop's cathedral church a body of clergy who would symbolise the far-reaching changes being made in the Scottish church as a whole. The Augustinian canons of St. Andrews wrote and preserved an *Historia Fundationis* of their house, whose text (followed faithfully, if selectively, by

---

[26] Wilson, loc. cit., p. 148, printed a charter of King Alexander I (*c.* 1120), which confirms the statement in the *Chron. Bower*, i, 316.

[27] *Chron. Melrose*, 31.

[28] *Chron. Bower*, i, 286; *Symeon of Durham*, ii, 205, corrected by Dowden, *Bishops of Scotland*, 2.

[29] Dickinson, op. cit., p. 120 and n. 5.   [30] Lawrie, *Charters*, no. 47.

[31] Its name is Eilean nam Bannaomh, 'isle of the holy women'.

Wyntoun) has survived, albeit in an unsatisfactory copy.[32] To the author of this narrative, writing before 1152, it was quite clearly Alexander's grant to the church of St. Andrews of the land called the Boar's Raik, 'so that the religious life might be established in that church',[33] that began the long process of founding the Augustinian cathedral priory, which culminated successfully only in 1144. Although not explicitly stated, it is almost certain that the king had Austin canons in mind, for his grants to St. Andrews were probably made shortly before his death in April 1124, and it was in this period that he appointed as bishop of St. Andrews, in succession to the unsatisfactory Eadmer, Robert, the prior of Scone. After a long interval, during which he experienced difficulties first in being consecrated, then in recovering church lands from lay impropriators, Bishop Robert sought the co-operation of Athelulf, the head of the community where he had first entered the religious life. By this time, as the *Historia Fundationis* points out, Athelulf was bishop of Carlisle as well as prior of St. Oswald's. With his help, Bishop Robert brought a canon from Nostell to Scotland to be prior of his proposed cathedral chapter, and this was eventually established (1144) at the instigation of King David.[34] We can see, therefore, that the placing of Austin canons at St. Andrews as the cathedral chapter compares very closely with the creation by Athelulf, 1133–6, of an Augustinian chapter to serve the newly-founded cathedral church at Carlisle.[35]

Earl David, youngest of Malcolm and Margaret's sons, and soon to become king, was associated with his brother in the grant of the Boar's Raik to establish the conventual life at St. Andrews.[36] Since the rest of this chapter will be concerned with a discussion of how King David I fulfilled, in superabundant measure, the aims of his mother and elder brothers, it will be useful first of all to present some account of his upbringing, connexions, and activity

---

[32] From the lost Great Register of St. Andrews Priory, in B. M. Harleian MS. 4628, printed by Skene, *Chron. Picts-Scots*, 183–93. Internal evidence shows that the narrative of the priory's foundation was written before 1152. For Wyntoun's version, see *Chron. Wyntoun*, iv, 372–7, 386–91.

[33] 'ut in ipsa Ecclesia constitueretur religio ad deo deseruiendum', Harl. MS. 4628, fo. 233ᵛ; *Chron. Picts-Scots*, 190, 193.

[34] Ibid., 191–3.   [35] Dickinson, op. cit., 246–50.

[36] *Chron. Picts-Scots*, 190.

as a monastic patron in the years before he succeeded to the Scottish throne.

David, born *c.* 1085, a sixth son, with no great expectations, had been brought up, presumably in the period after 1093, in the English court.[37] When Henry I became king of England and married David's sister Matilda, his prospects must have improved; but in the years 1100–14, when he is recorded as a witness to royal acts (e.g. to nine given in *RRAN*),[38] his name appears simply as 'David, the queen's brother', and, at least until 1107, he was not in his own right a baron of great standing. In this year, however, the death of his unmarried brother Edgar, who had apparently bequeathed him a great estate in southern Scotland,[39] must have turned David's attention northward and made the first big improvement in his personal position. A few years later came the second and more momentous change. At the end of 1113, or early in 1114, King Henry gave to David in marriage the Countess Matilda de Senliz, the richest widow in England, whose vast estates straddled the south-eastern midlands, from Northampton to Huntingdon, from Oxfordshire to Leicestershire. This marriage and all these lands came to David with the rank and title of earl,[40] and made him one of the most substantial magnates in the country.

As an immediate result, David now became patron of the Cluniac priory founded at Northampton by his wife's first husband, Earl Simon. In an act which may well belong to the

---

[37] William of Malmesbury, *Gesta Regum*, ii, 476–7.

[38] *RRAN*, ii, nos. 648, 689, 701, 703, 706, 818a, 828, 832, 833 (in two, simply as 'David').

[39] Ailred of Rievaulx, *De Bello Standardo* (Migne, *Patrologia Latina*, cxcv, 709).

[40] Anderson, *Early Sources*, ii, 147, n. 2, gives the two best authorities for the date of David's accession to the earldom, the Anglo-Saxon Chronicle, version H (ed. C. Plummer, i, 244–5), and a charter of Rohais, widow of Richard FitzGilbert of Clare, self-dated 1113, printed by G. Gorham, *History of St. Neots* (1824), ii, pp. cv–cvi, from P.R.O., K.R. Memoranda Roll, 3 Henry IV, Easter Term, ro. 22.

I have not found any certain evidence to support the statements of several historians (quoted in Lawrie, *Charters*, p. 266) that David had the title of earl from 1107 to 1114. He certainly did not have it six months after Edgar's death (B.M. Royal MS. 11 B ix, fo. 5ᵛ; *RRAN*, ii, nos. 832, 833). The reliability of the charter printed by J. H. Round, *Calendar of Documents in France*, No. 1377 (= *RRAN*, ii, no. 730), is questionable.

months immediately after David gained his earldom, we find him confirming the monks in their possessions.

David,[41] by God's grace earl, greets all his faithful men. I wish you to know the joyous tidings that I have granted to the monks of La Charité serving God at (the church of) St. Andrew of Northampton all whichsoever they hold of my fee, in churches, tithes, lands, men, and customs, to be possessed as honourably as they more honourably possessed them on the day on which I came to this honour.

The men who witnessed what may be the earliest of David's recorded acts must have a certain interest for both English and Scottish historians. They included Hugh of Leicester, the sheriff of Northampton, himself the co-founder of another house for Cluniacs of La Charité at Daventry. To this house also, at about the same time, the earl issued his confirmation.[42] But it was the monks of Northampton who were David's special responsibility, 'his own monks', as a contemporary writ of Henry I describes them.[43] The St. Andrew's Priory registers preserve copies of seven writs and charters of David in their favour, chiefly covering the period from 1114 to 1136.[44] It is consequently curious that the first religious house which David founded in his Scottish lands was not for the Cluniacs, but for monks from the austere community at Tiron, near Chartres, only recently brought into being (1109) by the reformer Bernard, who had himself revolted against the domination of Cluny.

Clearly, among the lay magnates of his time David was exceptionally sensitive to the many fresh and fast-multiplying currents of religious life and thought. The Tironensians' austerity of life, and their practice of the skilled crafts, may have attracted David after they had come to his notice through the royal court, for

[41] *RRS*, i, no. 1.

[42] Lawrie, *Charters*, no. 51 (in which the last witness's name should be read *Roberto filio Nigell'*).

[43] B.M. Cott. MS. Vesp. E xvii, fo. 17ᵛ (cf. *RRAN*, ii, no. 1409). King Henry orders Hugh of Leicester to put the monks of Northampton in possession of land in Stuchbury 'because I wish that Earl David and his monks (*monachi sui*) shall hold as well as his predecessor best held'.

[44] Lawrie, *Charters*, nos. 56–8, 60, 71; *RRS*, i, nos. 1, 10.

King Henry was by way of being a patron and benefactor to Bernard of Tiron.[45] David may well have heard about Tiron before he gained his earldom. Symeon of Durham says that the Tironensians came to England (and to Selkirk) in 1113.[46] But the Tiron connexion cannot have begun much before David became earl, for Geoffrey the Fat's *Life of Bernard of Tiron*, in a passage which seems to embody a nearly contemporary account, relates that David, '(chief) of the men of Lothian and Northampton', earnestly requested Abbot Bernard to send him some monks, whom when they came he endowed with land by the Tweed.[47] Some time later, according to the *Life* (and there seems to be no reason to doubt its substantial truth here, though the statement is unsupported by other evidence and contains an element of confusion), David actually travelled to Tiron to see Bernard, but in vain, for the saintly abbot had died before he arrived. On his return, David took with him to Selkirk a further twelve monks under an abbot.[48] This must have been in 1116 or 1117, and, indeed, it was probably in these years that Ralph, first abbot of Selkirk, was elected to succeed Bernard and was replaced by William (presumably the abbot who accompanied David back to Scotland). William in turn, in 1118, succeeded Ralph as abbot of Tiron, where he ruled for many years.[49] Thus, remote as it was, Tiron's Scottish daughter-house provided the parent community with her second and third abbots; and one of the earliest provisions of the Tironensian order must have arisen directly out of Abbot William's experience as head of the colony at Selkirk: in 1120 he enacted that Tironensian abbots from oversea need attend

[45] Migne, *PL*, clxxii, 1424.

[46] *Symeon of Durham*, ii, 247; cf. *Chron. Melrose*, 31. The colonisation of Selkirk, not St. Dogmael's, seems to be meant by this entry. See below, pp. 200–1.

[47] *PL*, clxxii, 1426. Selkirk is some miles from the Tweed, but the early endowments of the monks included land by that river at Melrose (Lawrie, *Charters*, no. 35).

[48] *PL*, clxxii, loc. cit. The *Life* says that David went to Tiron after he became king, and then brought back twelve monks with an abbot; but probably David made only one journey, *c.* 1116.

[49] Bernard died either in 1116 or 1117 (Anderson, *Early Sources*, ii, 159, n. 3). For the deaths of abbots of Tiron to 1122, see L. Delisle, *Rouleau Mortuaire du B. Vital, abbé de Savigny*, Plate XXXIII. *Chron. Melrose*, 31, has marginal additions giving the succession of early abbots of Tiron and Selkirk, which put William's translation to Tiron at 1118.

the annual general chapter only once every three years, foreshadowing a later Cistercian practice.[50]

The second witness to Earl David's charter to Northampton Priory, quoted above, was John, the (earl's) chaplain. This seems to be the earliest recorded appearance of the man who was to have such an eventful and momentous career as bishop of Glasgow. Whether or not John, who was a monk, as well as being David's tutor,[51] had any connexion with Tiron at this time is not known. In 1136, when he had fallen into disgrace with Pope Innocent II because, apparently, he had pushed his opposition to the Archbishop of York's jurisdiction to the extreme length of adhering to the anti-pope, Anacletus II,[52] Bishop John sought refuge from his difficulties by becoming a member of the convent of Tiron.[53] His choice of retreat would seem curious, unless there had been some previous connexion; but the link might have been provided by John's familiarity with the Tironensian monks who remained in his diocese at Selkirk until 1128, when they removed to Kelso. The bishop was recalled from Tiron in 1138, and his sojourn there bore fruit in the shape of a grant made to Tiron by King David c. 1140; perhaps also the founding in 1144 of a cell for Kelso at Lesmahagow, in the diocese of Glasgow—for which the king gave credit to the bishop, while the bishop gave credit to the king—resulted from John's stay at the French monastery.[54]

From 1114 to 1124 the number of religious houses with which Earl David was connected, either as a benefactor or in some less direct but nonetheless favourable capacity, was at least nine, and

[50] J. H. Round, *Calendar of documents in France*, no. 997. Professor Knowles sees in this evidence for triennial general chapters (*Monastic Order*, p. 202, n. 2), but Abbot William's act was surely meant as a concession to distant daughter-houses. Tiron seems to have had an annual chapter (*Gallia Christiana*, ed. 1744, viii, 1261). Cistercian abbots in Scotland were allowed to attend general chapters once every four years by a constitution of 1157 (*Statuta . . . Ordinis Cisterciensis*, ed. J. Canivez, 1933, i, 67).

[51] Lawrie, *Charters*, no. 50.

[52] This is my interpretation of the evidence of Richard of Hexham's statement regarding the Scottish clergy's attitude to Anacletus, *Chron. Stephen*, iii, 170, and of the letters of Innocent II to the English archbishops (1136), in *Historians of the Church of York* (Rolls Series), iii, nos. xlix and l, especially the latter. It is clear from the letters and from Lawrie, *Charters*, no. 141, that John did not leave Scotland until 1136 or after.

[53] *Chron. Stephen*, loc. cit.

[54] Lawrie, *Charters*, nos. 136–7, 172–3.

evidence of other connexions may yet come to light. These houses ranged, geographically and in character, from the reformed Benedictines of Tiron to the Austin canons of Lanthony on the march of Wales; from the Cluniac houses of recent foundation at Northampton, Daventry and Reading to the old-established abbeys of Ramsey and Westminster, and to two northern churches, Durham and St. Mary's, York, in which the monastic life had been revived in the previous century.[55]

When David was given the Honour of Huntingdon in 1114, one of the men with whom he was brought into contact was the sheriff of Huntingdon and Cambridgeshire, a Norman knight named Gilbert.[56] Gilbert was sheriff of Surrey also, and it was in this very year that he took Robert, the sub-prior, from the Augustinian priory of St. Mary, Huntingdon, to rule a new community of regular canons at Merton, south of London.[57] Unfortunately, the only extant cartulary of St. Mary's, Huntingdon, is an unsatisfactory production, and we do not know whether David, as earl, patronised this house, though as king he undoubtedly did so, as did also his son Earl Henry.[58] The black canons were certainly among those newer orders of religious which, on the whole, found most favour with David. We must not overlook the influence upon David in this period of his sister Queen Matilda. She was an active and influential supporter of the regular canons, and in 1107–8 founded the famous Austin priory of Holy Trinity, Aldgate. It is possible that David had already been a benefactor to this church before c. 1132, when, on his wife's death, he gave the church of Tottenham to the canons of Aldgate for the souls of the two Matildas, queens of England and Scotland.[59] To the canons' chagrin, the body of their foundress, who died in 1118, was buried in the abbey church of Westminster.[60] Earl David,

---

[55] A puzzling writ of Henry I commanding Earl David to assist the monks of Reading in respect of land at Cholsey, Berks., is in B.M. Harl. MS. 1708, fo. 17ᵛ (cf. *RRAN*, ii, no. 1423). David was also ordered, as lord of the honour of Huntingdon, to protect the monks of Ramsey; *Cart. Ramsey* (Rolls Series), nos. 168–9. Evidence for the remaining connexions is either discussed in the text, or is in Lawrie, *Charters*, nos. 29, 30, 32–4, 52.

[56] *Cart. Ramsey*, nos. 168–9; W. Morris, *Medieval English Sheriff*, p. 78; College of Arms, Arundel MS. 28, fo. 8ᵛ.

[57] Dickinson, *Austin Canons*, p. 117.   [58] *RRS*, i, nos. 20, 33.

[59] Lawrie, *Charters*, no. 98; *RRS*, i, no. 9.

[60] See Dickinson, op. cit., p. 111.

probably soon afterwards, made careful provision for the Westminster monks to celebrate his sister's anniversary, and also the
anniversaries of their father and mother, and the cost of this was
to be met appropriately—and economically—by a rent from the
estate of the late queen's chamberlain, Aldwin, which formed a
part of David's useful manor of Tottenham.[61]

It was apparently a chaplain of the English queen Matilda who
took a leading share in the beginnings of the Austin priory of
Lanthony, which was an early offshoot from Aldgate.[62] In the
period 1114 to 1124 Earl David and his countess recorded their
confirmation of a Bedfordshire tenant's grant of land to the canons
of Lanthony.[63] Queen Matilda, again, took a close and helpful
interest in Sheriff Gilbert's foundation at Merton,[64] a house which
was to play an important part in Scottish Augustinian development.

Among David's chaplains in the period c. 1118 to c. 1128 were
two clerks named Aelfwine or Alwin and Osbert.[65] In 1128 King
David founded a church, to be served by Augustinian canons, at
a site below Arthur's Seat, not far from the royal castle of Edinburgh, and Alwin, the king's chaplain, was made its first abbot.[66]
According to the fifteenth-century *Historia Fundationis* of Holyrood
Abbey, Alwin was then a canon of Merton.[67] It is curious that
modern Scottish historians have never realised that Holyrood
Abbey was formed by a colonisation from Merton in Surrey,
although this information has been available since the publication
in 1898 of A. Heales' *Records of Merton Priory*.[68] The actual
evidence is contained in the excellent *Historia Fundationis* of
Merton preserved in a manuscript at the College of Arms, and
the relevant passage, in which Edinburgh (Holyrood) is listed
third among Merton's seven daughter-houses, has been printed
by Mr. Dickinson.[69] The Merton parentage of Holyrood, which

---

[61] *RRS*, i, no. 6. [62] Dickinson, op. cit., p. 111.
[63] *RRS*, i, nos. 2, 3. [64] Dickinson, op. cit., p. 117.
[65] Lawrie, *Charters*, nos. 32, 35, 53; *RRS*, i, nos. 6, 7.
[66] *Chron. Melrose*, 32; *Chron. Holyrood*, 116, 128.
[67] *Book of the Old Edinburgh Club*, vii, 64.
[68] P. 6. Heales' reading and translation of his MS. source are faulty. In
Royal Commission on Ancient Monuments of Scotland, *Inventory of the City of
Edinburgh* (1951), p. 129, Holyrood is said to have been colonised from Scone,
on the authority of F. C. Eeles, *PSAS*, xlix, 91, but no source is given for the
statement.
[69] College of Arms, Arundel MS. 28, fos. 12ᵛ–13ʳ; Dickinson, op. cit.,

may with confidence be ascribed to the connexion between Merton and Huntingdon, need not surprise us, for both these churches were centres for the propagation of the Augustinian rule.

Alwin's fellow-chaplain, Osbert of Paxton, certainly belonged to Huntingdonshire. From an interesting charter (copied into the *Registrum* of Lincoln Cathedral) which was given by King David at Huntingdon between 1124 and 1128,[70] we learn that the parish church of Holy Trinity, Great Paxton, on David's demesne, was given an exchange of land by the king at the request of his chaplain Osbert and of Orgar the priest, apparently in order that, as the charter says, 'a prior and clerks should serve the church as regular canons'. The 'priory' of Paxton endured until *c.* 1140, when Osbert was prior, but after this nothing more is heard of it.[71] During the 1140s, however, we do hear of Osbert, prior of Holyrood,[72] and an identification of the Scottish with the English Osbert, which might seem far-fetched, is actually made probable by two further charters at Lincoln, which show that in or before 1162 Great Paxton church had been given by the Scottish king to Holyrood Abbey, and that by this time there was no longer a priory at Paxton.[73] Osbert evidently found it difficult to support the regular life at this small parish church, and taking, as it were, his title-deeds with him, seems to have migrated to the well-endowed royal abbey of Holyrood over which his former colleague Alwin now presided as abbot.

We may turn next to the two other Augustinian houses founded by King David, Jedburgh and Cambuskenneth.

In 1139, the year in which peace was made between David and Stephen after the first phase of war, we find for the first time in record mention of a prior of Jedworth (the later Jedburgh).[74] It

p. 118, n. 5. For Mr. Dickinson's 'inceptis fuit', I read 'incepcio fuit', which should perhaps be emended to 'incepto sunt'. The beginning of the next sentence I read 'Iamque ut ipsarum propagacionum ordinem teneamus . . .' It may be pointed out that the form 'Ednesburch' in the manuscript is further evidence that the narrative was composed in the twelfth century.

[70] *SHR*, xiv, 371–2; *Registrum Antiquissimum of Lincoln*, ed. C. W. Foster, iii, no. 800 (= *RRS*, i, no. 6).   [71] Ibid., no. 802.

[72] Lawrie, *Charters*, nos. 134 (dating possibly later than 1141), 182, 213; *Chron. Holyrood*, 121.

[73] *Reg. Antiquissimum of Lincoln*, iii, nos. 804–5 (cf. *RRS*, i, no. 197).

[74] Lawrie, *Charters*, no. 121. This prior, Daniel, also witnessed a charter of Earl Henry to St. Mary's, Huntingdon, given at Roxburgh *c.* 1140 or after; *RRS*, i, no. 20.

is possible that his priory (soon to become an abbey), which was founded by King David with the help of Bishop John of Glasgow, owed its existence to the bishop's wish to mark his reconciliation with the papacy. The legate Alberic had recalled him from his self-imposed exile at Tiron at the Carlisle council of 1138, and after his return nothing more is heard of his bitter dispute with York. According to John of Hexham, it was the bishop who had placed the regular canons in the church of Jedburgh, and it was in their church that he was buried in 1147.[75] In Spottiswoode's *Account* of the Scottish religious houses[76] the canons of Jedburgh are said, without authority cited, to have come from St. Quintin of Beauvais, the famous centre of Augustinian life and of its propagation. We have, however, the good authority of Ailred of Rievaulx that among King David's foundations was a house for canons of Beauvais,[77] and the evidence, by elimination, points to Jedburgh. But for the present, the identity of the mother-house of Jedburgh must remain uncertain.

One of King David's grants to Jedburgh touches on a point of some interest which has not been widely discussed.[78] When a small community of foreign clergy arrived in remote northern parts, not the least urgent of their needs must have been a supply of ready money. Money was probably scarce in Scotland, where so many revenues, even royal ones, were still paid in kind. David's solution was to make use of his English lands, apparently to provide temporary grants of money revenues which could later be exchanged for land in Scotland. In carrying out this plan, David's demesne manor of Hardingstone, by Northampton, for some reason bore an altogether disproportionate share of the burden. One of David's first acts on gaining his lands in southern Scotland was to restore the church and see of Glasgow, and, probably *c.* 1114, a rent of 100s. a year from Hardingstone was given 'ad edificationem et restaurationem' of Glasgow cathedral. At about the same time, ten librates of land in Hardingstone were given to

[75] *Symeon of Durham*, ii, 321.
[76] In Keith, *Bishops*, 392. So in J. Morton, *Monastic Annals of Teviotdale*, p. 3, perhaps following Spottiswoode.
[77] Migne, *PL*, cxcv, 714.
[78] For the following, see Lawrie, *Charters*, nos. 46, 74, 35 (cf. no. 194 and *Kelso Liber*, no. 241; *RRS*, ii, no. 62). David's *magnum negocium* may have been connected with the campaign of 1138–9.

the Tironensians settled at Selkirk, a grant which could only have been of use to them in the form of a money rent. Between 1124 and 1128, when King David was enlarging the endowments of Dunfermline so that a bigger church might be built there, the monks were given a rent of 100s. 'in England' (its source is not stated). These grants were not intended to be permanent. The Tironensians, for example, had to surrender their ten pounds a year for the king's 'important business' (*magnum negocium*) and were given the village of Traverlen (Duddingston) in exchange. This was almost certainly before the founding of Jedburgh, for one of King David's earlier grants to the Jedburgh canons was ten librates of land in Hardingstone, which were in turn exchanged, before 1153, for the estate of Rule Hervey (Abbotrule) in the Roxburghshire parish of Southdean.

No early writer has described the founding of the Augustinian abbey of Stirling, which was built in a crook of the Forth named Cambuskenneth, on the opposite side of the river from the king's burgh. In a paper on Carlisle cathedral,[79] Mr. Dickinson discussed the interesting fact that between 1136 and 1156 the Austin canons of the newly formed cathedral chapter of Carlisle obtained leave from Bishop Athelulf to adopt the order of Arrouaise, that is, the constitutions observed at the church of St. Nicholas, Arrouaise, already famous as a centre of the strict Augustinian life. Mr. Dickinson pointed out that the great Irish reformer, St. Malachy (Máelmaedóc Úa Morgair), visited both Clairvaux and Arrouaise on his journey to and from Rome in 1140. His purpose was to collect and learn the rules of the reformed religious orders so that he could plant them in his native country. On this journey, both going and coming, Malachy almost certainly passed through Carlisle, and Mr. Dickinson put forward the suggestion that the canons there were converted to the Arrouaisian observance through Malachy's influence.[80] More recently, M.

---

[79] 'The Origins of the Cathedral of Carlisle', in *CWAAS Transactions*, xlv, 134–43. As this paper is substantially included in the same writer's *Austin Canons*, my references are to that work.

[80] Ibid., p. 250; J. Wilson, *SHR*, xviii, 72–5. Abbot Gautier's historical narrative of Arrouaise (ed. from Gosse, *Histoire d'Arrouaise*, by O. Holder-Egger in *Monumenta Germaniae Historica* (*Scriptores*), xv, II, pp. 1117–25) says that Malachy took books and copies of the Arrouaisian use on his return to Ireland (ibid., pp. 1121–2).

Ludo Milis, in a lengthy study of the Arrouaisian order,[81] has put forward what seem to me to be convincing reasons for believing that it was Bishop Athelulf himself, and not the Irish reformer, who took the decision to adopt the Arrouaisian observance at Carlisle. He shows that Athelulf—evidently travelling south with the legate Alberic at the end of 1138 to attend the Lateran Council—must have made contact with the bishops of Thérouanne and Arras at the turn of the years 1138–9.[82] From this contact evidently sprang the decision—perhaps never fully, and certainly never permanently, implemented—to affiliate the cathedral priory of Carlisle to Arrouaise. The fact that St. Malachy visited Arrouaise and Carlisle on the journey to and from Rome seems therefore no more than a coincidence as far as Carlisle is concerned.

It is of greater interest to know that in this period King David took the first steps towards establishing an Arrouaisian community in Scotland, which became, a few years later (1147), the abbey of St. Mary of Stirling. Prior Gosse of Arrouaise, the eighteenth-century historian of his house, made the reasonable suggestion that the Scottish king's interest in this Picard abbey was due to the fact that his sister Mary, and her husband Eustace, count of Boulogne, had been its benefactors.[83] It should, however, be pointed out that the Countess Mary died in 1115, nine years before David even became king, and that in 1140 David would be most unlikely to favour a continental abbey simply on the grounds that King Stephen's father-in-law had been its patron. It seems more reasonable, therefore, to attribute David's connexion with Arrouaise to the influence of Bishop Athelulf of Carlisle or St. Malachy.

Hitherto, our knowledge that Stirling Abbey, or Cambuskenneth Abbey as it came to be called, was ever Arrouaisian has rested on a bull of Eugenius III of 30 August 1147.[84] This states that the 'ordo canonicus de Arrosia' had been instituted in the church of St. Mary, Stirling, by its first abbot, William, with the

[81] L. Milis, *L'ordre des chanoines reguliers d'Arrouaise* (2 vols., Bruges, 1969).
[82] Ibid., 324–7; and cf. the document printed on pp. 600–1.
[83] *Histoire de l'abbaye d'Arrouaise* (Lille, 1786), pp. 56–7.
[84] Lawrie, *Charters*, no. 180. Lawrie gives no authority for his statement, ibid., p. 401, that canons were brought from 'Aroise' to Stirling 'early in the reign of David I, perhaps in the reign of King Alexander'.

advice and help of Bishop Robert of St. Andrews. Thanks, however, to the survival at Amiens of Abbot Gautier's cartulary of Arrouaise, a fine production of the latter part of the twelfth century,[85] it has been possible to recover a charter given by Earl Henry, King David's son, at Carlisle, c. 1140–5.[86] This charter puts the connexion between Stirling and its French mother-house in a somewhat clearer light. From it we learn that King David had granted to the church of Arrouaise (probably c. 1140) half the hides and a quarter of the tallow of all beasts slaughtered at Stirling. M. Milis has shown, by a comparison of the papal privileges of 1164 and 1195 for Cambuskenneth[87] with that for Arrouaise itself (1181),[88] that King David's gift was intended— to begin with, at least—to benefit the mother house of Arrouaise, and not the community—which we may reasonably regard as a daughter-house—established at Cambuskenneth.[89] If this was so, it would provide a parallel to King David's grant of the annual customs dues from one ship at Perth to the abbey of Tiron, mother house of Selkirk-Kelso.[90] Yet it is difficult not to see this action by the king as part of the process whereby the Augustinian canons were effectively established at Cambuskenneth and their connexion with Arrouaise confirmed.[91] Between 1181 and 1195 the half-share of the royal hides and the quarter share of tallow of Stirling granted to Arrouaise had been transferred to the canons at Cambuskenneth.[92] They may already have been given the other quarter of the tallow since they are now seen to hold a half, the remaining half being in the possession of Dunfermline

[85] Bibliothèque Municipale d'Amiens, MS. 1077 (Catalogue Général des Manuscrits des Bibliothèques Publiques de France, vol. xlviii, p. 242).
[86] RRS, i, no. 35.   [87] Cambuskenneth Registrum, nos. 24, 25.
[88] J. Ramackers (ed.), Papsturkunden in Frankreich, iv (1942), Picardie, no. 249 (p. 402): 'medietatem coriorum et quartam partem arvine que vulgo sepum dicitur de animalibus que in Strivelin occiduntur, a regibus Scotie vobis et ecclesie vestre pia devotione concessam.'
[89] Op. cit., 331.   [90] Lawrie, Charters, no. 136–7; below, p. 209.
[91] We may note not only ibid., no. 143, which shows that the canons had acquired the land of Cambuskenneth in or before 1147 but also the statement in Abbot Gautier's History (loc. cit., p. 1121) that under Abbot Gervase (1121–47) Arrouaise sent out colonies not only to England, Burgundy and Poland, but also to Scotland. It may be noted that Alured, second abbot of Stirling, was in England in company with heads of other Arrouaisian houses, Bourne, Warter (?) and Harrold, c. 1160 (Reg. Ant. Lincoln, ii, no. 347).
[92] Cambuskenneth Registrum, no. 25 (p. 44).

Abbey—not for nothing was the story told of James I apostrophising his ancestor 'Saint' David as 'ane sair sanct for the Croune'.

Cambuskenneth Abbey seems to have been the Arrouaisian order's sole Scottish excursion.[93] If little or nothing in connexion with it was owed to St. Malachy, it may nevertheless be possible to suspect his influence in one of the earliest Cistercian foundations in Scotland.

On St. Malachy's return journey to Ireland in the autumn of 1140, he found King David keeping his court in one of his castles, probably Carlisle. With him was his only son, Earl Henry, who was so dangerously ill that his life was despaired of. Malachy, implored by the king to cure his son, attended Henry, bidding him have faith, and saying that he would not die on that occasion. The next day the prince recovered, to the intense joy of the royal household.[94] Nothing is more likely than that King David should have signalised his thankfulness for this event by endowing a religious community, and if this was done, and done, moreover, with Malachy's counsel, we should remember that he had come freshly from a visit to Bernard of Clairvaux. It is therefore conceivable, though there is no direct evidence on this point, that the Cistercian abbey of Newbattle, founded by King David and Earl Henry in November, 1140, as the first daughter-house of Melrose, owed its origin to this motive.[95]

So far, we have seen David as the patron in his own kingdom of the Benedictines of Canterbury at Dunfermline, and of Durham at Coldingham; of the monks of Tiron at Selkirk; and of several communities of Austin canons. This activity alone would make his work for the religious orders remarkable, but when we recall that in addition he founded three Cistercian abbeys, a Cluniac

[93] I am unable to accept M. Milis' arguments for adding St. Andrews Cathedral Priory to the list of Scottish Arrouaisian houses (op. cit., 327–30). The total silence of the considerable quantity of St. Andrews record must weigh against the rather weak evidence of the late Eckhout obituaries.

[94] Migne, PL, clxxxii, 1095–6. After this, we are told, both David and his son loved Malachy as long as he lived, as the man who had recalled (Henry) from death.

[95] The founding of Newbattle is usually acribed to King David alone, but a solemn privilege of Innocent II, of Feb.–Sept., 1143 (Newbattle Registrum, no. 263; cf. Jaffé-Löwenfeld, Regesta, no. 8369), links David and his son as making the initial endowments.

priory, and possibly a Cistercian nunnery,[96] to say nothing of his probable encouragement of the knights of the Hospital and Temple, the scale of his work is seen to be truly astonishing. It has been impossible within the limits of this chapter to discuss in equal detail all David's foundations. In particular, little has been said of the king's relations with the Cistercians, the more readily since Sir Maurice Powicke's work on Ailred of Rievaulx[97] has revealed in the clearest manner the close connexion between David and the white monks in the north of England, and has given us a vivid picture of the contemporary social background in which the founding of Melrose as a daughter of Rievaulx takes its natural place. It may, however, be useful to include a mention of David's sole Cluniac foundation, and of the two monasteries which he planted in Moray.

Henry I's favourite religious house was the Cluniac abbey of Reading, his own foundation, dating from 1121. A benefaction to its monks in memory of his former lord, in whose court he had been brought up, would be an act natural enough on David's part. Nothing, however, seems to have been attempted in the period immediately after Henry's death, and nothing could be attempted during the years of war and disturbance from 1138 to 1141. One might, indeed, have supposed that after the Rievaulx monks had colonised Melrose in 1136 the relations between David and Stephen, steadily deteriorating, would put an end for a while to further English monastic settlement in Scotland. But a good friend of the Scottish king, the faithful Brian Fitz Count, held command of the middle Thames valley throughout these gloomy years, and one of the first steps towards giving Reading a daughter-house in Scotland was recorded in a charter which King David addressed to Brian,[98] as well as to Abbot Edward and his convent. This was the grant of the estate of Rindalgros (now Rhynd), where the Earn flows into the Tay, made on the understanding

[96] Only the nunnery at S. Berwick can safely be ascribed to David I's time (D. E. Easson, 'Nunneries of Medieval Scotland', Scottish Ecclesiological Soc. *Tranactions*, xiii, II (1940–1), p. 35, n. 3).
[97] *The Life of Ailred of Rievaulx by Walter Daniel*, ed. and transl. by F. M. Powicke (Nelsons' Medieval Classics).
[98] Lawrie, *Charters*, no. 161, where the 'dominus Briencius' addressed by David can safely be identified with Brian Fitz Count, for whose personal connexion with Reading Abbey see J. B. Hurry, *Reading Abbey* (1901), p. 162.

that should the grant be sufficiently augmented Reading Abbey was to establish a convent there.

This was never carried out, but in these same years a community of monks from Reading, under their prior Achard, was in fact established on the lonely Isle of May, at the mouth of the Firth of Forth.[99] The service of the shrines of St. Ethernan and other saints on this bleak and foggy island, the haunt chiefly of rough fisherfolk who would not pay the tithes of their catches, must have contrasted dismally with the comparative luxuriance of the Thames valley, and the colonisation of the May is a token of the enthusiasm and devotion of the Reading Cluniacs.[100] Yet they were given some property and interests on the mainland, the lands of Pittenweem and St. Monance, a chapel in Perth, tofts in Berwick and Haddington, and they probably managed the estate of Rindalgros as well.[101] The priory of May never grew to wealth or independence of its mother-house; but it provides an interesting example of how the Scottish king placed in the custody of one of the foreign religious orders a shrine long associated with the veneration of a Celtic saint.[102]

The intensely Scottish province of Moray came under direct royal control in 1130, and the introduction of certain Anglo-Norman institutions followed with precocious speed. Protected by the king's newly-planted tenants, two religious communities of the new type were founded in the north before 1153. At an unknown date between 1130 and 1150 the Benedictines of Dunfermline were given land in Moray, and probably towards the end of this period established a dependent cell at Urquhart,[103] near the new burgh of Elgin. It is possible that in this period they made an abortive attempt to push still further north. A monk of

[99] Lawrie, *Charters*, nos. 155–6; and p. 387.

[100] St. Ethernan is mentioned in twelfth- and thirteenth-century record as *Yðerninus* (B.M. Egerton MS. 3031, fo. 62ᵛ) and *Etherninus* (*May Recs.*, no. 28). It is difficult to believe that St. Ethernan and St. Adrian of May, distinct in the Scottish Church calendar, were not one and the same. Malcolm IV ordered the fishermen of the May to pay their tithes, *c.* 1153–61 (*RRS*, i, no. 162).

[101] Lawrie *Charters*, nos. 155, 184, 202, 231; B. M. Egerton MS. 3031, fo. 611.

[102] Cf. A. A. M. Duncan, 'Documents relating to the Priory of the Isle of May, *c.* 1140–1313', *PSAS*, xc, 52–80.

[103] Lawrie, *Charters*, nos. 128, 255.

Dunfermline was made bishop of Caithness,[104] and a Dunfermline record shows us King David writing (*c.* 1139–51) on behalf of monks at Dornoch,[105] in the bishop's diocese. In the summer of 1150 a convent of Cistercians from Melrose was planted at Kinloss in Moray by the king,[106] the first of a number of communities of the more austere orders of religious which, as might be expected, predominated in the north.

In a review of this Scottish monastic development three features emerge with special prominence. First, it is remarkable how rapidly the successive phases of western religious life were reflected in this small northern kingdom, which though physically remote was, as we must agree, far from being socially or intellectually isolated. Secondly, despite the virtual monopoly of monastic patronage held by the royal house, we are struck by the wide variety of religious orders that found a place in Scotland. For this, most, though not all, of the credit belongs to David, who as earl and king fully merited a twelfth-century pope's description of him as 'princeps catholicus et Christiane fidei ampliator',[107] however much he may have diminished thereby the resources of the Scottish crown. Finally, whether or not we judge this flowering of monastic life to have been too sudden and even somewhat artificial, we must give credit to a remarkable ruling family for planting and fostering it by means of the fullest use of their resources and connexions.

[104] Dowden, *Bishops*, 232; *Chron. Picts-Scots*, 136.
[105] Lawrie, *Charters*, no. 132; Anderson, *Early Sources*, ii, 193, 213. The presence of the writ in the Dunfermline register suggests that the monks at Dornoch were from Dunfermline, but the wording of the writ does not, I think, necessary imply the existence of a religious house at Dornoch.
[106] *Chron. Melrose*, 35; Anderson, *Early Sources*, 210–11.
[107] Urban III; cf. *Glasgow Registrum*, no. 66.

6 Benedictines, Tironensians and Cistercians

I

The religious communities of monks, canons-regular and—to a notably lesser extent—of nuns set their stamp upon the medieval church in Scotland so profoundly and emphatically that whatever may be said of that church in praise or blame cannot, if it is to make any sense, leave the monasteries out of consideration. The religious were landowners on a scale so large that there cannot have been any part of the country outside the central and western highlands where a man was not the tenant, or the neighbour of a tenant, or at least the neighbour of a neighbour of a tenant, of some abbey or priory or hospital or preceptory. When, in the twelfth century, the wild hillmen from the uplands of Carrick drove their cattle down from the moors to the place where some royal officer waited to take possession of the king's tribute, they might or might not know that one beast in ten would be claimed by the Tironensian monks of distant Kelso. In 1845, there still survived a muddled tradition that the duke of Atholl, as proprietor of Stanley on the River Tay, was bound to pay one grilse annually to Dunfermline Abbey in respect of the old tower of 'Inchbervis'. In this we have an echo, faint but recognisable, of the grant made by King David I, seven hundred years before, to Andrew, bishop of Caithness, of the old church the Holy Trinity of Dunkeld, with its lands, including 'Inchethurfin' on the Tay (where Stanley now is), and of Bishop Andrew's subsequent grant of this property to Dunfermline Abbey, where he had once been a monk. Again, when the burgesses of Inverness went to their parish church of St. Mary, they could hardly be unaware that the patron of this church was the abbot and convent of Arbroath, many miles away to the south. These are merely random illustrations, which could be multiplied many times over, of the way in which different sorts of people up and down the country might find the religious houses impinging upon some aspect of their life.

Ubiquitous landlords, the monks and canons filled a place in early medieval Scotland whose importance was out of all proportion to their numbers. They set new standards of organised hospitality and charity, and above all new standards in the performance of the Divine Office, from which it followed that they brought in wholly new standards in the architectural setting required for a more continuous, more musical and in every way more splendid liturgy. They infused with a fresh vigour the monastic tradition in Scotland, the practice of the disciplined, communal life of devotion which at the outset of the twelfth century was almost certainly in decay in some parts of the country, and in others found no place at all. However far removed monastic life might be from the daily life of ordinary people—and one may suspect that it was more isolated in theory than in practice—the example set by the religious of whatever order must have made a profound impression. From the twelfth to the fourteenth century the monasteries cannot be ignored by the historian of politics, the constitution, the church, society or culture.

All this, the ubiquity and the manifold significance of the religious orders, is a commonplace of Scottish history, a point which needs no labouring. So true is it, indeed, that a special effort of the imagination is required to envisage the period, roughly from 1070 to the 1150s, when all this was not yet true, but was in process of becoming true. In 1070, the year of Lanfranc's appointment as archbishop of Canterbury, the probable year of Saint Margaret's marriage to the king of Scots, there was not a single religious community between Forth and Tweed—indeed, there was scarcely a monastery of any kind between the Forth and the English Fenland. In the midlands and south of England, slowly recovering from the shock of the Norman Conquest, religious life was characterised by the Benedictine abbeys, some at least of which were by no means so far gone in decay as continental reformers and innovators tended to suggest, and all of which were in any case shortly to undergo, with Norman inspiration or under Norman leadership, a phase of revival, re-invigoration and tremendous expansion. North of the Forth, the desolation which had settled upon Northumbria and the continental contacts and influences beginning to prevail in the south of England were alike unknown. There were religious communities, how many we do not know, but there was no monasticism of the Benedictine type and no sign of any movement within the church either to put new strength and fervour into the already ancient native tradition of collective or individual asceticism, or to adopt and introduce any of the forms of religious life which distinguished the christianity of western Europe in the second half of the eleventh century. Scotland at this time was going her own way, not it seems in any spirit of stubborn or chauvinistic independence, but simply because she was unaware that there was any other way to go.

In one of the most telling yet tantalising sentences of his *Life* of Queen Margaret, Thurgot observes in passing that in her time there were in the kingdom of the Scots—he means the country north of the Forth—very many men shut up in separate little cells in various places, who though they were living in the flesh practised denial of the flesh by severe asceticism.[1] Rarely can that indifference to topographical detail and proper nouns of every sort, which is the hallmark of the early medieval hagiographer, be more exasperating. If only Thurgot had given us the names of a few of those 'various places', or told us something in detail about even one member of that ascetic multitude! As it is, we can only speculate. It would not be rash to suppose that Loch Leven and Abernethy, with their communities of *célidé*, were two of the places which Thurgot had in mind. The queen and two of her sons, Edgar and Ethelred, were benefactors of Loch Leven, and when Ethelred's grant of Auchmuir to the Loch Leven *célidé* was confirmed by his brothers Alexander and David, an emphatic if unexplained Abernethy interest in the proceedings is shown by the attestation of the entire community of Abernethy who were present at the transaction, including Augustine, the priest of the *célidé* there.[2]

---

[1] *Vita S. Margaretae Scotorum Reginae*, ed. J. Hodgson Hinde, in *Symeonis Dunelmensis Opera et Collectanea*, i (Surtees Soc., 1868), p. 247: 'Quo tempore in regno Scottorum plurimi, per diversa loca separatis inclusi cellulis, per magnam vitae districtionem, in carne, non secundum carnem, vivebant: Angelicam enim in terris conversationem ducebant.'

[2] Lawrie, *Charters*, no. 14.

When in the twelfth century we begin to have record evidence to bear out the truth of Thurgot's jejune statement, we learn of several communities, e.g., the *célidé* at Muthil, Brechin and Monymusk, the *clerici* of Old Deer, the 'brethren of St. John the Evangelist of Inchaffray' under Isaac the hermit, all of which, if they already existed a hundred years earlier, would no doubt have qualified for a place among the ascetics whom Queen Margaret sought out, emulated and patronised. There is good evidence, too, of the existence of a solitary as well as of a collective eremitical tradition, in this case both north and south of the Forth. It is only casually that the names have been preserved for posterity of John the hermit at Loch Moy,[3] of Gilchrist Gartanach the hermit at nearby Ruthven beside the River Findhorn,[4] of Cristinus the hermit at Kingledoors in Tweeddale,[5] and of Gillemichel the hermit at Errol in the Carse of Gowrie,[6] with his plot of three acres—which, incidentally, with or without a cow, seems to have been something like a standard allowance for hermits. But we may be sure that John and Gillemichel and Cristinus and one or two others mentioned in early record stood towards the end rather than at the beginning of a tradition of the anchoretic christian life, and that their predecessors in this tradition were those whom Thurgot had in mind when he wrote of numerous isolated men living the life of angels upon earth in various parts of the Scottish kingdom.[7]

However much Queen Margaret might admire and venerate those *célidé* and hermits who had maintained their ancient austerity and observance, her conscience, and above all her consciousness of a wider European background, forbade her to leave the future of Scottish christianity entirely in their hands. In her view, the attitude of the leading men in the Scottish church must have seemed disturbingly insular and parochial. This was not essentially because of their deviations from catholic custom, or of their archaisms, e.g., in the observance of Lent. Some of the deviations were serious, others, such as the Scots' avoidance of the extremes of Sabbatarianism, seem to have been relatively trivial; none of

[3] *RRS*, ii, no. 142.   [4] *Moray Registrum*, no. 38.
[5] *Glasgow Registrum*, no. 104 (late 12th cent.), which also mentions Cospatric the hermit of Kilbucho.
[6] *Spalding Misc.*, ii, 307.
[7] Cf. D. McRoberts, 'Hermits in Medieval Scotland', *Innes Review*, xvi, 199–216.

them appears to have touched the fundamentals of eleventh-century catholic doctrine.[8] It was surely a deeper cause for anxiety in Margaret that her adopted country was unaffected by the great issues and personalities that were shaping the history of the universal church at this time. So far as we know, there was little contact with the papacy and no awareness of the implications for Church and State of the claims for greater papal authority now being vigorously pressed. In its organisation the Scottish church was anomalous, to say the least. That there was something of a pre-eminent quality about the see located at St. Andrews is almost certainly true; yet there was no bishop in Scotland who enjoyed either in practice or in acknowledged law a status which would be recognised on the continent or even in England as metropolitan. As for the other bishops, a serious if not wholly convincing attempt has been made to prove that Scotland was not ill-equipped in this respect,[9] but it remains doubtful whether there was anything which could be called a diocesan system. Thurgot's biography shows that it was possible to convene councils of the Scottish clergy, that these clergy had their recognised spokesmen, and that (as we should expect) their native vernacular, Gaelic, was adequate for the discussion of detailed matters of ecclesiastical and liturgical observance. But at this period the sister church of England, which could also be called backward and insular in some respects, had more than one point of contact with the papacy and with continental learning. It has been argued by Professor Donaldson that the irregularity or abnormality of the Scottish church may have been exaggerated, since, as he says, 'Queen Margaret, though critical of much else, had evidently no criticism to make of Scottish orders or organization.'[10] But we cannot be sure that the list of *corrigenda* given in Thurgot's biography was exhaustive—indeed, Thurgot himself implies that it was not by saying that the queen convened 'numerous councils' to bring about reform, while actually describing the proceedings at the principal one only.[11]

[8] Cf. D. Bethell, 'Two letters of Pope Paschal II to Scotland', *SHR*, xlix, 33–45, esp. pp. 37–44.
[9] Gordon Donaldson, 'Scottish Bishops' Sees before the reign of David I', *PSAS*, lxxxvii (1955), 106–17.
[10] Art. cit., p. 117, where 'late 12th century' is clearly a slip for 'late 11th century'.
[11] *Vita S. Margaretae*, p. 243: 'crebra concilia'.

Dr. Donaldson reminds us that according to the York writers the queen and King Malcolm sent the bishop of St. Andrews, Fothadh II, to Thomas of Bayeux, archbishop of York, to make profession of obedience.[12] This story is unsupported and comes from a biased quarter, but even if it is untrue we must remember that there were limits to what even the most determined and forceful of women could accomplish. Bishop Fothadh, after all, was no Stigand. He had done nothing to merit deposition; moreover, however inconveniently, he did not die until 1093, the year in which Malcolm and Margaret themselves died and their kingdom was plunged into anarchy and internecine strife.

Any move to reform the episcopate would have to begin with St. Andrews, and in this matter Queen Margaret was simply not given the opportunity that came to William the Conqueror in 1070. Thurgot's biography does not tell us that the queen wished to reform the episcopate, but there are two known facts which to my mind seem more significant than this omission. Between 1070 and 1089 Queen Margaret approached Archbishop Lanfranc for assistance in her work for the Scottish church; and in 1107, soon after his accession, the queen's son Alexander I, who was undoubtedly inspired by a wish to carry on his mother's work, appointed her biographer and confidant, the Benedictine monk Thurgot, prior of Durham, to the bishopric of the Scots, or (as it came to be called in the twelfth century) the bishopric of St. Andrews. These two facts alone, the approach to Lanfranc and the appointment of an English Benedictine intimately associated with Queen Margaret to the highest ecclesiastical office in Scotland, would in my view outweigh the argument from silence that Margaret 'initiated no reforms in the administration or organisation of the church' and 'concerned herself only with relatively trivial matters'.[13] But what was the assistance which the queen asked Lanfranc to give her? The archbishop's letter is our sole evidence for this, and the relevant passage deserves to be quoted in full:

In answer to your request, I am sending to you and your husband our dearest brother Goldwine, and two other monks,

[12] Art. cit., p. 117.
[13] *A Source Book of Scottish History*, ed. W. C. Dickinson, G. Donaldson and Isabel Milne, i (1952), p. 42. In the second edition (1958, p. 57) the wording has been slightly altered but the sense of the passage remains the same.

since he could not by himself fulfil all that should be done in God's service and yours. I ask earnestly that you should endeavour resolutely and successfully to complete the work you have begun for God and for your souls. And if you can or should wish to fulfil your work through others, we greatly desire that our brothers should return to us, because their services are needed by our church. But let it be according to your will.[14]

Until recently the significance of this passage has been missed, and it has even been argued that Goldwine was sent to Scotland to support the queen in her debates with the native clergy. But Lanfranc's letter, with its allusion to a work evidently of some duration, for God and for the souls of the queen and her husband, must be related to Thurgot's statement that Margaret founded at Dunfermline, for the redemption of the king's soul and her own, a church dedicated to the Holy Trinity.[15] Christ Church or Holy Trinity of Dunfermline was, I believe, affiliated from the very beginning to Christ Church or Holy Trinity of Canterbury. It was surely to this church of Dunfermline that Saint Anselm, between 1100 and 1107, sent monks from Canterbury at King Edgar's request, afterwards asking King Alexander to protect them;[16] it was Peter, the prior of this church, whom King Alexander sent as an envoy to Canterbury to negotiate the appointment of the Christ Church monk Eadmer to the St. Andrews see;[17] it was to this church, surely, that Archbishop Ralph d'Escures referred when he asked King Alexander's favour towards the monks of Canterbury who were in Scotland;[18] finally, it was the prior of this church who between 1124 and 1128 obtained a brieve from

[14] Lawrie, *Charters*, no. 9.

[15] *Vita S. Margaretae*, pp. 238–9: 'mox in loco ubi ejus nuptiae fuerant celebratae, aeternum sui nominis et religiositatis erexit monumentum. Triplici enim salutis intentione, nobilem ibi ecclesiam in Sanctae Trinitatis aedificavit honorem; ob animae videlicet regis et suae redemptionem, atque ad obtinendam suae soboli vitae praesentis et futurae prosperitatem.' Although Thurgot does not name the place, the passage clearly refers to the church of Holy Trinity, Dunfermline.

[16] Lawrie, *Charters*, no. 25 (p. 21).

[17] Eadmer, *Historia Novorum*, ed. M. Rule (Rolls Series, 1884), p. 279. The use of the term 'prior' may itself be significant, since its introduction into England was peculiarly associated with Lanfranc (E. John, *Land Tenure in Early England* (1960), p. 109).

[18] Lawrie, *Charters*, No. 38 (p. 33).

King David I ordering the king's grieve (or thane?) of Fothrif (i.e. West Fife) to see that private subjects in that district paid their dues to Dunfermline and assisted with the building operations which had begun there.[19] When, a year or two later, King David wrote to the archbishop of Canterbury, William of Corbeil, and to the cathedral convent, asking for a monk who should become first abbot of Dunfermline, he explained that 'the first foundation of the monastery of Dunfermline took from the church of Canterbury, with the advice and assistance of monks of that church, both its way of life and the pattern of its order'.[20] This letter, which came to light and was published a few years ago, constitutes the final evidence required to confirm the hypothesis that Queen Margaret founded her church at Dunfermline as a daughter-house of Christ Church, Canterbury, and that Goldwine and his fellows formed the nucleus or advance party usual on these occasions, of what in time became a full Benedictine convent under a prior. Later still, after 1128, when Geoffrey, prior of Christ Church, Canterbury, was made first abbot of Dunfermline by David I, this house grew into the wealthiest and most renowned Benedictine abbey in Scotland.

In a short book on the Church and Nation of Scotland through sixteen centuries, which has deservedly reached a wide public, Dr. Donaldson resumes his previous disparagement of Queen Margaret, and writes that her 'programme had at the best been a limited one . . . She did nothing, apart from bringing a few Benedictine monks to Dunfermline, to foster and endow new institutions.'[21] This view, which must be respected, represents a substantial shift in the traditional emphasis. It is grounded upon an entirely healthy disposition to be critical, even sceptical, of Thurgot's hagiography. Nevertheless, though I may be alone in this, I cannot help finding the change in emphasis a little odd, and wondering whether Dr. Donaldson, in spotlighting some individual trees, has thrown the wood as a whole into darkness. It would not be entirely untrue to say of Ethelbert, the heathen king of Kent, that his programme had at the best been a limited one, and that he did nothing, apart from bringing a few Benedictine

[19] Lawrie, *Charters*, no. 85 (Lawrie's date, '*c*. 1130', is some years too late).
[20] *RRS*, i, no. 8. Cf. *SHR*, xxxi, 18–19.
[21] G. Donaldson, *Scotland: Church and Nation through sixteen centuries* (1960), 18.

monks to Canterbury, to foster and endow new institutions. But any history of England which dismissed the conversion of the southern English in this fashion would read very strangely. I remain unrepentantly of the opinion that no history of Scotland in the eleventh and twelfth centuries would be adequate if it failed to recognise that in associating Lanfranc with her reforming activity in Scotland, in introducing, under Cantuarian auspices, a wholly new kind of religious life north of the Forth, above all in inspiring in her sons, her husband's successors, a zeal and devotion towards the forms of religious life and ecclesiastical observance familiar in Norman England and on the continent. Queen Margaret was knowingly and deliberately instigating changes which for both Church and Nation were of fundamental, far-reaching significance.

Before leaving Dunfermline, a footnote on the connexions between early twelfth-century Scotland and Canterbury may not be without interest. When Eadmer, the English monk from Canterbury, the friend and biographer of Anselm, came to Scotland in 1120 as bishop-elect of St. Andrews, Dunfermline, as we have seen, was the home of a small community of Canterbury monks, some of whom must surely have been known to Eadmer personally. King Alexander I declared that Eadmer had been recommended to him by many people:[22] from whom was the king more likely to have heard these testimonials than from Eadmer's fellow-Cantuarians at Dunfermline? But it has not been noticed before that Eadmer himself gives us a clue which suggests that some at least of his uneasy months in Scotland were spent at Dunfermline. In his little tract on the miracles of Saint Anselm, Eadmer tells the following story:

When I had been transferred to Scotland to the bishopric of St. Andrews, and living there for some time had become known and acceptable to the people of the country, it happened that a certain married woman of noble English descent, named Eastrild, well-known as a staunch Christian, fell ill of a malady so grave that all who saw her were certain that she was at death's door. She had previously heard of the fame of Anselm's

[22] *Historia Novorum*, ed. Rule, 279: 'quandam personam a plerisque mihi laudatam, Edmerum scilicet monachum.'

holiness, but when I informed her of it more fully she allowed to be put round her Anselm's girdle, though by this time she would have welcomed death. As soon as this was done she began to get better, and in a few days, to everyone's astonishment, was restored to perfect health. I was present at this event and witnessed it, and I and many others rejoiced at it greatly and gave thanks to God.[23]

Now, in the early thirteenth-century obituary or necrology of Christ Church, Canterbury, which of course contains names from a much earlier period, and arranges them methodically in four columns, we find the following names.[24] In column 1 (reserved for kings and archbishops and for abbots considered important at Canterbury), Geoffrey (II), abbot of Dunfermline; in column 3 (other abbots), Patrick, abbot of Dunfermline; and in column 4 (for lay men and women), the name of Estrild of Dunfermline, 'our sister'. In the story of this forgotten, indeed virtually unknown Englishwoman of good family, we see fortuitously linked and interwoven Christ Church, Canterbury, its noble saint and archbishop Anselm, its patriotic Kentish historian Eadmer, and the two Scottish churches, Dunfermline, which thanks to Queen Margaret was the daughter-house of Canterbury, and St. Andrews, whose need for reform was the reason for Eadmer's presence in Scotland. Estrild, moreover, was not the only Englishwoman connected with Dunfermline who was remembered at Canterbury. Joined to her name in the obituary is that of Ligiva, also described as 'our sister'. It so happens that there is preserved in the Dunfermline Abbey cartulary a copy of a brieve issued by David I, the gist of which is as follows:

I command and order the good men of all my land that wherever this woman Levif may be able to discover any of her

---

[23] Ibid., 434–5; also in F. Liebermann, *Ungedruckte Anglo-Normannische Geschichtsquellen* (Strasburg, 1879), 311–12. The woman's name is given variously as Eastrildis, Aestrildis, Estryldis, and represents the O.E. personal name Eastorhild.

[24] *Scottish Historical Review*, xxxi (1952), p. 27 and n. 10, p. 28 and nn. 1 and 2.

fugitive neyfs they are to be justly restored to her, and no-one is to detain them unjustly against my prohibition.[25]

The brieve proves that Levif was a landowner, and its presence in the Dunfermline Abbey cartulary shows that her land came into the abbey's possession. The names Ligiva and Levif are twelfth-century forms of the Old English woman's name Leofgifu. It is evident that as with Estrild so with Leofgifu we are dealing with an English member of the resident aristocracy of early twelfth-century Fife, closely connected, as would be only natural, with the English Benedictines at Dunfermline and their mother-house at Canterbury.

II

The monks of Dunfermline were not the only English Benedictines active in Scotland in the early decades of the twelfth century. King Duncan II and King Edgar both made endowments to the monks of Durham cathedral priory, and it is certain that long before the formal emergence of Coldingham Priory, c. 1139, there were monks from Durham administering the priory's estates in Berwickshire. Of the Durham Benedictine Thurgot something has been said above. He was already an old man in 1109 when he was consecrated bishop of St. Andrews, and between then and his death in 1115 little is recorded of his activity.[26] When King Alexander I and Eadmer could not resolve their differences over the question of Canterbury's alleged authority in Scotland, the king gave the St. Andrews bishopric to a custodian or 'tulchan' named William, apparently a monk of the renowned abbey of Bury St. Edmunds but hardly an adornment of his order.[27] A fourth great Benedictine house of England appears fleetingly in Scottish record in 1127, when Geoffrey, abbot of St. Albans, was evidently a visitor to the

---

[25] Lawrie, *Charters*, no. 158, where 'unuscunque H. leuif' should read 'ubicunque hec Leuif'. A more accurate text of the brieve is in *Dunfermline Registrum*, no. 20.

[26] For a small but important addition to our knowledge of Thurgot's episcopate see now D. Bethell in *SHR*, xlix, 33–45.

[27] Eadmer, *Historia Novorum*, ed. Rule, 283. Apparently William, to whom I can find no other reference, had already been in charge of the bishopric after the death of Thurgot.

court of King David.[28] As far as the old 'unreformed' Benedictinism was concerned, however, it was the Canterbury-Dunfermline
link which proved most far-reaching in its effects on Scottish
monastic development. At this point it will be useful to turn from
England to France, and see how a new current of monasticism,
colder perhaps at first and more astringent, flowed in from a
region where revolutionary movements were disturbing the even
tenor of the older Benedictine life.

Twenty years after Queen Margaret's death, seven years before
Eadmer came to Scotland, the queen's youngest son David
brought to Selkirk, in the heart of the great tract of wild moorland
and pastoral valleys which he held of his brother King Alexander,
a small body of monks from the austere community which Bernard
of Poitiers had gathered round him only four years earlier at
Tiron, in the forest country of Perche north of Chartres. Tiron
was in France, not in Normandy, and at the date of the colonisation David of Scotland, though high in the favour of Henry I, was
not yet an English landowner. The Tironensians could hardly
have been brought to Tweeddale without King Henry's approval,
but it is a point worth emphasising that the earliest settlement
anywhere in Britain of any of the communities of 'reformed' Benedictines—Cistercians, Tironensians, Savignacs and others—
through which the religious life of western Europe underwent so
profound a transformation was the abbey of Selkirk in Scotland,
which fifteen years after its foundation migrated down the River
Tweed to the 'limestone heugh' (*calc hoh*, Calchou = Kelso) opposite the king's castle and town of Roxburgh. This first crossing
of the Channel by any of the 'new orders' (the term is Professor
Knowles's) is in itself a memorable fact of British monastic history.
But there is perhaps a special and additional reason why it should
be emphasised. Owing to confusion and editorial ineptitude, it has
never stood out as clearly and firmly as it should. It is true that in
the late Dr. Easson's book on *Medieval Religious Houses* we find *circa*
1113 as the date of the founding of Selkirk,[29] but the '*circa*' is
rather unhappy, and in the footnotes there is worse to follow,

[28] Lawrie, *Charters*, no. 73. Abbot Geoffrey may have been in the north to
visit Tynemouth priory, a dependency of St. Albans, but we cannot rule out
'political' motives in view of the facts related by D. Nicholl, *Thurstan archbishop
of York* (York, 1964), 96, 103, 197.
[29] Easson, *Religious Houses*, 59, 60.

alternative dates mentioned, and sources which have no independent value cheek by jowl with those which do.[30] Professor Knowles,
writing of course as the historian of English monasticism, holds, in
accord with most modern authorities, that the date 1113, which
comes from Simeon of Durham, refers to the founding of St.
Dogmael's Abbey in West Wales; he merely adds that Kelso was
'an early plantation from Tiron'.[31]

We should try to get nearer the truth of the matter, and I
believe that we can do so. Our knowledge of Selkirk's origins
depends almost exclusively on certain additions to the basic text
of Symeon of Durham's *History of the kings of England*. This is contained in a Corpus Christi, Cambridge, MS., which despite the
name Symeon of Durham, seems to have strong Hexham and
Scottish connexions.[32] The annal for 1113 is on the back of folio
122. A sign at the year-number refers the reader to a note added at
the foot of column 2 of the same folio: 'The monks of Tiron came
to the land of David king of Scotland at Selkirk and remained
there fifteen years.'[33] This note must be read in conjunction with a
second note, on folio 128 *recto*, written in the same (non-text) hand,
and connected by a virtually identical sign, referring to the annal
for 1123: 'Stephen count of Boulogne afterwards king of England
gave to Abbot Geoffrey of Savigny the manor of Tulket in the
district called Amounderness, to build an abbey for his order on
the banks of the Ribble. This was in the time of Pope Calixtus (II),
and they remained there about three years.'[34] After fifteen years

[30] Ibid. The *Scotichronicon* has no independent value for the date of twelfth-
century events, and the quoted remarks of Spottiswoode and Lawrie are not
helpful.

[31] M. D. Knowles, *The Monastic Order in England* (2nd edn., 1949), 227, n. 2.

[32] Corpus Christi College, Cambridge, MS. 139, described in M. R. James,
Descriptive Catalogue of MSS. in Corpus Christi College, Cambridge, i, pp. 317–23;
see especially p. 323. The fact that the volume belonged to the Cistercian
abbey of Sawley in the West Riding of Yorkshire has been established by
P. Hunter Blair, 'Some observations on the *Historia Regum* attributed to
Symeon of Durham', in *Celt and Saxon: studies in the early British Border*, ed.
N. Chadwick (1963), 63–118. This does not seem to me to affect the question
of Hexham and Scottish connexions.

[33] 'Monachi Tironenses in terra Dauid regis Scocie apud Seleschirche
uenerunt . . . et ibi per annos quindecim manserunt.'

[34] 'Stephanus comes Bononicensis postea rex Anglie dedit abbati Gaufrido
Sauinniensi uillam scilicet Tulket in prouintia que uocatur Agmundernes . . .
super ripam fluminis Ribble ad abbatiam construendam ordinis sui . . .
tempore Kalixti pape et ibi fere per tres annos permanserunt.'

the Tironensians, as we have seen, moved from Selkirk to Kelso. After three or four years, the Savignacs moved from Tulket to Furness. In their early years there was a close connexion between Tiron and Savigny, amounting to something like rivalry, or at least pious emulation. It is not fanciful to see this rivalry in a third footnote added to Symeon's text, again in the same handwriting as the two mentioned already. This third addition is on the foot of folio 123 *recto*, but the sign which precedes it shows that it refers back to folio 122 *verso* and the annal for 1113. It says 'the monks of Tiron came to England ten years before the monks of Savigny came to England.'[35] It should not have required exceptional editorial perspicacity to grasp the working of the annotator's mind. 'The Tironensians came to Selkirk in 1113; the Savignacs came to Tulket in 1123; *therefore* the Tironensians came ten years before the Savignacs. Q.E.D.' (*Anglia*, incidentally, is what one would expect in a MS. of this date for English-speaking Tweeddale and Teviotdale: it is not what one would expect for West Wales.) Unfortunately, Arnold, the editor of Simeon for the Rolls Series, made a muddle of these additions, and his text and notes have led all subsequent scholars astray.[36]

To sum up this lengthy but, I believe, necessary excursion. At a date after 1135 someone knowledgeable about events in the north, someone interested in and informed about the orders of Tiron and Savigny, someone who knew the correct spelling of Selkirk, added to the text of a history book probably kept either at Hexham Priory in Tynedale or at Sawley Abbey in Yorkshire, the statement that it was in the year 1113 that the Tironensian monks came to Selkirk, following it with the mild boast that they were ten years ahead of the Savignacs. This statement may be accepted as authoritative, and it may also be accepted that it has nothing whatever to do with Robert Fitz Martin's foundation at St. Dogmael's, which the best authorities assign to *circa* 1115.[37]

[35] 'Monachi Tironenses in Angliam uenerunt decem annos antequam Sauinienses uenerunt in Angliam.'

[36] *Symeonis Monachi Opera Omnia*, ed. T. Arnold (Rolls Series, 1885), ii, 247, 267. Arnold transposes the additions on fos. 122 and 123, says wrongly that the addition narrating the Tironensians' arrival at Selkirk has no reference to the date, and, on p. 267, fails to point out that the Savigny-Tulket addition is in the same handwriting as the additions relating to the Tironensians.

[37] M. D. Knowles and N. Hadcock, *Medieval Religious Houses, England and Wales* (1953), p. 102.

It is from a work composed in the middle of the twelfth century at Tiron itself—Geoffrey the Fat's *Life of Bernard of Tiron*[38]—that we have the amplified statement that 'David (chief) of the men of Lothian *and* Northampton, afterwards king of Scots, brought to himself a considerable number of monks of Tiron, and built a monastery for them on a suitable site beside the Tweed, in Lothian (which on one side touches Albany of the Scots and on the other side is joined to the borders of Northumbria). This monastery he liberally enriched with large possessions and revenues.' Geoffrey goes on to say that David journeyed to Tiron to see Saint Bernard, who, however, had died before his arrival. Later, after his accession to the Scottish throne, David again visited Tiron, knelt before Bernard's tomb, took back with him to Scotland an abbot and twelve monks, and still further enlarged the possessions of their monastery.[39]

The more one studies this passage the more one feels that Geoffrey, for all his readiness to display geographical knowledge, was indifferent to or ignorant of the exact chronology of the course of events which produced in turn the monasteries of Selkirk and Kelso. His first description of David of Scotland fits the year 1114, when David got the earldom of Northampton-Huntingdon, but not 1113. His account of David's foundation surely applies not to Selkirk but to Kelso—beside the Tweed, close to the English border. His actual language is echoed closely by yet another marginal addition to Symeon of Durham's *Historia Regum* in the Corpus Christi manuscript, which at the year 1128 says 'Selkirk Abbey was moved to Kelso beside Roxburgh, and the church of St. Mary was founded for the Tironensian monks, which the pious King David enriched with great gifts, embellished with many ornaments, and nobly endowed with large estates and possessions.'[40] The story in Geoffrey's biography of Saint Bernard is obviously correct in substance, but its failure to be correct in detail

[38] In Migne, *Patrologia Latina*, clxxii, cols. 1367–1446.
[39] Ibid., cols. 1426–7.
[40] C.C.C., MS. 139, fo. 130ᵛ. This note is not in the text-hand, but is in the same rather ugly hand as a marginal note on the Savignac house in Byland (fo. 132ᵛ) and an important gloss on King David I opposite the passage narrating his death (fo. 148ᵛ): 'Hic pius Dauid rex Scottorum et pater dulcissimus religiosorum pauperum et peregrinorum . . . sidusque angelorum Domini uisionem quam sepius optauerat adeptus est.'

makes one hesitate to accept his account of *two* visits by David to Tiron. They may have taken place: our verdict must remain 'not proven'; but it is difficult to reject the story altogether, and it seems likely that at least one visit was made. If so, the abbot brought back to Scotland by David was probably Abbot William. William went north to replace Ralph, first abbot of Selkirk, who in 1116 or 1117 had been elected by the monks of the mother-house of Tiron to succeed their founder Bernard.[41]

The history of the Tironensians in Scotland—the richest single chapter in the history of medieval Scottish monasticism—has yet to be written. By way of contribution to the materials for such a history, this chapter will conclude with a discussion of three questions which arise naturally in connexion with the Tironensians' early years in Scotland: (1) What led David to choose Tiron in preference to several other possible sources for the first monastery he founded? (2) What endowment was made to the first Tironensians? (3) What was the place of Kelso in the early history of the order of Tiron?

It is only speculation, but perhaps not wholly wild speculation, that the very remarkable man who served David as tutor and chaplain in his early days, and whom David at some date between 1114 and 1118 made bishop of Glasgow or Cumbria, was responsible for the choice of Tiron. John, Earl David's chaplain, witnessed one of his lord's earliest acts, probably in 1114,[42] and he is described in the historical preamble to the famous Inquest of David as a monk who had given David his education.[43] The Tironensians arrived at Selkirk before John could have become bishop, but Selkirk was situated in territory, previously claimed by the bishop of Durham, which now, through the direct action of David personally, found itself in the diocese of Glasgow. David may well have meant to place this territory under his new bishop's charge some time before John's formal appointment, which was made 'by the counsel of [his barons?] and with the assistance of his clergy.'[44] After David's accession Roxburgh at once became a chief centre of royal government, and the migration of the

---

[41] See above, p. 175.   [42] *RRS*, i, no. 1.

[43] Lawrie, *Charters*, no. 50: 'quendam religiosum virum qui eum educauerat.'

[44] Lawrie, *Charters*, no. 50: '. . . . consilio clericorumque suorum auxilio in episcopum elegit', where the illegible word is probably 'nobilium' or the like.

Tironensians to Kelso—which was clearly thought of as a suburb of Roxburgh[45]—may very possibly have been prompted by the same desire to have a royal monastery close to a royal burgh which put the Benedictines at Dunfermline and the Augustinians at Holyrood, Cambuskenneth and Scone. But David's great charter to Kelso expressly says that the migration was by the advice and on the urging of John, bishop of Glasgow, because Selkirk was not a convenient site for an abbey, and this at least shows that John took an active interest in the Tironensians. Some years later, in 1136, Bishop John, having persistently refused to yield to papal and other pressure to make his profession of obedience to the archbishop of York, fell into disgrace with the pope, Innocent II, and sought asylum by becoming a member of the convent of Tiron, where he stayed two years. Soon after John's recall to Scotland King David and his son Earl Henry made a direct benefaction to Tiron—Earl Henry's original charter is still extant in the archives at Chartres[46]—and in 1144, again on the advice of John, bishop of Glasgow, King David established at Lesmahagow, in the bishop's diocese, the first of Kelso's daughter-houses. Thus, three years before Bishop John of Glasgow's death, the Tironensian monks in whom he seems to have taken a more than perfunctory interest, and whose life he had shared, were brought back to his diocese in which they had originally made their first Scottish home.[47]

It is worth spending a few paragraphs discussing the early endowment of the Scottish Tironensians, because here again we have a story which our modern works of reference do not tell as fully or as clearly as they might. It is true that the extant sources cannot be made to yield a complete account of events, but far from absolving us from trying to discern the truth, it should stimulate enquiry and urge us to extract what truth we can. Our starting point must of course be the charter recording the first endowment of Selkirk

[45] 'Kelso beside Roxburgh' (see above, p. 32) was already a 'vill' before the end of David I's reign, but in 1165–71 a royal charter grants strictly limited market privileges to the abbey's tenants in Kelso, who are still for certain purposes subject to the burgh of Roxburgh and bound to use its market: *RRS*, ii, no. 64.

[46] Archives du département d'Eure-et-Loir, Chartres, Chartes de l'abbaye de Tiron, charte d'Henri, comte de Northumberland; Lawrie, *Charters*, nos. 136, 137.

[47] On the foregoing see above, pp. 175–6.

Abbey, issued by David before his accession, in the period 1114–24, probably nearer the end than the beginning of that decade.[48] Owing to the characteristic imprecision of the phrases by which the charter indicates boundaries, and also to the disappearance of a number of crucial place-names, it does not seem possible to give any exact definition of the 'land of Selkirk' which formed the principal item of endowment.[49] It is, however, clear from the name 'Selechirche' that there was or had been an ecclesiastical foundation at this place, perhaps an ancient quasi-monastic church of the same type as had evidently existed at Jedburgh.[50] In other words, the choice of Selkirk as the site for his first abbey is likely to have been due to a deliberate wish on David's part that the new monks should occupy a site which already possessed significant if decaying religious associations.

If this is so, it is all the more remarkable that the site chosen was not Melrose, where the traditions of Saint Cuthbert were still very strong. In fact, Earl David did bestow part of Melrose—'my whole demesne of Melrose'[51]—upon the Tironensians, as well as the neighbouring 'toun' of Eildon, but apparently without any thought that the ancient and venerated traditions of early Scottish

[48] Lawrie, *Charters*, no. 35. I see no grounds for supposing with Lawrie (ibid., p. 277) that the list of witnesses is 'the invention of the writer'; his alternative suggestion, that the charter is a composite record of a number of separate earlier grants, seems quite reasonable.

[49] 'As the burn descending from the hills flows into Yarrow as far as that burn which, descending from "Crossinemara", flows into Tweed, and beyond the burn which falls into Yarrow a certain parcel of land between the road which runs from the castle to the abbey on the one side and Yarrow on the other, i.e. in the direction of the old toun.' This is intelligible only on the assumption that in the twelfth century what is now called the Ettrick Water from Yarrow mouth to Tweed was called Yarrow. The first burn referred to was probably the Batts Burn in Selkirk and Galashiels and 'Crossinemara' (alias 'Crossanesmer') may have been Faldonside Loch. See *Hist. Mon. Comm.* (*Selkirk*), 7, 32; R. P. Hardie, *Roads of Mediæval Lauderdale* (1942), pp. 1–11.

[50] Anderson, *Scottish Annals*, 60, no. 8, p. 97, no. 5. The name Selkirk (Selechirche, Seleschirche) appears to contain along with O.E. *circe*, 'church', the O.E. word *sele*, 'hall', or possibly the O. Norse word *selia*, 'sallow' (i.e. scrub willow). Suggested derivations from a word cognate with German *selig*, 'holy', and even from the root *selg* of the tribal name Selgovae are more picturesque than probable.

[51] 'My whole demesne of Melrose by the middle road [*vicus*] and by the middle well as far as the ditch and as the ditch divides, falling into Tweed.' This is one of those definitions which describe a place only to those who know it already.

and Northumbrian christianity would be revived on the spot. We can only speculate on the reasons for this surprising decision. At some date in the 1070s, probably around 1075, Thurgot, in one of the earlier stages of his career as a leader in the revival of the religious life in Northumbria, had come to Old Melrose with his companion. Aldwin of Winchcombe. The place was then deserted. They refused to take an oath of fealty to the Scottish king, and their bishop, Walcher of Durham, threatened them with excommunication if they did not return to 'St Cuthbert's Land'. Within a few years they were called to a more notable and splendid task, when Bishop William of St. Calais restored the monastery at Durham (1083) and made Aldwin its first prior, an office to which Thurgot succeeded four years later. For thirty years, therefore, before David of Scotland established the Tironensians at Selkirk, Benedictine monachism had had a firm footing at Durham, for thirty years the cult of Saint Cuthbert had been cherished and extended by a series of powerful bishops and by a great cathedral monastery growing in numbers and renown. Although the Scots kings had succeeded in ousting the bishop of Durham and his dignitaries from the exercise of the authority they had formerly claimed throughout Teviotdale, they could not keep out the pervasive influence of Saint Cuthbert, whose cult was observed beyond the Forth[52] and far into Galloway.[53] They themselves were not to be outdone in reverence for the saint by Normans or Englishmen. Hence the liberal grants made to Durham first by King Duncan II and afterwards, more fruitfully, by King Edgar. It is not impossible, therefore that Earl David was at first reluctant to place the site of the old monastery of Melrose in the hands of foreign monks, when Durham's claim to it was still strong. It was not until c. 1136 that this claim was surrendered. By a charter still preserved at Durham,[54] King David granted the monks of Saint

[52] Above, p. 64, n. 280.

[53] The church and clergy of Kirkcudbright provide the most obvious example; there is another Kirkcudbright in south Ayrshire.

[54] Lawrie, *Charters*, no. 99, where the date is given as '1130–1133'. The absolute limits are 1128 and 1147, but if the original part of the Melrose 'foundation charter' (ibid., no. 141) is compared it will be seen that there are six witnesses common to both, including the rather infrequent Esmund, clerk or almoner (for whom see also *RRS*, i, no. 7). It is likely that the exchange was necessitated by the founding of Melrose Abbey and that both documents were issued at about the same time, c. 1136.

Cuthbert the church of St. Mary in Berwick 'in exchange for the church of Melrose and the rights and property they had there'. At the date of this charter, the king had either taken the first steps to bring the Cistercian monks from Rievaulx to Melrose, or had at least decided to do so. Contrary to anything that might have been expected in the early decades of the twelfth century, it was not to be the Benedictines of Durham or the 'reformed' Benedictines of Tiron who were to represent in Scotland, *par excellence*, the traditions and the cult of Saint Cuthbert, but the Cistercians of Rievaulx.

It is obvious that the establishment of a new abbey at Melrose, endowed from the beginning with 'the whole land of Melrose and the whole land of Eildon', must either have been made possible by a major rearrangement of the Tironensians' early endowments or else have precipitated such a rearrangement. The curious thing is that none of our surviving documents says anything of the Tironensian surrender either of Eildon or of their share of the old demesne at Melrose. The probability is that once they had been moved to Kelso and received a whole array of fresh and rich endowments in and around Roxburgh and Berwick, the Tironensians were prepared to sacrifice property of which they had failed, perhaps through no fault of their own, to make the most appropriate use. Nevertheless, a number of surviving documents do make it plain that King David went to great trouble to ensure that once the Cistercians were settled on land which had previously belonged to the Tironensians, there would not be dispute between the two houses. In this praiseworthy endeavour he was not entirely successful. As late as 1202 we are told that there had been a controversy for many years between Kelso and Melrose over the marches of Melrose on the one hand and Bowden, belonging to Kelso, on the other. King William, by whose decision both parties had sworn to abide, caused an inquest to be made by the 'good and ancient men of the countryside', and their verdict was formally promulgated in the king's court at Selkirk on Sunday after the close of Easter (9 May), 1204.[55] The old men's verdict speaks well for King David's conscientiousness. He had drawn the boundary between the Cistercians and the Tironensians from the ford

---

[55] *Kelso Liber*, no. 19 (= *RRS*, ii, no. 440). The two parties made a formal agreement by chirograph which received the king's confirmation before 1211 (ibid., no. 412 = *RRS*, ii, no. 493).

on the Bowden Burn in the vicinity of Whiterig across country in a north-westerly direction to the head of the Sprouston Burn and up to Eildon Mid Hill. On the summit of this hill he had had ditches dug. Below the hill on the west, he had caused a wood to be cut through to carry on the boundary, which then continued by Cauldshiels Loch and down into the Tweed between Abbotsford and Faldonside. At various points along the march there were crosses and ditches and oak trees with crosses cut in them. As far as can be judged, King David's boundary is substantially the present parish boundary between Melrose on the one side and Bowden and Galashiels on the other. The monks of Kelso had given up Eildon and Melrose apparently without a murmur: the subsequent controversy, however protracted, turned merely on the precise line of the boundary.[56]

The order of Tiron was scarcely represented in England. In Scotland, by contrast, it provided one of the best-known forms of Benedictine monachism, widely distributed across the country, at Kelso, Lesmahagow, Kilwinning, Lindores, Arbroath and Fyvie. The remarkable vigour and renown of the order in Scotland were not, I think, due to accident. For the first sixty or seventy years of the order's history the importance of its Scottish daughter-house at Kelso and her family was recognised by Tiron itself. Far from there being an early loss of contact because of the difficulties of communication, the first two abbots of Selkirk, Ralph and William, became in turn abbots of Tiron. William was abbot for many years, and only the brilliant success of the Cistercians at this period, and the over-shadowing pre-eminence of Bernard of Clairvaux, have prevented the order of Tiron and Abbot William from finding the place they deserve in twelfth-century history as exponents of 'reformed' Benedictinism. Like Cîteaux and possibly even earlier than Cîteaux, Tiron adopted a system of annual general chapters, and like Cîteaux Tiron was obliged to modify the obligation of annual attendance for abbots from distant

[56] For the boundaries in detail see *Melrose Liber*, no. 145. There is a pleasant passage on this in R. L. G. Ritchie, *The Normans in Scotland* (1954), 220–1, and the topography has been carefully investigated by E. B. Lyle, 'A Reconsideration of the Place-Names in "Thomas the Rhymer",' *Scottish Studies*, xiii, pt. 1 (1969), 65–71. For other instances of King David personally taking part in or supervising the perambulation of marches, see Lawrie, *Charters*, nos. 90, 146; *RRS*, i, no. 29.

daughter-houses. As early as 1120, only two years after he had left Selkirk, Abbot William decreed that Tironensian abbots from oversea need attend only once every three years.[57] Not only was this concession considerably earlier than similar concessions made by the Cistercians, it must surely have arisen directly out of Abbot Ralph's and Abbot William's toilsome journeys from the Forest of Selkirk to the Forest of Perche. In 1140, as we have seen, Tiron was given a small but direct stake in the Scottish economy—a grant of one ship annually free of customs duty wherever it may put in in Scottish territory and whether its men choose to fish or not. On this Sir Archibald Lawrie wrote, 'Tiron is a quiet inland monastery in rural France, far from the sea . . . and this seems a privilege of which the monks would never have the opportunity of getting any advantage.'[58] But the abbey did not regard the grant as negligible or derisory: they persuaded King Malcolm IV to commute it into an annual grant of three merks from the customs of Perth.[59] Over a century later, in 1267, King Alexander III told his provosts of Perth to pay these three merks to Kelso Abbey as proctors for Tiron, and even as late as 1302 John de Soules, guardian of Scotland on behalf of John Balliol, commanded the sheriff and bailies of Perth to make up two years' arrears of this annual payment.[60]

Unfortunately, neither Kelso nor Tiron seems ever to have produced a chronicler. One of the last, yet in some ways the most significant of all pieces of evidence on the connexion maintained between the two abbeys comes in the form of a laconic statement in the *Chronicle of Melrose* that in 1176 a dispute arose between Walter abbot of Tiron and John abbot of Kelso over the matter of subjection, and as to which of them should take precedence of the other.[61] The outcome of the quarrel is not known, but coupled with the fact that Abbot John won the privilege of the mitre from Pope Alexander III in 1165,[62] the Melrose annal shows that John, who ruled over Kelso for twenty years, was ambitious for the honour and position of himself and his house within a Tironensian

[57] J. H. Round, *Calendar of Documents in France*, no. 997.
[58] Lawrie, *Charters*, no. 136 and p. 372.   [59] *RRS*, i, no. 223.
[60] *Kelso Liber*, nos. 398, 397.
[61] *Chron. Melrose*, 41: 'Facta est contentio inter Walterum abbatem Tironensem et Johannem Kalcoensem de subieccione, quis eorum videretur esse maior.'
[62] *Chron. Melrose*, 37.

'order' which was still intact. As for their place in Scotland, the Tironensians' record in the twelfth century speaks for itself. Of the early abbots of Kelso, Herbert became bishop of Glasgow, and Arnold, though he survived for only two years after his consecration, was the first bishop of St. Andrews to be made papal legate in Scotland and the founder of the great medieval cathedral church at St. Andrews. In 1152, when King David's son Earl Henry, 'king-designate' of Scotland, died, it was to Kelso, not Dunfermline, that his body was taken for burial. Two out of the three most notable monastic foundations of the Scottish royal family in the second half of the twelfth century—St. Andrew of Lindores and St. Thomas the Martyr of Arbroath—were daughter-houses of Kelso, and so was Kilwinning Abbey in Cunningham, founded by a private subject, Hugh de Morville the constable, who was very closely connected to the royal house. To match their institutional distinction and prominence, the Scottish Tironensians made use of an architecture of 'powerful simplicity' which has made a rich contribution to Scotland's modest repertory of early medieval building.[63] It would be no exaggeration to say that although the Tironensians' way of life became more and more closely assimilated to the ordinary practice of the black monk houses, they gave a distinctive character to Benedictine monachism in twelfth-century Scotland, something which was not quite the way of the Cistercians nor yet the way of the black monks, possessing features of both yet informed by their own individual tradition.

It is dangerously easy for the historian to impose on the past a pattern which did not exist when the past was still the present. At this remove of time we can see that one of the recurrent rhythms in Scottish history has been the alternate reception of influences, ideas, and culture now from the west, now from the east. The Scottish kingdom of the 'high middle ages' had turned its back, as it were, on its immediate, western, Celtic past; it was emphatically an eastward-looking North Sea country, entering into the closest

[63] Stewart Cruden, *Scottish Abbeys* (1960), p. 59: 'The architecture of the four great Tironensian abbeys is characterised by a powerful simplicity. The basic forms of arch and pier, wall, window and buttress, are handled with a sure and bold sense of scale, which, as a common characteristic of a group, is altogether exceptional. As far as one may judge from a heritage of architecture which is largely ruinous one may justly acknowledge a Tironensian style.'

relations with the other lands round that sea, Norway, Germany, Holland, and more especially Flanders, France and England. In one sense, the introduction into Scotland of new forms of religious life between 1070 and 1153 was but part of a general re-orientation of the country. This was one of those profound changes which no individual or group of individuals could produce or control—a tide in the affairs not of men but of peoples. But the particular character assumed by the ecclesiastical changes in Scotland, the choice of one model rather than another, was due to the deliberate decisions of a few individuals, almost exclusively members of the royal house, Queen Margaret, Edgar, Alexander I, David I, Henry the 'king-designate'. We miss the significance of this remarkable development if we do not see it as a whole, if we fail to grasp the unity of purpose which inspired it. 'He illumined in his days', wrote Andrew Wyntoun of David I in a famous couplet, 'his land with kirks and with abbays.' But this illumination, complete as it might seem by the middle of the twelfth century, had been no sudden flood of light. It was a steady diffusion from the moment when through the agency of Queen Margaret and with the encouragement of Lanfranc the first small community of Benedictine monks was successfully established upon Scottish soil.

7 The clergy at St. Andrews

It has long been a commonplace of Scottish ecclesiastical history that the culdees or *célidé*[1] at St. Andrews, who held a place in the cathedral church in the earlier part of the twelfth century, survived for a further two hundred years. The most authoritative statement of this belief is still to be found in the work of Dr. William Reeves (later Bishop of Down), whose paper on 'The Culdees of the British Islands' was read to the Royal Irish Academy at Dublin in 1860, and published there as a book in 1864.[2] Reeves's paper discussed very fully the origins and later history of the culdees in the British Isles, especially in Ireland and Scotland; and it is of some interest to recall that since the author was a vicar-choral of Armagh cathedral he belonged to a corporation which could claim to have directly represented, since the seventeenth century, the older body of culdees attached to the mother church of St. Patrick.[3]

Reeves's account of the St. Andrews *célidé* may conveniently be prefaced by a brief notice of the establishment of the cathedral chapter there in the twelfth century. An Augustinian canon, Robert, had been consecrated bishop, probably in 1127;[4] and the Augustinian priory was founded at St. Andrews in 1144, its canons forming from the outset the chapter of the cathedral. At this period, as, indeed, for some centuries before,[5] there was a

[1] 'Culdee', although still a more familiar spelling, is historically and linguistically indefensible and the more correct *célidé* is preferred here. In Scottish medieval records the usual form is *kel(l)edeus*, and its cases.

[2] In 1863, a paper by David Laing was published in *PSAS*, 76–86, entitled 'Historical Notices of the Provostry of Kirkheugh', covering, with regard to St. Andrews, some of the same ground as Reeves, and reaching some of the same conclusions. Laing noted, correctly, that the *célidé* community had become a collegiate church by the reign of Alexander II (1214–49); ibid., 79.

[3] Reeves, op. cit., 12–19.

[4] Dowden, *Bishops*, 5; cf. *Chron. Holyrood*, 132–3, n. 7.

[5] The St. Andrews *célidé* are first mentioned in records relating to the year 943; Anderson, *Early Sources*, i, 447; *Chron. Picts–Scots*, 151.

body of *célidé* attached to the church of St. Andrew. When the bishop, assisted by king David I, instituted his chapter of regulars, it was intended that the older community should be absorbed by them. The existing *célidé* had the option of becoming regular canons themselves or of keeping their prebends for life. Ultimately, however, each place in the church formerly held by a *céledé* was to be filled by a regular canon, the purpose being, as king David's writ put it, 'that all the estates and all the lands and alms which the *célidé* have shall be converted to the use of the canons'.[6]

Here we may take up Reeves's account of the situation at St. Andrews in 1144:[7]

'There were now two rival ecclesiastical bodies in existence at St. Andrews—one the old corporation of secular priests, who were completely thrown into the shade, and shorn of many of their privileges and possessions; and the other, that of the regular canons, who virtually represented the secularized portion[8] of the old institution, and entered into the enjoyment of their estates.'

Reeves then describes king David's provision, backed by a similar one from the pope, that regular canons should eventually replace the culdees, and continues:

'But the Keledei were able to withstand the combined efforts of king, pope, and bishop; for we meet with a recurrence of this provision under successive pontiffs until 1248; and yet we find the Keledei holding their ground. Nay, in 1160, King Malcolm actually confirmed them in a portion of their estates. In 1199 we find them engaged in a controversy with the prior of the other society, which terminated in a compromise by which the tithes of their own lands were secured to them, they at the same time quitting claim to all parochial fees and oblations. . . . And it was not until 1273 that they were debarred from the prescriptive right to take part in the election of a bishop. They met with like treatment in 1279, and again in 1297, when William Comyn, provost of the Keledei, went to Rome and lodged a protest against the election then made, on the ground of their exclusion; but Boniface VIII decided against him. In 1309 the Keledei were still in possession of their lands in the Cursus Apri. In 1332, when

---

[6] Lawrie, *Charters*, 188, no. 233.   [7] Reeves, op. cit., 39–41.

[8] I.e., the *personae* of the church who had become secularised. They were distinct from the *célidé*.

William Bell was chosen bishop, they were absolutely excluded from taking any part in the election, and the claim does not appear to have been ever after revived. Nor does the name Keledei occur again in existing records, although the corporation still continued in the enjoyment of their privileges and possessions.'

In the same year as Reeves's work was published there appeared Father Augustin Theiner's great collection of papal letters and other documents relating to Ireland and Scotland, taken from the Vatican archives.[9] Among these were several documents which threw a good deal of light on the continued existence of the *célidé* at St. Andrews throughout the thirteenth century. The work of Reeves and Theiner has formed the essential basis of all subsequent discussion of the subject. William Skene, for example, drew largely on both works for his account of St. Andrews in his *Celtic Scotland*, first published in 1877. After summarising some of the relevant documents printed by Theiner, he wrote,[10] 'It is evident from these deeds that the Keledei asserted their claim to be considered as canons, and did not submit without a struggle to be deprived of the right of participating in the election of a bishop, from which they were finally excluded in the year 1273.'

A similar belief in this culdean struggle for survival was expressed by bishop Dowden, in his introduction to the Inchaffray Abbey Charters,[11] where he says:

'The stronger Celtic communities, as, for example, the Keledei of St. Andrews, continued, though with ever diminishing power, to survive for many years side by side with the newly established communities destined eventually to absorb them . . . The claim of the Keledei to have a voice in the election of the Bishops of St. Andrews, which continued to be made for over a century, is another piece of evidence contributing to the conviction that the Keledei of St. Andrews formed a community of considerable vigour and purpose.'

The late Dr. Hay Fleming, whose sympathies scarcely lay with the medieval Church, found his imagination captured by the notion of a handful of conservative Celts, obstinately and success-

---

[9] *Vetera monumenta Hibernorum et Scotorum historiam illustrantia*, etc., Rome 1864, referred to henceforth as *Vet. Mon.*
[10] Op. cit., ii, 387.   [11] *Inchaffray Chrs.*, pp. xxv and liii–iv.

fully resisting an ecclesiastical revolution. In his excellent *Handbook to St. Andrews*[12] we have this account of the *célidé*:

'For nearly a century [i.e. from *circa* 1150], however, the representatives of the Celtic clergy continued to take part in the election of the Bishop; and for nearly another century declined to give up this prescriptive right at the bidding of Bishop, Pope or King. By the middle of the thirteenth century this Culdean establishment was presided over by a Provost, and so may be regarded as one of the earliest Provostries, or Collegiate churches, in the kingdom, and before the end of that century it was a Chapel Royal.'

The conclusion to which these passages all point seems broadly to have been accepted by modern scholars.[13] And, indeed, it is undeniable that we continue to hear of *célidé* at St. Andrews in records until 1332. Yet, in the light of what can be learned of the origins and policy of the bishops of St. Andrews in the late twelfth and early thirteenth centuries, it would be remarkable if the Celtic clergy should have endured at St. Andrews, the ecclesiastical centre of the Scottish kingdom, even as late as the early thirteenth century, and still more remarkable that they should have clung to their position until 1332 or later in defiance of 'bishop, pope, and king'. Moreover, apart from the intrinsic improbability of such a survival, several pieces of documentary evidence from the thirteenth century should lead us seriously to question the accepted view, and should stimulate a careful re-examination of all the available evidence in order to get at the truth of what happened to the St. Andrews *célidé* during the twelfth and thirteenth centuries.

In the first place, we learn from a papal letter of 27 April 1217,[14] that on some occasion between 1202 and 1216 the bishop of St. Andrews, William Malvoisin, absolved the *célidé* of St. Andrews from the sentence of excommunication passed against them, at

[12] I have used the edition of 1927, in which the passage quoted appears on p. 87.

[13] See, e.g. D. E. Easson, 'Foundation Charter of the Collegiate Church of Dunbar A.D. 1342', in *SHS Miscellany*, vi (1939), 81, and n. 1. 'In 1342, at least one collegiate church—St. Mary's-on-the-Rock, St. Andrews—was already in being; the "Culdee" community, in self-defence, had adopted the form of a secular college c. 1250.' Cf. J. A. Duke, *History of the Church of Scotland* (1937), 87; W. D. Simpson, *The Celtic Church in Scotland* (1935), 116; and the Ordnance Survey *Map of Monastic Britain* (1950; North Sheet, Introduction, 5).

[14] *Vet. Mon.*, no. 6.

the instance of the prior and chapter of the cathedral, by papal judges-delegate. Then again, on 7 August 1220,[15] Honorius III commissioned his legate in Scotland, Master James,[16] to settle the case between the prior and convent of St. Andrews on the one side, and, on the other, bishop Malvoisin; 'certain clergy of St. Andrews commonly called *célidé*';[17] Master H[ugh] of Milbourne, Master Adam Ovidius, Master Adam of Scone; and the clerks Henry of Weles and Roger of Huntingfield; together with certain others.[18] The dispute concerned a wide variety of matters in which the prior and canons complained that they had suffered injuries at the hands of their opponents. Chief among these disputed matters they listed churches, possessions, pensions and other rents, liberties, estates, and prebendal lands.

Thus in the second decade of the thirteenth century, we find that the *célidé*, instead of defying their bishop, were first protected by him, and then closely associated with him and two of the most prominent members of his *familia*.[19] Moreover, far from defying

[15] *Vet. Mon.*, no. 37. Evidently the case had, at least in part, been committed previously to the abbot of Melrose. The bishop, his clerks, and the steward, of St. Andrews had been freed from his jurisdiction in the case by a letter dated Viterbo, 4 March 1220 (NLS, MS. Adv. 15.1.19, no. vi; *St. Andrews Liber*, pp. xlii–xliii).

[16] For the legation of Master James, canon of St. Victor, cf. *Vet. Mon.*, no. 35 and *Chron. Melrose*, 72, 75.

[17] *Quosdam clericos de S. Andrea, qui Keledei vulgariter appellantur.*

[18] These included the bishop and archdeacon of Dunblane and Hugh of Nydie, who may have been the bishop of St. Andrews' steward.

[19] Master Hugh of Milbourne, with whom we may safely identify the Master 'H. de Meleburne' of *Vet. Mon.*, no. 37, appears often as a member of the episcopal *familia* in the time of Bishop Malvoisin and his successor David Bernham. See, e.g. *St. Andrews Liber*, 156–7, 160–1, 163–8, 281, 306; *Dunfermline Registrum*, no. 119. His surname may have been from Milbourne in Ponteland, Northumberland.

Master Adam Ovidius was also a prominent clerk of Bishop Malvoisin's *familia* (*Arbroath Liber*, i, nos. 153–9, 161–7; *St. Andrews Liber*, 266, 316). He had some interest in Hobkirk church in the diocese of Glasgow (*Glasgow Registrum*, no. 114), of which see Malvoisin had been bishop from 1200 to 1202.

Master Adam of Scone was a royal chaplain (*Arbroath Liber*, i, no. 136) and possibly a canon of Dunkeld (*St. Andrews Liber*, 296).

Master Henry de Welles, 'scholar of Oxford', occurs in record of Lincoln diocese, associated with Bishop Hugh de Welles, in 1228 (*Rotuli Hugonis de Welles* (Canterbury and York Society, 1907–9), ii, 145).

Roger of Huntingfield, presumably a member of the English baronial family of that name, was incumbent of Lathrisk, Fife, to which he would have been presented by the family of de Quinci (*St. Andrews Liber*, 156, 336; *Rot. Litt.*

the pope, the culdees obtained a confirmation of their possessions from Innocent IV, who, in August 1249,[20] placed under papal protection the 'provost and chapter of St. Mary of St. Andrews'. It will be seen shortly that it was the *célidé* who were described by this new corporate designation. As to their acting in defiance of the king, the thirteenth-century evidence points to exactly the opposite being the case. On 20 July 1255,[21] Pope Alexander IV sent a letter to the prior and chapter of St. Andrews, in which he declared that no prejudice should arise to them or their church in their right, on account of the fact that [in 1239] at the election of David [Bernham, the king's chamberlain], and again [in 1255] at the postulation of Master Gamelin [the king's chancellor], as bishops of St. Andrews, two of the *célidé* of the church of St. Mary of Kilrymont[22] of the city of St. Andrews, 'who call themselves canons',[23] were admitted to the proceedings at the instance of, respectively, king Alexander II and king Alexander III. On two occasions, that is to say, during the century, it was the king who compelled the reluctant and, indeed, protesting canons to admit certain *célidé* to ceremonies at which what was doubtless the king's choice of prominent civil servants for the St. Andrews see was formally approved.

So far the evidence does not readily fit in with any notion of the Celtic culdean community 'surviving' at St. Andrews in opposition to any authority except the prior and canons of the cathedral. There is at least one further document which seems to make such a notion altogether untenable. We have the record,[24]

Claus., i, 110b); he died, incumbent of Keyston in Huntingdonshire, before 1255–6 (*Rotuli Roberti Grosseteste* (Canterbury and York Soc., 1913), 511.

[20] Papal registers are missing for 1249; but this privilege is contained in a declaration by an auditor at the *curia*, a copy of which is NLS, MS. Adv. 15.1.18, no. 32, printed by Reeves, op. cit., Appendix M 16. The privilege was dated Lyons, 21 August, seventh pontifical year of Innocent IV (i.e. 1249).

[21] *Vet. Mon.*, no. 177.

[22] In Theiner's text, as also in La Roncière, *Les Régistres d'Alexandre IV*, i, 185, no. 608, the name is spelt *Kiltemont*. Kilrymont (*Kilrimund, Kilrimuned*, etc.), was the old name of the site of the church dedicated to St. Andrew. It is interesting to find it used as late as 1255 in connexion with the *célidé* whose church of St. Mary may have stood nearer the site of the older, pre-twelfth-century church than did either of those built for the Augustinian canons.

[23] *Qui se canonicos nominant.*

[24] NLS, MS. Adv. 15.1.18, no. 30. The best and most accessible printed text is in Reeves, op. cit., Appendix M 15, which, however, is not entirely free from errors.

luckily preserved among Sir James Balfour of Denmylne's collections in the National Library of Scotland, of a formal monition and appointing by papal judges-delegate of a day for hearing the case brought by the prior and convent of St. Andrews against the *célidé*, dated 7 November 1250.[25] In this are given the names of seven *célidé* of the church of St. Mary of the city of St. Andrews who, it is said in the document, were 'acting as canons'. These seven evidently did not comprise the entire community, since the dispute was also concerned with 'every other *céledé* acting as a canon' and included the vicars who, it seems, performed the *opus dei* for the *célidé* in their church of St. Mary.

We have some evidence for the status and careers of five of the *célidé* whose names are given. The first, Master Adam Makerston,[26] 'acting as provost', was one of the most prominent thirteenth-century Scottish clergymen not to hold episcopal office. A graduate either of Paris or Oxford,[27] he was associated with bishop Bernham in 1240 and at various later dates,[28] evidently as a member of his *familia*. In 1253 we find him exercising a kind of 'voluntary jurisdiction' on behalf of a well-known Fife laird, and in 1259 and 1260 he appears as the bishop of St. Andrews' Official.[29] In the previous year he had been one of the two envoys sent by king Alexander to negotiate with the king of England.[30] In 1263 he was appointed a papal chaplain,[31] and at the time of the collection of the papal tenth in 1275–6 we hear of his paying a certain sum 'for all his churches'.[32]

Richard Weyrement,[33] the next *céledé* to be named, was also a

[25] The morrow of St. Leonard.
[26] Magister Adam de Malkarwistun. The name appears variously as Malcarueston, Malcaruistun, etc., and represents the present-day Roxburghshire village of Makerston.
[27] Cf. 'Letters of a Scottish Student at Paris and Oxford', ed. N. R. Ker and W. A. Pantin, in *Oxford Formularies*, ii (ed. H. E. Salter, W. A. Pantin and H. G. Richardson, Oxford Historical Society, 1942), 485, no. 9. Adam of Makerston (here Malcalstratn') may have studied at both Paris and Oxford.
[28] *St. Andrews Liber*, 168, 169, 281.
[29] *Lindores Chartulary*, nos. 64 and 110 respectively. Cf. also SRO, GD 241/381/1.
[30] *Cal. Docs. Scot.*, i, nos. 2126–7.   [31] *Cal. Papal Letters*, i, 391.
[32] A. I. Dunlop, 'Bagimond's Roll: a statement of the Tenths of the kingdom of Scotland', *SHS Misc.*, vi (1939), 36, 65.
[33] In Reeves' text the name is given as Weytement. The correct reading is as given above.

fairly prominent figure in his day. When David Bernham was elected bishop of St. Andrews in 1239 at a ceremony at which, as we have seen, two of the *célidé* participated, the news of the election was sent to the pope by three proctors of the cathedral chapter. Two of these, who were canons-regular of the priory, failed to reach Rome, one dying on the journey, the other falling seriously ill. The third proctor, who reached the *curia* successfully, was Master Richard Vairement, described at the time as a 'secular canon'.[34] Six years later (13 September 1245), at the request of the Queen of Scots, Master Richard Veirement, her chancellor, and parson of Tannadyce,[35] was dispensed to hold an additional benefice with cure of souls.[36] In May 1251, as we learn from a papal letter dated 7 June of that year, Master Richard Verment, a *céledé*, was the defendant in a case heard at the papal *curia*.[37] The appellants were the prior and chapter of St. Andrews. They claimed that a vacant culdean prebend ought, in accordance with privileges issued by eight popes, from Lucius II[38] to Honorius III, to have passed to them; instead, it had been wrongfully obtained by Master Richard. The defendant did not wish to contest the case against the canons, from whom, he said, he had received many favours.[39] He resigned the prebend into the hands of the judge,[40] who awarded it to the canons. This is not the last occasion on which we hear of Richard Vairement in record, for

[34] *Vet. Mon.*, no. 100.

[35] This church had been granted to the canons of St. Andrews priory by Richard de Malluvel (=Melville?) before 1187 (*St. Andrews Liber*, 64, 152, 231).

[36] *Cal. Papal Letters*, i, 220.

[37] *Vet. Mon.*, no. 145. The identity of Richard Weyrement in the list of *célidé* with Master Richard Verment is made clear, ibid., p. 54, col. 2.

[38] Although the priory had received privileges from all the popes named, there is no extant bull of Lucius II which mentions the *célidé*, the earliest to do so being one of Eugenius III, 1147.

[39] As we have seen, in 1245 he was parson of a church belonging to the priory.

[40] This was the English cardinal-priest John of Toledo (of St. Laurence in Lucina); cf. A. Chacon, *Vitae . . . Pontificum, etc.* (edn. of 1677), ii, cols. 118–19. It is tempting to identify the cardinal's chaplain, Richard, an Englishman, who was provided to the see of the Isles (Sodor) in 1253 and was a canon of St. Andrews, with Richard de Noffertuno (of Nafferton?) who acted in the case referred to above as the priory of St. Andrews' proctor; and also with Richard, canon of St. Andrews, who acted as the priory's proctor in 1252 or 1253 (*St. Andrews Liber*, 26; *Vet. Mon.*, no. 145; Dowden, *Bishops*, 278).

there are references to him in the diocese of St. Andrews in 1265 and in 1267.[41]

William Wishart, whose name appears after Vairement's, had a rather more amply documented career. Like Makerston, Master William Wishart was probably a graduate of Paris or Oxford or both.[42] From 1254 to 1271 he was archdeacon of St. Andrews,[43] and chancellor of the kingdom for very nearly the same period. In 1273 he became bishop of St. Andrews, and died in 1279.

The other two *célidé* of 1250 about whom we have any knowledge were Robert de Insula and Patrick of Muckhart (Patricius de Muchard). The former we find associated with bishop Malvoisin, probably as one of his clerks, *c.* 1230, and also, as a clerk of bishop Bernham, in 1246.[44] Patrick of Muckhart seems also to have been an episcopal clerk; at least, a person called 'Sir P. de Mukard' witnessed as a clerk of bishop Bernham two strictly contemporary documents of *c.* 1245.[45] And although there does not appear to be any further evidence regarding the other two *célidé* whose names are given, Michael Black (*Niger*) and Michael Reid (*Ruffus*), it is probable that their status was similar to that of their fellows.

Thus we find the *célidé* in 1250 forming a small collegiate church, whose membership comprised a provost and more than six canons, together with the vicars who celebrated divine office on their behalf. The provost was a clergyman of considerable note, a prominent member of the bishop of St. Andrews' household and a trusted servant of the king. Four of the canons were episcopal or royal clerks, two of them being persons of some importance in contemporary Scotland.[46] It is hard to see in what

[41] *Arbroath Liber*, i, pp. 187, 269; *St. Andrews Liber*, 312–13, respectively.

[42] *Oxford Formularies*, ii, 485–6, 489–90, nos. 7, 11, 18.

[43] *Cal. Papal Letters*, i, 296; *St. Andrews Liber*, p. xliii, no. 12; Dowden, *Bishops*, 306.

[44] *St. Andrews Liber*, 157, 169 respectively. An unprinted charter of Bishop Bernham (SRO, 'Black Book of St. Andrews', fo. 35) was also witnessed by Robert de Insula.

[45] *St. Andrews Liber*, 281; *The Study of Medieval Records: essays in honour of Kathleen Major*, ed. D. A. Bullough and R. L. Storey (Oxford, 1971), 129–30. Muckhart was a living in the collation of the bishop of St. Andrews (*Cal. Papal Letters*, i, 30).

[46] Skene thought it possible that Richard Vairement was the author of a fabulous history of Scotland included in the lost Great Register of St. Andrews Priory, and that he was the 'Veremondus' or 'Veremond' cited as an authority

sense these influential churchmen can be regarded as 'representatives of the Celtic clergy', nor does their church seem
obviously to be a survival from the twelfth and earlier centuries.
Yet survival in some sense there must have been. Evidence for
it can be adduced from a number of sources. For example, we
have preserved in a notarial transumpt of the fifteenth century a
copy of a charter by which Master Adam Makerston, the provost,
and the chapter of the Blessed Mary of the city of St. Andrews
feued out to John, son of William Lambin's son,[47] the whole land
of Lethin with Kyninnis (the present-day Lambieletham, south
of St. Andrews). Now the culdees had been given Lethin (in
exchange for part of Strathkinness) as early as *c*. 1160,[48] and they
were said to be holding Lethin with Kininnis at various dates
between then and the period 1189–98, and again in 1199.[49]

Again, according to the *Book of Assumptions* of the sixteenth
century, the provostry of St. Mary's (or, as it was known in later
medieval times, the 'Lady College Kirk') was said to hold the
lands of Kinkell,[50] which we know the *célidé* held in the period
1172–8,[51] as well as in 1199.[52] And George Martine of Claremont,
who wrote his *Reliquiae Divi Andreae* in the latter part of the
seventeenth century, says that the prebends of the Lady College
at the end of the sixteenth century included those of Cameron
and Cairns, and Kinglassie and Kingask,[53] which plainly represent the twelfth-century culdean holdings (as preserved in the St.
Andrews Priory Register) of Cambrun, Kernes, Kilglassin, and
Kingask.[54]

by Hector Boece and David Chambers of Ormont in the sixteenth century;
Chron. Fordun, i, pp. xxxviii et seq. and n. 1. There does not seem to be any
evidence to decide the point.
  [47] *Laing Chrs.*, no. 15. In the twelfth century Lambin had been a burgess of
St. Andrews (SRO, 'Black Book of St. Andrews', fo. 35). His son William
floruit c. 1190–1220 (*St. Andrews Liber*, 45, 268, 316). A person called H(ugh)
Lambin was apparently a particular friend of Master Adam of Makerston
(*Oxford Formularies*, ii, 485, 489, nos. 9 and 17).
  [48] *St. Andrews Liber*, 203.   [49] Ibid., 131, 143, 145, 150, 318.
  [50] George Martine, *Reliquiae Divi Andreae* (see below, n. 53), 217, citing the
Book of Assumptions of Thirds of Benefices of 1561.
  [51] *The Study of Medieval Records* (ed. Bullough and Storey), 119.
  [52] *St. Andrews Liber*, 318.
  [53] Op. cit., 216, 217. This work was dedicated in 1683 to Archbishop
Burnet. The first printed edition was published at St. Andrews in 1797.
  [54] *St. Andrews Liber*, 318.

But by far the most striking evidence of continuity between the mid-twelfth century and the early part of the fourteenth has always been the fact that the term 'the *célidé*', in one or other of its contemporary forms,[55] was used throughout the period to describe apparently one body of clergy.[56] Our only account of the St. Andrews culdees *c.* 1144[57] describes them as a community of thirteen, holding office hereditarily.[58] Though they held a place in the church of St. Andrew, they did not serve its chief altar, that of the Apostle. Following their custom, they celebrated divine office 'in a certain corner of the church',[59] presumably at a side altar. These *célidé* held their prebends individually; they were also supported by personal offerings, and held only their poorer property in common. From the acts providing for their replacement by regular canons it seems that they were broadly equated by the reformers with those bodies of secular canons which in the first half of the twelfth century were being very widely replaced by Augustinians.[60]

Yet although this equation might be made in 1150, it is a far cry from Gillecrist the abbot and the hereditary *célidé* of Kilrymont in the twelfth century,[61] to Master Adam Makerston the provost and the prebendaries of the collegiate church of St. Mary of Kilrymont of the city of St. Andrews in 1250. The foregoing evidence, in short, presents us at first glance with a serious conflict. In the twelfth century, the *célidé*, a community whose name, character, and personnel bear witness to its origin in the older, Celtic church, were regarded as old-fashioned and un-

[55] See above, p. 212, n. 1. *Calledei* is sometimes a variant in papal documents.

[56] *Vet. Mon.*, passim; *St. Andrews Liber*, pp. xxxi–xxxii (1309); *Chron. Bower*, i, 360–3 (1271–1332).

[57] This is to be found in B.M., MS. Harl. 4628, fos. 240ff., taken from the lost Great Register of St. Andrews Priory. I have used Skene's edition (*Chron. Picts–Scots*, 183–93), but in some respects the partial edition of Reeves (*Culdees*, Appendix M 2) is more accurate and satisfactory. The title used by Skene, 'Legend of St. Andrew', and his date for its composition, '1279', obscure the fact that the last part of the account is a *Historia Fundationis* of St. Andrews Priory written, probably by a canon of the house, before 1153.

[58] *Chron. Picts–Scots*, 188: 'Habebantur tamen in ecclesia Sancti Andreae, quota et quanta tunc erat, tredecim per successionem carnalem, quos Keledeos appellant . . .'

[59] *Chron. Picts–Scots*, 190.

[60] See, e.g. Dugdale, *Mon. Angl.* (New), vi, Part I, p. 305, No. VII; *Gallia Christiana*, vol. xi (Paris, 1874), *Instrumenta*, col. 238, no. XI.

[61] For Abbot Gillecrist, see below.

becoming to the principal church in the kingdom, and provision was made for their replacement by Austin canons. But a hundred years later the *célidé* were still at St. Andrews, though no longer in the cathedral church. Far from being either Celtic or old-fashioned, they formed a small college of highly-placed secular clerks closely connected with the bishop and the king.

This is a conflict which is not resolved by positing an exceptionally tenacious conservatism on the part of the *célidé*, or even by Dr. Easson's explanation, quoted above, that the *célidé* had taken the form of a secular college 'in self-defence'; or that they had merely 'conformed to Roman ways'.[62] Yet despite the paucity of the evidence, which makes it impossible to pronounce with certainty, it is, I think, possible to suggest a reasonable solution of the problem. The validity of this solution depends partly on the documents already cited, together with what is known of the policy of the bishops of St. Andrews, Roger de Beaumont (1198–1202) and William Malvoisin (1202–38), and also of what was happening in their time at a number of other cathedral churches in England and Ireland where there were chapters of regular clergy.

Put briefly, the hypothesis is that either bishop Beaumont or bishop Malvoisin, or possibly both working successively towards the same end, and no doubt with the compliance of the king, effectively converted the old culdean community, with its lands and revenues intact, into a secular collegiate foundation, separate from the cathedral priory; and that they did this chiefly if not entirely by collating the prebends of this church to clerks of their own *familiae*, or to clerks for whom the king may have wished provision to be made.

This conversion need not have been effected by a single drastic act of expropriation. By the close of the twelfth century it is quite possible that a number of the culdean prebends had become vacant through the death of their incumbents, and had not been filled up in the manner (whatever it was) in which they had been accustomed to be filled in earlier times. The Celtic *célidé* were evidently still a legally recognised body in the period 1172–8, when their abbot, Gillecrist, feued out certain lands to the bishop's

[62] Above, p. 215, n. 13; *The Society of Friends of Dunblane Cathedral, Annual Report*, 1941, 134.

steward.[63] The abbot of the *célidé*, this time unnamed, occurs again
in record of the following decade.[64] We next hear of an individual
céledé in the period 1200–9, when 'Johannes Keledeus' witnessed
an agreement between the priory of St. Andrews and a tenant
with the highly Celtic name of Gellin, son of Gillecrist mac
Cussegerri.[65] The order of names in the testing clauses of early
thirteenth-century charters is not usually haphazard, though
it would be wrong to put too much weight on evidence of this
sort. But it is perhaps significant that the name of John the *céledé*
appears among the laymen. He was no doubt a member of the
older Celtic community, and if he was regarded as being a
clergyman his status as such was not thought very prominent.

Rather earlier than this, however, we have the record of an
agreement which may be assigned to the years 1198–9,[66] between
the prior and convent of St. Andrews and the *célidé*. This agreement seems to have an important bearing on our enquiry, and
deserves describing in some detail. By it the canons granted the
célidé the right to all teinds in the latter's lands, which lay south
and east of St. Andrews, but all parochial revenues, that is from
marriages, purifications, oblations, baptisms, and burials, were
to be retained by the canons. For their part, the *célidé* surrendered
the lands of Strathtyrum, west of St. Andrews, but were allowed
to keep the obventions of Kinglassie, again save for the character-
istically parochial dues from baptisms and burials. What the
agreement did was to consolidate the culdean holdings in a fairly
compact block of land, give them a secure and, be it noted, an
ecclesiastical, income, and deprive them of any parochial status.
That this agreement was regarded as being of more than transitory
importance seems plain. It was to be confirmed by the king and
by bishop Beaumont. It was authenticated by the seals of the prior
and convent for their own part and, and this seems significant, of

---

[63] *The Study of Medieval Records* (ed. Bullough and Storey), 119.
[64] *St. Andrews Liber*, 353 (*c.* 1180–8).
[65] Ibid., 329. Gellin seems to have been connected with the old church of
St. Andrews, since the canons gave him the right to bear the *Morbrac* (a
reliquary?) as his predecessor had done before.
[66] *St. Andrews Liber*, 318–19. It dates in the time of Prior Gilbert, the years of
whose priorate are uncertain. If we read *xxxiv* for *xxiv* in Book VI, cap. 50 of
Scotichronicon (*Chron. Bower*, i, 367) we might take it that Gilbert became prior
in 1196 and died in 1198–9; he was apparently dead by 1200. Bishop Beaumont, though elected in 1189, was not consecrated until early in 1198.

bishop Beaumont on the part of the *célidé*. The list of witnesses is unusually impressive. Besides Beaumont himself they included three bishops (Aberdeen, Dunkeld, and Dunblane) and one bishop-elect (Brechin). The laymen were headed by the king's brother, David, earl of Huntingdon; Duncan, earl of Fife, and his three sons; Gilbert, earl of Strathearn, with his brother; Gilchrist, earl of Angus, with his son; Murdoch, earl of Menteith; and Robert of London, the most prominent of the king's bastards. Clearly no trivial agreement was recorded by this document. And if Beaumont's role in the matter was simply that of an aloof arbitrator, which is unlikely to have been the case, it still seems hard to believe that he would have set his seal to a deed which was meant to give permanence to the existence at St. Andrews of a community unchanged from the days of the Celtic church. In fact, the agreement seems to be the starting-point of a fresh departure, and to usher in a new act of this prolonged drama in which king and bishop give their support to the *célidé*, if need be against the established chapter of the cathedral. It may mark the beginning of the process by which the old culdean community became a secular collegiate church.

So far we have discussed the problem of the survival of the *célidé*. We may now turn to the related problem of their participation in episcopal elections. As we have seen, throughout the thirteenth century, from 1239 onwards, the *célidé* put in a claim to take part in such elections, although the only occasions on which any of their number are recorded as having done so were in 1239 and in 1255. But when and how did this claim arise? Earlier writers on the subject seem to have taken it for granted that the *célidé* had had this right under the older Celtic dispensation. Reeves, and following him Hay Fleming, speak of their 'prescriptive right'.[67] But there is really no evidence that the Celtic *célidé* did participate in episcopal elections, and it would be

---

[67] Above, pp. 24–5. So much was this right taken for granted that Sir Archibald Lawrie, printing Eugenius III's privilege of 1147 in his *Early Scottish Charters* (no. 181), entitled it 'Bull . . . giving the right of electing the Bishop of St. Andrews to the Prior and Canons . . . *instead of to the Keledei*' (my italics). The bull does not mention the *célidé* in connexion with episcopal elections, and the formula by which it conveys the privilege of episcopal election to the canons is the standard formula employed generally at this time; cf. W. Holtzmann, *Papsturkunden in England*, vol. 2 (ii, *Texte*), Berlin 1936, nos. 20, 48, and 57, of 1139, 1146, and 1148 respectively.

surprising to find that they had ever done so. From all we know of the bishops in early times it is most probable that they were not elected but appointed. Eadmer, it is true, relates that he came to St. Andrews to be bishop in 1120 *eligente eum clero et populo terrae*;[68] but this is the account of a stickler for canonical procedure, who only a little before says that he owed his appointment to the request of king Alexander and to Henry I's consent to that request.[69] It is likely in fact that Eugenius III's privilege of 1147 giving the Augustinian canons the right of free canonical election of future bishops introduced an entirely new element into the constitution of the cathedral church; and as late as 1178, when the canons tried to exercise this right without consulting the king, it caused a dispute that lasted ten years.

The first occasion on which we hear of the *célidé* taking part in an episcopal election was in fact in 1239, when David Bernham was chosen. This culdean participation was at the king's instance.

It was followed by further claims to participate in elections, and we may note the pertinacity with which the prior and convent opposed them. In the end the canons were successful, but for our enquiry the most interesting record is provided by the struggle which led to that success. In 1252, the year after Master Richard Vairement's case had been settled at the *curia*, the prior and canons renewed the conflict. They obtained papal letters addressed to the bishop of Brechin, the abbot of Arbroath and the prior of May ordering them to cite peremptorily not only 'the provost and *célidé* of the chapel of St. Mary',[70] but bishop Bernham also, to appear, or be represented by proctors, before the pope within three months of the publication of their summons—i.e. before 13 July 1253.[71]

The prior and convent were unlucky in their citation of their

---

[68] *Historia Novorum* (Rolls Series), 282.   [69] Ibid., 279–81.

[70] The difference in the terminology used respectively by the prior and convent and the *célidé* is worth remarking. The former were careful to style themselves the 'prior and canons (or convent) of the cathedral chapter of St. Andrews', while they called the collegiate church of the *célidé* the 'chapel' of St. Mary, and its occupants '*célidé*', or '*célidé* acting as canons'. The *célidé*, on the other hand, never seem to have so styled themselves in the thirteenth century; their official style was 'The provost and chapter of the church of the Blessed Mary of the city of St. Andrews', and by *c.* 1290 the legend on their common seal read SIGILLVM CAPITVLI S. MARIE CAPELLE DOMINI REGIS SCOTORVM (*Laing Chrs*, no. 15).   [71] *St. Andrews Liber*, 26.

bishop, for Bernham died in April 1253, and the whole business had to be begun afresh. On 7 June 1253, they issued a declaration narrating the foregoing events, concluding somewhat plaintively:

'We were about to proceed, as was just, in this case, and the papal judges-delegate had cited the bishop of St. Andrews and the provost and culdees according to the tenor of the papal mandate; now, since our bishop has died, we declare our citation superseded. When our church is provided with a bishop, we shall prosecute our right in the said cause by another citatory letter'.[72]

Three weeks later, and acting apparently without the royal *congé d'élire*, the canons elected the dean of Dunkeld, Robert de Stuteville.[73] The king wished the archdeacon of St. Andrews, Master Abel, to be made bishop. It is not surprising to learn that when, on the day before they elected Stuteville, the canons pleaded strenuously with Master Abel to agree to their choice his response was unfavourable.[74] Both Abel and a proctor for the *célidé* went to the pope and protested that the election was invalid because of their exclusion. The pope's official reply, embodying Master Abel's arguments together with some of those of the prior and canons, is in some ways the most interesting, as it is certainly the most tantalising, document concerning the *célidé* in thirteenth century record.[75]

According to Abel and the *célidé*, the election of Stuteville had been invalid because the canons had performed it without their due participation and vote. To this the prior and canons answered that neither archdeacon nor *célidé* had any right in episcopal elections. Formerly, only the canons-regular had elected the bishop; they had held this right 'beyond memory', and still possessed the papal privilege giving them the right of electing a bishop and declaring that on the death of the *célidé* canons-regular should replace them. The archdeacon's argument follows, and it was largely historical also. There had been, he said, an archidiaconal dignity in the church before the canons had been introduced.[76] 'And', he continued, 'although, when the *célidé* left the church of St. Andrew, and entered the church of St. Mary,

---

[72] Ibid. [73] *Chron. Bower*, i, 360.
[74] *Vet. Mon.*, no. 162. [75] Ibid.
[76] This was true, in that there was an archdeacon of Lothian in or before 1144; but no archdeacon of St. Andrews itself appears until *c.* 1150.

retaining their prebends, liberties and rights in their entirety, canons-regular might have been introduced, nevertheless the archidiaconal dignity never disappeared, but remained, and the archdeacon remained in the church with the canons, as he had been wont formerly.'[77] He added that his predecessor (Master Laurence) had taken part in the postulation to the St. Andrews see of Geoffrey, bishop of Dunkeld;[78] this the prior and canons admitted, but declared that he took part not as archdeacon but as advisor (*consiliarius*). Abel further added that bishop Bernham had collated the archdeaconry to him, and assigned to him (or to it?) a stall in choir and place in chapter.[79]

The archdeacon was a papal chaplain, and had been in the pope's confidence for some years.[80] It is not surprising that Innocent took his part and, quashing Stuteville's election as invalid, himself appointed Abel as bishop. Yet the pope did not effectively answer the points raised by the priory; and its tradition, embodied in the later accounts of Wyntoun and Walter Bower,[81] that Abel obtained the see unjustly, is difficult to discount. The prior and canons were probably telling the truth when they claimed that in the past (if we except 1239) elections had been performed only by themselves.

The problem which most concerns us is to decide what period Abel referred to when he described the *célidé* leaving the church of St. Andrew and entering that of St. Mary. If he meant 1144, his account cannot be accepted as it stands. The *célidé* were certainly regarded as having a place in the cathedral church after the priory had been founded,[82] and even as late as 19 June 1248, which was the date of the last papal privilege copied into the

[77] 'Et licet exeuntibus Calideis de predicta Sancti Andree ecclesia, et intrantibus prefatam ecclesiam Sancte Marie, prebendas, libertates et iura sua integre retinendo Canonici regulares in ipsam ecclesiam Sancti Andree fuerint introducti: Archidiaconalis tamen dignitas nunquam ibi evanuit, sed perseveravit ibidem, et Archidiaconus in eadem remansit ecclesia cum ipsis Canonicis regularibus, sicut ibi consueverat prius esse.' The Latin does not seem free from ambiguity as to whether it was the *célidé* or the canons who retained their rights. I have taken it to mean the former.

[78] In 1238 (Dowden, *Bishops*, 13).

[79] 'Subiunxit . . . quod . . . David Episcopus Sancti Andree sibi . . . Archidiaconatum eundem contulerat, stallo in choro et loco in Capitulo ipsius ecclesie assignatis.'   [80] *Cal. Papal Letters*, i, 244–5.

[81] *Chron. Wyntoun* (Laing), ii, 255; *Chron. Bower*, i, 360.

[82] Lawrie, *Charters*, nos. 181, 233.

St. Andrews Priory Register which provided for the substitution, in the church of St. Andrews, of regular canons in the place of deceased *célidé*.[83] In fact it may not be a coincidence that 1249 is the earliest year in which we find mention of the church of St. Mary. Master Abel may have been referring to recent history. In any case, it seems clear from his account that it was the formal transference of the *célidé* from the cathedral into another church, retaining their prebends and rights, that was responsible for the mid-thirteenth century collegiate church of St. Mary—the earliest collegiate church in Scotland.

Although this formal transference and erection of a collegiate church may not have taken place before 1248–9, the evidence outlined in the foregoing pages provides some grounds for believing that the first moves of the process whereby the *célidé* became a secular college were made by bishop Roger Beaumont and his successor. Whether the object from the outset was the creation of a separate collegiate church, which would in effect strengthen the bishop's hand against his chapter of regulars, is not certain. But if that was not the intention, it was undoubtedly the result. It is inconceivable that William Malvoisin, a typical school-trained prelate of his time, should have permitted a body of hereditary Celtic clergy to continue at his own episcopal see, and it is unlikely, in view of his generally restrictive attitude towards the established religious orders, that he would willingly have seen any of the culdean prebends pass into the hands of the regular canons of the priory. It is surely more probable that in the period 1202–16, when Malvoisin absolved them from excommunication, and again in 1220, when they were fellow defendants with Malvoisin and his clerks, the *célidé* were already themselves episcopal clerks, to whom the bishop had collated the prebends of the older Celtic foundation.

It is worth glancing, at this point, at some contemporary developments at other cathedral churches with chapters of regular clergy. The most widely known of ecclesiastical disputes in England in the last twenty years of the twelfth century concerned the attempt by the two archbishops of Canterbury,

---

[83] *St. Andrews Liber*, 98–102; unfortunately there does not seem to be any later bull of general confirmation to compare with this; ibid., 103–6 is of the same date.

Baldwin and Hubert Walter, to found a college of highly-placed learned secular clerks near Canterbury, ostensibly in honour of St. Thomas, but having for its ulterior purpose the creation of a second chapter of the cathedral to offset the authority of the prior and monks and enhance that of the archbishop and his suffragans.[84] There is, as far as I am aware, no evidence to link either Beaumont or Malvoisin with this Canterbury scheme; but they must have known about it, and the ensuing conflict, which became, as Professor Knowles has put it,[85] 'a *cause célèbre* familiar to the whole of Christian Europe'.

The Canterbury episode, lasting intermittently from 1186 to 1200, was not an isolated one. At Coventry, for example, bishop Hugh of Nunant actually expelled the monks of his chapter in 1189–90, and between then and 1198, when Hugh died and the monks were restored, there was a chapter of secular canons at the cathedral church.[86] Of greater interest, however, from the standpoint of comparison with St. Andrews, was the contemporary development at Dublin. There, the native Irish archbishop, Lorcan Ua Tuathail (Laurence O'Toole), had turned the existing cathedral clergy of Holy Trinity (Christ Church) into a chapter of Augustinian canons of the order of Arrouaise *circa* 1163.[87] The first Anglo-Norman archbishop, John Comyn, a trusted servant of Henry II, was appointed in 1181, and consecrated in the following year. He enlarged the foundation of the existing cathedral of Holy Trinity, but it is of especial interest to note that within eight years of becoming archbishop, he took over the old parish church of St. Patrick in the south of Dublin, and re-established it as a secular collegiate foundation for thirteen prebendaries of honest life and learning—no doubt clerks of his own *familia*.[88] This new collegiate church of St. Patrick was

---

[84] See Stubbs's introduction to his edition of the *Epistolae Cantuarienses* (Rolls Series); and D. Knowles, *The Monastic Order in England* (1949), 318–22, 325–6.

[85] Ibid., 319. [86] Ibid., 322–4.

[87] See P. J. Dunning, 'The Arroasian Order in Mediaeval Ireland' in *Irish Historical Studies*, iv, no. 16 (1945), 308. Father Dunning points out that the exact date of St. Laurence's foundation is not certain.

[88] See the article on Comyn by Tout in the *Dictionary of National Biography*, and the references there cited, especially W. M. Mason, *History of St. Patrick's* (1820); cf. also G. H. Orpen, *Ireland under the Normans* (1911), ii, 62–5. St. Patrick's was consecrated on 17 March 1191.

certain to be a serious rival to the older Augustinian cathedral chapter. It is not surprising to find that *circa* 1220 Comyn's successor, Henry of London, transformed St. Patrick's into a full cathedral foundation, with a dean, precentor, treasurer and chancellor and other *personae*, his act being confirmed by Honorius III in a letter dated from the Lateran, 6 March 1221.[89] As a result, there were two cathedral churches and chapters at Dublin, the favoured secular foundation of John Comyn and Henry of London[90] assuming a status almost of equality with the older Augustinian priory. For much of the thirteenth century, the situation at St. Andrews must have borne a close resemblance to that at Dublin, with two bodies of clergy, the one secular and closely connected with the bishop, the other of Augustinian canons, both claiming to be capitular clergy of the cathedral church.

In the thirteenth century, the *célidé* of St. Andrews were closely connected with the bishop and in some cases with the king. Before the close of the century, indeed, they formed a royal chapel, and may have held this position in effect if not in name considerably earlier. On various occasions throughout the century, from 1239 onwards, the *célidé* claimed a voice in episcopal elections. The most reasonable explanation of their claim seems to lie not in a 'prescriptive' right directly inherited from the days of the Celtic church, for which there is no clear evidence, but in the fact that the king of Scotland or the bishop of St. Andrews considered it advantageous that this virtually new foundation of episcopal and royal clerks should act, in this capacity at least, as capitular clergy. There seems to have been no legal break between the *célidé* of 1150 and the so-called '*célidé*' of 1250, who held the prebends of the older Celtic community. Consequently the members of the 'church of St. Mary of the city of St. Andrews' could claim that in a sense they were as much cathedral clergy

---

[89] Mason, op. cit., *Appendix*, IV; *Vet. Mon.*, no. 45.

[90] It may perhaps be mentioned that archbishops John and Henry had a clerk named Master Peter Malvoisin, canon of St. Patrick's, and from 1221 to 1230 bishop of Ossory. I have found no evidence to connect Master Peter with his namesake at St. Andrews. (See the cartularies of St. Thomas's and St. Mary's, Dublin, ed. Gilbert (Rolls Series), references in indices; *Cal. Papal Letters*, i, 67; *Vet. Mon.*, no. 41; PRO, Chancery Masters' Exhibits, Lanthony Cartulary, vol. A 8, third and sixth charters in section I.)

as the Augustinian canons. The obstacle to this claim, and it was a major one, which eventually brought victory to the priory, was the explicit provision both by David I and by successive popes from Eugenius III to Innocent IV that the regular canons should enjoy a total occupation of the cathedral church and its endowments. In spite of this, the priory was never able to appropriate all the culdean prebends and estates, and in the thirteenth century the 'culdean' foundation was actually enlarged.[91] Moreover, the church of St. Mary may have been founded to circumvent the papal decrees regarding the substitution of regular canons for *célidé* in the cathedral. But on the head of episcopal election, the lawyer-pope Boniface VIII in 1297–8 decided in favour of the priory, and his decision was evidently final.[92] The collegiate church of St. Mary, however, remained at St. Andrews with its property intact and its prestige almost unimpaired until the period of the Reformation. The fact that the name *céledé* or 'culdee' was often given to its members at least until the fourteenth century should not be taken to mean that there was any survival of the older, Celtic church. Nevertheless, the history and function of their community in the thirteenth century, when they formed the earliest collegiate foundation in Scotland, provide a highly interesting example of episcopal and royal policy at the most important church in the kingdom.

[91] The rectory of Ceres was annexed to the provostship of St. Mary's during the century.

[92] *Chron. Bower*, i, 361–3; cf. *Vet. Mon.*, no. 362; *Cal. Papal Letters*, i, 578.

8 The clergy in the war of independence

Historians on both sides of the border have never been slow to acknowledge that in the War of Independence from 1296 to 1328 the church in Scotland played a part of critical importance. It would probably be true to say that this is given more emphasis by Scottish than by English writers. Sir Maurice Powicke believed that 'King Edward [I] had more reason to fear the ecclesiastics than the barons. The ecclesiastics were both more rooted in the land and wider in their outlook; more alert to meet any danger to their independence and better able to rally the lairds and gudemen of the country-side in resistance to English claims.'[1] The acute and entertaining John Hill Burton, writing a century ago that 'the cause of Scotland must have been well supported at the Court of Rome', felt that this was 'probably due to a pretty loud participation in the national wailings, by a body who knew how to be heard at Rome, and whose voice would find ready sympathy there. The Church of Scotland was in danger—or rather, the churchmen.'[2] The result of this, in Hill Burton's view, was that the Scottish clergy busied themselves with valuable propaganda at the court of Boniface VIII. Among more modern Scottish historians, Andrew Lang took, perhaps, a special pleasure in declaring that 'Scottish independence was in part the gift of "Baal's shaven sort", Knox's "fiends" and "bloudie bishops".' 'The Churchmen [he says] were united, and always had been, in resistance to England. The clergy saved Scotland's freedom. They later preached for it, spent for it, died for it on the gibbet, and imperilled for it their immortal souls by frequent and desperate perjuries. Without them Bruce must have warred in vain.

[1] F. M. Powicke, *The Thirteenth Century* (1953), 585.
[2] J. H. Burton, *History of Scotland* (2nd edn, 1873), ii, 207–8.

Times were to alter, creeds were to change, but we must never forget these unequalled services of the Churchmen to the national cause.'[3] With this judgement of Lang's Evan Barron, the latest historian of the War of Independence, was in full accord. 'It was beyond question the Church of Scotland which inspired and kept alive the spirit of resistance to England throughout the long and bitter years of the War of Independence, and she it was who preached the sacred duty of war against the English yoke and in the persons of her bishops and her priests often led the way on the field of battle itself.' Dr Barron believed that 'it is not too much to say that Scotland owed her independence to the Catholic clergy of the thirteenth and fourteenth centuries more than to any other class or body of men in the kingdom'.[4]

In recent years other candidates have been put forward for the position of Most Powerful Single Factor contributing to the Scottish victory, but I am not aware that anyone has tried to belittle the church's share in the national struggle. Yet historians have been remarkably content to rest their case for the church upon the activities of a handful of bishops and abbots and a very small number of individual clergymen of lesser rank. Abbot Maurice of Inchaffray, with his few well-chosen words on the morning of Bannockburn; Bishop Sinclair of Dunkeld personally beating off an English invasion of Fife; David Murray, who as bishop of Moray exhorted his flock by preaching that it was more meritorious to fight the English than the Turks and Saracens; and, of course, the two leading prelates, Lamberton of St. Andrews and Wishart of Glasgow, who were lucky to suffer nothing worse than iron fetters for their part in Bruce's coronation—these, and a few others, are in all the history books. We hear virtually nothing of the clergy who were less prominent, less heroic or less picturesque. Moreover, there has been general agreement among historians that, while the Scottish clergy may or may not have been exceptionally patriotic, what they were anxious for above all else was *ecclesiastical* freedom, and that few things aroused their alarm and resentment more than Edward I's policy, from 1296, of filling Scottish benefices with English incumbents. Dislike, in other words, of the prospect of submission to

[3] A. Lang, *History of Scotland* (1900), i, 165.
[4] E. M. Barron, *The Scottish War of Independence* (2nd edn, 1934), 27, 378.

York or Canterbury, and fear of wholesale unemployment, sent the Scots clergy flocking to the national standard.

This unanimity among the historians has depended upon a belief, or at least upon an assumption, that the church formed a completely separate homogeneous body within the feudal kingdom, composed of like-minded individuals who were invariably churchmen first and only secondarily Scotsmen or Bruces or Comyns or northerners or southerners or parish chaplains or university men or royal clerks or whatever else they might be. The habit dies hard among Scottish medieval historians of personalising the church, and giving it, along with a capital C, a clear policy, an opinion, an attitude distinctively its own. Suppose, on the contrary, that the Scottish church did not form a sharply distinct, unassimilated, element in the nation, that Scotsmen in clerical orders were not markedly different from Scotsmen out of them, that they were neither more nor less heroic and patriotic than their fellow-countrymen, but that, being literate and members of a highly organised corporate institution they could, if need arose, exploit those advantages, as knights and merchants and peasants could exploit theirs, this, I believe, would be a truer hypothesis and would explain more intelligibly the part taken by the clergy in the struggle with England. Chronicle and record evidence suggests that the Scottish nation—the *communitas regni Scotie*—possessed a majority which waited for a lead from others, and an articulate minority accustomed to giving a lead. Within that minority there were conflicts of interest and loyalty, but from 1286 to 1291, again from *c.* 1294 to 1304, and again from *c.* 1307 onwards, the initiative within the minority lay with those who wished above all to protect the 'royal dignity' and preserve the independence of the kingdom. That state of affairs was reflected in the church, which had an inarticulate majority and a dominant minority that was itself divided by conflicts of loyalty and interest. The main question which this chapter will try to answer—in rather more detail than has been usual—is: How were the power and influence of the dominant minority within the Scottish church used during the period between the death of King Alexander III in 1286 and the opening years of Robert I's reign?

We must look first at the bishops of Scotland, to whom even

Sir Maurice Powicke paid the grudging tribute that their 'general level of ability and character was higher than might be expected'.[5] The fact that the Scottish church formed a single province, with the pope in the position of absentee metropolitan, gave its bishops what Sir Maurice has called 'their sense of confident independence'. Nevertheless, we should note an Orwellian feature of their relationship: they were all on a footing of equality, but the bishops of St. Andrews and Glasgow were emphatically more equal than the rest. Indeed, the bishop of St. Andrews enjoyed in all but constitutional formality the pre-eminence of a primate, and only on William Fraser's death in 1297 did the bishop of St. Andrews cease to style himself on his seal EPISCOPUS SCOTTORUM. Even so, every episcopal appointment in Scotland had to be confirmed by the pope, and Scottish bishops-elect were consecrated at the papal *curia* or by papal legates or by other Scottish bishops acting by special papal authority.

Between 1286 and 1306 there were fourteen effective episcopal appointments in the twelve Scottish dioceses.[6] It is worth emphasising that in this troubled period eleven out of fourteen bishops were consecrated at Rome, one in Scotland, one (of Whithorn) at York, and one (of Sodor) probably in Norway. Of these fourteen appointments, only two were made by Edward I or with his clear approval, and they were in the remotest dioceses of Sodor and Caithness. Five appointments can be assigned to John Balliol as king of Scotland, but, since they all belonged to 1295 or 1296, they are less likely to reflect the influence of Balliol himself than of the council of twelve which had been imposed upon him. One appointment—Thomas of Dalton to the see of Whithorn— strikingly reveals Balliol's weakness, for it was made in spite of his protests through the influence of the competitor Bruce of Annandale. The six remaining, and for our purposes most interesting, appointments were made by or with the approval of the guardians

---

[5] Powicke, op. cit., 584.

[6] Unless otherwise indicated, the authority for statements about episcopal appointments is Dowden, *Bishops*, Watt, *Fasti* and *Vet. Mon.* The fourteen effective appointments were—ST. ANDREWS: Lamberton 1298: DUNKELD: Crambeth 1288; MORAY: David of Moray 1299; BRECHIN: Nicholas 1296, Kinninmonth 1298; DUNBLANE: Alpin 1296, Nicholas 1301; ROSS: Thomas of Dundee 1295; CAITHNESS: Adam 1296, Andrew 1297, Bellejambe 1306; SODOR: Alan 1304–5; WHITHORN: Dalton 1294; ARGYLL: Andrew 1300.

established by the community of the realm. In 1288, Master Matthew of Crambeth, dean of Aberdeen, was made bishop of Dunkeld. Master Matthew, despite his cloth, was heir to the small barony of Crambeth, now Dowhill, on the slope of the Cleish Hills overlooking the royal burgh of Kinross.[7] The later medieval ruins of Dowhill Castle still stand, and obviously interested the Commissioners for Ancient Monuments, though they were unaware that Dowhill had been the home for many generations of the Crambeths of that ilk. In 1292, Matthew was among Bruce's forty auditors in the competition for the throne,[8] and three years later was one of the four ambassadors who negotiated the crucial alliance between King John and King Philip the Fair. There is no evidence that he returned to Scotland before 1304, the year following that in which he appears as one of the Scottish leaders at the French court.[9] In the intervening decade he may well have served as a permanent Scottish representative in France.

The senior ambassador to France in 1295 was the bishop of St. Andrews, William Fraser, who belonged to a baronial family, of the second rank, established in East Lothian, Stirlingshire and Tweeddale.[10] Fraser never came back to Scotland, but died at Auteuil near Paris in 1297. One of his last acts was to appoint two vicars-general, Master William of Kinghorn and Master Peter de Champagne (Champney), who, in Fraser's absence and on the orders of King John and his parliament, expelled twenty-six

[7] *Cal. Docs. Scot.*, ii, no. 1530. For the identification of Crambeth with Dowhill, see Keith, *Bishops*, 82, and *Dunfermline Registrum*, no. 193, which describes the marches between Crambeth and Outh in 1231.

[8] Statements about membership of the panels of auditors in 1291–2 are based on two significantly different lists. The first (Palgrave, *Docs. Hist. Scot.*, Illustrations, pp. v–vi=*Foedera* (1816), i, 767) gives the names of the eighty persons formally appointed to serve as auditors, 5 June 1291. The second (*Chronica Willelmi Rishanger*, ed. H. T. Riley (Rolls Ser., 1865)), gives the names of those who actually performed the auditors' duties, at any rate at one of the later sessions of the court at Berwick, Thursday, 6 November 1292. It appears from a comparison of the lists that a number of magnate auditors, especially ecclesiastics, were represented at sessions of the court by *magistri*.

[9] *Acts Parl. Scot.*, i, 454; *Cal. Docs. Scot.*, ii, nos. 1363, 1455, 1528; Barrow, *Bruce*, 177 and n.

[10] The bishop was brother of Simon Fraser the elder, who seems to have died between June 1291 and November 1292 (Stevenson, *Documents*, i, 154; ii, 93, 96; Palgrave, *Docs. Hist. Scot.*, Illustrations, p. vi; Rishanger, 263).

English incumbents of Scottish benefices in 1296, to prevent them forming a fifth column.[11] On 5 November 1297, by the direction of William Wallace and (presumably) Andrew Murray, the St. Andrews chapter elected in Fraser's place the chancellor of Glasgow, Master William Lamberton. The slight biographical evidence we possess, though inconclusive, suggests that the new bishop was of the Lambertons of Linlathen near Dundee, landowners in Aberdeenshire as well as Angus.[12] Consecrated at Rome in 1298 and returning with difficulty, Lamberton served as guardian from 1299 to 1301, entered into a pact with Robert Bruce in 1304, and two years later played a decisive part in his coronation at Scone. The small see of Brechin, which stood to St. Andrews in much the same relation as Rochester to Canterbury, was likewise given a new bishop at Rome in the summer of 1298, with the consecration of Master John Kinninmonth, archdeacon of Brechin. The Fife family of Kinninmonth of that ilk, hereditary stewards of the cathedral priory, had been connected with the church of St. Andrews for a century and a half; one former bishop of Aberdeen and two later ones were members of the family, so that if we know little else about Master John we know that ecclesiastical preferment was in the blood.[13] In 1299, under the joint guardianship of Bruce and Comyn, David Murray (*de Moravia*, 'of Moray'), parson of Bothwell and canon

[11] *Chron. Fordun*, i, 325 (which has *Patrick* de Campania, wrongly); cf. J. Raine, *Priory of Coldingham* (Surtees Soc., 1841), 248, 251. In 1296 Master William of Kinghorn was parson of the bishop of St. Andrews's church of Kirkliston, and Master Peter de Champagne parson of Kinkell (*Cal. Docs. Scot.*, ii, p. 194).

[12] Linlathen was granted to Alexander de Lamberton by King William the Lion for knight-service (*RRS*, ii, no. 564), and Alexander seems to have been the characteristic Christian name of the family. Sir Alexander Lamberton of Angus appears prominently in the period 1296–1305, presumably the Sir Alexander Lamberton who was a prisoner in Edinburgh Castle in 1304 (*Cal. Docs. Scot.*, ii, references in index), and presumably also the great-grandfather of Margaret Leslie who inherited Linlathen from him (*Reg. Mag. Sig.*, i, no. 247). In 1327 a deed of Bishop Lamberton was witnessed by his brother Sir Alexander Lamberton, knight (*Holyrood Liber*, no. 90), presumably the Alexander Lamberton, knight, who served on an Angus inquest in 1322 (*Reg. Mag. Sig.*, i, App. 1, no. 29). Between 1209 and 1228 Alexander son of William de Lamberton appears as laird of Bourtie, Aberdeenshire, and a benefactor of St. Andrews Cathedral priory (*St. Andrews Liber*, pp. 235, 267–8).

[13] Cf. G. W. S. Barrow, 'The early charters of the family of Kinninmonth of that ilk', in *The Study of Medieval Records*, ed. Bullough and Storey, 108–15.

of the cathedral church of Moray at Elgin, was elected and consecrated bishop of Moray. He was evidently the brother of Sir
William Murray of Bothwell—Sir William 'the Rich'—and uncle
of Wallace's colleague Andrew Murray.[14] David Murray was
consistently hostile to Edward I, and though Bruce was supported
at his coronation by only three bishops, David Murray was one
of them. The Scottish guardians may be judged responsible for
two other appointments, a Dominican, Andrew, to the see of
Argyll in 1300, and Nicholas, abbot of Arbroath, to Dunblane in
1301. But this was unimportant when set beside the fact that three
major sees, including the key position of St. Andrews, had fallen
vacant during periods of guardianship, and had been filled by
candidates wholeheartedly committed to the national cause.

Except for Fraser, the bishops already in office in 1286 have so
far been left out of consideration. Among them I shall mention
only those two who lived right through the War of Independence—Henry le Chen (Cheyne) of Aberdeen and Robert
Wishart of Glasgow. Henry Cheyne belonged to a prominent
Aberdeenshire family whose successive heads, the elder and
younger Reginald Cheyne of Inverugie, were among Edward I's
most consistent Scottish supporters. What evidence we have
suggests that the bishop of Aberdeen also was not sympathetic to
the guardians in the period before 1306.[15] But, in any balance-
sheet, Cheyne of Aberdeen was more than offset by Wishart of
Glasgow, in many ways the most interesting figure among the
Scottish bishops of his time.

Master Robert Wishart, bishop of Glasgow since 1273, and
previously archdeacon of Lothian, was nephew of William
Wishart who had been a graduate of Oxford (and perhaps also
of Paris),[16] archdeacon of St. Andrews, chancellor of Scotland and
bishop of St. Andrews. The Wisharts, whose origin is unknown,
though the name—Guiscard, Wiscard, Wishart, 'cunning'—is of

[14] The probabilities regarding David Murray's family relationships are set
forth by E. M. Barron, *Scottish War of Independence*, 204–5, and in Barrow,
Bruce, 163–4.

[15] For most of Bruce's reign Bishop Cheyne seems to have been his loyal
supporter, but none of the documents summarised in *Cal. Docs. Scot.*, ii, *passim*,
suggests that Cheyne gave any support to the Guardians between 1297 and
1304, and several show him actively supporting Edward I.

[16] *Oxford Formularies*, ii (ed. Salter, Pantin and Richardson, Oxford Historical Soc., 1942), 486, 489.

Iᴋs

course Norman-French, were already a well-established family in Angus and Mearns. Their main estate was Conveth, in the parish of that name now called Laurencekirk.[17] Robert Wishart served as guardian from 1286 to 1292; he was one of Bruce's auditors in the Great Cause, though in the end he declared himself convinced by the arguments for Balliol;[18] in 1297 he and James the Stewart were the only leaders of national resistance who had had experience of government. Wishart's tergiversations after 1297, to which historians, especially English historians, have repeatedly drawn attention, have been exaggerated or misinterpreted. On this point Edward I and Edward II are surely better witnesses. On 16 June 1306 Edward I wrote to Aymer de Valence to say that he was almost as pleased at Wishart's capture as if it had been Bruce himself. He was to be treated without regard for his status as prelate or priest. Edward II, who freed Lamberton and others to make use of them, released Wishart only when the disaster of Bannockburn forced him to do so.

There was perhaps one moment, in the summer of 1296, when Edward I might have summoned the whole bench of Scottish bishops before him and impressed on them the extent of his power and the seriousness of his intentions. But in fact the English king received the homage not of twelve but of only three Scottish bishops, one of whom, Thomas of Dalton, bishop of Whithorn, was in any case a suffragan of York, and another Henry Cheyne of Aberdeen, who was never his opponent. The third was Wishart of Glasgow, on whom the ceremonies perhaps sat more lightly than they might have done on others. St. Andrews and Dunkeld were in France, Caithness in Italy, Ross was certainly vacant, Brechin and Dunblane were probably vacant, and for an unknown reason no homage is recorded for either Moray or Argyll.

[17] The family were later known as the Wisharts of Pitarrow. Conveth was acquired by John son of John Wishart from the abbot and convent of Arbroath in feu-ferm in 1242 and 1245 (*Arbroath Liber*, i, nos. 271, 272), confirmed by Alexander II by a charter of 21 June 1246 (Fraser, *Carnegies*, ii, 477–8). The family must have been established in Kincardineshire before this, since John Wishart senior was sheriff of Mearns in the early decades of the thirteenth century (*Arbroath Liber*, i, nos. 138, 261).

[18] Rishanger, 264. It was Wishart and Matthew of Crambeth who, in June 1291, issued the significant *inspeximus* of Edward I's guarantee that the Scots magnates' visit to Norham should not prejudice the status of the Scottish realm (Barrow, *Bruce*, 48).

So much for the bishops as a group. I will only make the point that if they used their influence in support of national resistance this did not follow automatically from the fact that they were churchmen: it was due primarily to the fact that most of the key positions in the episcopate were deliberately captured by the national party, often in the face of strong opposition from England. This could never have been achieved without the active assistance of a pope, Boniface VIII, who, until 1302, pursued a markedly pro-Scottish policy. Papal benevolence was fortuitous and fickle, but as long as it lasted the Scots took full advantage of it.

The bishops were few. They had to co-operate with the other lords, and above all they depended on trained assistants. The church set high standards both of liturgical and administrative efficiency which were expensive to live up to. The Scottish dioceses could not afford any great multiplication of dignities and offices. Able or influential clerks must have competed for what was available, but they also had a tendency to gather several benefices at once. In this they were only following the universal custom of western countries, but it is worth remarking that owing to the small size of the *Ecclesia Scotticana* there was little trace of provincialism in the higher ranks of its clergy: local and family influence were obviously important, but the clergy moved easily from one diocese to another. The remarkable invasion of the great south-western diocese of Glasgow by a small group of east-country clergy is an illustration of this statement. At various dates within the 1280s and 1290s, when Robert Wishart was bishop, the dean of Glasgow was Thomas Wishart,[19] the archdeacon of Glasgow may have been John Wishart,[20] and the archdeacon of Teviotdale was Master William Wishart.[21] William Wishart, incidentally, was also a canon of Dunkeld, and as such one of the electors of Bishop Matthew of Crambeth. Of Dean Thomas nothing seems to be known save that his successor was Bruce's brother Alexander, but

[19] *Vet. Mon.*, 256 (at a date subsequent to 9 July 1286). The date at which he was succeeded by Bruce's brother Alexander is not known for certain, but it was later than 1292 (Watt, *Fasti*, 153).

[20] John Wishart was archdeacon of Glasgow in 1321 (*Glasgow Registrum*, no. 268) and is described as 'formerly archdeacon of Glasgow' in an English record of 1310 (*Foedera* (1818), ii, 106). He had probably been archdeacon of Glasgow in the last decade of the thirteenth century.

[21] *Vet. Mon.*, no. 306, shows William already archdeacon in 1288; for his surname, see *Glasgow Registrum*, no. 252 (1297).

both archdeacons, John Wishart and William Wishart, were imprisoned and deprived of office by the English in 1306 or 1307.[22] The sub-dean was Master Thomas of Dundee, related to Master Ralph of Dundee, a prominent clerk of King Alexander III.[23] Thomas of Dundee was dean of Brechin, and a canon of Ross, of which see he became bishop in 1296. The chancellor of Glasgow, until his election to St. Andrews in 1297, was Master William Lamberton. The Official of the archdeacon of Teviotdale, Master Walter Cammoys, is described as Bishop Wishart's clerk, and his attachment to the bishop is shown by the fact that he acted as go-between in the surrender negotiations which Wishart, the Stewart and Bruce conducted with Percy and Clifford in July 1297.[24] Among these east-country figures the Official of Glasgow, Master Alexander Kennedy, seems an odd-man-out. His name shows that he belonged to the ruling clan of Carrick, and one might suppose that he would follow the lead of Robert Bruce, who became earl of that province in 1292. But Kennedy may already have been a canon of Glasgow, possibly already the Official, before this date.[25] Any close Bruce connection seems to be ruled out by the fact that at the moment of Balliol's surrender in July 1296, when the Bruces were in Edward I's following and at the end of a period when the national party had held power, Master Alexander Kennedy was actually chancellor of Scotland.[26]

What looks like a Wishart influence may be seen in the diocese at large if we look at the principal churches in the bishop's gift. The parson of Stobo was Michael of Dundee[27] who, as a canon of Dunblane, was voter in the election in 1296 of Master Alpin

---

[22] *Foedera*, ii, 106; *Cal. Docs. Scot.*, ii, no. 1934; iii, nos. 37, 288.

[23] *Glasgow Registrum*, nos. 238, 244. For Master Ralph of Dundee and his probable close relationship to Master Thomas, see *Highland Papers*, ii, 115–17, 223–5. For other particulars, see Dowden, *Bishops*, 214.

[24] Stevenson, *Documents*, ii, 200, 220. 'Wautier Cammays, clerk of Roxburghshire' did homage in 1296 (*Cal. Docs. Scot.*, ii, p. 208).

[25] *Glasgow Registrum*, no. 237, an undated deed which may be earlier than 1292. It bore the seal of the Officiality and the third witness was Master Alexander Kennedy, canon of Glasgow. Kennedy was certainly Official in 1295 (Theiner, *Vet. Mon.*, no. 349). Cf. *Paisley*, p. 228, of 1280.

[26] Stevenson, *Documents*, ii, 61. As royal chancellor Kennedy had replaced Master Thomas of Hunsingore, presumably a Yorkshire nominee of John Balliol.

[27] *Cal. Docs. Scot.*, ii, 212.

of Strathearn, one of Balliol's auditors in 1292, to the see of Dunblane.[28] The parson of Ancrum, where the bishop of Glasgow had his palace, was John of Conveth,[29] who was an auditor for Bruce in 1292, and who may conceivably have been John Wishart archdeacon of Glasgow under an alternative name. We may also note that the vicar of Walston in 1296 was Robert Lamberton,[30] probably the Master Robert Lamberton who appears as archdeacon of St. Andrews in 1319,[31] and possibly earlier.[32] Walston was a parish in which the national party had a predominant influence: the dean and chapter of Glasgow were patrons of the rectory and the Morays of Bothwell patrons of the vicarage.[33] Possessing such a close-knit group of east-country clergy presumably taking their cue from Robert Wishart, the diocese of Glasgow was in a strong position to use its wealth and influence in the national cause.

Exactly the same clannishness and holding of key places by men of common purpose may be seen at St. Andrews. With William Fraser bishop, we are not surprised to find John Fraser as archdeacon. In that capacity he voted for Lamberton in the crucial election of 1297.[34] Edward I's grant of the archdeaconry, in 1299, to his clerk Roger of Kingston may imply Fraser's deprivation, but even in Scottish eyes he cannot have held office after 1301, when Adam of Machan had succeeded, and it is possible that by 1299 John Fraser was already dead. The archdeacon of Lothian from 1285 to 1305 or later was Master William Frere.[35] He resembled his predecessor, Adam of Gullane, in being a regent master in the university of Paris, but whereas Adam's subject was theology William Frere's was law. The Scots have seldom found theology irrelevant in a crisis, but in the age of Accursius and Boniface VIII there was something to be said for a legal training. Frere took part in the election of Lamberton in 1297, and in 1301

[28] *Vet. Mon.*, no. 355; Rishanger, p. 263. Master Alpin had been Treasurer of Scotland; above, p. 93, n. 32. He perhaps belonged to the family of the earls of Strathearn.

[29] *Cal. Docs. Scot.*, ii, p. 210; cf. Rishanger, 265, for 'J. de Coverweythe' [*sic*] among Bruce the Competitor's clerical auditors.

[30] *Cal. Docs. Scot.*, ii, p. 212.

[31] *Dryburgh Liber*, no. 293.   [32] Watt, *Fasti*, 305.

[33] *Origines Parochiales*, i, 131–2.

[34] *Vet. Mon.*, no. 362. Fraser's surname (Fresel) is given in *Rot. Scot.*, i, 25.

[35] *Newbattle Registrum*, no. 59; *Foedera* (1816), i, 975.

was the leader of the delegation sent to the pope by the guardian John de Soules.[36] The immediate purpose of this delegation was to rebut the claims to superiority over Scotland made by Edward I in his letter of May 1301, but it had the more general and important duty of arguing the Scottish case at the bar of papal, and, by implication, of European, opinion. The Scots' reply to King Edward represented the high-water-mark of the conservative or Balliol phase of the independence struggle. Presumably William Frere's part in the business was not insignificant, but contemporary documents and later Scottish tradition agree to attribute the lion's share to Master Baldred Bisset, the 'wys and cunnand clerk' of Andrew Wyntoun's verse, and, with the exception of Duns Scotus, surely the most remarkable of all the Scottish clergy of this period below the rank of bishop. At the start of his recorded career, in 1282, Baldred Bisset was Official of St. Andrews, an office which he still held three years later, and perhaps for somewhat longer.[37] He seems to have belonged to the knightly family of Bisset holding land in the neighbourhood of Stirling. He was a canon of Caithness,[38] and he held the rectory of Kinghorn a rich living in crown patronage.[39] He was ousted from this by Edward I in favour of Peter of Dunwich, an English royal clerk active in Scotland from 1296. For a man who could plead his country's cause at Rome it was nothing to plead his own at Bologna, and between September 1301 and early in 1305 Baldred protested formally to the bishop of Bologna against his deprivation.[40] It is surely to 1301 or at the very latest 1302 that we should assign an undated letter which thus reported on conditions in Scotland to King Edward I:

[36] *Chron. Fordun*, i, 332, where the mission is wrongly assigned to the year 1300. See Barrow, *Bruce*, 166–7.

[37] *Cambuskenneth Registrum*, no. 3; *Newbattle Registrum*, no. 59. Professor Robert Brentano shows that as late as 1296 Durham Priory was still paying an annual retainer of £5 to Baldred Bisset, Official of St. Andrews, in respect of a lawsuit in which he had acted as sub-delegate over ten years previously (*York Metropolitan Jurisdiction* (1959), 126, 159). But it is not clear that Baldred was Official as late as 1296; between 1289 and 1295 the officiality was held by Alpin of Strathearn and Robert de Montfort.

[38] Brentano, op. cit., 233.

[39] Master Baldred was already parson of Kinghorn on 19 September, 1289 (NLS, MS. Adv. 15.1.18, no. 43).

[40] *Nat. MSS. Scot.*, ii, Pl. xii.

The bishop of St. Andrews has shown the people a letter sealed
with the king of France's seal (whether counterfeit or not I
cannot say), declaring that there will never be peace between
you and the king of France if the Scots be not included. The
people have put all their trust in this and in the success which
may be obtained by Master Baldred (*Mestre Baudre*) their
procurator at the Court of Rome. They say for certain that the
whole affair is the work of the bishop of St. Andrews.[41]

The *processus Baldredi*, the case presented at Rome by Bisset and
his colleagues, has often been studied for its bearing on the
legendary origins of Scotland and the fable of the Stone of
Destiny, but it is perhaps more remarkable for its concentration
on recent events, its reiteration and expansion of the points which
must have been made to the pope by the Scots as early as 1299
before he issued the bull *Scimus, fili*.[42] The mission to the *curia*
caught the popular imagination in an age which dearly loved 'a
bonny fechter'—in the schools and courts as much as in a joust or
on the battlefield. If Scotland possessed in William Wallace a
military champion, she could also boast a forensic champion in
Master Baldred Bisset. In November 1306 Edward I issued a
safe-conduct at the instance of Sir William Bisset, constable of
Stirling Castle, to Master Baldred 'the Scot', coming to the constable from oversea. William Bisset was commanded to bring
Master Baldred to the king.[43] Whether the meeting ever took
place does not seem to be known; if it did, one would give much
for a record of the conversation.

After Baldred and the two archdeacons, the most significant
member of the St. Andrews clergy from our point of view was
Master Nicholas of Balmyle, who exhibits in his career all the
characteristics of the 'key man'. He may for a time have been
the archdeacon of Lothian's Official,[44] and he was certainly par-

---

[41] *Cal. Docs. Scot.*, ii, no. 1431 = P.T.O., S.C.1/21/166. Bain places this
under 1303, but 1301 or 1302 seems much more likely, and in any case it must
be earlier than the Anglo-French treaty of May 1303.

[42] Barrow, *Bruce*, 85–6, 165–6.   [43] *Cal. Docs. Scot.*, ii, no. 1848.

[44] *Newbattle Registrum*, no. 172 (1293): Master Nicholas of St. Andrews,
Official of the archdeacon of Lothian. No doubt this was the 'Master Nicholas
of Balmyle called "of St. Andrews"' appearing in 1295 (*Cambuskenneth Registrum*, no. 111). Master Nicholas of St. Andrews was Official of the archdeacon
of Lothian before 1285 (Raine, *North Durham*, no. 418).   [*Footnote continued*

son of West Calder in Midlothian in 1296, it being perhaps worth mentioning that Bishop Wishart of Glasgow had a grant of the presentation to West Calder, one of the earl of Fife's manors, from 1294.[45] Nicholas of Balmyle had the alternative and unhelpful designation of Nicholas 'of St. Andrews',[46] and if, on the strength of that, we merged all our references to Master Nicholas of St. Andrews and Master Nicholas of Balmyle we should have to assign him a career after graduation of fifty-seven years—a lengthy, but not an impossibly long span. Associated with Bishops Gamelin, Fraser and Lamberton, and promoted to the see of Dunblane at the end of 1307, Nicholas of Balmyle enters the recorded course of national history at three points. In 1292 he was one of Balliol's auditors.[47] During the critical vacancy in the see of St Andrews following Bishop Fraser's death, Master Nicholas was appointed Official of St. Andrews by the prior and chapter, and in the chapter's name exercised the jurisdiction of the see effectively throughout the diocese.[48] In 1303, the year of Bisset's mission to Rome, he appears as chancellor of Scotland,[49]

Among the numerous occurrences of Master Nicholas of Balmyle *alias* of St. Andrews in contemporary record, it is especially interesting to find him associated with an agreement made at Scone, 18 February 1293, presumably in King John's first parliament, between William Moray of Bothwell and Bishop Wishart of Glasgow (*Glasgow Registrum*, no. 239).

[45] *Cal. Docs. Scot.*, ii, p. 213; ibid., no. 700. There was apparently some defect in the original grant, which was amended, with specific inclusion of the right of presentation, by a warrant dated 26 August 1295 (P.R.O., C 47/22/7(4b)).

[46] *Cambuskenneth Registrum*, no. 111. Balmyle is a small estate in Meigle, Perthshire, which passed into the possession of Coupar Angus Abbey, apparently by the grant of Simon, son of 'Euard', of Meigle in the twelfth century (*Coupar Angus Rental*, i, 343, no. 70: a grant of land between Balbrogie grange and Meigle). See *RRS*, ii, no. 201 for Simon of Meigle. Michael of Meigle, laird of Meigle in the period 1203–10, had a brother and a son named Simon (*Coupar Angus Chrs.*, i, no. 16). Master Nicholas's surname suggests that his family were tenants of Coupar Abbey, possibly connected with the Meigles of that ilk. There is, however, another Balmyle, in Kirkmichael.

[47] Rishanger, 263 (Master N. of St. Andrews).   [48] *Chron. Bower*, i, 362.

[49] *St. Andrews Liber*, p. 120, an act of Bishop Lamberton, which has been thought to be the sole evidence of Nicholas's chancellorship. But in an unpublished record of an agreement of 1312 between Nicholas, then bishop of Dunblane, and the abbot and convent of Arbroath, it is stated that Nicholas had been suing Arbroath abbey for arrears of money due to him 'ratione feodi sui pro tempore quo fuerat Cancellarius Scocie' (BM MS. Add. 33245, f. 86ᵛ). This not only provides additional evidence of Nicholas's tenure of the office, but also throws valuable light on how the Guardians met the salaries of their major officers.

and served as an envoy to the abortive Anglo-French negotiations at Canterbury.[50] Here we are taken into the heart of the darkest, yet in some ways most fascinating, period of the war of independence, when John de Soules as sole guardian was not only pressing for the return of John Balliol, and evidently counting at least on the succession of Edward Balliol,[51] but was also behaving in Scotland as though John Balliol had already been restored, issuing acts of government running in the name and style of King John with his regnal years correctly calculated from November 1292. Since the missions to Rome, Canterbury and France were parts of a single policy whose agents included prominent St. Andrews clergy, it cannot be doubted that William Lamberton, despite his resignation from the guardianship, was still committed to the view that the survival of the Scottish kingdom and monarchy depended on the restoration of John Balliol, the only lawfully constituted, hereditarily legitimate, king whom the community of the realm could as yet recognise. It is clear that even in the stormy days of Wallace there had been no lack of experienced clerks to draft, write and seal acts of government according to the ancient forms. But it is surely no coincidence that we find no chancellor till 1301, or that when we do find him it is as witness to a deed executed by Bishop Lamberton, and also witnessed by two of the three members of the delegation to the papal *curia*—Archdeacon Frere, and Master William of Eaglesham, doctor of canon law, parson of Dunbarney, himself to become archdeacon of Lothian by 1317.[52]

Two more names from this document, which in effect gives us Lamberton's *familia* in 1301, help to illustrate the striking preponderance among the influential clergy of men from the country between Tay and Spey. Master Robert de Montfort, who had

[50] *Cal. Docs. Scot.*, ii, no. 1244 (where 'Balnul' is an error for 'Balmil').
[51] This is strongly suggested by the negotiations for Balliol's future which were being conducted at this time by the pope and the French king, of which the Scots were doubtless fully cognisant; by the terms of the document printed by Professor E. L. G. Stones, *SHR*, xxxiv (1955), 123–4 (late 1301 or early 1302); and by the terms of one of the acts issued by John de Soules as Guardian but running in the name of King John, 'these present letters to be valid at the will of us or of our beloved son Edward or of John de Soules Guardian of our realm' (S.R.O., Scrymgeour-Wedderburn, Dudhope Muniments, Box 40, Bdle. 1, no. 309; 10 July 1301).
[52] *St. Andrews Liber*, p. 120; *Kelso Liber*, nos. 310, 315.

been official of St. Andrews in 1295,[53] was parson of Kinneff in Mearns, doubtless because he belonged to the old family of Montfort of Kinneff, to whom the lands had been granted by King William the Lion in the 1190s. Master Stephen of Dunnideer, though his family had some links with Glasgow,[54] presumably took his name from Dunnideer in central Aberdeenshire. In 1301 he was parson of Conveth, the family living of the Wisharts. As early as 1309 King Robert I made Stephen of Dunnideer his chamberlain, and vicar and custodian of the see of Glasgow, of which he was a canon, on behalf of Robert Wishart.[55] Stephen came near to succeeding Wishart as bishop, but the pro-English pope, John XXII, withheld confirmation of his election, and he died at Paris before a decision could be reached. Finally among the St. Andrews *magistri* we may mention Master Nicholas of Lochmaben, who occurs in record between 1285 and 1305. His surname implies a Bruce connection, but he worked mainly in the St. Andrews diocese, being Official of the archdeacon of Lothian in 1283.[56] Master Nicholas appears in the printed *Rotuli Scotiae* for 1296 as parson of 'Strivelin', that is, Stirling. But Stirling was a vicarage, not a rectory, and the fact that the writ for the restitution of Nicholas's temporalities went to the sheriff of Peebles shows that we should read, as, indeed, the formation of the letter on the roll itself permits us to read, Scrivelin, that is Skirling, a tiny parish on the borders of Tweeddale and Clydesdale whose rectory was in the patronage of a branch of the Lindsays.[57] That Master Nicholas of Lochmaben was active for the guardians and the community of the realm is made probable by an entry in the escheator's account, rendered to Edward I for 1302–4, of 'the lands of the rector of Skirling, a rebel'.[58]

Between them, the dioceses of St. Andrews and Glasgow accounted for nearly half the population of medieval Scotland. If we look at one further sizeable diocese, Dunkeld, and find there

[53] NLS MS. Adv. 15.1.18, no. 8.

[54] Richard of Dunnideer appears among the burgesses of Glasgow in 1270 (*Glasgow Registrum*, no. 220), and as one of the provosts at a slightly later date (ibid., no. 236).

[55] *Glasgow Registrum*, no. 258.

[56] Raine, *North Durham*, no. 511 ('1286', correctly 1283). This is the earliest mention of Master Nicholas of Lochmaben I have been able to find; the latest is *Dunfermline Registrum*, no. 338 (29 October 1305).

[57] *Origines Parochiales*, i, 183.   [58] *Cal. Docs. Scot.*, ii, p. 425.

the same clerical clannishness, the same overlapping of personnel with other dioceses, and a similar small number of well-placed clerks in the service of the bishops and magnates who upheld the national cause, we shall have a pattern of clerical activity which will hold good for well over half the country. The position and career of the bishop, Matthew of Crambeth, have been indicated already. Remembering the Wisharts at Glasgow and the Frasers at St. Andrews, we look automatically for the name of Crambeth among the higher clergy of Dunkeld and are not disappointed. At the time of his promotion in 1288, Bishop Matthew had been dean of Aberdeen, and within three years we find this office filled by Master Hervey of Crambeth.[59] By 1296, Master Hervey had joined his kinsman and become dean of Dunkeld.[60] If, as seems probable, the bishop was absent from 1295 to 1304, the dean would have held an unusually important position in the diocese, and in fact we find him acting in place of the bishop in a trans-action dating between 1300 and 1303,[61] in association with John Comyn of Badenoch, the former guardian, Robert Wishart bishop of Glasgow, Thomas of Dundee bishop of Ross, and Henry abbot of Scone—the same abbot, incidentally, who assisted at Bruce's coronation. The archdeacon of Dunkeld until 1304, when he seems to have succeeded Hervey of Crambeth as dean, was Master Matthew of Kinross, whose name, since Crambeth and Kinross are but three miles apart, suggests Crambeth influence. But it is not clear that Matthew of Kinross had been associated with the guardians, since a document of 1304 tells how he had been captured by leading Scottish patriots who were trying to hold him to ransom for £200 contrary to the terms of the Scots' surrender.[62]

The disconnected and inadequate character of the available sources means that we are given only occasional glimpses of the careers of men who are not necessarily beneath our notice simply because they are now obscure. The subject, as must be abundantly obvious, bristles with problems of identification. One of these

[59] *Aberdeen Registrum*, ii, Plate II, no. 3 (at end), the legend reading s. HERVEI D CRABETH. 'Henry', dean of Aberdeen, an auditor for Bruce the Competitor in 1291 (Palgrave, *Docs. Hist. Scot.*, Illustrations, p. v), is a mistake for Hervey.

[60] *Cal. Docs. Scot.*, ii, pp. 195, 212.

[61] *Coupar Angus Chrs*, i, no. 69; cf. ibid., no. 73 (9 February 1303).

[62] *Cal. Docs. Scot.*, ii, nos. 1473, 1573.

problems may be allowed to conclude our brief glance at Dunkeld. We have record in this period of Thomas of Preston, canon of Dunkeld, and Master Thomas of Bunkle. The adjacent and now conjoined parishes of Bunkle and Preston in Berwickshire were in the diocese of Dunkeld, Bunkle at least, if not Preston also, being one of the bishop of Dunkeld's mensal churches. It does not take a student of British medieval history long to discover that the rule that names are given in order to distinguish is not without its exceptions. Were these two different names for two different men, or for only one man? Thomas of Preston, canon of Dunkeld, took part in the election of Bishop Matthew. Master Thomas of Bunkle acted with Bishop Matthew and Sir Alexander of Bunkle as an auditor for Bruce in 1292. Again, Master Thomas of Bunkle, who had duly done homage to Edward I in the great round-up of 1296,[63] served along with Nicholas of Balmyle and two lay lords as a Scottish envoy to the Canterbury negotiations of 1301.[64]

So much for the secular clergy. Of the religious there is less to be said because less is known. It was not uncommon in Scotland at this time for monks and canons-regular as well as friars to become bishops, though it looks as though they could hope only for the poorer sees. But constitutionally the collective importance of the heads of religious houses in the community of the realm is not in doubt. It is shown convincingly in the list of sponsors of the treaty of Birgham, in Balliol's forty auditors, who included seven abbots and one cathedral prior, and on the Ragman Roll of 1296, where fifty-five heads of religious houses—not counting the English, or the Master of the Templars and Warden of the Hospitallers—were surely much more fully representative of their class than the three bishops, eight cathedral or diocesan dignitaries, sixty-eight parsons and twenty-nine vicars were of theirs. It is often impossible to determine the political sympathies of the

[63] *Cal. Docs. Scot.*, ii, p. 207, where Thomas Bonequil appears among the Berwickshire clergy. The homage of Thomas of Preston, canon of Dunkeld, is also recorded (ibid., p. 212), but this of itself does not disprove the identity of the two Thomases, since there is undoubtedly duplication of names on the roll of homages. The balance of probability, however, seems to weigh against their identity. Thomas of Preston acted in the election of Bishop Sinclair in 1311 or 1312 (*Vet. Mon.*, no. 398).

[64] *Cal. Docs. Scot.*, ii, no. 1244.

religious, and it is therefore all the more valuable to have some evidence for the three great abbeys of Teviotdale—Melrose, Kelso and Jedburgh. Patrick of Selkirk, abbot of Melrose, a supporter of Bruce in 1292, served as envoy to the French court in 1299 along with John [Morel] abbot of Jedburgh.[65] Richard abbot of Kelso, who was on Balliol's side in 1292, was said, in August 1299, to have been long absent from his monastery of his own free will as an aider, abettor and counsellor of King Edward's enemies. The king therefore replaced him with an English monk, Thomas of Durham,[66] whom Robert Wishart many years later described as 'a dilapidator of the goods of the priory of Lesmahagow [a cell of Kelso] while he governed it, as well as of the monastery of Kelso during the time that by usurpation he there bore the name of abbot'.[67] Perhaps the most famous name among the monks belongs to a man whom we may suspect to have been a late recruit to the religious life—Bernard of Linton, parson of Mordington in Berwickshire in 1296,[68] who very quickly became Robert I's chancellor and then abbot of Arbroath, and who may well have been the author of the Declaration of Arbroath of 1320.

Of the lesser clergy we catch only casual glimpses, which cannot justify any generalisations. That the 'false preachers' who a few months before Edward I's death were travelling through the countryside north of Forth exhorting the people with Merlin's prophecies of the day when Celt should triumph over Saxon included friars and minor clergy is more than likely.[69] Even so, we should not expect too much in the way of independent action and *savoir-faire* from parish priests and chaplains who could be ignorant and simple. At the very time that the prophecies of Merlin were being noised abroad, a rascally English Bethlehemite, touring occupied Scotland to collect funds, was able to pose as the recipient of a commission from the pope to such good purpose that he extorted (among other things) six stones of cheese—to meet the pope's necessities—from the parson of Slamannan, and 36s. from the prioress of Haddington because she was detected possessing property of her own.[70] Yet even in the ranks of the obscure we may see men whose actions were as straws in the wind. The marshal's

[65] Ibid., no. 1071.
[66] Stevenson, *Documents*, ii, 392–3.
[67] *Kelso Liber*, no. 188.
[68] *Cal. Docs. Scot.*, ii, p. 207.
[69] *Cal. Docs. Scot.*, ii, p. 537.
[70] *The Stewarts*, ix, no. 4 (1954), 325–6.

court of the English army which overran Scotland in 1296 had before it one Thomas, chaplain, of Edinburgh, who, asked why he had presumed to excommunicate the king of England publicly with bell and candle, admitted that he had done it out of hostility and disrespect.[71]

In conclusion, we may ask whether any conclusions can be drawn from these scattered biographical details. The sources tell us of a body of clergy led by a majority among the bishops, most of whom seem to have had their origin among the lairds and lesser barons. They were well provided with benefices, and many of them were university graduates. Controlling the machinery of ecclesiastical administration, and in any case forming the class from which the Scottish crown had long been accustomed to draw its educated servants, they applied their particular skills and capacity, intellectual and clerical as much as spiritual, to the service of the guardians and the community of the realm of Scotland. Nothing suggests that the clergy held ideas on the struggle for independence which differed appreciably from those held by the laity. What these ideas were may be deduced, firstly, from a number of leading documents—the treaty of Birgham of 1290, the protestation to Edward I in 1291,[72] the bull *Scimus, fili* of 1299, the case presented by Baldred Bisset in 1301, and the Declaration of Arbroath of 1320; secondly, from the language of the official written acts issued by the guardians. These documents follow one or both of two different lines of argument. According to the historical line, Scotland's independence of England was implicit in the entirely separate mythical migrations which gave rise to the two kingdoms—Scota, Pharaoh's daughter, being a lady quite independent of Brutus of Troy. The second, more empirical line of argument was based on the observable facts of the recent past: for example, the existence of Scottish kingship, and the contrast between Edward I's failure to behave like a feudal overlord in 1286 and his emphatic claims of 1291. Documents following this line of thought used terms such as *regia dignitas*, and 'la bone gent Descoce'—surely an echo of the technical term, *probi homines*, in which, ever since the days of David I, the free subjects of the king

[71] *Cal. Docs. Scot.*, ii, p. 190.
[72] Printed by E. L. Stones, *SHR*, xxxv (1256), 108–9, and republished in Stones, *Documents*, no. 16.

of Scots in the widest possible sense had been comprehended. They also made great play with the expression *communitas regni Scotie*, in a manner which leaves little doubt that by it was meant the entire body of persons who composed the feudal kingdom, especially when it lacked a king. The authorship of most of these documents is unknown. No doubt they were clerical products in the sense that their actual drafting and composition were the work of educated clerks, perhaps of clergy of high rank. But they were certainly not produced by a clerical minority working in isolation from the laity.

In the guardianship which ruled the country from 1286 to 1291 the bishops had equal representation with the earls and the barons. In 1291 the clergy doubtless shared sponsorship of the protest against Edward I's claims, but they did not make any special representations. The decisive mission to Paris in 1295 was composed of two churchmen and two laymen. When Edward I defeated the Scots in 1296 and fealty was sworn to him by about 2,000 Scotsmen, something like a tenth of this total (about 190) were clergy. In the revolt of the following year, the chief leaders at the outset, who professed to speak for the whole community of the realm,[73] were one bishop, one earl and one baron, and the same balance of representation was maintained from 1299 to 1301, when the practice of multiple or joint guardianship was abandoned. Down to 1303 or 1304 the evidence suggests that the clergy supporting the national cause were as fully committed as the laymen to the three principles which, with or without his own connivance, were denied to Robert Bruce: French support, papal support, and the retention of John Balliol as king of Scots. But what was the later position? Lamberton allied with Bruce in 1304, it is true, but that was after the cause of Balliol had been proved hopeless, and when it was clear that only revolutionary action could save Scottish independence. The clergy as a whole certainly did not flock to Bruce in 1306. They must have doubted, as the laymen doubted, whether Bruce could possibly succeed against tremendous odds, and they must have been as dismayed as the laymen at the prospect of changing horses in midstream even though one of them was obviously drowning. During his early years, Bruce had to work as hard to gain the clergy as he had to

[73] Stevenson, *Documents*, no. 447 (p. 193).

win over the influential laymen, and the tale of episcopal appointments, with a hostile, pro-English papacy, is in sharp contrast with the period from 1292 to 1302. The successive promulgations of the Scottish Church's support for Bruce (1309, 1310 and (?) 1314) point to King Robert's difficulties rather than to his rapid success in winning the clergy over.[74] From 1296 to 1314 there were some clergy who supported the king of England, and some so closely connected with one or other of the great families involved, Comyn, Bruce or Balliol, that their actions seem to have been motivated by this fact.[75] But the clergy in general, and certainly its dominant element in particular, supported the national cause for the same reasons and with the same constancy as the laity. If there was any difference between laity and clergy in the extent of their commitment to the cause of independence, the explanation surely lies in the difference in their composition. Unlike the laymen, the clergy formed an artificial group who owed their existence to the exercise of patronage and deliberate acts of appointment. For this reason, I believe it would be as wrong to explain the Scottish clergy's part in the War of Independence by some natural clerical propensity for patriotism or freedom as it would be to portray Wallace as a leader of democratic nationalism or Bruce as a desperate, self-seeking adventurer. In their different ways, Wallace, the middle-class conservative, Bruce, the aristocratic revolutionary, and the clergy, who after many years of loyalty to King John rallied, not without hesitation, in support of King Robert, were all acting in response to an idea of the community of the realm which was the distinctive thirteenth-century contribution to the constitutional development of Scotland.

[74] Barrow, *Bruce*, 262, 378–9.

[75] Of these the most interesting and prominent was Master William Comyn, provost of the chapel-royal of St. Mary at St. Andrews (i.e. provost of the '*célidé*'). There has not been space here to discuss his position and career.

PART III   SOCIETY

9 Rural settlement in central and eastern Scotland

Evidence relevant to the study of rural settlement in early medieval Scotland is of four chief types, archaeological, geographical, documentary and onomastic (with special reference to place-names). This chapter is based on the third and fourth types of evidence, and deals chiefly with the period from *c.* 1100 to *c.* 1300. Regionally, it is limited to the area from the Tweed to the Dornoch Firth, leaving out of consideration the Northern Isles and Caithness, most of the West Highlands and Western Isles, and the south-west, including Galloway. The area thus described has in the past been relatively neglected by the student of early medieval agrarian and social organisation, although it corresponds to the most populous and most centrally-governed part of the medieval Scottish kingdom.

For rural settlement, the traditional or 'historical' divisions of Scotland have an obvious relevance, but precisely what this relevance amounted to remains an unanswered question. For W. F. Skene, at the time he published his famous book, *Celtic Scotland* (1876–80), matters seemed much simpler than they seem now. He drew a sharp division between 'Saxon' Scotland, south of the Forth and east of the Clyde-Tweed watershed, and 'Celtic' Scotland, and for him the twain would never meet. The evidence is more complex than he allowed it to be, more evidence has become available since his time, and in particular the whole trend of modern research is stressing more and more not the contrasts but the underlying resemblances and parallels between areas of 'Saxon' and areas of 'Celtic' settlement. An intensive study of the English agrarian scene has made us all familiar with the 'highland' *versus* the 'lowland' zone, the former with its scattered townships and small, compact holdings, the latter with its large nucleated villages built in a great open plain of arable, which was divided into two or three 'fields' and cultivated according to a two- or three-field system of rotation of crops. The analysis of the English evidence has become more and more intensive. Regional studies show a much more complicated pattern than any simple 'highland' and 'lowland' zone division might suggest. It is conceded that open fields and nucleated villages were general in districts where agriculture predominated, e.g. the eastern midlands. But they might well be found in suitable places in the hilly west country, while in many parts of the 'lowland' east, e.g. Kent, Essex and parts of East Anglia, they were rare or developed very late. An eminent student of English agrarian history has written 'Norman England was a land of greater local variety, and rather less marked regional contrasts, than I had previously conceived it to be'.[1] It was tempting for older scholars to apply the English lesson to Scotland, and assume a clear-cut division between the highlands and the far north, on the one hand, and the lowlands (especially the south-east) on the other. In the one there were scattered townships and small compact holdings; in the other, nucleated villages and open fields. The results of recent English studies should warn us in Scotland not to look for simplicity where there was local variety. At the same time, Lennard's phrase about 'rather less-marked regional contrasts' may prove to be applicable to Scotland as well as England— especially if we include (as we must) in our 'Scottish' regions the country between Tweed and Tees.

The nucleated village settlement is undoubtedly a reality for the lower-lying, flatter parts of south-eastern Scotland. The pattern is, as we should expect, that of Northumbria, not that of midland England. A number of nucleated villages, often having parochial status at an early date, often associated with lord's ownership, are to be found in this region in the twelfth and thirteenth centuries.[2] Frequently we find them linked to outlying

---

[1] R. Lennard, *Rural England, 1086–1135* (1959), p. v.

[2] E.g. Greenlaw, Smailholm, Swinton, Edrom, Old Cambus (Merse); Oldhamstocks, Innerwick, Spott, Stenton, Tynninghame, Whittinghame, Athelstaneford (E. Lothian). Several of these villages have names indicating an early origin, such as Auldhame, Oldhamstocks, Tynninghame, Coldingham and Whittinghame (which was possibly the *Hruringaham* (*al. Hrutlingaham*) mentioned in the anonymous *Life of St. Cuthbert* as the home of Cuthbert's

settlements, much as their counterparts in Northumberland, Co. Durham and north Yorkshire will be found linked to outlying settlements. Where nucleus and outliers formed a sizeable group it would normally be called a 'shire', as in northern England. Thus we have Coldingham and Coldinghamshire, Bunkle and Bunkleshire, Haddington and Haddingtonshire.[3] This practice may be seen further west, for Edinburgh and Linlithgow were both shire-centres at an early date, and so was Stirling. In between the last two was Callendar, which, though not styled a 'shire', has every appearance of being one. Shire unity was to be found not so much in the peasantry who dwelt in the shire as in the shire-centre and the lord—usually the king, a bishop or abbot, or some great layman. It was also expressed in the officer who administered the shire and yet at the same time was virtually its hereditary tenant, the thane. The thanes of Lothian and Teviotdale referred to by David I and Earl Cospatric in the early twelfth century cannot be envisaged apart from shire centres or other important royal or comital estates. We happen to know most about just those shires or vill-groups which were most likely to have lost their thanes at an early date, under pressure of royal reorganisation (Haddington) or ecclesiastical reorganisation (Coldingham). But vestigial shires may be seen in later ecclesiastical agreements anent mother churches and their dependencies, e.g. Edrom with Nisbet and distant Earlston (Berwickshire) or Ednam and Newton (Roxburghshire).[4] The shire pattern relates to a time when lords reckoned to consume the products of their estates, whether in cereals or live-stock, in a relatively unconverted form.

Turning to the smaller units of settlement, the villages and hamlets and farmsteads, the earliest documentary evidence that we have (not earlier than the twelfth century) shows what seems to be a pattern closely similar to, if not identical with, that found in the English northern counties. The arable lies open in a large tract round the village nucleus, and individual holdings consist of a number of rigs scattered about in the arable fields. The word

foster-mother, ed. B. Colgrave, p. 90). Longniddry and Tranent, which fit into this south-eastern pattern of nucleated villages, have British names (*Nodref*, 'new settlement', *Tref yr neint*, 'dells' sttlement') which cannot have been formed later than *c*. 630, and the same seems to be true of Treverlen, *alias* Duddingston.   [3] See above, pp. 28–31, 35
[4] Lawrie, *Charters*, nos. 117, 213 and p. 449; and no. 212.

'acre' is used, presumably to refer to the rig or to a group of rigs. By *c*. 1200 the equivalent French word *raye* itself creeps into Latin documents, in the form *reia*. The southern English (really French) word 'selion' for a rig is extremely rare, but in the form *seyillun* it occurs in record of 1226 relating to Hailes in Midlothian.[5] No word for a furlong is common, though 'furlong' itself (in place-names) and its Latin equivalent *cultura* appear occasionally.[6] The Scandinavian 'wang' or 'wong' never seems to occur. David I granted to Kelso Abbey half a carucate in Selkirk, and when Malcolm IV confirmed this grant he said: 'Whereas this half-carucate in King David's time lay scattered about the field (*per campum dispersa*), and was not very convenient, I now grant the same quantity of land lying all in one piece.'[7] This text introduces us to what was the universal, standard term in Latin documents for the major unit, the carucate (Scots, ploughgang, ploughgate), throughout south-eastern Scotland. It also shows that the English concept of an abstract carucate was familiar in Tweeddale (and presumably also in Lothian and the Merse) in the mid-twelfth century. Race fitz Malger (late twelfth century) grants to Jedburgh Abbey half the land of Shortbutts (*Scortebuttes*) in Liddesdale, in the territory of Sorbie (*Sourebi*), with one acre of arable next to Shortbutts on the east; and the whole shaw (*scawe*) of Sorbie, with one acre lying next to the shaw and belonging to it; with common pasture for 40 cows and their followers up to one year old, and two bulls, and 10 oxen and two horses.[8] Shortbutts looks like the name of a furlong; the *territorium* of Sorbie was presumably the whole arable ground of the vill.

In the grant to Kelso above we have an instance of favoured treatment meted out to a religious house, but it is clear that great landowners could not always expect their arable to be consolidated, and, conversely, that peasant holdings were on the

[5] *Dunfermline Registrum*, no. 218.

[6] A good example is in *Holyrood Liber*, no. 34, a grant of six acres of Gorgie 'which are within the *cultura* of Saughton beside the Water of Leith' (late twelfth century). Occasionally, however, *cultura* might refer to an oxgang or merely 'arable'; cf. Adam of Lamberton's charter of *c.* 1190, *Hist. MSS. Comm.*, *Milne-Home of Wedderburn* (1902), 223–4.

[7] *RRS*, i, no. 187.

[8] SRO, Crown Office Writs, no. 5. *Sourebi* is now lost, but is represented by the name Sorbietrees near Newcastleton (in Castleton, Roxburghshire), Mangerton, close by, may contain the name of Race fitz Malger's father.

same pattern (though of course not on the same scale) as lords' holdings. We have relatively few 'peasant' documents for the area in the early period, but a charter of *c*. 1250 given by a member of the lesser gentry will show how small holdings might be made up. Cicely of Mow grants 26 acres of arable in her demesne of Mow in Roxburghshire as follows: in *Hauacres* to the east of Gilbert Avenel's land 9 acres, with a ½ acre lying next to the Atton-burn (*Aldetuneburn*)—these acres lie in parcels (*per particulas*); 2 acres through *Souhside*, and 1 acre next to the exit going towards Percy Law; 1 acre west of *Benelaun*; 9 acres and 1 perch in *Dederig*; 3 acres below *Parvula Hoga*; a half-acre in *Kydelauuecrofth*; and 8 acres of meadow, viz., 4 between the arable land of *Hauacre* and the ploughed furrow dividing it from Gilbert Avenel's meadow, and other 4 below Percy Swire between ploughed furrows.[9]

Along with the arable in rigs and acres, the meadow adjacent to the arable, and the common pasture near the village settle-ments and on the arable when not under crops there went, com-monly, stretches of hill grazing, which were exploited in the summer months in the form of shielings. The shieling system is well seen on Lammermuir, where the parish boundaries are highly instructive. The villages which huddle below the edge of the higher ground have territory reaching far back on to the muir, where names like Penshiel and Gamelshiel preserve the ancient use of this uncultivated grazing.[10] Shielings were to be found in the southern uplands generally and in the Cheviot Hills, e.g. in King David I's time the shielings of Riccalton (in Oxnam, Roxburghshire) went with the low-lying estate of Whitton.[11] It is highly probable that the enormous expansion of the wool trade in the twelfth and thirteenth centuries made devastating inroads into the old shieling system, for the religious houses and other great landowners tried (often successfully) to acquire and keep

[9] *Kelso Liber*, no. 148 (slightly abridged). Since this land went with the toft and croft of one William of Molhope, it may in fact have formed an individual peasant holding. Most of our earliest 'peasant' documents are to be found in *Kelso Liber*, *Melrose Liber* and Raine, *North Durham*.
[10] Note especially the parochial boundaries of Whittinghame, Stenton, Spott, Innerwick, Oldhamstocks and Longformacus. The shielings of Bothwell (*Bothkil*) in Spott (seven miles from Spott church) are mentioned *c*. 1164 (*RRS*, i, no. 217). [11] Ibid., no. 42.

huge tracts of hill-pasture for themselves and their own flocks exclusively. There was a serious dispute over hill-pasture rights in the late twelfth century between Melrose Abbey and the men of Wedale (the valley of the Gala Water). We do not know its details, but it would not be rash to guess that the abbey was seeking to encroach upon or monopolise ancient shieling grazings.[12]

There is no indication in early documents of any system of 'infield' and 'outfield' cultivation, although the texts are not incompatible with the existence of such a system. The *terra* (*arabilis*) of which they speak over and over again would in that case be the infield of later times, kept under more or less constant cultivation, while outfield would often appear as pasture. The twelfth and thirteenth centuries were a period of steadily growing population and there was pressure on available land and a steady process of winning new arable from waste. Thus we hear of the 'new land' of Crailzie (*Karelzi*) at Harehope above Peebles.[13] The men dwelling on the moors above Borthwick who had to be reminded of their obligation to pay teind sound more like pioneers than refugees,[14] and the same was evidently true of the crown's tenants in 'Elrehope' whom King William I removed to his waste land of Selkirk.

The ecclesiastical organisation of the south-east bears out the picture of the area as made up chiefly of nucleated village settlements, with or without a pattern of 'shires' of Northumbrian type. In Lothian, at least from Midlothian eastward, the church was usually located in the village settlement, close to the lord's hall or castle. In the twelfth century we find an established and often hereditary parish clergy, who were unquestionably members of the local aristocracy, men of standing in the community, like Uhtred the priest of Lilliesleaf who took his dispute over land in Lilliesleaf (*versus* Ansketill of Ryedale, a knight) to the Roman *curia* in the 1150s and 1160s[15] or Peter, parson of Stobo and dean of Clydesdale, whose son David inherited his lands if not his livings.[16] Such men compare closely with the forebears of Saint

---

[12] For this dispute, see Anderson, *Early Sources*, ii, 307; *Melrose Liber*, no. 112.

[13] 307; *Melrose Liber*, nos. 82–5. This new land was evidently meant to be used in conjunction with hill sheep grazing.

[14] *RRS*, ii, nos. 124, 367 (p. 363).   [15] *RRS*, i, no. 312.

[16] *Kelso Liber*, nos. 112, 113; for Peter, see *Origines Parochiales*, i, 197.

Ailred of Rievaulx, hereditary priests of Hexham in Tynedale. It may be added that many parish churches of the south-east were endowed with as much as a whole carucate of land, some with more.[17]

How, if at all, does this picture change north of the Forth? There the basic social unit was the township, relatively widely dispersed. Often there seems to have been no obvious nucleus of settlement, and the church may be located in a site which appears to have no clear relevance to any other major feature of the parish. Yet the differences may be exaggerated. In the flatter and lower-lying parts of Scotland benorth Forth, especially in Fife and the Carse of Gowrie, it looks as though the arable of any particular settlement might lie more or less in one piece, and be cultivated in rigs and acres. A charter of 1284, e.g. speaks of a ditch between the meadow and the arable land of the village of Markinch (Fife).[18] Early in the thirteenth century, William the Lion gave to John Waleran the land held by William Carpenter in *Ballebotlia* (now represented by Babbet in Kingsbarns), namely 'the fifth rig' (*quintam reiam*) of the whole half of Ballebotle; and 'in the fields of *Dreinin* (cf. Drony Road, in Kingsbarns) the land held by Roger of the Chamber; and the whole land of Airdrie (*Ardarie*) which William de Beauvoir held, viz., that land which is on the east of the burn flowing past the land of Geoffrey the chaplain as far as that well in the direction of Crail which in Gaelic is called *Tolari* (Toldrie).'[19] Here the 'fifth rig' presumably means 'every fifth rig', a good instance of an early runrig tenement. William, Bernard's son (late twelfth century) granted to Arbroath Abbey two bovates of arable in the *territorium* of Catterline (Mearns), viz., 7 acres lying together and adjacent to the abbey's existing property on the north side, and 19 acres lying together and near those 7 acres, beside the sea to the east, namely within the furlong (*cultura*) called *Treiglas*.[20] These examples

---

[17] Many examples of parish churches endowed with one carucate may be found in collections of twelfth-century charters, starting with Lawrie, *Charters*, no. 50 (p. 46). *Holyrood Liber*, nos. 17, 33, are examples of half-carucate churches (Livingstone, Bolton). Airth had its endowment brought up to two carucates by King David I (Lawrie, *Charters*, nos. 92, 153).

[18] *St. Andrews Liber*, 420–1.   [19] *RRS*, ii, no. 469.

[20] *Arbroath Liber*, i, no. 124. *Treiglas* is Gaelic *tràigh ghlas*, 'grey (or green) strand'.

show the existence north of Forth of large tracts of arable attached
to settlements, Markinch, Crail and Catterline, divided into rigs
and furlongs, such as we have seen to be the case in the south.[21]

Nevertheless, the differences between north and south remain.
At this point, we must grapple with problems of terminology.
Besouth Forth, the largest visible, physical unit of agrarian exploitation was the 'field' (*campus, territorium, tellus*),[22] sometimes
divided into furlongs, everywhere divided into rigs or acres,
equally visible and physical. Unless we have positive evidence to
the contrary, it is safe to assume that every *campus* or field belonged
(in the social and geographical sense) to some village or similar
settlement—often, but not always, a nucleated village. Similarly,
we may assume that every rig and acre belonged (in the legal or
tenurial sense) to some individual or family or corporate proprietor. Alongside and overlapping these visible, physical units
of field and rig were the semi-tangible or wholly intangible units
of ploughgate and oxgang. Originally, no doubt, the ploughgate
and the oxgang would have been as tangible and concrete as field
and acre. Even in the twelfth and thirteenth centuries, it is clear,
there were a number of oxgangs and ploughgates besouth Forth
which were actually physical entities. This was either by survival
from a primitive period, or because the acres of which they were
composed had been treated collectively for so long that the area
which formed their total had acquired a physical reality. The
consolidated half-carucate formed in Selkirk by Malcolm IV
(referred to above) shows how this could happen. But in this
period, as a rule, ploughgate and oxgang were essentially abstract
concepts, expressions used to denote an approximate area, or
rather, approximate capacity. The ploughgate was what one
notional team of eight oxen could deal with, including what they
actually ploughed and what they could not plough, in any one
year. The oxgang was an eighth part of this, the contribution of a
single notional ox. Mr. Andrew McKerrall has said that the
difference between Celt and Saxon was that the latter had an
idea of superficial measurement in the acre, the oxgang of 13

[21] A late-twelfth-century charter speaking of half a carucate 'in Whitefield'
(in Cargill) seems to have reference to a pattern of this sort (*RRS*, no. 377).

[22] The first two terms are more common, but *tellus* in this sense of arable
ground occurs in a document of 1170 relating to Tranent (*SHR*, xxx, 44).

acres, and the ploughgate of 104 acres; whereas the Celt was incapable of grasping the idea of superficial measurement.[23] The Saxons were surely not so much more precocious than the Celts as Mr. McKerral would have us believe. The English acre, oxgang and ploughgate were far from being standard, accurately measured areas. The acre was thought of primarily as an actual fixed piece of ploughed or ploughable ground, and acres varied considerably in area not only in different parts of the country but even in the same field or furlong. Hence we have reference to 'full' or 'complete' acres, implying the existence of 'incomplete' acres. Whatever the nature of the gulf between Celtic and Anglian Scotland, it did not lie here.

North of the Forth we find a different usage with regard to the ploughgate, and this is where terminology becomes of crucial importance. Practically all our documents are in Latin, and their authors had a preference for Latin or thoroughly latinised words. In south-country documents of the twelfth and thirteenth centuries the words 'ploughgate' and 'oxgang' never (as far as I know) appear. Instead, we have *carucata* (*terre*) for the former, *bovata* (*terre*) for the latter. This is entirely on all fours with the usage in northern England, from the River Welland northwards. North of the Forth, the Latin documents of the twelfth century, with very few exceptions, use *carucata*, and occasionally *bovata*. We may give the following examples:

1. 1 carucate called Balrymonth (St. Andrews, Fife).
2. 1 carucate in Naughton (Balmerino, Fife), called *Melchrethre*.
3. 1 carucate in Errol called *Le Murhouse* (Muirhouse).
4. ½ carucate west of Invergowrie church called Dargie.
5. 4 carucates of arable in Conveth (Laurencekirk, Mearns).
6. 1 carucate in Durno (Chapel of Garioch).
7. 2 measured carucates in Kennethmont (identifiable as Ardlair).
8. ½ carucate measured in Rayne, known as (Easter) Tocher.[24]

[23] A. McKerral, 'Ancient denominations of agricultural land', *PSAS*, lxxviii, 41, 46.

[24] 1. *The Study of Medieval Records* (ed. Bullough and Storey), 128; 2. *RRS*, i, no. 228; 3. *Coupar-Angus Chrs.*, no. 47; 4. *RRS*, i, no. 251; 5. *RRS*, ii, no. 344; 6. *Hist. MSS. Com., Mar and Kellie* (1904), p. 3; 7. *Aberdeen Registrum*, i, pp. 9, 218; 8. ibid., 8, p. 10.

With these instances from the late twelfth and earlier thirteenth centuries may be compared the endowments of the Augustinian canons of Scone made by Alexander I in the early twelfth century: Innerbuist, 5 carucates, Banchory with 3, Fodderance (Lintrose) with 1, Kinnochtry with 1, Fingask with 1, Durdie with 3, Clien with 3, Liff with 6, Gourdie with 10, Invergowrie with 3.[25] It would be needless to multiply examples of texts which speak unblushingly and without hesitation of carucates north of the Forth. But attention has to be drawn to one notable difference. In six of the examples given, the carucates had names attached to them. It would be rash to state that carucates never have names south of the Forth, for we have at least one example in 'the carucate on the Peffer Burn called *Porhoy*' (Prora, in Athelstaneford, E. Lothian).[26] But in general the formula south of the Forth is: '*x* carucate(s) in the vill of A', while north of the Forth it is: '*x* carucate(s), by name B, C, D, etc. (in the vill of A)'. The naming of a carucate does not by itself prove that it formed no part of an open-field pattern, any more than the fact that a carucate had fixed boundaries proves this. But when, over and over again, carucates appear with names permanently attached to them and with fixed marches, the presumption is strong that such carucates are not abstract units of measurement but compact pieces of arable which are not and never have been composed of rigs or acres scattered across a large undifferentiated plain of cultivable ground.[27] We may proceed, more warily, to a further presumption. In documents relating to the country benorth Forth, *carucata* may have been merely the most seemly, respectable term available to the latinising clerks who wrote our documents. Thus, northern 'carucates' might not be the same as southern, though they would have borne some relation to them.

There is some evidence to support this hypothesis. First, *carucata* is commoner in twelfth-century texts than in thirteenth, commoner in thirteenth-century texts than in fourteenth. It is commoner in royal texts than in private. Occasionally in the twelfth century, more commonly in the thirteenth century, quite

---

[25] Lawrie, *Charters*, no. 36.   [26] *Registrum Newbattle*, no. 69.
[27] Sir Frank Stenton long ago drew attention to a named bovate in the English Danelaw, observing that it was probably composed of adjacent acres (*Danelaw Charters* (1920), p. xxxiii, n. 3).

commonly from the fourteenth century, a more exotic, more definitely vernacular term finds its way into our Latin documents. This is the word davoch, Irish, *dabhach*, a vat or tub or large measure of volume. It is a fair assumption that the davoch of land was not introduced into Scotland as late as the twelfth century. Its relative absence from texts of that period is best explained by clerical reluctance to use a term so uncouth and strongly vernacular that it was a century or more before it was made tolerable in the form *davata (terre)*.[28] Secondly, we find the carucate and davoch existing side by side across the same stretch of territory, though with the carucate growing rarer as we go north, the davoch growing rarer as we come south. Thirdly, there are hints dropped by the texts themselves. The Crailshire document, cited above,[29] speaks of 'half a Scottish carucate' of arable, proving that the clerk was aware of a difference between southern and northern carucates. There is some evidence that his 'Scottish carucate' was merely periphrasis for 'davoch'. Whether or not this is so, it does seem to be true that the characteristic unit of agricultural capacity south of Forth was the carucate, north of Forth the davoch.

At this point we may cite a few examples of davochs from relatively early texts, to set beside our examples of carucates:

1. 2 davochs of *Uactair Rosabard* (xi cent.).
2. *Dauach Icthar Hathyn*, with common pasture (xii cent., probably in Fife).
3. 7 davochs in Mearns, viz., the two Tipperties, Glenfarquhar, Kinkell, *Culbac*, Monboddo (xii cent.).
4. 10 half-darochs in Strathavon (Stratha'an), Banffshire, all named (xiii cent.).
5. 1 davoch in Strathardle named Tullochcurran (*alias Petcarene*) (xiii cent.).
6. 5 davochs in Mearns, viz. Balmakewan, *Ackwendochan*, Balbegno, *Lacherach-geigh*, *Dauochendolach* (xiii cent.).

[28] As, for example, Robert I's grant to Thomas Randolph of the earldom of Moray, under obligation of rendering Scottish service 'from the several davochs' (*singulis davatis*), or Robert II's charter of Badenoch, described as *sexaginta davatas* (*Moray Registrum*, no. 264 and Carte Originales, no. 21).

[29] *RRS*, ii, no. 469; 'Scottish' in texts of this date means pertaining to Gaelic-speaking Scotia, north of the Forth.

7. 1 davoch called Inverquharity (Angus) (xiii cent.).

8. Whole davoch of Resthivet (Chapel of Garioch) (xiii cent.)[30]

In western Moray, in what is now Inverness-shire, the two adjoining parishes of *Dulbatelach* (Dunballoch, now Kirkhill) and Convinth (*Coneway*) were said to contain nine and eleven davochs respectively. Dunballoch contained the davochs of Dunballoch, Fingask, *Moreweyn* (Lovat?), *Lusnacorn*, Moniack, the other Moniack and the three davochs of *Ferge*. Convinth had its own two davochs together with the davochs of Bruiach *Muy*, the other *Muy*, Dounie, Phoineas, Erchless, Buntait, Comar and Guisachan.[31] If I have identified these places correctly, it is clear that there was enormous disparity in area, but probably not in agricultural capacity, among these highland davochs.

There has been argument as to the meaning of davoch as applied to land. Mr. McKerral believed in 1943 that it was originally arable, and that according to the progress made in arable it would consist of a varying number of ploughgates.[32] He reinforced this in 1947 by an apt quotation from Sinclair's *General View of the Agriculture of the Northern Counties*, to the effect that Inverness-shire arable farms were reckoned by the davoch or daugh, the *auchten* (eighth) and the boll (forty-eighth).[33] Unhappily, McKerral's later view seems to go back on this sound position, and to contain the belief that the davoch was originally and essentially a large fiscal unit. 'When the davochs . . . ceased to function as fiscal units, and their original significance was forgotten, the terms became fluid, and were used as denominations for various kinds of agricultural holdings',[34] sometimes pasturage, sometimes ploughgates of arable. The late W. J. Watson, though of course he was well aware that *dabhach* meant a vat or vessel, nevertheless thought that as applied to land it was a unit of souming, that is, of pastoral capacity. Yet his illustration tells

[30] 1. Lawrie, *Charters*, no. 1 (p. 2); 2. *St. Andrews Liber*, 290–1; 3. *RRS*, ii, no. 346; 4. *Moray Registrum*, no. 16; 5. Ibid., no. 79 and *Coupar-Angus Chrs.*, no. 38; 6. *RRS*, ii, no. 497; 7. Scot. Rec. Office, J. M. Thomson Photographs, no. 10; 8. BM, Cotton Charter xviii, 23.

[31] *Moray Registrum*, nos. 21, 51. Lovat is alternatively known as *a' Mhormhaich*, to which Moreweyn may be an approximation. In Convinth we must assume that one other name, in addition to Convinth itself, embraced two davochs.   [32] McKerral, art. cit., 52.

[33] *PSAS*, lxxxii, 50.   [34] *PSAS*, lxxxv, 61.

against this view: Pennant, writing of Lochbroom in the late eighteenth century, said 'Land is set here by the davoch or half-davoch; the last consists of 96 Scotch acres of arable, such as it is, with a competent quantity of mountain and grazing ground'.[35]

It may be a noteworthy contrast that the English preferred to estimate their cultivated land in terms of the instrument which went into the soil at the start of the crop-growing process, while the Scots reckoned in terms of the amount of corn which was sown, or which emerged at the other end of the process. Even so, there can be little doubt that the davoch, whenever it began to be used of land, was a strictly agricultural unit, a measure of arable capacity.[36] Of course it carried pasture with it, for men of the early Middle Ages were incapable of thinking of arable apart from the pasture and grazing that accompanied it. A suggestive pointer to the strictly arable character of the davoch is to be found in documents of the middle of the thirteenth century and later. *C.* 1260, the earl of Strathearn granted certain land in upper Glenalmond 'to be held by its rightful marches *cum omnibus fortyris et communibus pasturis'*. Between 1250 and 1256, Alan Durward granted the two davochs of Clintlaw and Balcashy (Angus) *cum molendino et fortyris ad dictas dauahcs spectantibus.*[37] Some fourteenth-century charters from Ross associate 'le fortyr' of Strath Sgitheach with the davochs of both Easter and Wester Foulis, 'le fortyre' of 'Badgarwy' with the davoch of Katewell, and 'le fortyr' of Ardoch with the davoch of Contullich (in the parishes of Kiltearn and Alness).[38] The word *fortir* is not well-attested in documentary sources, yet its meaning of 'upper land', 'over land', seems clear. In this sense it would correspond with the Welsh word *gorthir*, 'higher land',[39] and it is of some interest to recall that on the

---

[35] *CPNS*, 235 and n.

[36] It is not clear whether the davoch was in origin a measure of seed-corn or of corn-yield. By the twelfth century the term had come to denote a quantity of ground, and had lost its direct connection with measurement of volume. See K. Jackson, *The Gaelic Notes on the Book of Deer*, 116–17.

[37] Fraser, *Grandtully*, i, 125; *Coupar-Angus Chrs.*, i, no. 55.

[38] *Munro Writs*, nos. 5, 6, 11, 15. I have to thank Mr. and Mrs. R. W. Munro for this reference.

[39] See T. Richards, *A Welsh and English Dictionary* (Merthyr Tydfil, 1839). It should also be compared with *gwrthtir*, 'upland', for which see *The Mabinogion* (Everyman edn, ed. G. Jones and T. Jones), p. 68, where 'uplands of Ardudwy'

great manor of Taunton in Somerset the ancient customary freehold tenures were of two kinds, 'Bondlands' and 'Overlands', and on the latter it was said that 'anciently no dwelling stood'.[40] The distinction between the *fortirs* and the main estates with which they were carefully associated suggests on the one hand terrain which was either never or at least not regularly under the plough and on the other hand the principal arable lands which were relied on to produce regular staple crops.

The relationship of davoch to social unit (township, village, or farmstead) has never been clearly established. Davoch-names in *pett-* and *bal-*, of which there are numerous instances, suggest equation of davoch with township, but there are also davoch-names in *achadh-* (field). The davoch was too large for a peasant holding: only sizeable landowners held whole davochs. Yet the davoch possessed some unity; it was tangible, physical, concrete. It was commonly named, and had fixed boundaries. Its unity must surely have lain in the fact that its nucleus was a single stretch of arable, the north-country equivalent of the large fields of the south. The families who were dependent on this arable with its grazing would dwell close to it or round it, forming the township or homestead, the *pett* or *baile* to which a distinctive name would be given. Within this general pattern, the lord's land might well be distinct from the land of the peasantry. Thus Swain, Thor's son, lord of Ruthven near Perth (late twelfth century), speaks of meadow on the Lochty Burn 'beginning at the place which on the east is adjacent to the neyfs' land' (*terre rusticorum*);[41] John of Inchyra (Carse of Gowrie, early thirteenth century) speaks of one full acre of arable at the end of the haugh on the west, next to the cottars' acres;[42] the bishop of St. Andrews (*c.* 1200) refers to Nydie as *Nidin Ecclesie* and *Nidin Rusticorum*—now Nydie and Bond Nydie;[43] the Kirkton of Arbuthnott, in the same period, had numerous petty tenants called *scoloc* (perhaps equivalent to the

translates *gwrthtir Ardudwy*; and *An English and Welsh Dictionary*, ed. D. Silvan Evans, ii, 1027, s.v. 'upland pasturage', *porfa orthtir*. I am grateful to Mr. G. R. J. Jones for help with these Welsh references.

[40] J. Toulmin, *History of Taunton* (ed. Savage, 1822), 50.

[41] *Scone Liber*, no. 21. Swain's own land bore the name *Ahednepobbel*, 'field of the shieling'.

[42] *Scone Liber*, no. 118.

[43] BM, MS. Harl. 4628, ff 240 et seq.

gresmen of the south) living pastorally in return for rents of cheese and dun cows—the lord evicted them one after the other and began to plough their land as he ploughed his own adjacent land;[44] a mid-thirteenth-century charter speaks of the land of *Bondes* near Inverurie.[45]

It has often been remarked that davochs, like carucates, lent themselves to fractionalisation. Many scholars have mentioned the halves, thirds, quarters, fifths and eighths (to go no further) into which davochs might be subdivided. Surviving fractions may here and there betray the existence of a vanished davoch. Trianafour in Glenerrochtie (Perthshire) was presumably the upland 'pasture third' of a lost davoch of Glenerrochtie, while Coignafearn and the other 'coigs' at the head of Strathdearn seemingly formed fifths of the davoch of Sevin[46] or Shevin. But it does not seem to have been realised that among fractions the half-davoch seems to have held a special place, standing in its own right as an established permanent unit, much as the bovate/oxgang stood in relation to the carucate/ploughgate. Thus, we have the revealing place-names, Lettoch (Black Isle), formerly Haldoch or *Lethdabhach*; Lettoch near Grantown, and Halfdavoch (both Moray); Haddo in Fyvie and Haddo in Methlick (Aberdeenshire). There is also the evidence of the documents, especially many in the *Registrum Episcopatus Moraviensis*. Among these may be cited the ten half-davochs enumerated and named in Strathavon,[47] the half-davoch in Stratherrick called Boleskine,[48] the half-davoch of *Kyncarny*,[49] the half-davoch of Urquhart (Inverness-shire) 'which is called the half-davoch of the church',[50] and the half-davoch 'in which is situated the church of Insh' (in Badenoch).[51] If Pennant is to be relied on for the eighteenth-century equation $\frac{1}{2}$ davoch $=96$ Scotch acres, we might hazard the inference that a half-davoch was roughly the same as a south-country carucate of 104 Scotch acres. It is suggestive of the capacity of the davoch and its relationship to the carucate that the common endowment of

---

[44] *Spalding Misc.*, v, 209–13.   [45] *Lindores Chartulary*, no. 116.

[46] L. Shaw, *History of Moray*, 98, 205; *Exchequer Rolls*, vi, *passim* (references in index). This upland davoch was crown property, and its name seems to be preserved today in the name of three hills on its marches, Carn na Saobhaidhe, *Saobhaidh* meaning 'lair of wild beasts'.

[47] *Moray Registrum*, no. 16.   [48] Ibid., no. 73.

[49] Ibid., no. 80.   [50] Ibid., no. 83.   [51] Ibid., no. 76.

north-country parish churches seems to have been half a davoch,[52] while a few possessed a whole davoch (e.g. Laggan in Badenoch, St. Peter of Strathavon, and Lhanbryde).[53] South of the Mounth we have churches endowed with half a carucate (e.g. Longforgan, Invergowrie),[54] while south of the Forth it was common enough for parish churches to possess a whole carucate. It would be extraordinary if parish churches in Moray should have been, in general, much better endowed than their counterparts in the Carse of Gowrie or in Lothian, and the inference is strong that a half-davoch was not greater than a south-country carucate. If we allow for a less efficient plough in the north and smaller 'acres', we should arrive at a relationship which at least seems reasonably acceptable. The historian, however, must pose the question of whether *carucata* in his texts always meant the same thing even in the same region; it might have been used in the earlier period for a whole davoch, later on for half a davoch. Duldauach (now Culdoich, in Strathnairn) appears as a half-carucate in a royal charter of the late twelfth century, and as a half-davoch two generations later.[55]

The geographical distribution of the davoch also raises interesting questions. It is not found anywhere south of the Forth-Clyde line, nor, in fact, was it general throughout the area to the north of this line. It is not found in Argyll, Lennox or Menteith, nor is there much evidence of its use in Strathearn. It can be found in Fife,[56] Gowrie, Stormont and Atholl, and was evidently general throughout the country north of Tay as far as the Dornoch Firth area. Its absence from the Scandinavian north (Caithness and the Northern Isles) may, it has been argued, be due simply to the replacement of a Celtic by a Scandinavian term, leaving the older 'substance' of the davoch in being.[57] In the west highlands its distribution is hard to trace because of the scarcity of early

[52] I have counted (probably not exhaustively) sixteen parish churches in the dioceses of Aberdeen and Moray endowed with a half-davoch each, referred to in *Moray Registrum*. They are Abernethy, Abertarff, Abriachan, Altyre, Botarie, Dallas, Daviot, *Drumdalgyn*, Dumbennan, Essie, Glass, Kincardine, Kinnoir, Rathven, Rhynie and Urquhart.

[53] *Moray Registrum*, nos. 41, 46.   [54] *RRS*, i, nos. 122, 251.

[55] *Moray Registrum*, nos. 3, 31; *RRS*, ii, no. 142.

[56] *St. Andrews Liber*, 290-1; *Dunfermline Registrum*, no. 339; NLS, MS. Adv. 34.6.24, pp. 248-9 (referring to Blebo in Kemback).

[57] H. Marwick, 'Naval Defence in Norse Scotland', *SHR*, xxviii, 1-11.

texts; it occurs in Lochaber,[58] and in late documents which refer to 'fiscal' davochs it is applied to Glenelg, Skye, the Small Isles and the Outer Isles.[59] Despite the apparently Irish origin of the word, there seems to be something inescapably Pictish about the use of the davoch of land.[60]

Davochs usually had names, but the word itself does not enter frequently into place-names. Its use here should be compared with English place-names in *hīd* (hide, 'household') and *hiwisc* with the same meaning.[61] Such names would seem to be later than primary settlement, for they must belong to a time when the reckoning of a place at so many davochs was well established. The word davoch never seems to have been used as a synonym for *baile* or *pett*, and in place-names it may have been attached to a settlement or piece of agrarian exploitation which was essentially subordinate to, dependent upon, some older or larger settlement. Thus Phesdo (Mearns) might have been the 'firm davoch', *fas dabhach* (or 'empty davoch', *fàs dabhach*?), of some neighbouring centre (Kincardine?), while Dochfour, south of Inverness, was perhaps the 'pasture davoch' of some centre which also possessed Dochnalurig and Dochgarroch. Fendoch was possibly the 'white davoch' (*fionn dabhach*) of Glenalmond. Very few davoch-names refer to places of parochial status; Auchindoir in upland Aberdeenshire is one rare example (*Davachendor*, perhaps meaning 'davoch of water or streams'). There survive in Banffshire and Aberdeenshire a number of davoch-names of a rather different type, e.g. the Daugh of Carron (also of Kinermony, Grange, Corinacy, Banffshire), and the Daugh of Invermarkie (also of Aswanley and Cairnborrow, Aberdeenshire). As found at present, these davochs look like the hill pasture or rough grazing attached to townships which are now and must always have been chiefly pastoral. But this hardly contradicts the general thesis propounded here that the davoch was in origin and in essence an agricultural unit. The word must have been adapted to

[58] At least in the place-name Gargawach (*CPNS*, 235), and by implication, fiscally, in *Moray Registrum*, no. 264.

[59] *Reg. Mag. Sig.*, i, App. I, no. 9; cf. also *Cal. Docs. Scot.*, ii, no. 1633.

[60] Mr. Ralegh Radford has made the helpful observation that the distribution of the davoch corresponds closely to that of the Pictish symbol-stones.

[61] E. Ekwall, *Concise Oxford Dictionary of English Place-Names* (4th edn, 1960), under Fyfield, Fifehead, Hyde, Hewish, Huish, etc.

semi-pastoral and wholly pastoral districts, and its survival in the areas mentioned may be due partly to their remoteness and partly to that superfluity of nomenclature which is so attractive a characteristic of north-eastern Scotland.

In Strathearn, writers of early documents seem to have been chary of using any word for a large arable unit, preferring *villa* or *terra* and giving the name of the place. Acres are found, and there are the familiar acres or rigs in big fields, e.g. '2 acres in the *villa* of Pitlandy' described as lying *in agro qui dicitur Fitheleresflat* (early thirteenth century).[62] '1 toft plus 1 acre of land plus land added elsewhere in the field (*in agro*) to make up 4 acres',[63] and '16 acres on the east side of the field called *Langflat*'.[64] The 13-acre bovate appears in Strathearn,[65] and there is at least one text showing that even if the davoch or carucate was not used in Strathearn, nevertheless a subdivision of the davoch, the *rath*, was known there. An early-thirteenth-century charter speaks of the quarter of *Dunphalin* known as *Rath* (now Raith in Trinity Gask),[66] and this is to be compared with charters of the late twelfth century which speak of 2 bovates in Catterline (Mearns) called *Rath*.[67] Apparently a *rath* was a quarter of a davoch, and it looks as though *Dunphalin* formed a davoch even if it was not so called.

Lennox is well-known to have been the home of the *arachor*, a word fittingly preserved in the name of the village of Arrochar at the head of Loch Long. Like carucate, *arachor* has an obvious etymological connection with ploughing, and the texts leave no doubt that *arachor* was in fact a Gaelic term for the ploughgate. 'Three-quarters of *Ackencloy Nether* which in Gaelic is called *arachor*, namely *Clouchbar, Barauchan* and *Barnaferkelyn*',[68] formed three-quarters of one whole *arachor*. Two connected texts give us, first, 'the half-carucate in Strathblane, where the church is built, which in Gaelic is called *arachor*' and, secondly, 'the half-carucate in Strathblane, where the church is built, which in Gaelic is called *Leth-arachor*',[69] and a further text has 'Half a carucate in Killearn, where the church is built, which in Gaelic

---

[62] *Inchaffray Charters*, no. 56. [63] Ibid., no. 57. [64] Ibid., no. 99.
[65] *Lindores Chartulary*, no. 68 (Forgandenny, early thirteenth century).
[66] *Inchaffray Charters*, no. 52. *Dunphalin*, now lost, is represented by Millearn in Trinity Gask. [67] *Arbroath Liber*, i, nos. 67–9.
[68] *Hist. MSS. Comm., Second Report*, App., 166, no. 14.
[69] *Hist. MSS. Comm., Third Report*, App., 386, nos. 7, 9.

is called *Leth-arachor*.'[70] Here, clearly (despite the muddle or error in the first example), carucate = *arachor*, half-carucate = *leth-arachor*. Quarters as well as halves were common in the Lennox, indeed, perhaps we should note that they were especially common, showing a parallel with Argyll. There were other fractions also, and Blackthird, e.g., was doubtless the muirland or unploughable third part of the *arachor* of Darleith (in Cardross). In a markedly pastoral territory such as the Lennox, where rents were paid in cheeses and cattle, the presence of an arable unit, the *arachor*, is noteworthy. If pastoralism did really predominate in early medieval Scotland, still the arable tail seems to have wagged the pastoral dog.

It goes without saying, perhaps, that arable settlements north of the Forth were associated with areas of common pasture, not only in ground adjacent to the settlements themselves, but also in stretches of muir and hill grazing used as shielings. David I, e.g. granted the Dunfermline monks at Urquhart in Moray the land of Penick, by Auldearn, together with the shielings of Fornighty (in Ardclach).[71] The granter of an interesting charter of the middle of the thirteenth century (noted by Watson,[72]) has this to say of the muirland which in his day stretched from the great Roman camp at Ardoch to the ancient village of Muthill, in Strathearn: 'The land called *Cotken* (Gaelic, *coitcheann*, 'common') in *Kathermothel* has been in the time of all my predecessors free and common pasture to all the men dwelling round about it, so that no one may build a house in that pasture or plough it or do anything which might hinder the use of the pasture.'[73] The distinction between local pasture and shieling is well brought out by a late-twelfth-century charter in the Arbroath Cartulary, in which Humphrey de Berkeley, granting the lands of Balfeith (Mearns), with common pasture there and in his fief of Kinkell and Conveth, for up to 100 cattle with their progeny and as many swine and horses as required, adds: 'The monks of Arbroath and

---

[70] Ibid., no. 11. An illustration of how exasperating the evidence can be is provided by the fact that Buchanan, called one carucate, did forinsec service of one cheese from each cheese-making household, while Luss, called two arachors, did service of two cheeses from each cheese-making household (*Hist. MSS. Comm., Third Report*, App., 387, No. 28; *Lennox Cartularium*, Addenda, pp. 96–8).   [71] Lawrie, *Charters*, no. 255.
[72] *CPNS*, 136; cf. above, p. 52.   [73] *Lindores Chartulary*, no. 28.

their tenants may have a shieling from Easter to All Saints for these same beasts, wherever they please in Tipperty, Corsebauld or Glenfarquhar.'[74] In a contemporary royal charter, Humphrey de Berkeley is granted forest rights over seven davochs in Mearns, including by name the two davochs of Tipperty and one davoch of Glenfarquhar.[75] Here, indeed, about these highland reaches of the Bervie Water, as in upper Strathdearn, we may have an instance of davochs whose character was that of summer pasture and game preserve rather than arable farming.

Although it is not strictly relevant to rural settlement, it is impossible to discuss the agricultural units without some reference to the fiscal use to which these units were put. Not only may this throw light on the nature of the agrarian unit, but the tax-collector was a more precocious record-maker than the farmer, and consequently we have a fair amount of documentation of this fiscal aspect. South of the Forth, the Crown's forinsec service was levied according to the capacity of the taxpayers' land measured in carucates, and perhaps in bovates. Benorth Forth, forinsec service—called variously 'Scottish service', 'Scottish army', 'common army' or just 'army'—was levied *according to the number of carucates or the number of davochs*. Examples of the fiscal carucate may be found at Cassingray,[76] Airdrie in Fife,[77] Cambo,[78] and St. Andrews,[79] while Allardice (Mearns) did 'common service' for thirteen bovates.[80] Examples of the fiscal davoch are more numerous, but among them we may mention Balcormo, Morton of Blebo, Bruckly and Nydie (Fife), Blairgowrie (co. Perth), Lour, Kincriech, Inverquharity and Old Montrose (Angus).[81] Beyond the Spey, examples could readily be multiplied, and the student is referred to the *Registrum Episcopatus Moraviensis* for numerous instances.

[74] *Arbroath Liber*, i, no. 89 (*Tubertach, Crospath, Glenferkaryn*).
[75] *RRS*, ii, no. 346.   [76] *RRS*, ii, no. 286.
[77] *RRS*, ii, no. 469 (half a Scottish carucate in shire of Crail).
[78] *RRS*, ii, no. 131.
[79] SRO, Transcripts of Royal Charters, 1214–49, text of charter abridged in *Reg. Mag. Sig.*, iii, no. 2132 (exemption from service due from a certain carucate).   [80] *Hist. MSS. Comm., Fifth Report*, App., 629.
[81] *Acts Parl. Scot.*, i, 101 (Balcormo); NLS, MS. Adv. 34.6.24, pp. 248–9 (Blebo); *Cal. Docs. Scot.*, ii, no. 1350 (Bruckly and Nydie); *Scone Liber*, no. 67 (Blairgowrie); *Coupar-Angus Chrs.*, no. 10 (Lour, Kincriech); SRO, J. M. Thomson, photographs, no. 10 (Inverquharity); *Hist. MSS. Comm., Second Report*, 166, no. 17 (Old Montrose).

In the Fife examples, it is very tempting to suppose that the term *carucata* was simply being used interchangeably with davoch. This would explain the use of the phrase 'Scottish carucate' in the Cambo and Airdrie examples, while it would also make intelligible the otherwise puzzling assessment of Cassingray in Kellie-shire at a ½ carucate and of Balcormo (surely also in Kellie-shire?) at 1½ davochs. But the Blairgowrie document (1235) tells us that Scone Abbey had its assessment reduced from 6 to 5 davochs because 2½ carucates had been taken away from its estate there.[82] If 1 carucate = 1 davoch, the canons of Scone were rather hard done by, but if 1 carucate = ½ davoch their treatment was not so harsh. Perhaps, here, the carucate represented the hard facts of the agricultural situation as it obtained at Blair in the 1230s, while the davoch assessment belonged to a much older period and had grown out-of-date. Otherwise, this may be additional evidence that *carucata* was used for a half-davoch.

When we study the documents relevant to Scottish agriculture which have survived from the twelfth and thirteenth centuries, we are rather like palaeontologists trying to reconstruct the whole body of an extinct form of life from a chance survival of imperfect fossils. It is here that we badly need the help of archaeology, geography and of the technological historian. We need to know much more about types of plough and of ploughing techniques, field shapes and sizes, corn yields, kinds of stock reared and so forth. A big heavy plough in the south would produce a quite different 'ploughgate' from a small light plough in the north. Rearing cattle and sheep for local consumption or for milk and cheese would lead to very different conditions from those which obtained when the export of wool and hides became an important feature of the economy, and we need to know when these developments took place. To some of these questions we shall never know the answer, but we can go further than we have yet done. The preliminary contribution of the student of documents is that already *c.* 1100, when his sources largely begin, the social and agrarian pattern of Scotland both south and north of Forth appears to be of very long standing. A fiscal system based on the traditional agrarian units was well established, probably fairly

[82] *Scone Liber*, no. 67

ancient. It may have been copied from one or more of the Anglo-Saxon kingdoms, on the model of the hidage, or it may have been developed independently. In general, the peasant population met its obligations to its lords and clergy by rendering a cross-section of their produce more or less on the spot, or at least to some not very distant shire-centre. For the king, if not for lesser mortals, there may have been some degree of specialisation; place-name evidence, at least, seems to suggest as much. There are, for instance, at least three localities benorth Forth which take their names from the *conveth* (*coinnmed*), the hospitality given to a visiting lord.[83] In Ayrshire there is the old settlement of Sorn, which apparently has the same significance.[84] In Kinglassie (Fife), in what was the old royal demesne of Fothrif, there is the estate of Goatmilk, which evidently means what it says in the earliest recorded form of the name (*Gatemilc*),[85] while just north of the Lomond Hills, also on former royal demesne, is the estate of Cash, which looks like what would be made out of goatmilk and other kinds of milk as well (Gaelic *cais*, 'cheese'). These names, and the cheese and cattle rents of Lennox and Mearns and other parts, remind us of the importance of pastoralism in early medieval Scotland. But davochs, carucates, and arachors, the prevalence of malt and *prebenda* in crown revenues, and the abundant references in every settled part of the country to mills and multures show that already by the twelfth century and probably long before, the pattern of rural settlement was chiefly determined by the amount of ground that could be ploughed and sown, and of the crops that could be harvested.

[83] Above, p. 47.
[84] Above, p. 47. There is also Sornfalla (in Douglas), Lanarkshire.
[85] Lawrie, *Charters*, no. 74.

10 The beginnings of military feudalism

The legal and military aspects of feudalism in twelfth-century Scotland received notable attention from scholars at the turn of the century.[1] In 1954, we were given the results of the late R. L. Graeme Ritchie's life-long study of Norman influence upon Scotland before 1165.[2] While Professor Ritchie's book does not treat of Scottish feudalism as such, it contains many passages relevant to feudal ideas and institutions. It is not intended here to re-examine these legal, military and (as they may perhaps be called) cultural aspects of the subject, though it will be impossible to avoid going over some of the same ground. The purpose of this chapter will be, first, to establish, as far as possible, a fairly correct chronology of the introduction into Scotland of military feudalism; secondly, to give some account of its salient features; and, thirdly, to try to estimate its relative importance in the constitution of the early medieval Scottish kingdom. The evidence reviewed will relate almost entirely to the period from 1124 to 1214.

That Norman feudalism had made some headway in Scotland before 1124 was urged by Graeme Ritchie; but the evidence for it, which he surveyed very thoroughly, does not in sum appear impressive.[3] A small party of Norman knights were in Macbeth's service from 1052 to 1054, when they were all slain in battle. Forty years later, the Scots, having rebelled against King

---

[1] G. Neilson, 'The Motes in Norman Scotland', *Scottish Review*, xxxii (1898), 209–38; 'Tenure by Knight-service in Scotland', *Juridical Review*, xi (1899), 71–86, 173–86; Ella S. Armitage, *The Early Norman Castles of the British Isles* (1912), pp. 302–22.

[2] *The Normans in Scotland* (Edinburgh, 1954).

[3] *The Normans in Scotland*, pp. 1–175, esp. pp. 160–75.

Duncan II, agreed to accept him on condition that he would not further introduce Englishmen or Normans, nor allow them to perform military service for him.[4] This hardly seems to point conclusively to a feudal settlement before 1094. The evidence from the reigns of Edgar and Alexander I (1097–1124) suggests at most that the Scottish crown was not hostile to the military feudalism already established in England. There is no indication that it regarded castle-building, the regular use of professional cavalry, the knight's fee, or homage and fealty, as essential props of royal authority. Between 1099 and 1107, a baron from England, who had fought for King Edgar, tried to build a castle on the land in Lothian, near the English border, with which the king had rewarded him, and which possibly formed a fief.[5] An envoy of King Alexander in 1120 was described as a knight,[6] and the expeditions made by that king in 1114–15 to Wales and the far north of Scotland probably involved the use of cavalry. Shortly after David I's accession in 1124, he was required to settle a dispute between the Celtic clergy of Saint Serf's Island in Loch Leven and a knight named Robert of Burgundy, who was, it seems, already a landowner in the neighbourhood.[7] Robert of Burgundy was clearly an exotic importation, and it is possible that his estate was a knight's fee created by Edgar or Alexander I. Beside this evidence, however, we should set the speech ascribed by Ailred of Rievaulx to Robert Brus in 1138. Brus reproaches King David for ingratitude towards his Norman retainers, reminding him that it had been the fear of David's Anglo-Norman barons which had forced Alexander I to yield possession of David's inheritance in southern Scotland.[8] Even if this report were Ailred's invention, it would have little point unless it was generally believed that King Alexander did not maintain, at least during his early years, a force of heavy-armed cavalry.

This reference to the knightly vassals of Alexander I's brother David brings us to the first significant evidence of military feudalism in Scotland. That David I was responsible for its

[4] Florence of Worcester, *Chronicon ex chronicis* (ed. Thorpe), ii, 32; cf. ibid., i, 210, 212.

[5] *Chron. Fordun*, i, 225.   [6] Eadmer, *Historia Novorum*, 279.

[7] Lawrie, *Charters*, no. 80.   [8] Migne, *Patrologia Latina*, cxcv, col. 709.

introduction on a wide scale and with lasting effect has long been an unchallenged fact of Scottish history. The most frequently cited illustration of his policy is the grant to Robert Brus of Annandale and Annan castle as a fief, which he probably, and his descendants certainly, held for the service of ten knights.[9] It is well-known also that Hugh de Morville, who became the king's hereditary constable, was enfeoffed on the east with Lauderdale, on the west with Cunningham; and that Walter son of Alan, who became hereditary steward, was enfeoffed on the east with land in Tweeddale, on the west in Renfrew and the Ayr valley. It was evidently in like manner that Eskdale was given to Robert Avenel[10] and Liddesdale to Ranulf de Sules.[11] It is probable that similar provision was made by King David for a number of other Anglo-Norman barons who regularly attended him, for example, William de Somerville, Robert Corbet, William and Walter of Lindsey, and Robert de Burneville.[12] Save for Brus's charter of Annandale, not a single direct record of this colonisation has survived. We know, solely by inference, of what appears to have been a fairly systematic plantation of Anglo-Norman or Breton barons across the middle of southern Scotland, who, it may reasonably be supposed, held their lands by military service. The truth of this inference is confirmed by the two explicit charters of infeftment for knight-service which are all that survive from David I's reign. By the first,[13] the king granted Athelstaneford by Haddington to Alexander of St. Martin for the service of half a knight, adding, 'and I shall pay him yearly from my chamber 10 marks of silver until I shall have made up for him the full fee of one knight'. By the second,[14] Walter of Ryedale (Riddell) was enfeoffed in Whitton and Lilliesleaf in Roxburghshire for one knight's service, to hold 'as one of my barons of that neighbourhood best and most freely holds his fief'. In short, in the later part of his reign King David was in process of creating knights' fees, and the knight's fee was already familiar at least in the area of Roxburgh.

[9] Lawrie, *Charters*, no. 54; *RRS*, ii, no. 80.   [10] *Melrose Liber*, no. 39.
[11] SRO, Crown Office Writs, nos. 1–4.
[12] These men are named because there is good evidence that they settled in Scotland permanently.
[13] Lawrie, *Charters*, no. 186.
[14] Lawrie, *Charters*, no. 222 = *RRS*, i, no. 42.

All this merely underlines what every Scottish historian has fully recognised, that David I, himself trained as a knight under Henry I of England and, in virtue of his double earldom of Northampton-Huntingdon, the lord of scores of infeft knights in eleven midland shires, did much to reproduce in his own realm the pattern of feudal tenure prevailing in Norman England. Yet this familiar picture of David I as the feudaliser of Scotland may overstate the thoroughness of his achievement, and antedate a process which was in fact to continue for the rest of the twelfth century and beyond. In the first place, the infeftments mentioned were all carried out south of the Forth–Clyde line, in Lothian and Cumbria, and not in the country considered in the twelfth century to be Scotland proper. Secondly, even in this southern third of the kingdom, there must still have been in David I's time wide tracts of land wholly innocent of castles and owing the crown nothing whatever by way of knight service. For example, King David did not eliminate the substantial Northumbrian aristocracy native to the soil of Tweeddale, Teviotdale and Lothian. It would be unsafe to assume that he was able in one generation to convert these thanes and drengs into knights on the Norman model. On the contrary, his military tenants were incomers to the land, some from his own honour of Huntingdon, others drawn to his service from afar by his personal reputation and the prospect of territorial reward. Such considerations seem to make all the more interesting the meagre yet reliable scraps of evidence which show us that David I not only began to create feudal holdings north of the Forth, but also brought into strictly feudal relationship with himself one of the greatest of the native Scottish magnates. A charter of William the Lion, of date 1166 × 1172,[15] confirmed to William, son of Freskin, for two knights' service, the lands of Strathbrock in West Lothian together with Duffus and neighbouring lands in Moray, 'which his father held in the time of King David'. From his name, Freskin was almost certainly a Fleming.[16] His holding of land in a district remote from the normal centres of Scottish government has always been associated,

[15] *RRS*, ii, no. 116.

[16] T. Forssner, *Continental Germanic Personal Names in England* (Uppsala, 1916), 95. For the Flemish character of the suffix *-kin*, cf. J. Mansion, *Oud-Gentsche Naamkunde* (1924), 217, and *Complete Peerage* (ed. G. White), xii, pt. I, 537, n. d.

no doubt rightly, with the king's annexation of Moray after the defeat and death of its last native mormaer in 1130. From another reliable copy of a charter of William I,[17] we learn that David I granted West Calder in Midlothian to Duncan, earl of Fife, in return for knight-service. This, the earliest known military enfeoffment of a native Scottish lord, is remarkable enough, but its interest is overshadowed by an original charter of Alexander II,[18] fortunately extant, which shows that King David granted to this same Earl Duncan the earldom of Fife itself and that the grant was recorded by a charter in which a fixed service was specified. This grant, as a fief and by charter, of an ancient Scottish earldom cannot have been made much later than 1136, and would therefore have been contemporary with the earliest known grant of a feudal earldom by the charter of an English king, the grant of the earldom of Essex to Geoffrey de Mandeville in 1140.[19] It provides striking testimony to the lengths to which David I was able to go in the introduction of feudalism into Scotland. Yet it should not be regarded as typical. Duncan of Fife belonged to a family which was closely allied to the royal house by personal loyalty and probably by blood relationship.[20] To suppose, as Skene supposed in his study of Celtic Scotland,[21] that King David was able to treat the other ancient earldoms as he treated Fife is to go beyond anything warranted by the evidence. Across the Forth, in fact, David I had made a significant beginning; but the task was to be completed only by his successors.

The enquiry must therefore be projected into the reigns of Malcolm the Maiden and William the Lion. With the second half of the twelfth century, the picture of a steadily expanding feudalism grows clearer and more detailed. The impression which the whole of the evidence now seems to convey is, that over much and perhaps most of the country effectively ruled by the king,

---

[17] *RRS*, ii, no. 472.   [18] *Nat. MSS. Scot.*, i, Pl. L.
[19] *Complete Peerage*, v, 115, n. b.
[20] This is suggested by the earls' personal names, and by the fact that Malcolm Canmore's son Ethelred was earl of Fife (Lawrie, *Charters*, no. 14). R. L. G. Ritchie, *Normans in Scotland*, 273, strangely speaks of 'the prevalence of Norman names in the family' of the earls of Fife. The prevailing names were in fact Duncan and Malcolm.
[21] *Celtic Scotland*, iii (1880), 63–71.

military feudal tenure had become the normal mode by which his greater lay subjects held their lands. To this conclusion, at least two serious objections might be raised. In the first place, a late twelfth-century document's chance of survival is considerably better than that of any produced before 1153. If, it may be argued, the evidence for the more widespread granting of fiefs becomes plentiful only for the reigns of Malcolm IV and William I, it does not follow that the practice itself was newly developing in their time. There seem to be two answers to this objection. First, there is the nature of the evidence, the composition of the royal charters of infeftment. Between *c.* 1150 and 1214 there seems to have been a definite progress towards greater precision and the use of stereotyped formulas. While the infeftments of David I and his eldest grandson show some variety of wording, the thirty or more documents of this class surviving from the reign of William the Lion are so alike in style and language[22] as to leave little doubt that their issue has become a familiar activity—one may even say, a routine activity—for the clerks of the king's writing-office. The second answer is a matter of geographical distribution. If we consider the infeftments made before 1214 and explicitly recorded either in charters whose texts survive or in reliable references, we see that those of David I relate to two border counties and Lothian, together with one example from Moray. Three of the six knight-service and serjeanty charters of Malcolm IV concern lands north of the Forth. Under William I the proportion becomes twenty-five for the north to nine for the south. If instead of counting the charters we count the number of knights and serjeants for whose service they stipulate, the ratios are admittedly somewhat different: under Malcolm IV, six knights and one serjeant from the south against three knights from the north; under his brother, $36\frac{1}{2}$ knights and one serjeant produced from southern fees against $27\frac{5}{6}$ knights and four or five serjeants from northern fees. Yet however this evidence is analysed, it points unmistakably to a steady feudalisation of the Celtic regions beyond the Forth and Tay in the second half of the twelfth century. There is a contrast here with the direct and indirect

---

[22] This is an impression formed by the writer from a study of the charters of infeftment known to him, now published in *RRS*, ii, *passim*. Its truth can be tested only when the charters have been compared.

evidence for the reign of David I which can scarcely be attributed merely to the incidence of survival.

The second objection is that in an enquiry into knight-service and serjeanty tenements not enough weight may be given to the number and importance of enfeoffments made in return for unspecialised, non-military services. It will be best to hold over any attempt to meet this objection until a survey has been made in some detail of military feudal tenements in Scotland prior to the death of William the Lion.

We may find some confirmation of the belief that the years from 1153 to 1214 formed a period of more intensive military feudalism than Scotland had previously experienced, if we turn from statistics to personalities. Malcolm the Maiden and William the Lion belonged more completely than their grandfather to the Frankish aristocracy which in their time dominated western Europe. It is clear that they both felt the powerful attraction of this society, with its knightly code, its passion for tournaments, and its large and growing literature of chivalry. An anonymous writer said of them, in a passage often wrongly quoted as applying to all the twelfth-century rulers of Scotland, that they held themselves for Frenchmen, not only by race (their mother was a Warenne) but also in manners, language and culture, and that they kept only Frenchmen in their household and following.[23] Jordan Fantosme says much the same of King William, that he held only foreigners dear and would never love his own people.[24] Within five years of Malcolm IV's accession, Henry II of England was able to exploit politically his young cousin's ardent desire to be made a knight.[25] It would not have been honourable for the king of Scots to have been knighted by anyone of lesser rank than the English king, and besides, there was almost certainly a wish to maintain a family tradition: Henry I had bestowed knighthood upon David I, David in turn had knighted Henry of Anjou. Malcolm was kept waiting until the summer of 1159, when, with his brother William, his steward Walter son of Alan, and other barons, he joined the English king's abortive expedition to

[23] Walter of Coventry, *Memoriale* (ed. Stubbs), ii, 206.
[24] *Chronicle of the War between the English and the Scots* (ed. F. Michel, Surtees Soc., 1840), lines 641–3.
[25] See *RRS*, i, 10–12.

Toulouse.[26] The failure of the siege of Toulouse probably mattered less to the eighteen-year-old king of Scots than the fact that in the Bishop's Meadow at Périgeux King Henry at last girded him with the belt of knighthood.[27] This episode is usually cited for its evidence that the relationship between the two kings was that of lord and vassal. No doubt the two boys who represented the Scottish royal house were mindful of their feudal obligations; but it seems at least as likely that they were glad to join the Toulouse expedition because of the opportunity for knightly adventure. There is, in fact, some curious evidence for the almost pathetic pleasure which King Malcolm took in being knighted. In four of his surviving acts, normally businesslike and matter-of-fact documents, the king prefaces the substantive part of the text with the words, 'Know that after I received the arms of knighthood. . . .'[28]

It is an especially valuable part of Graeme Ritchie's work that it has emphasized the social aspect of early Scottish feudalism when its importance was in danger of being overlooked. After all, the feudal host which could be mustered by the twelfth- and thirteenth-century kings of Scotland could never, at its greatest extent, seriously challenge any major cavalry force from south of the border. It was doubtless useful to deal with rebellion in the remote and ungovernable parts of the kingdom, in the far north and west. But even here, William I found it easier on one occasion (1212) to ask for mercenaries from England to suppress an insurrection.[29] But to keep his countenance before the rulers of England and France, of Flanders and Brittany, a king of Scots must have a sizeable entourage of trained knights. In a country where money was scarce, it was not only more honourable, it was actually easier, to maintain its members by enfeoffments of land than to raise the cash needed to pay the wages of professional hired soldiers. We have good evidence of William the Lion's fondness for jousting. In the year of his accession, he crossed to France and attempted 'certain feats of chivalry'.[30] In 1175, after his capture by Henry II, he brought a large company to a

---

[26] That Walter son of Alan the Steward accompanied the king on the Toulouse expedition seems to be shown by his witnessing an act given by Malcolm IV at 'Andele', i.e. Andely in Normandy (*RRS*, i, no. 55), the only known act of King Malcolm dated south of the Channel.
[27] Anderson, *Early Sources*, ii, 243.   [28] *RRS*, i, nos. 183, 184, 195, 198.
[29] *RRS*, ii, 19–20.   [30] *Chron. Melrose*, 37, ad annum 1166.

tournament in Normandy fought out between knights of France, England and Normandy on one side, and of Anjou, Maine, Poitou, Brittany and Scotland on the other. The best of the Scots knights was reckoned to be Philip de Valognes, who, according to the biographer of William the Marshal,

> Fu armez si trés cointement
> Et si trés acesmeement
> E sus toz les autres plus beals,
> Si fu plus joinz ke nus oiseals,
> Que mainz chevaliers l'en esgarde.[31]

We know from Scottish sources that Philip de Valognes, a younger son 'who went to Scotland',[32] was the king's chamberlain, and held, among other property, half a knight's fee in Benvie and Panmure in Angus.[33] Even the engagement in front of Alnwick castle in 1174, where the Yorkshire barons captured King William, had much of the character of a tournament. Jordan Fantosme, in his lively fashion, tells us that four of the Scottish knights fought particularly well, Richard de Melville, William de Mortemer, Ralph 'Rufus', and old Sir Alan de Lascelles, 'who had not jousted for thirty years'.[34] These names occur frequently among the witnesses of William the Lion's charters.[35] Moreover, we know from surviving charters of infeftment that Richard de Melville held Granton by serjeanty, and Melville itself as a fief, perhaps for knight-service;[36] that Roger de Mortemer (to whom William de Mortemer was doubtless kin) held Fowlis Easter in Gowrie for the service of one knight;[37] and that Kinnaird in Gowrie was

[31] *Histoire de Guillaume le Maréchale* (ed. Meyer, 1891–1901), i, 44–56, especially lines 1319–29.
[32] J. Greenstreet, in *Notes & Queries* (6th Ser.), v, 143: 'Et Philippus tercius frater adiit Scociam'. Cf. J. H. Round, in *Ancestor*, xi (1904), 130.
[33] *RRS*, ii, no. 405.   [34] Op cit., lines 1856–90.
[35] *RRS*, ii, references in index.
[36] Ibid., nos. 45, 266 (Granton), and nos. 59 and 269, which state that lands at Liberton and Leadburn formerly held by Malbet (presumably including lands named after the Melville family) were to be held by Geoffrey de Melville, and after him by Richard de Melville, 'on the same condition and by the same service as are testified by the charter of King Malcolm (IV)'. This charter has not survived to show what the service was.
[37] Ibid., no. 302.

held by Ralph 'Rufus' for the same service.[38] These men, of course, were not Scots, but we know from similar charters of infeftment that King William might demand knight-service from native landowners, from the younger sons of Scottish earls, and even, in two instances, from earls themselves. Between 1172 and 1184, Ardross in East Fife was granted for one knight's service to Merleswain, whose family were not newly-settled in the district.[39] The Ogilvy family has its origin in the grant which King William made before 1177 to Gilbert, a younger son of Earl Gilchrist of Angus, of the lands of Ogilvy and Kilmundie by Glamis and of Pourie near Dundee, likewise for the service of one knight.[40] Malise, a younger son of Earl Ferteth of Strathearn, was infeft for one knight's service in Muthil and other properties in the neighbourhood (1172 × 1178) and also, apparently, in Meikleour and Lethendy, which his brother Gilbert held later, after succeeding to the earldom.[41] Madderty formed a knight's fee for Earl Gilbert after c. 1185, when its previous holder had forfeited it for treason.[42] Earl Duncan II of Fife was confirmed in the possession of Strathleven, granted to him in return for the service of knights, apparently between 1165 and 1171.[43]

Among the knights captured at Alnwick was Waltheof son of Baldwin, lord of Biggar.[44] It seems probable that Waltheof's father, who first appears in record as sheriff of Lanark in 1162, was established at Biggar during the remarkable colonisation of Strathclyde carried out by Malcolm IV. There are hardly any original documents for a study of this event, and for our knowledge that it happened at all we depend on piecing together many scattered bits of indirect evidence. It is true that we have one original act of King Malcolm which shows that he ordered a large estate in lower Clydesdale to be perambulated for a new owner,[45] but this owner was the Cistercian abbey of Newbattle and not a lay feudatory. A firmer starting-point is given by a brief writ

[38] *RRS*, ii, no. 135.
[39] Ibid., no. 137. This Merleswain was the son of Merleswain son of Colban, who, c. 1160, gave to St. Andrews priory the church of Kennoway, together with its endowments, which in part at least had been granted by a third Merleswain at some earlier date (*St. Andrews Liber*, 258–9). The name recalls the prominent refugee who fled from England in 1068 and again in 1070 (Anderson, *Scottish Annals*, 88, 91).
[40] *RRS*, ii, no. 140.   [41] Ibid., nos. 136, 524.   [42] Ibid., no. 258.
[43] Ibid., no. 558.   [44] *Chron. Howden*, ii, 63.   [45] *RRS*, i, no. 198.

copied into a cartulary of Sawtry abbey in Huntingdonshire.[46] By this writ, David Olifard—King David I's godson, and ancestor of the Scottish family of Oliphant—renounced before his friends and peers his ancestral holding in Sawtry, a part of the honour of Huntingdon, because his lord King Malcolm had given him in exchange 'the land between the two Calders' (*inter duas Caledoures*), between, that is, the North Calder Water and the South Calder Water, two tributaries which fall into the Clyde on either side of Bothwell. This brief document, which has escaped the notice of the Scottish family historians, not only gives us the origin of the great medieval lordship of Bothwell, but also one of our very rare glimpses of the Scottish king transplanting into his own kingdom a baron of his honour of Huntingdon. Another private charter (in the Arbroath cartulary) shows that King Malcolm granted more land by the South Calder to a settler named Tancard, who was probably a Fleming and who has certainly left his name in Thankerton by Bothwell and Thankerton near Lanark.[47] Again, it was in Malcolm IV's reign that another man bearing a name outlandish in Clydesdale but not unfamiliar in Flanders, Wice or Wicius,[48] gave to Kelso abbey the church of his 'toun', *Wicestun*, now Wiston,[49] while, for contemporary and probably Flemish neighbours along these upland reaches of the Clyde, Wice of Wiston had, among others, Lambin in *Lambinestun* (Lamington) and Simon Loccard in *Simondestun* (Symington), in addition to Baldwin, lord of Biggar.[50] The Flemish character of this colony, which has long been recognised by genealogists and local

[46] Bodl. Library, MS. Rawlinson B. 142, fo. 16ᵛ (transcript of Sir Richard St. George).

[47] *Arbroath Liber*, no. 99; *Origines Parochiales*, i, 143.

[48] Forssner, *Continental Germanic Personal Names*, 259; Mansion, *Oud-Gentsche Naamkunde*, 95. They discuss the form Wizo. Neither gives the form Wice or Wicius, but Forssner, pp. 39–40, says that Azo (a name of similar development to Wizo) may occur as Ace. One should compare Lambynus *Asa*, probably the Lambin whose name is preserved in Lamington (*Kelso Liber*, p. 75).

[49] *Kelso Liber*, no. 336.

[50] *Origines Parochiales* i, 173 (Lamington), 144–5 (Symington). Compare also Roberton (ibid., 148), from Robert, brother of Lambin. For Baldwin, sheriff of Lanark, see *RRS*, i, no. 198, and for his line, *Kelso Liber*, no. 186.

It is probably significant of the deliberate and symmetrical character of the plantation of upper Clydesdale that in 1359 the baronies of Biggar, Covington, Symington, Roberton, Lamington and Wiston each owed the same amount of castle-ward at Lanark Castle (*Exchequer Rolls*, i, 582).

historians, finds a curious echo in a part of Britain quite unconnected with Scotland. In the first half of the twelfth century a substantial number of Flemings were planted in the west of modern
Pembrokeshire. There in the 1130s we find Wizo the Fleming and
his settlement of Wiston; there too Tancard the Fleming, castellan
of Haverfordwest, whose name may be preserved in Tankredston
near St. Davids; there too we even come upon a settler with the
uncommon Flemish name of Freskin,[51] recalling for the Scottish
historian his namesake who founded the great baronial families of
Moray and Sutherland.[52] This oddly close parallel is not without
the value which a comparison may sometimes afford where the
evidence is meagre or obscure. But by far the most arresting clue
to the 'plantation of Strathclyde' seems to be given us by King
Malcolm himself in a remarkable charter[53] which he issued shortly
before his death in favour of the cathedral church of Glasgow. In
this charter, the king recorded his gift to the cathedral and its
clergy of Kinclaith[54] (now Glasgow Green), for the remission and
absolution of all the transgressions committed by his grandfather,
his father and himself against the church of Glasgow—'if', the
king is careful to add, 'if it be that we have transgressed in any
point'—'and specifically', he continues, 'in respect of those lands
which, up to the time when I took the staff of a pilgrim to Saint
James, I granted to my barons and knights, from which lands the
church of Glasgow had been accustomed to receive rents and
"cain".' It is not often that a twelfth-century royal charter
speaks so candidly about the remorse of conscience by which,
from time to time, a king might be afflicted. But for the purposes
of our enquiry, it is of greater consequence here to emphasise
that Clydesdale contained a number of estates of which the church
of Glasgow had once held the lordship but which it did not
possess at the end of the twelfth century.[55] The particular value

[51] B. Charles, *Non-Celtic Place-names in Wales*, 44 and 28; *Pipe Roll, 31
Henry I*, 136 (for 'Witso Flandrensis' and 'Fresechinus filius Ollec'); and
Giraldus Cambrensis, *Opera* (Rolls Ser.), vi, 85–6.

[52] R. L. G. Ritchie noted this parallel between Pembroke and Clydesdale
(*Normans in Scotland*, 376, n. 4).

[53] *Glasgow Registrum*, no. 15 (=*RRS*, i, no. 265).

[54] 'Conclud'. Cf. R. Renwick, *History of Glasgow*, i, 37, 287.

[55] Lawrie, *Charters*, no. 50.
Even if we cannot accept all the identifications proposed by J. T. T. Brown
(*Inquest of David*, 1901), we ought not to adopt the excessive scepticism shown

of this charter consists in its implication that the feudal colonisation of the Clyde valley was a deliberate and forcible stroke of royal policy.

With the settlement of Clydesdale, we may compare the better attested process by which knight's fees and serjeanties were created in Gowrie, Angus and Mearns. The evidence shows this to have been the work of William I, and there is nothing to suggest that any considerable feudalisation had taken place in these districts before 1165. Some of the evidence for Angus and Gowrie has already been noted, and some will be referred to later.[56] Here we may mention briefly a few surviving charters which show King William establishing feudal holdings in a region which under David I was probably still dominated by the native magnates. Between 1195 and 1200, William Giffard, already possessing a considerable holding in East Lothian, was granted Tealing in Angus with Powgavie in Gowrie by the same marches as those by which Ferthnauh (presumably a native predecessor) had held that land. The service was fixed at one knight.[57] C. 1173–80 the king's chamberlain Walter de Berkeley was infeft in

by Lawrie (op. cit., pp. 301–3). Mr. Brown was clearly right in thinking that the names in the Inquest are arranged in geographical groups. Working backward from the end of the list, we have:

(1) Morebattle.
(2) Traquair and Peebles.
(3) 'Treuergylt' (unidentified).
(4) 'Brumescheyd' (probably 'Brunschaith', 'Brunscayt', xiii. cent., *Melrose Liber*, nos. 205, 318, etc., associated with Auchencrieff and Dargavel near Dumfries; 'Brounskeath', etc., also so associated, xvii. cent., *Retours*, Dumfries, nos. 260, 232, etc.). Esbie; Trailtrow; 'Colehtaun' (? 'Coldanis abone Castlemilk', *Acts Parl. Scot.*, i, 716, now Cowdens); Dryfesdale; 'Abermelc' (Castlemilk or St. Mungo); 'Edyngaheym' (probably Edingham in Urr parish, the chapel of which was granted to Holyrood Abbey both by its lord and by the bishops of Glasgow, *Holyrood Liber*, nos. 52, 53, 67. It is 'Edinghaim' on Blaeu's map of 1654); Hoddom.
(5) Ashkirk; Lilliesleaf; 'Treueronum' (? 'Trarouny', *Melrose Liber*, no. 544, Troney Hill in Ancrum parish); Ancrum.
(6) Eddleston and Stobo.
(7) Thirteen other names, which include 'Cunclut' (Kinclaith), Carntyne, Carmyle, Wandell, 'Abercarf' (? mouth of the Garf Water, therefore Wiston), and Machan. It is extremely probable that the whole group from 'Carcleuien' to 'Planmichel' consists of places in Clydesdale, and very few of these are found in the possession of Glasgow cathedral church after the twelfth century.

[56] Above, pp. 287–8; below, p. 294.   [57] *RRS*, ii, no. 418.

the estate of Inverkeilor on the Angus coast, likewise for a single knight's service.[58] Between 1202 and 1208, King William confirmed to Walter de la Kernelle the land of Guthrie (near Forfar) for the service of half a knight 'as testified in the charter of Roger de la Kernelle', Walter's predecessor.[59] The family of de la Kernelle (Carnail) were tenants of the Honour of Huntingdon in Great Stukeley[60] but there is no evidence that any of them settled in Scotland before the time of William the Lion, to several of whose acts Roger de la Kernelle was a witness. Before 1174, the land of 'Rossin', perhaps Rossie by Montrose, had been granted to Henry, son of Gregory the clerk, for one knight's service.[61] In the period 1189 × 1199 the king issued charters of infeftment granting Benholm in Mearns to Hugh, brother of Elias the clerk, for half a knight's service, and Kinneff in Mearns to William de Montfort for one knight's service.[62] Between Benholm and Kinneff lie Arbuthnott and Allardice. The latter was confirmed by the king (1189 × 1199) to Walter, son of Walter Scott;[63] perhaps c. 1199, since Walter Scott, a neighbour of the lords of Arbuthnott and therefore doubtless the donee's father, was said to have been on the point of death not long before February, 1198.[64] The service for Allardice was one archer with horse and haubergel. Arbuthnott the king seems to have granted as a fief to Osbert Olifard, whose successor Walter Olifard sub-infeft Hugh of Swinton, ancestor of the baronial family of Arbuthnott.[65] The next parish west of Arbuthnott is Fordoun. Here, in the Howe of the Mearns, is Balfeith, which according to the oath of a local jury, 1198–9, belonged to the land given by King William to Humphrey de Berkeley for his homage and service. This land was evidently that described by Humphrey de Berkeley as his fief of Kinkell (in Fordoun) and 'Cuneueth' (i.e. Conveth in Laurence-kirk).[66] For lack of any surviving charter, we cannot tell whether

[58] RRS, ii, no. 185.   [59] Ibid., no. 473.

[60] W. Farrer, Honors and Knights' Fees, ii, 360–2. A Reginald de la Kernelle held land in Northants in this period: see Pipe Rolls, 34 Henry II to 6 Richard I (references in indexes), and in the thirteenth century a branch of the family held part of Earl's Barton of the honour of Huntingdon (V.C.H., Northants, iv, 117).

[61] RRS, ii, no. 151.   [62] Ibid., nos. 350, 335.   [63] Ibid., no. 404.

[64] Spalding Misc., v, 211 (shortly before the consecration of Roger de Beaumont as bishop of St. Andrews).

[65] Ibid., pp. 210–11.   [66] Arbroath Liber, no. 89.

the Olifards held Arbuthnott for military service. Documents recently brought to light prove that Conveth was held by the Berkeleys for half a knight's service.[67] Both direct and indirect evidence shows the crown establishing hereditary fiefs in the Mearns in the later years of the twelfth century.

It is chiefly in royal and private charters of the reign of William the Lion that we must look for answers in detail to certain questions naturally prompted by a study of the contemporary feudal scene in England. What, for example, can we learn of the size of a Scottish knight's fee? What was its value in money? What was the degree of subinfeudation carried out by the king's tenants-in-chief? What was the normal type of serjeanty in Scotland? Where mere acreage is concerned, it would obviously be absurd to look for uniformity, even if we could trace twelfth-century fees on the modern map, which for the most part we cannot. But might we expect some similarity in terms of social organisation, agricultural capacity or annual yield in cash? The English evidence, collected and discussed by Sir Frank Stenton, would counsel caution. 'It disproves', he says,[68] 'the existence of any general idea that the land which provided a knight's service should form an economic unit, or that manor and knight's fee should be identical.' And he goes on to show that in the middle of the twelfth century knights' fees of £10 a year were probably commoner than those assessed at £20, the rate which later became almost standard.[69] In asking whether the typical knight's fee was as elusive a concept in Scotland as it was in England, we should remember that a higher proportion of single fees seems to have been created in Scotland directly by the king, and that therefore we might reasonably expect somewhat less variety in size and value. So far as it goes, and it does not take us very far, the Scottish evidence does appear to bear out this expectation. It is true that estates scattered over several parishes were occasionally brought together by the king to form approximately the fief of one knight. Seton and Winton, east of Edinburgh, were in this way united with Winchburgh on the west to make one knight's fee for Philip of Seton.[70] Gogar, Pentland and Cousland, respectively west, south and east of

---

[67] *RRS*, ii, nos. 344, 345.
[68] *The First Century of English Feudalism* (2nd edn, 1961), 159.
[69] Ibid., pp. 166–8.   [70] *RRS*, ii, no. 200.

Edinburgh, made up a fee of one and a half knights for Ralph of Graham.[71] A group of townships spread out across ten or twelve miles of country on the marches of Strathallan and Strathearn were granted for one knight's service to Malise, the younger son of Earl Ferteth of Strathearn.[72] But beside these examples should be set the far more numerous cases where the knight's fee of the twelfth century seems to have consisted of a compact inhabited locality which, later at any rate, emerged as a distinct parish or village. We have noticed West Calder in David I's time; from Malcolm IV's infeftments we may cite Lundin in Fife, a knight's fee for Philip the chamberlain,[73] and also the knight's fee granted to the steward, consisting of the parish of Legerwood (with Birkenside), and Mow, which seems then to have been a parish.[74] Among the fees created by William the Lion were Lenzie in Dunbartonshire, for William Cumin;[75] Yester in East Lothian for Hugh and William Giffard;[76] and three villages in or bordering the Carse of Gowrie, Kinnaird for Ralph Rufus, Fowlis Easter for Roger de Mortemer, and Errol (a double fee) for William de Hay.[77] We may put in the same class Cargill on the Tay and Kincardine in Menteith, both afterwards parishes, which together made a knight's fee for Richard de Montfiquet (Muschet) before 1196.[78]

For the money value of these fees our evidence is quite exiguous. Among the royal archives lost after 1291 was a charter[79] by which William I granted to his sister Margaret, the widowed countess of Brittany, one hundred librates of land and twenty infeft knights. Later records show that this estate was located chiefly in the region of Ratho and Bathgate in West Lothian.[80] This source, as Dr. Neilson noted many years ago,[81] would suggest that a knight's fee at that time may have been equated with some such notional value as £5 a year. The same is implied in a charter[82] issued between 1177 and c. 1190 by Alan the Steward, son of

[71] Ibid., no. 125.   [72] Ibid., no. 136.
[73] RRS, i, no. 255: not the same person as Philip de Valognes.
[74] Ibid., no. 183.   [75] Wigtown Charter Chest, no. 1.
[76] RRS, ii, nos. 48, 459.   [77] Ibid., nos. 135, 204, 302.
[78] Ibid., no. 334. For the Muschets of Burnbank in Kincardine, 'the chief of that name now extinct', see Macfarlane, Geographical Coll., i, 339.
[79] Acts Parl. Scot., i, 116.
[80] Ibid., charters in the same pyx. Cf. Fraser Facsimiles, no. 27, and Hist. MSS. Comm., 5th Rept., p. 611, first item under 'Titles of Ratho'.
[81] Juridical Review, xi (1899), 71–86.   [82] Fraser, Lennox, ii, no. 2.

Walter, granting 'Kellebrid' (Neilston) to Robert Croc for the service of one knight in exchange for the 100s. worth of land owed to Robert by the grantor. A royal act of date 1166 × 1182[83] confirmed to Hugh Giffard for the fifth of a knight's service that part of Yester for which the previous holder had paid yearly 21s. 4d.— implying a knight's fee of eight marks, or £5 6s. 8d. These examples come from the south of Scotland and may all be referred to the first thirty years of William the Lion's reign. By themselves, they might encourage us to believe that the notional value of a Scottish knight's fee ran at roughly £5 a year. But there exists the charter of David I to Alexander of St. Martin, already mentioned, which gives him half a knight's fee and promises him 10 marks a year in addition until his half fee shall be made a whole one. The natural inference from this document is that a knight's fee of twenty marks, or over £13, was conceivable before 1153. A charter of Robert de Quinci, recently come to light, points to a valuation of £10 for a knight's fee in East Lothian.[84] Uhtred of Galloway's grant of Loch Kindar (New Abbey) to Richard son of Tructe (1162–75) seems to suggest a valuation of eight pounds of silver.[85] Thus, it may be that in Scotland, as in England, there were current during the twelfth century more than one notional valuation of the land needed to support a knight in the king's service.

After David I's time, the crown seems rarely to have granted out great tracts of land in return for the service of large numbers of knights. Its practice seems rather to have been to create single or even fractional knight's fees. One consequence of this was that as a class the barons of Scotland, the men who held in chief of the crown the small fees thus created, were men of considerably less substance than their counterparts in England. It may be suggested that the Scottish baronage, closely attached to the crown by feudal allegiance, was at the same time closer than the English baronage to the freemen of lower rank, and indeed, to the rest of the population. Nevertheless, there were large estates in Scotland held for military service, and within them there seems to have been a fairly systematic process of sub-infeudation. The great barons might choose to infeft their vassals with whole knight's

[83] *RRS*, ii, no. 85.   [84] SRO, GD 241/254.
[85] *CWAAS Transactions*, New Ser., xvii (1917), 218–19.

fees, but as often as not they appear to have created tenements to be held for a half, a quarter, an eighth, a tenth, or even a twentieth part of the service of one knight. There is no certain evidence for scutage in twelfth-century Scotland,[86] and the holders of fractional fees may either have performed the full service of a knight only once in so many years, or else have clubbed together to pay towards the wages of a knight, each in proportion to his holding. In general, the crown seems to have preferred round numbers in its infeftments. Single knight's fees were common, and double fees are occasionally found. Five knights were demanded from the steward's vast lordship,[87] ten from the Brus lordship of Annandale, ten from Earl David, King William's brother,[88] and twenty from the countess of Brittany in respect of the fees which were evidently inherited by her second husband's heirs, the Bohun earls of Hereford, in western Lothian.[89] The king's tenants-in-chief naturally operated on a smaller scale. When, between 1189 and 1196, Walter de Berkeley enfeoffed William son of Richard in 'Croswaldef'[90] (perhaps Carswadda in Kirkcudbrightshire), it was for the service of half a knight. The same was stipulated in the contemporary charter by which Waltheof, son of Cospatric, lord of South Queensferry, granted the lands of Dundas to Elias, son of Uhtred, ancestor of the ancient family of Dundas of that Ilk.[91] After Richard de Montfiquet had been granted Cargill, but before 1199, he created a sub-fief for William son of Alexander out other minor tenements. The service demanded was as little as the

[86] The only explicit references to scutage which I have been able to find in Scottish documents prior to 1214 occur in *Melrose*, nos. 116, 117, a charter of Walter of Windsor and its confirmation by William I. They include the word *scutagiis* in a clause of exemption along with *cornagiis*, another highly unusual term in twelfth-century Scottish record. Possibly the whole phrase was a piece of common form produced by a clerk accustomed to northern English terminology.

[87] *RRS*, i, no. 184.   [88] *RRS*, ii, no. 205.   [89] *Acts Parl. Scot.*, i, 116.

[90] Anderson, *Diplomata*, Pl. LXXVII. 'Croswaldef' is not certainly identified. Carswadda ('Corsuada', Blaeu, 1654), which seems a phonetically possible derivative from Croswaldef, is in Lochrutton parish. Walter de Berkeley for a time held land in Kirkgunzeon, the neighbouring parish, from Roland, son of Uhtred, a witness to the Croswaldef charter (B.M. Harl. MS. no. 3891, fos. 87ᵛ–88ʳ).

[91] *Acts Parl. Scot.*, i, 92. The Waltheof who gave this charter was presumably the son of Cospatric, son of Waltheof, addressed by Malcolm IV in a writ concerning the Queen's Ferry (*RRS*, i, no. 126).

of half a carucate *ad Withefeld* (Whitefield in Cargill), with some tenth part of half a knight, the fraction being doubtless so expressed because Cargill formed half a knight's fee.[92] So little is known in any detail about Scottish sub-infeudation that it may be useful to examine the evidence relating to two great feudal lordships, those of the Morvilles in Lauderdale and Cunningham and of Earl David of Huntingdon in Aberdeenshire and elsewhere. Their records are scattered and scanty, but nevertheless they show us something of the internal arrangements of a Scottish honour in the middle years and at the close of the twelfth century.

Some of the earliest Morville records are extant only in the inventory made by the first earl of Lauderdale, which was embodied in an act of parliament in 1661 as a statutory title-deed for the Maitland family.[93] Despite many blunders, the earl's attempt to summarise the numerous ancient charters which he had before him seems to have been entirely honest. According to the inventory, the first of the Morvilles, Hugh, granted Thirlestane near Lauder to Elsi, son of Winter, for three marks a year.[94] Between 1189 and 1196, this grant was confirmed by Hugh's grandson, William, to Elsi's son, Alan, 'for the service of a certain knight'.[95] The interest of these vestigial writs does not lie merely in the probability that through them we may trace the pedigree of the Maitlands of Thirlestane, Lethington and Lauderdale to a member of the native Anglian gentry of Northumbria. They show us also the money rent of a pre-feudal landholder being turned into the knight-service of his son, and a knight's fee being created, evidently without social dislocation, on the lordship of a great Scottish baron. The Lauderdale inventory contains evidence of several other grants made by the Morvilles to their vassals, but fortunately there are more reliable sources to illustrate the process of sub-infeftment for military service carried on by Hugh

[92] *RRS*, ii, no. 372, comment. There is so little documentary evidence on the private castle in twelfth-century Scotland that it is worth noting that William's fee included a toft and croft 'between the castle (*castellum*) and the church of Cargill'.

[93] *Acts Parl. Scot.*, vii, 138 et seq.

[94] Ibid., 111 marks, followed by *Scots Peerage*, v, 277, is obviously an error for iii. For Elzi or Elri, father of Alan, see Anderson, *Diplomata*, Pl. LXXV a. His name stands for an Anglo-Saxon Aethelsige or Aelfsige (cf. O. Feilitzen, *Pre-Conquest Personal Names in Domesday Book* and *V.C.H. Berks*, i, 292–3).

[95] *Acts Parl. Scot.*, vii, 138.

de Morville's descendants. Richard de Morville, Hugh's son, who succeeded his father in 1162 and died in 1189, obtained 'Gillemurestun' (Eddleston in Peeblesshire) at farm from Bishop Ingram of Glasgow (1164 × 1174),[96] and made it a knight's fee for Edulf, son of Uhtred,[97] who, to judge from his name, was, like Elsi, son of Winter, a native Northumbrian. Again, Richard de Morville enfeoffed Henry de Sinclair (de Sancto Claro) for a quarter of a knight's service in Herdmanston (East Lothian), previously held by Richard the chamberlain.[98] Both Richard de Morville and his son and successor William established a knight's fee in Cunningham when they enfeoffed James, son of Lambin, in the lands of Loudoun.[99] Eddleston and Loudoun, incidentally, are further examples of single fees which later became (if they were not already) parishes. The Morville fief in Scotland would certainly have counted among the largest of those held under the crown by private feudatories. It seems, moreover, to have been the only baronial honour in this period on which we find evidence for an officer with the title of vicecomes, sheriff. A charter of William de Morville, e.g., was witnessed by Henry de Sinclair, the grantor's sheriff (1189 × 1196).[100] In 1203, after the Morville fief had passed to the lord of Galloway by the marriage of William de Morville's sister and heir Helen to Roland, son of Uhtred, a judicial decision was witnessed by Roland's son Alan of Galloway, in company with a few Morville sub-tenants, including Alan de Clephan (Clapham), 'sheriff of Lauder'.[101] We may probably trace the office back before William de Morville's time, for two acts of Richard de Morville, of uncertain date between 1162 and 1189, were witnessed by Alan, son of the sheriff, and A., son of the sheriff, respectively,[102] while another act of Richard de Morville, confirming an agreement between the abbeys of Dryburgh and St. James by Northampton, and dating 1162 × 1177,[103] was witnessed by Elfius the sheriff. It may be conjectured that for Elfius we should read Elsius, and that Alan the sheriff's son

---

[96] Glasgow Registrum, no. 44.   [97] Ibid., no. 45.
[98] Anderson, Diplomata, Pl. LXXV b.
[99] Stevenson, Illustrations, no. VIII. Cf. Scots Peerage, v, 488.
[100] Glasgow Registrum, no. 46.   [101] Kelso Liber, no. 143.
[102] Glasgow Registrum, no. 45; Anderson, Diplomata, Pl. LXXV b.
[103] B.M. Cott. MS. Tiberius E v. fo. 88. There is no copy of this document in the Dryburgh Liber.

was identical with Alan, son of Elsi of Thirlestane, who was witness to a number of surviving Morville charters.[104] Professor W. C. Dickinson, who referred only to the example from 1203, suggested that *vicecomes* here means no more than 'constable', the officer in charge of Lauder castle.[105] If this was true of Alan de Clephan, it may also have been true of the earlier Morville sheriffs. But it is worth noting that the baronial sheriff is a well-attested figure in twelfth-century England, where he was not necessarily a purely military officer.[106] The late Graeme Ritchie accepted without comment Mrs. Armitage's view that the Morvilles' 'chief seat is not even known by name'.[107] Yet there is considerable, if not conclusive, evidence that Lauder was the *caput* of the Morville lordship, and if this was so, an officer described as sheriff of Lauder might well have had wider duties than the maintenance and defence of his lord's chief castle.[108]

Our starting point for the history of the lordship created in Scotland for Earl David of Huntingdon must be the charter which his brother the king issued between 1179 and 1182,[109] granting to David the earldom of Lennox (temporarily), Dundee and other places in Angus, Longforgan and Pitmiddle in Gowrie, Morton near Edinburgh, and the district of Garioch, in the middle of what is now Aberdeenshire, all for the service of ten knights. The feudalisation of the Garioch which evidently followed this grant is especially interesting because this was a completely Celtic region, remote from the main centres of royal power frequented by the twelfth-century kings, though it lay athwart one

---

[104] Some references are given in *Scots Peerage*, v, 277.

[105] *Fife Court Bk.*, 371–2.

[106] Stenton, *First Century of English Feudalism*, 67–8.

[107] *Early Norman Castles*, 317; cf. *Normans in Scotland*, 292.

[108] The evidence for the pre-eminent position of Lauder in the Morville fief is too scattered to be brought together here. But it may be noted that Richard de Morville's castle of Lauder was important enough to be included in the list of eight Scottish-held castles during the war of 1173–4 given by Roger Howden ('Benedict of Peterborough', *Gesta Henrici*, ed. Stubbs, i, 48–9).

In 1296, Helen la Zouche (widow of Roger la Zouche, the grandson of Helen de Morville) was said to have held as part of her dower one third of Lauder and one third of Lauderdale for one knight's service. It might perhaps be inferred that the Morvilles held Lauder and its dale in the twelfth century for three knights' service (*Calendar of Inquisitions Post Mortem*, iii, no. 363).

[109] *RRS*, i, no. 205.

of the natural overland routes into Moray from the south. The *caput* of Garioch was fixed at Inverurie, where Earl David founded a burgh and no doubt constructed (from a natural mound) the stout *motte* at the confluence of the Urie with the Don, preserved today under the name of the Bass of Inverurie. An extremely botched record of some of the earl's enfeoffments has survived in an old inventory among the muniments of the earls of Mar and Kellie.[110] There are, e.g. notices of grants of Durno with a toft in Inverurie burgh to Simon and Robert de Billingham, and of Ardoyne below Bennachie to (?) Henry de Bovill or Boyville.[111] These fragments alone would give no proof that the division of Garioch was carried out in return for fixed amounts of military service. It is therefore valuable to have three complete charters of Earl David, two of which certainly, and the third of which may, relate to this district. By the first,[112] Malcolm son of Bertolf was enfeoffed in Leslie for one knight's service. By the second,[113] David de Audree (from the honour of Huntingdon) was given the whole davoch of Rescivet (in Chapel of Garioch parish), 'rendering to the earl as quittance for every secular service, custom, exaction and demand' the tenth part of the service of one knight. That so small a fraction of a knight's fee could be created in the remote region of Garioch at the turn of the twelfth and thirteenth centuries is a testimony to the highly developed notions of military feudalism taken, as it seems, for granted at least by the lord of an especially large and doubtless well-organised fief and by his knightly vassals. The third charter is among the Yester House writs.[114] It records the enfeoffment of

---

[110] *Hist. MSS. Comm., Mar and Kellie* (1904), pp. 3 et seq.

[111] Robert de Billyngam's land is referred to in B.M. Cott. Ch. xviii, 23, cited below. The '. . . Bommill' and his heirs mentioned in the Mar and Kellie inventory may be identified with Henry de Bouill or Boyville, and his family, vassals of Earl David and Earl John of Scotland (*Lindores Chartulary*, nos. 3, 5, etc.; *Hist. MSS. Comm., 4th Rept.*, 493).

[112] SRO, Rothes Charters, No. 1. The grant included 'Mache' and 'Hachennegort' (? Auchnagorth in King Edward parish, next to land held by Walter de Leslie in 1369, *Reg. Mag. Sig.*, i, no. 300).

[113] B.M. Cott. Ch. xviii, 23. For the de Aldri fee in the Honour of Huntingdon, see *Sir Christopher Hatton's Book of Seals* (1950), nos. 200, 220. David 'de Audereye' (de Andreya, etc.) and Henry de Boyville witness acts of Earl John of Scotland, *Lindores Chartulary*, no. 17, *Hist. MSS. Comm., 4th Rept.*, p. 493.

[114] *Yester Writs*, no. 4.

Hugh Giffard by Earl David in 'Fintre' (apparently Fintry in Angus), in augmentation of the other fee which Hugh held of the earl and in return for half a knight's service for the two fees together. The charter is interesting evidence of the earl creating a knight-service tenement for a baron who was already a tenant-in-chief of the king.[115]

A fractional fee might occasionally represent the less expensive service of a light-armed soldier or mounted archer. William I granted Gilberton to his clerk Michael 'Flerdius' (read *Flandrensis*) towards the end of his reign, 'for the service of one serjeant on a horse with a haubergel', and Alexander II confirmed this grant, to his clerk Michael 'Flandrence'. But when the same lands were confirmed by Alexander II or Alexander III to Michael's son Archibald, it was for a quarter of a knight's service.[116] In thirteenth-century Scotland feudal service had doubtless become the largely fiscal concept which it had become in England in this period. A quarter of a knight's fee may have been equated fiscally with a serjeanty. At the same time, we should note that William of Dallas, described as a knight, was confirmed by Alexander III (1279), for a quarter of a knight's service, in the upland territory of Dallas, near Forres, 'in which King William infeft his forebear William de Rypely'.[117] The tenure of Michael the Fleming seems to have been typical of Scottish serjeanties of the twelfth century. William I infeft Gregory de Melville in Granton for the service of one archer with a horse,[118] and, as we have seen, one archer with horse and haubergel was owed for the lands of Allardice.[119] John Waleran was given land near Crail by King William for one serjeant on a horse with a haubergel.[120] Private serjeanty infeftments followed this pattern closely. Robert de Neuham held Cambo near Crail of the Countess Ada (King William's mother), for one foot soldier in the king's army.[121] Robert of London, the king's bastard son, granted to Ralph Frebern (1189 × 1199)

[115] Dr. K. J. Stringer has taken the subject of Earl David's Scottish lordship much further in his Cambridge Ph.D. thesis on David earl of Huntingdon, shortly to be published by Cambridge University Press.

[116] For the foregoing, see *Acts Parl. Scot.*, vii, 144.

[117] SRO, Royal Charters, no. 58. It is possible that 'Dolaysmykel' (Dallas) was not the only estate with which William de Rypely had been endowed; but it was this fief which gave their name to the knightly family of Dallas.

[118] *RRS*, ii, no. 45.   [119] Ibid., no. 404.   [120] Ibid., no. 469.
[121] Ibid., no. 131.

Couston, Balmule and Montquey 'in his fief of Aberdour', for one serjeant on a horse with a haubergel in the royal army.[122] Before 1214, Hugh Freskin, lord of Sutherland, infeft Master Gilbert of Moray (archdeacon of Moray, and later to be bishop of Caithness) in Skelbo and other lands in Sutherland, for the service of one archer.[123] Fergus, earl of Buchan, infeft John, son of Uhtred, in Fedderate (New Deer parish), described as three davochs, for the free service of one archer and for the performance of three capital suits to the earl's court of Ellon, 'as any earl may freely infeft a vassal in Scotia'.[124] The language of this latter document, incidentally, is highly feudal in tone, and the grant shows clearly that the concept of feudal tenure could be understood and applied by a native earl in a remote region before the death of William the Lion.

As evidence for active subinfeudation, these private charters do not stand alone but could be paralleled from the contemporary records of the Countess Ada of Northumberland's fiefs in East Lothian and East Fife, of the Brus fief of Annandale, and of the Stewart's estates in Renfrew, Ayrshire and the Merse.[125] That knight-service had become, by the early thirteenth century, a burden which might be permanently attached to a particular piece of land we know casually from the terms of an exchange transacted between 1204 and 1228, by which Reginald de Warenne fully released to Laurence of Abernethy the lands of 'Coventre' (near Abernethy)[126] save for the king's forinsec service, on condition, however, that Reginald would answer on Laurence's behalf for the amount of knight-service belonging to that land. We also know, from less oblique evidence, that castle-ward, a highly characteristic obligation of the knight in the first century of English feudalism, was associated in Scotland also with the knights who held fiefs of the crown. At Christmas, 1160, King Malcolm IV infeft Berewald the Fleming in the lands of Innes and (?Nether) Urquhart for the service of one knight in Elgin castle.[127] When William I confirmed Annandale to Robert Brus, he

[122] *Spalding Misc.*, v, 242, no. 3.   [123] *Fraser Facsimiles*, no. 30.
[124] *Aberdeen-Banff Coll.*, 407–9.
[125] See below pp. 337–61 for the Stewart's estates.
[126] Fraser, *Douglas*, iii, 349–50, no. 281. 'Coventre' doubtless = 'Covintrie' in the barony of Forgandenny, *Retours*, Perth, nos. 202, 853.
[127] *RRS*, i, no. 175.

exempted him from the ward of his castles.[128] An extremely instructive royal charter of the early years of Alexander II, discussed by Dr. Neilson,[129] commuted for 20s. a year the castle-ward owed at Roxburgh by Bernard of Hadden, nephew and heir of a prominent baron of William the Lion, Bernard, son of Brien. By the terms of this charter, Bernard might pay 20s. instead of performing castle-ward unless there was war or a state of emergency, while if he had to go at the king's command north of the Forth or south of the March, or if he should pay the aid for his fee when a common aid was levied throughout the realm, he need not pay his 20s. that year or do his castle-ward (recalling the last clause of Magna Carta, chapter 29).

The point has now been reached at which the other side of the story—the incidence of non-military infeftments—may usefully be considered. It would clearly help us to decide the relative importance of military tenure in the second half of the twelfth century if we could form some idea of the scale of infeftments made in the same period in return either for straightforward money rents or for services which were vague or in no sense military. For a realistic comparison, we should consider among unspecific or unmilitary grants only such as involved substantial holdings of land or persons who were socially equal or superior to barons, knights and serjeants. Church property held in alms, and burgage tenements, each forming a specialised class of tenure, will not be included. Nor will special mention be made of infeftments in frank marriage, since they would not have formed a true exception to a prevailing system of knight-service and serjeanty tenures. In a number of instances, we have reasonably good evidence of a grant of land made by a twelfth-century king, but no record of its terms: e.g. a grant by Malcolm IV to William, son of Nigel, of land in Ednam,[130] and by William I to Adam Hasteng of the lands of Kingledoors.[131] It will be impossible to make use of this sort of evidence here, but it is necessary to bear in mind that we now possess only a fraction, probably a very small fraction, of the enfeoffments originally recorded in writing in the period before

[128] *RRS*, ii, no. 80.

[129] *Juridical Rev.*, xi, 173 et seq. Dr. Neilson showed that this charter is really an act of Alexander II, though purporting to be one of Robert I. It is printed in *RMS*, i, App. I, no. 55.

[130] *RRS*, i, no. 297.   [131] *RRS*, ii, no. 561.

1214. The assumption underlying the comparison made here is that there seems no obvious reason why, so far as large estates are concerned, written infeftments for military service should have survived in significantly larger numbers than those for non-military service.

The first group of landholders to be taken into account in discussing non-military tenants of the crown must be that of the earls, because of their obvious political and social importance. We have already seen how David I established a strictly feudal relationship between himself and the earl of Fife, Duncan I. We cannot be certain that the service due from the earldom was military, but both Earl Duncan I and his son Earl Duncan II were tenants-in-chief of the crown for knight-service, at least for their fiefs of West Calder and Strathleven.[132] It seems unlikely that the earldom of Strathearn was held for knight-service, or even on feudal terms, in the middle of the twelfth century. We cannot be sure that Earl Gilbert of Strathearn, at the end of the century, owed knight-service for his earldom, though he was the king's tenant by knight-service for lands in or near Strathearn.[133] The wording of the charter by which William I granted the earl Kinveachie[134] 'to be held as freely and quit as Earl Gilbert holds the earldom of Strathearn', is inconclusive and in marked contrast not only with the precisely worded conditions in contemporary knight-service charters but also with Alexander II's confirmation of the earldom of Fife to Earl Malcolm I, 'performing therefor the service which is owed to us from that earldom'.[135] The earldom of Lennox was presumably part of the great estate for which King William's brother David owed him the service of ten knights;[136] but David held this earldom only temporarily, and when, in 1238, Alexander II confirmed it to Earl Maoldomhnaich, he was to hold it 'as freely and quit as any of our earls more freely and independently hold and possess their earldoms, performing for it the forinsec service in armies and aids which belongs to our other full manors (*plenarias villas*)'.[137] Thus there is not only no requirement of knight-service; there is a distinct implication that anything more than forinsec service would be an

132 Above, pp. 283 and 288.   133 *RRS*, ii, nos. 258, 524.
134 *RRS*, ii, no. 206.   135 *Nat. MSS. Scot.*, i, Pl. L.
136 *RRS*, ii, no. 205.   137 *Lennox Cartularium*, no. 1.

exceptional burden upon a Scottish earldom. For the other ancient earldoms, the evidence is insufficient. The agreement made in the king's court in 1213 regarding the earldom of Menteith[138] says nothing about service, though it is clear that the earldom was regarded as being held of the king, to whom it was surrendered, and who could adjudge it to its rightful heir after making a temporary subtraction from its lands. As for the rest, Caithness, Ross, Buchan, Mar, Angus, Atholl and Lothian or Dunbar, there is (so far as I am aware) no direct record whatever for the period under review.[139] It is doubtful if Moray was regarded as an earldom in this period, and, in any case, it was in the hands of the king. Gowrie was certainly an earldom, but it, too, was in royal hands, and the feudalisation of Gowrie, of which some evidence has been given, was but part of a general royal policy, applicable to the territory of Gowrie simply because it was, in effect, crown demesne.

In conclusion, we may say that there seems to have been a tendency to bring the earldoms into a strictly feudal relationship with the crown, but the vagueness or reticence of the documents even as late as the thirteenth century suggests that they were not held in return for specified amounts of knight-service. It must, however, be emphasised that this did not mean that an earl might not be a tenant-in-chief of the crown by knight-service.

When we turn from a consideration of the earls to men who were, or may have been, of baronial or knightly status, we find relatively few surviving enfeoffments which do not demand the service of knights or serjeants. There are preserved at Durham two copies[140] of a grant of Swinton made by David I to his knight Hernulf or Arnulf as an hereditary fief to be held 'as freely and

---

[138] *Cal. Docs. Scot.*, i, nos. 2275, 2276.

[139] The earldoms of Ross, Menteith and Atholl were evidently granted by royal charter in the thirteenth century (*RMS*, i, Appendix II, nos. 1, 4, 5).

W. F. Skene (*Celtic Scotland*, iii (1880), 446–7), prints a charter purporting to have been issued by William I and restoring the earldom of Mar to Morgrund, son of Gillocheri (=*RRS*, ii, no. 119). He is of the opinion that this charter (certainly not genuine) was forged in favour of William, earl of Mar, in the reign of Alexander III. Though spurious, its clause giving the service due from the earldom may be significant: 'Faciendo inde ipse et heredes sui mihi et heredibus meis forinsecum servicium videlicet Servicium Scoticanum sicut antecessores sui mihi et antecessoribus meis facere consueverunt.'

[140] Lawrie, *Charters*, nos. 100 and 101.

honourably as any of my barons holds', in return for a payment of
40s. to the monks of Durham. While this was not the creation of a
knight's fee, and while Swinton seems to have been part of the
'Patrimony of Saint Cuthbert', the fact that Hernulf is described
as the king's knight proves that King David was obtaining
knight's service from him, whether in return for Swinton or not.
The gift may have been a reward for a hitherto landless knight,
and therefore a disguised knight's fee, or it may have been an
augmentation of land which he held as a knight's fee elsewhere.
Before 1189, King William granted, for an annual rent of 20s., to
Andrew, son of Uviet, Whitslaid, the upland glen which forms the
head of the valley of the Ale Water.[141] The land involved here
was no doubt considerable in area, more than an oxgang or two,
but we do not know whether Andrew counted as a man of
knightly or serviential rank.[142] Robert, son of Maccus, of whose
status we have insufficient knowledge, owed the same rent merely
for one carucate in 'Lesedwin' (Lessudden, Roxburghshire) c.
1200.[143] Hugh Giffard, almost certainly of baronial rank, was
granted part of Yester by Malcolm IV, but as the original charter
has not survived we do not know the service. When the grant was
confirmed by William I, between 1165 and 1171, no knight-
service obligation was mentioned;[144] but the king enfeoffed Hugh
Giffard in another part of Yester for the fifth of a knight's service,
and when he confirmed the whole of Yester and Lethington to
Hugh's son, William, the land formed the fee of one knight.[145]
It was evidently this same William Giffard who received a royal
charter (1189 × 1199) for the lands of 'Stradhehhan' (Strachan
on Deeside), to be held *in forestam* for nine marks yearly.[146] In
area, Strachan may well have been equal to any estate formed into
a knight's fee in this period. But much of the parish is mountainous, and the fact that it was granted 'in forest' suggests
relatively poor agricultural resources.

The most remarkable series of surviving non-military enfeoffments to a person who was undoubtedly of baronial status is that
by which, between 1153 and 1184, Orm, son of Hugh, obtained

[141] *RRS*, ii, no. 145.
[142] It seems probable that Andrew son of Uviet was identical with Andrew
of Synton, first of a line of hereditary sheriffs of Selkirk (ibid., nos. 581A, 582).
[143] Ibid., no. 422.   [144] Ibid, no. 48.   [145] Ibid., no. 459.
[146] Ibid., no. 340.

grants or confirmations of the abbey of Abernethy, and the lands of Dunlappie and Inverarity in Angus and Glenduckie and Balmeadow in Fife.[147] Malcolm IV's charter of Dunlappie has apparently not survived, but his grant was confirmed to Orm's son, Laurence, in free forest and no service was mentioned[148] Inverarity and the Fife lands were granted between 1165 and 1171, the king in each case specifying no *reddendo* but merely adding 'saluo mihi seruicio meo quod ad terram illam pertinet'.[149] The Fife lands were actually quitclaimed to Orm by Earl Duncan II of Fife in exchange for 'Balebrenin' (Balbirnie in Markinch). The transaction was contemporary with the king's infeftment of the earl, for knight-service, in Strathleven, of which Markinch presumably formed a part. It may, therefore, have been the result of a scheme to put the earl in total possession of the lands of this fief by buying out the other landholders.[150]

The grant of Abernethy (1172 × 1184) stands in a somewhat different case. The abbey was confirmed 'as it was in the year and on the day when King David was alive and dead', fully, save for ten librates of land which King William had granted to Henry Revel in marriage with Orm's daughter (from which, incidentally, the king required half a knight's service),[151] and freely, save for common aid, common army and common labour-service (*communi operatione*). For all this, including the usual jurisdictional rights of lordship, Orm was to render the large sum of £20 a year. The chief contrast between this grant and the others lies in the fact that Abernethy was an ancient ecclesiastical foundation, to which clergy were still attached and of which Orm, son of Hugh, was abbot, though to all intents and purposes a layman. He was probably the hereditary abbot, for the grant was made in the form of a confirmation, and his son Laurence held the position of abbot after his father's death. That Abernethy was still regarded as in some sense a religious institution is made clear from the arrangements whereby, between 1189 and 1194, much of the strictly ecclesiastical property of the lordship was transferred to

---

[147] Ibid., nos. 14, 152; *RRS*, i, no. 311.   [148] *RRS*, ii, no. 565.
[149] The order of words is slightly different in ibid., no. 14.
[150] *PSAS*, lxxxvii, 55.
[151] *Balmerino Liber*, no. 2; cf. nos. 3–6. It would probably be unsafe to take this as evidence for a knight's fee of £20 per annum. It was a grant in marriage, and the service imposed may therefore have been lenient.

the king's new abbey of Arbroath.[152] It is quite possible, therefore, that knight-service was thought an inappropriate tenure for the abbot of Abernethy, even though he was a lay and hereditary abbot. Nevertheless, the lordship was large and valuable, and this was reflected in the rent of £20, an exceptionally high rent for the period.

We may notice, in conclusion, a number of infeftments of relatively small amounts of property in return for money rents, or service which we may surmise to have been a form of serjeanty, or for no apparent service at all. Wormieston by Crail was evidently granted by William I to a certain Winemer for 2d. blench ferm every Whitsun.[153] Winemer had been a prominent retainer of the Countess Ada in the Crail district.[154] It is likely that the land outside Crail to which he seems to have given his name was granted to him in return for his services to the countess and (after her death) to her son. Between 1189 and 1199, William I granted Cassingray in Carnbee parish to Robert the butler, son of Henry, merely in return for the forinsec service of half a carucate of land in the 'shire' of Kellie.[155] The fact that the grantee is styled *pincerna* suggests that we may here have to deal with a disguised serjeanty. We may perhaps put in the same class the grant made by David I to Master Robert the ironsmith 'for his service' of two carucates in Newbattle (Masterton),[156] and the grants made by Malcolm IV of half a carucate in Sprouston to his clerk Serlo and of land in Manor, in the forest of Selkirk, to Norman the hunter.[157]

The practice of making substantial grants of landed property, or grants of any kind to persons of high rank, in return for non-military service, does not seem to have been comparable in range or scale to that which created the knight-service and serjeanty infeftments of the period. The earldoms formed a notable exception, but even there we have seen that two important earls are known to have been knight-service tenants of the crown, and we cannot be sure that none of their fellows was in the same position.

It may be worth estimating, at this stage, what difference, if any, was produced by planting across much of the Scottish

[152] *Arbroath Liber*, i, nos. 34, 35.   [153] *RRS*, ii, no. 196
[154] Stevenson, *Illustrations*, no. XIII; J. Hodgson, *History of Northumberland*, Pt. II, vol. iii, p. 17; *St. Andrews Liber*, 208.
[155] *RRS*, ii, no. 286.   [156] *Newbattle Registrum*, no. 2 (=*RRS*, i, no. 69).
[157] Ibid., nos. 295, 298.

kingdom the military aristocracy of which some account has been given. Was the military service which they rendered something entirely new, and did their settlement make warfare a more familiar occurrence? On the contrary, the Scots seem to have fought among themselves more frequently before the reign of David I than between 1124 and 1286, and they had certainly recognised an obligation of military service to the crown. It was the great pre-feudal magnates, the mormaers or earls, who had the duty of calling out and leading the host when the king went to war. The amount of this service was based upon the unit of arable, the carucate of the south, the arachor of the middle west, the davoch of the east and north. Abundant references are made to it in the records of the period, under the terms 'forinsec service', 'Scottish service', or 'common army'.[158] What it might mean on one estate may be judged from two charters by which Maoldomhnaich, earl of Lennox, granted to his namesake Maoldomhnaich, son of Gillemoire, and to his son after him, the lands of Luss on Loch Lomond. They were to be held for a render to the earl and his heirs 'in the common army of the lord king' of two cheeses from every house on the estate in which cheese is made, and by contributing towards royal aids as much as pertains to two arachors of land in the earldom of Lennox.[159] These documents are comparatively late in date (c. 1224 × 1260), but it seems unlikely that the conditions which they outline were the invention of the thirteenth century. The Lennox was a Celtic and conservative region, where older customs might be expected to linger long after their abandonment elsewhere. It scarcely needs emphasising that a system under which a free and hereditary tenant could acquit himself of the military service owed to the king by the despatch of two cheeses from each cheese-making household on his estate belongs to a society which was markedly different from that of the Anglo-Norman feudatories brought into Scotland by the kings of the twelfth century.

It has been said that in Scotland in the thirteenth century 'rents and services of all kinds existed, but not an articulated system of knight-service'.[160] In the light of the twelfth-century evidence

---

[158] See *RRS*, ii, 54–7.
[159] *Lennox Cartularium*, Addenda, pp. 96–8; cf. *Fraser Facsimiles*, no. 36.
[160] F. M. Powicke, *The Thirteenth Century* (1953), 576.

summarised in the foregoing pages, this view suggests a question. How did it come about that what appears to have been, before 1214, an organised system of feudal tenements, which linked the crown to its tenants-in-chief and them to their tenants by fixed amounts of knight-service and serjeanty, and of which evidence exists for most of governed Scotland, broke down in the reigns of the two Alexanders? Before asking this question and trying to find the answer, it may be necessary to reserve judgement until the whole of the evidence for the thirteenth century is set beside that for the twelfth. It might then appear that between 1214 and 1286 the kingdom of Scotland remained what it had begun to be under David I, what it actually became under Malcolm the Maiden and William the Lion, a feudal kingdom in the same narrow and specific sense in which that term is by general agreement applied to England between the Norman conquest and the reign of Edward I.

Tables of charters of infeftment for knight-service and serjeanty surviving in the original, or in good copies, or reported in reliable sources.

TABLE 1 KNIGHT-SERVICE CHARTERS, ROYAL

Feoffee	Fief	Service	Date	Source
Robert de Brus	Annandale	(? 10 kts.)	c. 1124	Lawrie, *Charters*, no. 54.
Alexander of Saint Martin	Athelstaneford, etc.	½ kt.	?1141 × 1153	Ibid., no. 186.
Walter of Ryedale	Whittons, half (?) Chatto & Lilliesleaf	1 kt.	× 1153	Ibid., no. 222 (= *RRS*, i, no. 42).
Duncan I, earl of Fife	West Calder	kt(s.)	c. 1136 × 1153	*RRS*, ii, no. 559.
Freskin	Strathbrock, Duffus, etc.	(? 2 kts.)	1130 × 1153	Ibid., no. 116.
Berewald the Fleming	Innes and 'Ether Urecard' (? for icthar, i.e. nether Urquhart)	1 kt. in Elgin castle	1160	*RRS*, i, no. 175.
Walter, Alan's son	Birkenside, Legerwood & Mow	1 kt.	1161	Ibid., no. 183.
Walter, Alan's son	The same, *plus* Renfrew, Paisley, Pollok (other places in Renfrewshire), Hassendean, Innerwick, Stenton	5 kts.	1161	Ibid., no. 184.
Philip the Chamberlain	Lundin	1 kt.	1161 × 1164	Ibid., no. 255.
Ralph Frebern	Dunduff, Rosyth & Masterton in Newbattle	1 kt.	1162 × 1164	Ibid., no. 256.
William de Vieuxpont	Carriden, Horndean (and lands in England)	4 kts.	1165 × 1170	*RRS*, ii, no. 84.
William, son of Freskin	Strathbrock, Duffus, etc.	2 kts.	1166 × 1171	Ibid., no. 116.
Robert de Brus	Annandale	10 kts.	1165 × 1173	Ibid., no. 80.
Henry, son of Gregory	'Rossin'	1 kt.	1165 × 1174	Ibid., no. 43.
Gilbert, son of earl of Angus	Pourie, Ogilvy & Kilmundie	1 kt.	1166 × 1174	Ibid., no. 140.

TABLE 1—continued

Feoffee	Fief	Service	Date	Source
Henry Revel	Coultra	½ kt.	1173 × 1178	Ibid., no. 147.
Duncan II, earl of Fife	Strathleven & W. Calder	(? 2) kts.	1165 × 1171 (?)	Ibid., no. 559.
Ralph de Graham	Cousland, Pentland, Gogar	1½ kts.	1165 × 1174	Ibid., no. 125.
Malise, son of earl of Strathearn	Muthil, Kincardine, etc., in Strathearn	1 kt. (to E. Gilbert)	1172 × 1173	Ibid., no. 136.
Ralph 'Ruffus'	Kinnaird, less Pitmiddle	1 kt.	1172 × 1174	Ibid., no. 135
Margaret, countess of Brittany	? Ratho, Bathgate, land in Kirkliston	20 kts.	(c. 1175)	Ibid., no. 554.
Merleswain, son of Merleswain	Ardross	1 kt.	1172 × 1174	Ibid., no. 137.
Philip de Seton	Winton, Winchburgh & Seton	1 kt.	1177 × 1185	Ibid., no. 200.
David, brother of K. William	(earldom of Lennox), Lindores, Dundee, Longforgan, Newtyle, Garioch, etc.	10 kts.	(c. 1178)	Ibid., no. 205.
William de Hay	Errol	2 kts.	1178 × 1182	Ibid., no. 204.
Walter de Berkeley	Inverkeilor	1 kt.	1173 × 1180	Ibid., no. 185.
Walter de Berkeley	'Neutun' (Longnewton, or Newton in Forgandenny?)	½ kt.	1173 × 1182	Ibid., no. 171.
Richard de Montfiquet	Cargill & Kincardine in Menteith	1 kt.	1189 × 1195	Ibid., no. 334.
Roger de Mortemer	Fowlis Easter	1 kt.	1189 × 1194	Ibid., nos. 302, 338.
Hugh, brother of Elias the clerk	Benholm	½ kt.	1189 × 1195	Ibid., no. 350.
William de Montfort	Kinneff	1 kt.	1189 × 1199	Ibid., no. 335.
Gilbert, earl of Strathearn	Madderty	1 kt.	1187 × 1189	Ibid., no. 258.
William de Valognes	Benvie & Panmure	½ kt.	1198 × 1200	Ibid., no. 405.
William Giffard	Tealing & Powgavie	1 kt.	1196 × 1201	Ibid., no. 418.
Walter de la Kernelle	Guthrie	½ kt.	1205 × 1207	Ibid., no. 473.
William Giffard	Yester	1 kt.	1202 × 1207	Ibid., no. 459.
William Cumin	Lenzie	1 kt.	× 1214	Ibid., no. 557.
Gilbert, earl of Strathearn	Meikleour & Lethendy	1 kt.	1214	Ibid., no. 524.
Richard Revel	Coultra & 'Ester Ardint'	(? ¼ kt.)	× 1214	Ibid., no. 573.
William de Rypely	Dallas	½ kt.	× 1214	Ibid., no. 576.
Alexander de Lamberton	Linlathen	½ kt.	× 1214	Ibid., no. 564.

TABLE 2 KNIGHT-SERVICE CHARTERS, PRIVATE

Feoffee	Fief	Service and Lord	Date	Source
Alexander of Saint Martin	Athelstaneford, and lands in E. Lothian and E. Fife	1 kt. Countess Ada	1153 × 1178	Laing Chrs, no. 2.
Richard, son of Tructe	Loch Kindar (New Abbey)	1 kt. Uhtred, son of Fergus	1161 × 1174	CWAAS Trans. (1917), 218–19.
Henry de Sinclair	Herdmanston	¼ kt. Richard de Morville	1162 × 1189	Anderson, Diplomata, Pl. LXXV b.
Edulf, son of Uhtred	Eddleston	1 kt. Richard de Morville	1164 × 1189	Glasgow Registrum, no. 45.
Pagan de Hedleia	Adniston and (?) Penston	1 kt. Robert de Quinci	1165 × 1185	SRO, GD 241/254.
Malcolm, son of Bertolf	Leslie	1 kt. Earl David	1172 × 1199	Hist. MSS. Comm., 4th Rep., 493
Hugh Giffard	Fintry, Angus	½ kt. Earl David	1185 × c. 1190	Yester Writs, no. 4.
Adam, son of Gilbert	Tarbolton and other places	1 kt. Alan the Steward	1177 × 1204	Fraser, Lennox, ii, no. 1.
Robert Croc	'Kellebrid' (Neilston)	1 kt. Alan the Steward	1177 × 1204	Ibid., no. 2.
Helias, son of Uhtred	Dundas	½ kt. Waltheof, son of Cospatric	c. 1180	Acts Parl. Scot., i, 92.
Alan, son of Elsi	Thirlestane	1 kt. William de Morville	1189 × 1196	Ibid., vii, 138.
James, son of Lambin	Loudoun	1 kt. William de Morville	1189 × 1196	Illustrations of Scottish History (Maitland Club), no. 8.
William, son of Richard	'Croswaldef'	½ kt. Walter de Berkeley	1189 × 1196	Anderson, Diplomata, Pl. LXXVII.
William, son of Alexander	land in Cargill	$\frac{1}{20}$ kt. Richard de Montfiquet	1189 × 1199	SRO, J. M. Thomson's photos of charters, no. 6.
David de Audree	davoch of Rescivet, in Garioch	$\frac{1}{10}$ kt. Earl David	1185 × 1214	B.M. Cott. Ch. xviii, 23.
Ivo of Kirkpatrick	land in fee of Pennersaughs	⅛ kt. William de Brus	×1214	Fraser Facsimiles, no. 23.
Adam of Carlisle	'Kynemund'	¼ kt. William de Brus	×1214	Ibid., no. 24.
Hugh de Crauford	¼ of Stevenston	½ kt. Alan, son of Roland	(? ×1214)	Dumfries House, Ayrshire, Bute Muniments, Loudoun Charters, no. 4.

TABLE 3 SERJEANTIES

Feoffee	Fief	Service and Lord	Date	Source
Gregory de Melville	Granton	1 archer with horse in army William I	1166 × 1171	RRS, ii, no. 45.
Robert de Neuham	Cambo	1 man in army Countess Ada	1153 × 1178	Ibid., no. 131.
Ralph Frebern	Couston, Balmule and Montquey	1 serjeant on horse with haubergel Robert of London	1189 × 1199	Spalding Misc., v, 242, no. 3.
Walter, son of Walter Scott	Allardice	1 archer with horse and haubergel William I	1199 × 1200	RRS, ii, no. 404.
Michael Fleming, clerk of the king	Gilberton	1 serjeant on horse with haubergel William I	c. 1195 × 1214	Ibid., no. 560.
John Waleran	fifth rig in 'Ballebotla' (? Babbet), and other land in Crailshire	1 serjeant on horse with haubergel William I	c. 1195 × 1214	Ibid., no. 469.
John, son of Uhtred	Fedderate	1 archer Fergus, earl of Buchan	× 1214	Aberdeen–Banff Coll., 407–9.
Master Gilbert, archdeacon of Moray	Skelbo and other places in Sutherland	1 archer Hugh Freskyn	× 1214	Fraser Facsimiles, no. 30.
Yothre [? Rothre] mac Gillhys	Meft, a house in Elgin castle and a net in River Spey	1 serjeant in the army William I	1165 × 1214	RRS, ii, no. 589.
—	Balcormo (Fife)	1 serjeant with haubergel	? × 1214	Acts Parl. Scot., i, 102.
Ranulf, falconer, son of Walter de Loutorp (? Lowthorpe, Yorks., E.R.)	'Kingower' in Gowrie and 5 davochs in Mearns (Halkerton)	service of own body, failing which 1 archer in army William I	c. 1195 × 1214	RRS, ii, no. 497.

11 Scotland's 'Norman' families

In all our modern histories of Scotland the Normans have their assured place. They form a bridge between the Celtic kingdom of Malcolm Canmore and the Scotland which was capable of waging the wars of independence against the first three Plantagenet Edwards. With the Normans, whether we view them with favour or disfavour, we feel that we know where we are. Our mental picture of them is one of the fixed points in our historical consciousness. Hard of face and of fist, restless, rapacious, ruthlessly efficient, they were the men who dragged Scotland, struggling and kicking, into the middle ages. The list of structures, institutions, functionaries and ideas indispensable to the medieval state which the Normans are alleged to have introduced into Scotland is so formidably comprehensive that it tends to erect a barrier between us and the immediately pre-Norman age. It is not only historical artists who seem to have a notion of the Scotland of Macbeth and Canmore as a land whose inhabitants were clad in rough skins and whose sole form of commerce was primitive barter. For some reason we all remember Thurgot's statement about Queen Margaret:

> She caused merchants to come by land and sea from various regions and to bring very many precious wares that were still unknown in Scotland. The Scots were compelled by the queen to buy clothing of different colours and various ornaments of dress.[1]

We overlook another contemporary statement, which surely relates to a date earlier than Saint Margaret's accumulation of

[1] *Vita S. Margaretae* (Surtees Society, 1868), 241–2.

sumptuous luxuries. In 1075 King Malcolm and his queen received Edgar the Atheling with 'great gifts and many treasures consisting of skins covered with purple cloth and robes of marten's skin and of grey fur and ermine and costly robes and golden vessels and silver' and then, when poor Edgar had been shipwrecked and nearly all these precious gifts had been lost, Malcolm and Margaret again gave him 'immense treasure' before sending him off to King William in Normandy.[2]

Nevertheless, even if we are apt to give the Normans and their *protégés* rather too much credit for transforming the character and quality of Scottish life, their achievement remains impressive. Their latest and best apologist, the late Professor Graeme Ritchie, began his book on *The Normans in Scotland* with the plain assertion: 'There was a Norman Conquest of Scotland.'[3] Sheriffs or *vicomtes*, castles, justiciars, burghs, abbeys and cathedrals, above all perhaps the mail-clad, cone-helmeted *chiualer* or knight, all these and many other phenomena bear witness to an alien settlement which was creative as well as destructive, indeed arguably more creative than destructive.

With these wider aspects of the Norman impact upon Scotland this chapter is not concerned. They have been delightfully and shrewdly discussed by Ritchie, and since I have called him an apologist for the Normans it is only fair to add that he had no illusions about his heroes. 'All Normans', he reminds us salutarily, 'were not Normanizers, Conquistadors, exponents of efficiency, land-improvers, missionaries of culture, arbiters of *élégance*, social reformers. Some stood in need of reform themselves.'[4] Here we may address ourselves to certain narrower questions. There is a crying need to get down to some basic archaeology. The Norman penetration of Scotland was effected by the physical migration of individuals, families and groups. Our general histories take this whole slow, difficult and perhaps painful process of migration too much for granted. Not only do all continental incomers get lumped together as Norman—which many of them were not—the impression is also given that all these 'Normans' poured into Scotland

---

[2] *The Anglo-Saxon Chronicle. A revised translation*, ed. Dorothy Whitelock, D. C. Douglas and Susie I. Tucker (1961), 156.
[3] R. L. Graeme Ritchie, *The Normans in Scotland*, p. xi.
[4] Ibid., 216.

at the same time, there to establish, almost overnight, their feudalism, their administrative system and their motte-and-bailey castles. The general historians have shown little interest in the precise origins of particular families: that was a task proper to the genealogist and family historian. Unfortunately, with a number of honourable exceptions, the family historians have made a fearful mess of things, indulging in idle speculation or piling error upon error. Take almost any article in the *Scots Peerage*[5] dealing with a family whose origins lay—or were believed to lie—in Normandy or its neighbouring regions: will not its first page bring a blush to the cheek of the conscientious antiquary?

Even so careful and learned a scholar as George Black, whose *Surnames of Scotland*[6] gives us an unrivalled starting-point for research into Scottish family history, was not free from the bad old habit of assigning a family with a Norman-sounding name to some place in France, preferably Normandy, with more or less the same name. We may take three entries from Black, chosen almost at random: 'CARVEL. From Carville in Normandy. Roger *de la* Keruel [my italics] witnessed a charter by William the Lion to [Arbroath abbey]. Thomas Caruel was burgess of Arbroath in 1461.' There is a place called Carville in Normandy, not far from Vire, but not a shred of evidence to link it with the Arbroath Carvels of the fifteenth century. As for Roger de la Keruel, it should be sufficient to point out that place-names in '-ville' do not take the definite article. We shall return later to this obscure and interesting surname.

The second example reads: 'SINCLAIR. This Caithness surname is of territorial origin from St. Clare in the arrondissement of Pont d'Evêque [*sic*], Normandy.' Presumably this refers to St. Clair-de-Basseneville, formerly St. Clair-en-Auge, but no evidence is adduced in support of the categorical assertion. The Caithness Sinclairs may be traced back to the thirteenth-century Sinclairs of Roslin, who in turn may be traced with reasonable certainty to the Sinclairs who in the twelfth century were prominent tenants and vassals of the de Morville lords of Lauder and

---

[5] See, e.g. in *Scots Peerage*, the beginnings of the articles COMYN Lord of Badenoch, COLVILLE of Culross, DOUGLAS Earl of Douglas, MONTGOMERIE Earl of Eglinton, GORDON Earl of Huntly.

[6] G. F. Black, *The Surnames of Scotland* (New York, 1946).

Cunningham. On general grounds a more likely candidate for this family's place of origin would be St. Clair-sur-Elle, north-east of St. Lô in the department of La Manche. After the Angevin conquest of Lower Normandy in 1143, the lordship of this St. Clair was held by Robert of Gloucester, Henry I's son, and a family of Sinclairs from this place held the manor of Hamerton in Huntingdonshire surrounded by lands of the Honour of Huntingdon on which the de Morvilles were prominent barons.[7] Nevertheless, no connexion between St. Clair-sur-Elle and the Scottish Sinclairs has been established.

Thirdly there is Quinci. 'QUINCI. . . . The name is territorial from Quinci (now Quinçay) in Maine, France.' Again, there is no evidence to associate the de Quincis with Quinçay, and in an invaluable work unfortunately not published until five years after Black's *Surnames*, Lewis Loyd showed that 'in all probability' the de Quincis came from Cuinchy near Béthune in the Pas de Calais.[8] It is worth a moment's digression to observe the method of enquiry which produced Loyd's authoritative entry—no more than five lines long—on de Quinci. He noted that the family first appear north of the Channel as landholders at Long Buckby in Northamptonshire, where they were tenants of the family of de Chokes. It was established beyond doubt by Round and Farrer that de Chokes derived from Chocques, near Béthune, and that this was one of a small group of Flemish families which were well-endowed with land in Northamptonshire after the Conquest. Cuinchy is only a few miles from Chocques. The reasoning which thus links de Quinci to Cuinchy may not seem to justify the description 'method of enquiry'—it seems no more than plain common sense. Yet it is astonishing how very few family historians apply this same common sense when dealing with remote and admittedly sketchy medieval evidence. Perhaps a footnote may be added to Loyd's economical entry. Before the end of Malcolm IV's reign (1165) Robert de Quinci, younger brother of Saher II of Long Buckby—probably through his father's marriage to a de Senlis and through his own tenure on the Honour of Hunting-

[7] L. C. Loyd, *The Origins of some Anglo-Norman Families* (ed. C. T. Clay and D. C. Douglas, Harleian Society, 1951, hereafter cited as Loyd, *Origins*), 88–9. Cf. also W. Farrer, *Honors and knights' fees* (London and Manchester, 1923–5), ii, 287–91.

[8] Loyd, *Origins*, 84.

don—had become an important figure north of the Border.[9] An agreement which he made with Newbattle abbey (Midlothian) in 1170 was witnessed—right at the end, after the notables and locals, by one Alan de Cureres.[10] A glance at the map of French Flanders shows that sixteen kilometres from Cuinchy is the commune of Courrières, and the mid-twelfth-century forms of this name correspond exactly to that found in the Newbattle document.[11] Moreover, of the comparatively few surviving Scottish charters of Robert de Quinci, one (hardly datable more narrowly than 1165–97) was witnessed by Robert of Béthune (de Betunia),[12] possibly the ancestor of the Scots family of Beaton or Bethune, while another, of c. 1170, was witnessed by Robert 'de Carvent' and Hut' 'de Lens'. Carvent is a recorded medieval form for Carvin in the *arrondissement* of Béthune, while Lens (to whose bailiary Carvin was formerly attached) is of course a well-known town some twenty kilometres south-east of Béthune.[13]

Before examining the origins of any more families in detail, it will be as well to clarify our terms of reference. By 'Scotland's "Norman" Families' is meant those families whose immediate origin lay in north-west Gaul or Francia, who settled permanently within the Scottish kingdom between 1100 and 1250, and who succeeded in retaining their identity as families. Ritchie showed clearly from what a wide area might come the men and women whom we in modern times—once they are north of the Channel—tend to call 'Norman'. He also wrote,

it is seldom possible to ascertain their continental home, whether in the Duchy or in Flanders or in Brittany or elsewhere, and the precise connection which their forebears had with [what he finely called] Duke William's Breton, Lotharingian, Flemish, Picard, Artesian, Cenomannian, Angevin, general-French and Norman Conquest.[14]

---

[9] See Dr. G. G. Simpson's unpublished Edinburgh Ph.D. thesis on Roger de Quincy, Earl of Winchester.   [10] *SHR*, xxx (1951), 45.
[11] *Dictionnaire topographique du département du Pas de Calais* (1907), 112–13.
[12] *St. Andrews Liber*, 354.
[13] SRO, GD 241/254; *Dict. top. du dép. du Pas de Calais*, 89, 220. The family of 'de Carvent' evidently survived in the late thirteenth century (*Cal. Docs. Scot.*, ii, 201 and no. 857).
[14] Ritchie, *Normans in Scotland*, 157.

The majority of the families we call Norman do seem to have originated within the Duchy of Normandy, but the inverted commas in the title of this chapter serve as a warning that the Normans have tended to monopolise the credit (perhaps also the discredit) for a highly significant migratory movement. How it was possible for this fairly small region to produce a sufficient surplus population possessing both the urge to emigrate and the necessary technical means is certainly a proper question for the historian, but before addressing himself to it he should try to discover as much as possible about the numbers and origins of those who migrated. Another proper question—which has always occupied students of comparable modern migrations, e.g. to America and Australia—is what sort of reception awaited the immigrants, how much land was available for their settlement, how much displacement did they produce among existing groups and communities, to what extent did they bring with them their wives and children. The point was well put in an anonymous review of Professor David Douglas's recent book on *William the Conqueror*.

> Here surely was the greatest achievement of all, the initial miracle of William's reign, to get his followers and their followers, families and household gods, all parked out and peaceful in England's green and pleasant land. Yet of this process, to which Domesday Book stands as did Bradshaw to the railway mania, not a vestige of a trace remains.[15]

Yet, even if we cannot embark here on these large and fascinating questions, there remain other questions which we may be able to answer and there certainly remains in most of our history books a vagueness which we should try to bring into sharper focus, a muddle which we should tidy up. Broadly speaking, there were two periods of relatively rapid and intensive Norman settlement in Scotland. The first period ran from 1107 to the 1140s. It was associated with Alexander I (1107–24) and David I (1124–53), and it affected most of Scotland south of the Forth–Clyde line and east of the valleys of Nith and Doon. The second period ran from about the middle of Malcolm IV's reign—say *c.* 1160—and

[15] *The Times Literary Supplement*, 20 August 1964, 738.

lasted until the turn of the century. Since these periods are so close together, and since it is unlikely that Norman immigration ceased during the few intervening years, it may be questioned whether the periods can be thought of as distinct. The difference seems to have lain in the source of immigration and in the character of the settlement in Scotland itself. Period I saw David I, before and after his accession, bringing Norman barons from his own Honour of Huntingdon and granting them very large lordships stretching right across the face of southern Scotland. Period II saw immigration from a much wider variety of sources. The estates with which settlers were endowed in this second period were much more widely scattered across Scotland, reaching far into the south-west and the north. They were also, in general, much smaller.

The figure of King David dominates the scene down to mid-century, and in this context two facts about him seem especially relevant, first that for more than twenty years before his accession he enjoyed the closest friendship with Henry I, and secondly that for more than ten of these years he held the Honour of Huntingdon. We need to recall that whereas Duke William's Normans had helped him to conquer England, King Henry's Normans had helped him to conquer Normandy. Henry's lordships and friends belonged emphatically to Lower (i.e. Western) Normandy. The families of this region had not profited from the Conquest of England anywhere near so richly as the families of Upper Normandy. When Henry became king and defeated the Bellême gang they saw their chance and expected their reward. Much of southern and midland England was already staked out and occupied, but north of the Trent and especially north of the Tees there was still plenty of room. It was inevitable that a man of David's upbringing should introduce Normans into Lothian, Teviotdale and Cumbria. It was overwhelmingly probable that these Normans would either be re-exports from the Honour of Huntingdon or else be immigrants from Henry I's sphere of influence, the Cotentin, the Avranchin and the eastern borders of Brittany. The special position held by David I thus set the pattern for Period I, when settlement took place on a scale large enough to make any previous continental immigration seem like a thin and irregular trickle.

The familiar names from this prodigal period are Bruce, Morville, Somerville, Corbet, Burneville, Soules, Avenel, Ridel, Lindsay and (lacking a surname) Walter 'le filz Alain', first of the Stewarts. Despite Ritchie's pessimism we are reasonably sure of the provenance of five out of these ten families. Loyd considered that the evidence deriving Bruce from Brix, arrondissement and canton Valognes, dép. Manche, 'hardly seems sufficient',[16] but really this is one of our certainties. Bruce fiefs in Cleveland were held at an early date by dependants from Sottevast close to Brix.[17] We have record of the gift of the parish church of Brix to the nearby priory of La Lutumière by Adam de Bruis, whose links with the English and Scottish Bruces are clearly established.[18] What I believe is not known is the origin of the Bruce family in Normandy itself, but the fact that Brix and its forest were important parts of the ducal demesne, and the high favour which Robert de Brus I enjoyed with Henry I suggest that the Bruces were closely related to the ducal house either by blood or by service or both.

In connexion with the Bruces we should look at one of the minor mysteries in the career of David I. A charter whose text survives in a copy entered into the cartulary of Wetheral priory in Cumberland, a cell of St. Mary's abbey, York, records the confirmation by Earl David (before he became king) of the gift made to St. Mary's by Robert de Brus of the vill called Karkarevill and its church.[19] Antiquaries have searched in vain for Karkarevill on the north side of the Channel. Sir Archibald Lawrie, realising that it was not in Scotland, said it must have been some land of the Bruces of which Earl David was overlord, possibly in the earldom of Northampton.[20] Archdeacon Prescott, unable to find it in

[16] Loyd, *Origins*, p. viii.

[17] *Cartularium prioratus de Gyseburne*, ed. W. Brown (Surtees Society, 1889–94), i, 203; ii, 7–8.

[18] *Recueil des actes de Henri II . . . concernant les provinces françaises et les affaires de France*, ed. L. Delisle and E. Berger (1909–27), i, 331. For Adam de Brus, Adam 'I' by English numbering, and his son Adam 'II', see Farrer, *EYC*, ii, 11–16.

[19] Dean and Chapter of Carlisle, MS. Cartulary of Wetheral Priory (saec. xiv), fo. 71ᵛ, Karkareuil' (in contemporary table of contents, on *verso* of twenty-second leaf, Kyrkareuil, and, in the rubric to the actual charter on fo. 71ᵛ, either Karkareuil' or Kirkareuil'). The charter has been printed in Dugdale, *Monasticon Anglicanum* (New edn.), iii, 583; in J. E. Prescott, *Register of the priory of Wetherhal* (1897), 194–5; and in Lawrie, *Charters*, 47, no. 52.

[20] Lawrie, *Charters*, 305.

England, supposed that it lay in Annandale in Scotland.[21] But early twelfth-century place-names ending in '-vill(e)' must be exceedingly rare north of the Channel. An early Bruce charter for Guisborough priory in Cleveland was witnessed by Robert 'de Kirchevile'.[22] This place was undoubtedly Querqueville near Cherbourg, whose church, at some date between c. 1195 and c. 1251, passed into the possession of the Norman abbey of Grestain.[23] I suspect that for the identity of Karkarevill we should look to Querqueville, formerly Kercavilla, Kirkevill.[24] The 'kirk' from which Querqueville takes its name is an old tenth-century structure; its change of ownership from Wetheral to Grestain (if it ever did belong to Wetheral) might have happened at the time of the loss of Normandy (c. 1204), either by agreement or by *force majeure*. But if I am right in thinking that David of Scotland confirmed a Bruce grant of a Norman church and manor, it poses a problem regarding David's earlier years, about which so little is known, and it might strengthen the belief that the great favour he showed to Robert de Brus owed more to personal considerations than to the rather small tenure which Brus held on the Honour of Huntingdon.

Morville is from Morville, a few kilometres south-west of Brix, and the Morvilles were prominent tenants on the Honour of Huntingdon.[25] The family's main stem were vassals of the Norman Honour of Vernon, which had its *caput* at Néhou a few miles further south.[26] The closeness of the Scottish Morvilles to the Norman and Wessex lines of the family is shown by the fact that Morville charters in Scotland were witnessed by Alexander de Néhou,[27] Richard de Néhou,[28] and William de Néhou.[28a] Richard was perhaps Richard the clerk, brother of William de Néhou, who witnessed a mid-twelfth-century grant of the chapel

[21] *Register of Wetherhal*, 195, no. 2.   [22] *Guisborough Cartulary*, ii, 7–8.
[23] Bouquet, *Recueil des historiens des Gaules et de la France*, xxiii, 530. For the date, cf. A. Longnon, *Pouillés de la province de Rouen* (1903), pp. lvii–lviii (I am indebted to Professor de Boüard for this reference, and for help in establishing that the date at which Grestain acquired Querqueville must have been between c. 1195 and c. 1251. Unfortunately, I have not been able to discover any record of the grant of the church to Grestain).
[24] Delisle-Berger, *Recueil des actes de Henri II*, ii, 302; *Rotuli Scaccarii Normanniae*, ed. T. Stapleton (1840), i, 278.
[25] Farrer, *Honors and knights' fees*, ii, 356–8.   [26] Loyd, *Origins*, 70.
[27] Anderson, *Diplomata*, Plate LXXXI.   [28] Stevenson, *Illustrations*, 15.
[28a] Marquess of Bute, Dumfries House, Loudoun Charters, no. 1.

of Bradpole in Dorset to Montebourg abbey by William de Morville,[29] who himself seems to appear in Scottish record as a witness to the famous charter by which David I conveyed Annandale to Robert de Brus.[30]

In the train of the Morvilles we must place, among others, Sinclairs, Clephanes,[31] and of course Haigs. I have suggested that St. Clair-sur-Elle seems a likely provenance for Sinclair, in view of its western situation and Angevin connexions, but this remains unproven. Clephane seems at first sight a puzzle. It is evidently a place-name, and Black identifies it with Clapham in Sussex. Clephan(e) often ends in 'n' in good sources and only rarely shows any trace of the 'clop' (= 'hillock') symptomatic of English Claphams. Dr. Grant Simpson, however, has been able to trace the Scots surname to the Pennine village of Clapham in the West Riding of Yorkshire.[32] As for the Haigs, Lewis Loyd proved conclusively that the first of the family in Scotland came from the district of La Hague, the extreme north-west corner of the Cotentin peninsula, best known perhaps for Cap de la Hague.[33] We also find William de Morville witnessing a charter with Adam de Gundeville, whose name seems to be from Gonneville, near Cherbourg.[33a]

Somerville is probably to be connected with the de Lacy family, but the place of origin seems to be unknown.[34] Corbet is traceable only as far as the Honour of Huntingdon.[35] It would be tempting to derive Robert de Burneville from either Besneville or Binniville, both formerly Bernevilla, if only because of their proximity to Morville, Néhou, etc. But the most reliable forms of the name in Scottish record seem to point to Burnovilla, now

[29] *Calendar of documents preserved in France, illustrative of the history of Great Britain and Ireland*, ed. J. H. Round (1899), no. 885; cf. Loyd, *Origins*, 70.

[30] Lawrie, *Charters*, no. 54.

[31] For a very brief notice of this family, see M. Stuart and J. Balfour Paul, *Scottish Family History* (1930), 129; and for early records relating to the family, cf. *Acts Parl. Scot.*, vii, 153, col. 2.

[32] I am grateful to Dr. Simpson for providing me with this information. For one document showing the Morville connexion with Clapham cf. *Cal. Docs. Scot.*, i, no. 195.

[33] Loyd, *Origins*, 49–50.   [33a] Anderson, *Diplomata*, pl. LXXVII.

[34] The early forms for Sommervieu (dép. Calvados) and Semerville (dép. Eure) do not encourage identification with a twelfth-century 'Sum(m)er-villa' which must have given rise to this surname.

[35] Farrer, *Honors and knights' fees*, ii, 386.

Bénouville, between Caen and the sea.[36] Black and Ritchie, on unstated evidence, say Bourneville (canton Quillebeuf), near Pont-Audemer.[37] The origins of Ridel of Cranston Riddell and of Lindsay remain unsolved problems, but it may be pointed out that the Frankish character of the Lindsays, despite their Lincolnshire surname, is corroborated by correcting the printed witness-list of an early Melrose charter to read not 'Arosine de Lindeseia' (attractive as that name may sound) but 'Drogone de Lindeseia', i.e. Drogon or Dreux, a highly characteristic name of north-west Francia.[38] This witness must be the Drew or Drogo de Lindsay found in contemporary English record.[39]

With Avenel and Soules we are on surer ground. The Scottish Avenels, lords of Eskdale, probably belonged to a well-known family of this name who were landholders in the Avranchin, especially in the county of Mortain.[40] Ranulf de Soules, to whom King David granted the lordship of Liddesdale and probably the office of butler in his household, held Great Doddington in Northamptonshire on the Honour of Huntingdon, adjoining Earls Barton which would have been one of King David's chief residences in England.[41] Ranulf's surname is from the commune of Soulles a little south of St. Lô, and a knightly family of this name remained at Soulles at least until the fourteenth century. It is appropriate to put Hay or de la Haye in the company of Soules, although the Scottish Hays belong to Period II rather than Period I. Garter King of Arms has demonstrated with a wealth of learning that the Hays of Erroll came from the small seigneurie of La Haye-Hue, now called La Haye-Bellefonds, almost adjacent to Soulles.[42] The first of the Scottish Hays, William, was the

[36] Lawrie, *Charters*, nos. 93, 99. These charters are originals, and have *Burnovill(-e, -a)*; cf. *Dictionnaire topographique du département du Calvados* (1883), 23.

[37] Black, *Surnames*, 118; *Normans in Scotland*, 156 and n. The early forms, which include *Burnevill(-e, -a)*, do not rule out this identification; cf. *Dictionnaire topographique du département de L'Eure* (1877), 33.

[38] *Melrose Liber*, i, no. 12. The true reading was established by examining the original charter, SRO, Melrose charters, no. 12.

[39] Farrer, *Honors and knights' fees*, ii, 376; *St. Bees Register*, no. 15.

[40] *Rotuli Scaccarii Normanniae*, ii, 539, 543, 545, 548; Delisle-Berger, *Recueil des actes de Henri II*, i, 136, 179, 187; ii, 155, 302.

[41] *RRS*, i, 34.

[42] Sir Anthony Wagner, 'The origin of the Hays of Erroll', in *Genealogists' Magazine*, 1954, 1955.

nephew and the knight of Ranulf de Soules, and his son or grandson used the same arms, three escutcheons, as were used by the de la Hayes of La Haye-Hue and their cadets the de la Hayes of Les Agneaux near St. Lô. Striking corroboration of the links between Soules and Hay in Scotland and the Norman families of de Soulles and de la Haye is to be found in a Liddesdale charter of c. 1200 issued by the younger Ranulf de Soules (the original of the Wicked Lord Soulis of legend) and witnessed by William des Aigneus.[43] William, incidentally, may be regarded as the first of the Scottish Agnews.[44]

Ultimately the most famous of all the families of Period I were the Stewarts, whose origin, as is well-known, was not Norman but Breton.[45] Their ancestor Walter was a younger son of Alan son of Fla(h)ald son of Alan, who was seneschal of the bishops of Dol in the eleventh century. The family was richly rewarded for its support of Henry I and understandably took a strongly pro-Angevin line in Stephen's reign. It is precisely from families such as these that one would expect David of Scotland to draw his foreign followers. A closely comparable recruit was Walter de Bidun, the king's last chancellor, whose family's original home seems to have been one of the two places called Bidon respectively west and east of Dol. The de Biduns were tenants of the Honour of Huntingdon and also held the small lordship of Lavendon, where the remains of their castle still overlook the main road from Bedford to Northampton along which King David and his son and grandsons must have ridden many times.[46] Walter the Stewart and Walter the Chancellor belonged to an East Breton–South West Norman group of families which loyally supported Henry I. Others in this same group took their names from St. Hilaire-du-Harcouët and St. James-de-Beuvron near the Breton border.[47] While these two families did not come north, among the Scottish Norman families of Period

---

[43] R. C. Reid, 'Some early de Soulis Charters', in *Dumfriesshire Trans.*, 3rd Series, xxvi (1949), 155–6.

[44] Correctly derived by Black, *Surnames*, 10, from Les Agneaux.

[45] J. H. Round, *Studies in peerage and family history* (1901), 115–31.

[46] Farrer, *Honors and knights' fees*, ii, 1–5; B.M., MS. Cotton Tiberius E v, f. 159; MS. Cotton Vespasian, E xvii, f. 238; *VCH, Bucks*, iv, 380.

[47] C. T. Clay, *EYC*, v (1936), 86–7; J. H. Round, *Studies in peerage and family history*, 124–5; *VCH, Northants*, i, 362.

II, apparently established in Berwickshire under William the Lion, was that of Landells or Landale (de Landelles).[48] There is a commune of this name north of Vire, but a more likely provenance for the Scottish family (one of whom, incidentally, was bishop of St. Andrews for forty-three years in the fourteenth century) would be the adjacent parishes of St. Martin and St. Brice-de-Landelles, just west of St. Hilaire-du-Harcouët. The earliest generation of Scottish Landells included a man with the extremely rare name of Sequard,[49] and it is a curious fact that the debateable land of Chalandrey a short way north of Landelles was granted to Savigny abbey in the twelfth century by Geoffrey son of Wimund and his three sons, Alan, Juhel and Sequard.[50]

Norman families did not of course all arrive in Scotland as part of a tidy and logical process, nor can they all be fitted into a pattern centred upon King David and his English estates. Their immigration might be due to the chance of war or of a royal marriage. In 1136 or shortly afterwards, a 'Norman' (actually a Flemish) lord of North Devon and Somerset, Robert of Bampton, whom the bishop of Bath and Wells described as a 'winebibber and gourmand, devoted in peace-time only to gluttony and drunkenness', rebelled against King Stephen and was forced to flee to the king of Scots' court, where he is said to have stayed for a long time.[51] It was indeed his son who allegedly incited King David to make war on King Stephen in 1138.[52] Whatever the truth of this, and whether or not any of Robert of Bampton's kinsmen remained permanently in the north, one family well-known in Scotland for nearly two centuries, the Lovels of Hawick, do seem to have migrated as a result of Robert of Bampton's rebellion. In 1138 one Ralph Lovel had charge of Robert's castle of Cary in Somerset, which Stephen forced him to surrender, and only a few years later Ralph's son and heir Henry appears as the earliest of the Scottish Lovels, and his descendants were lords of Hawick and Castle Cary in the middle of the thirteenth century.[53]

[48] *Kelso Liber*, nos. 322, 401; cf. *Cal. Docs. Scot.*, ii, pp. 200, 203.
[49] *Kelso Liber*, no. 322.
[50] Delisle-Berger, *Recueil des actes de Henri II*, ii, 181.
[51] *Gesta Stephani*, ed. K. R. Potter (1955), 18–20; R. H. C. Davis, 'The authorship of the *Gesta Stephani*', *EHR*, lxxvii, 219. [52] *Gesta Stephani*, 36.
[53] *Gesta Stephani*, 44–6; Davis, art. et loc. cit.; *St. Andrews Liber*, 261; *Cal. Docs. Scot.*, i, no. 1740. See also I. J. Sanders, *English Baronies* (1960), 27–8.

One bridge between Period I and Period II was provided by the marriage of Earl Henry, King David's son, to Ada de Warenne, daughter of Earl William II de Warenne. This great family was in the first rank of the nobility of Upper Normandy and came into the Conquest of England on the ground floor. It was unlikely that many of its richly endowed dependants would find much to tempt them in Scotland, but a few of the Countess Ada's vassals did settle there and found notable families. Among them pride of place must go to the Giffards of Yester, who gave their name to Gifford in East Lothian and who are still represented by the family of Gifford-Hay, Marquess of Tweeddale. These Giffards were probably a branch of the main clan of Giffard based upon Longueville-la-Gifart in the arrondissement of Dieppe, only a few miles from Bellencombre, the Norman seat of the Warennes.[54] Other Warenne dependants who settled in Scotland were Alexander of St. Martin, presumably a kinsman of the St. Martins who are to be found on Warenne estates in England,[55] and Hugh de Balliol, first of the earlier family of Scottish Balliols.[56] The early Balliols were not related to the famous Balliols, being Normans from Bailleul-Neuville, about thirty kilometres north-east of Bellencombre,[57] whereas King John Balliol's family came from Bailleul-en-Vimeu in Picardy.[58]

During the reigns of Malcolm IV and William the Lion, the Period II of my classification, Norman settlement in Scotland continued unabated. It is much harder to trace any pattern either in its sources or in the character which it took north of the Border. We have many more names to deal with—so many, in fact, that only a fraction of them can be mentioned here. But it would be rash to assert that the pace and volume of foreign settlement had greatly increased. What seems to have happened is that since the south of Scotland had been largely occupied the newcomers tended to move into the extreme south-west or else into the lands north of Forth and Tay, and especially into the royal

[54] Ritchie, *Normans in Scotland*, 276; Loyd, *Origins*, 45.
[55] Ritchie, *Normans in Scotland*, 275; C. T. Clay, *EYC*, viii (The Honour of Warenne), 78, 132; *Cartulary of St. Mary, Clerkenwell* (ed. W. O. Hassall, Royal Historical Society, Camden Third Series, vol. lxxi, 1949), 20.
[56] *SHR*, xxx, 48.
[57] Loyd, *Origins*, 11, benefactors of the Warenne foundation of Lewes Priory, Sussex.   [58] *Origins*, 11.

demesne of Fife, Gowrie, Angus and Mearns. Oddly enough, King David seems to have retained the royal lands of Clydesdale mostly in his own hands. His grandson, Malcolm IV, may be said to have inaugurated Period II by dividing up much of this property—and church property as well—into knight's fees, which he bestowed mainly on Flemings whose origins are either very poorly documented or not documented at all.[59] Theobald the Fleming in Douglasdale, William Finemund in Cambusnethan, Baldwin the Fleming lord of Biggar, Hugh of Pettinain (who has left his name in the Renfrewshire Houston) and his sons Reginald, Arkenbald and Boderic—of whom the last has given his obscure Flemish name to Botherickfield in Houston parish[60]—Thankard of Thankerton, Lambin of Lamington, his brother Robert of Roberton, Wice of Wiston, Simon Lockhart or Flockhart of Symington, all these men, although they were the very foundation of the lairds class in medieval Lanarkshire, are scarcely more than names. A clue to the general region from which they may have come is possibly given us by the name of their contemporary, Philip de Vermeles, lord of Romanno, of whom Baldwin of Biggar's vassal Hugh of Houston held a fief.[61] Vermeles is Vermelles, a commune in the same canton (Cambrin) as Cuinchy, the de Quincis' probable place of origin, and indeed we find Philip de Vermeles and his son in association with Robert de Quinci.[62] Just as Soules of Normandy and Northamptonshire seems to have brought Hay and Agnew direct to Scotland, so may de Quinci, of Flanders and Northamptonshire, have brought Vermelles and other Flemish settlers. In any event, Flemish settlement was not confined to Period II. The two greatest Scottish families which sprang from it were Murray and Douglas. The founder of the house of Murray was a Fleming named Freskin who was granted Strathbrock in West Lothian and Duffus in Moray by David I.[63] Although William, the first of the Douglases, does not appear till the 1170s, his family, replete with Christian names such as Arkenbald (Archibald) and Freskin, was undoubtedly related to the Murrays and was surely Flemish in origin.[64]

[59] Above, pp. 288–91.
[60] G. Crawfurd, *History of the shire of Renfrew* (1710), 71.
[61] *Newbattle Registrum*, 93–4.   [62] *Newbattle Registrum*, 52.
[63] Above, p. 282.   [64] *Origines Parochiales*, i, 155–6.

The Duchy of Normandy itself continued to be well represented in Period II. In some cases we may see the probable connecting link which led a man—often doubtless a younger son out to make his fortune by skill in arms—to seek the king of Scotland's patronage. 'We recommend to you', wrote Gilbert Foliot, bishop of London, to King Malcolm, 'our near kinsman Elias, whom we hope you will take into your service. If he finds favour in your sight he will bring many more to your service who will be no charge on your generosity. His father', the bishop significantly added, 'lost his patrimony through his loyalty to your father and grandfather.'[65] Of Elias Foliot we hear no more in Scottish record. It seems probable, despite the bishop's statement about his father's loyalties, that he remained on the Honour of Huntingdon and took service with the Senlis earls, the rivals of the royal house of Scotland. At all events, he is found witnessing charters of Earl Simon III de Senlis and his wife Alice de Gant, dating to the years c. 1160–85.[66] David Olifard, King David's godson, whose ancestral estate on the Honour of Huntingdon was confiscated by Earl Simon II de Senlis and devoted to the founding of Sawtry abbey, may be compared and contrasted with Elias Foliot. To David Olifard, already holding Smailholm in Roxburghshire, King Malcolm gave the land between the North and South Calder Waters and thus created the great lordship of Bothwell.[67] The Olifards had been on the Honour of Huntingdon from the late eleventh century, but where they came from before that is not known.[68] Another example may be seen in Raoul de Clères, who acquired the baronies of Mid Calder in Midlothian (Calder Clere) and Cambusnethan in Clydesdale, apparently from Malcolm IV or William I.[69] Clères, now in the arrondissement of Rouen, was a fief dependent on the ancient and wealthy honour of Tosny in the Seine valley.[70] Raoul IV de Tosny married Earl Waltheof's younger daughter, and was thus King Malcolm's great-uncle.[71] At the very time that Raoul de Clères was building his castle at Mid Calder Master Simon de Tosny, perhaps a

[65] *RRS*, i, no. 320.

[66] *Cartularium abbathiae de Rievalle*, ed. J. C. Atkinson (Surtees Society, 1889), pp. 48, 115–16; Farrer, *EYC*, ii, 438.

[67] Above, p. 289.   [68] Ritchie, *Normans in Scotland*, 279.

[69] *Kelso Liber*, nos. 272, 349.   [70] Loyd, *Origins*, 29.

[71] D. C. Douglas, *William the Conqueror* (1964), 86.

grandson of Raoul IV de Tosny, was a monk at Melrose. After a period as abbot of Coggeshall in Essex, Master Simon returned to Scotland and was Bishop of Moray from 1172 until his death twelve years later.[72] It hardly seems rash to connect the appearance in Scotland of Raoul de Clères with the royal family's kinship to the de Tosnys. Little fleas have lesser fleas, and Raoul de Clères, a client of King Malcolm, had his own clients. A witness to a de Clères charter in Scotland was one Richard de Langetoft.[73] At first sight his surname looks thoroughly Northumbrian, but it is identical with the twelfth-century spelling of the place now called Lanquetôt in the arrondissement of Le Havre, some twenty-five miles west of Clères.[74]

The Crown itself was responsible for bringing into Scotland many individuals and families of Norman origin. Their number cannot be calculated with any precision, and we must remember that for every one of the greater men there would be a small company of dependants—kinsmen, knights, men-at-arms, servants, some expecting land and all requiring billets. Sometimes these lesser men may leave a clue as to their origin, but more often not.[75] It was to William the Lion's reign, and in particular to the period immediately following the Treaty of Falaise (1174), that later Scottish tradition, if correctly reported by Sir Thomas Grey,[76] assigned a sudden and massive tidal wave of Norman immigration into Scotland, bringing with it the families of Balliol, Bruce, Soules, Moubray, Sinclair, Hay, Giffard, Ramsay, Laundells, Bisset, Barclay, Valognes, Boys, Montgomery, Vaux, Colville, Fraser, Graham, Gourlay and several more. The list conflates, of course, the settlements of David I's time with those of his grandsons, but the mistake is not inappropriate, for surely there was never a more normanising king of Scots than William the Lion, who began his public career as 'William de Warenne, earl of Northumberland'?[77] One may accept from Grey's list the families of Moubray, Ramsay, Laundells, Valognes, Boys and Fraser as certainly or probably introduced under William the Lion. The Bissets (with whom we should associate the Grants)

[72] Dowden, *Bishops*, 146.   [73] *Kelso Liber*, no. 272.
[74] Loyd, *Origins*, 53.
[75] E.g. Robert 'de Clipanvile', of whom *Melrose Liber*, no. 137, gives us a fleeting mention, presumably came from Cliponville, dép. Seine-Maritime.
[76] *Scalacronica*, 41.   [77] *RRS*, ii, nos. 1, 2.

certainly came in with William the Lion.[78] Their district of
origin was the Pays de Caux. The inclusion of Barclay can also
be justified, as we shall see. On the other hand, Grey leaves out
several names which are most familiar in the record of William's
reign, e.g., Lovel, Frivill (Frésville, arr. Valognes, dép. Manche),
Lascelles (possibly from Loucelles, arr. Caen, dép. Calvados),
de la Kernelle, de Montfiquet or Muschet (Montfiquet, arr.
Bayeux, dép. Calvados), Montfort, Revel, and Normanville (with
which one should associate Menzies; Normanville and Mesnières
are both in the arr. Neufchatel, dép. Seine-Maritime). Here
there is space only to tell three cautionary tales, designed to illustrate the pitfalls which may trap the unwary, and also to fortify
the plea for more basic archaeology, to which it is earnestly to be
hoped that Norman as well as Scottish scholars will contribute.
The tales concern the families of Barclay, de la Kernelle and
Quarrantilly.

There are surely more published histories of the Barclays than
of any other Scottish family. The Barclay histories published in
this century are worse than those published in the eighteenth, and
those in turn are distinguished for the low level of their medieval
scholarship. It has been assumed, on no concrete evidence, that
the Scottish family of Barclay (de Berchelai, etc.), which first
appears at the end of Malcolm IV's reign in the persons of Robert
and Walter de Berkeley,[79] must be a branch of one or other of the
two Anglo-Norman families of de Berkeley of Berkeley in Glouces-
tershire. Despite this assumption, it has never been possible to
point to a single piece of evidence which would link the Scottish
and English families. Is it extravagant to look for an alternative
explanation? As with Lindsay and Ramsay, we have a Scottish
family with an English place-name for surname and a strongly
Norman flavour about the Christian names. Near Frome in
Somerset there is a small village called Berkley (in 1086, Ber-
chelei). In 1086 its overlordship belonged to a Norman named

[78] *Beauly Chrs.*, 17–25, 53.

[79] *RRS*, i, 283, n. 1. According to G. Crawfurd, *History of the shire of Renfrew*,
88, one Richard de Barclay was a witness to the foundation charter of the
abbey of Kilwinning, Ayrshire. The abbey's charters are now lost, but it is
generally held that this house was founded by Hugh de Morville the Constable,
who died in 1162. Richard may be an error for Robert; alternatively, he was
an otherwise unrecorded member of the family of de Berkeley.

Roger Arundel, whose tenant in Berkley—that is, the actual lord of the manor—was a certain Robert.[80] Roger Arundel's manors in Somerset—part of a barony whose *caput* was Poorstock in Dorset— were interspersed among those held by the Fleming, Walter of Douai, father of the gluttonous Robert of Bampton, and they included Cary Fitzpaine (in Charlton Mackerell), not far from Castle Cary.[81] Cary Fitzpaine seems to have been held by the same tenant as Berkley. At the very time when Henry Lovel of Castle Cary first appears in Scotland, we have the equally un-heralded appearance as witnesses to Scottish royal charters of Godfrey de Arundel[82] and Robert and Walter de Berkeley. There is surely a case for testing the possibility that the Scottish Barclays took their name from Berkley in Somerset because their ancestors were tenants there of the Arundels.

This, however, is not the whole story. The Barclay historians not only ignore a possible connexion with the Somerset Berkley, they ignore a fact of more fundamental importance. What has always been regarded as the main line of the Scottish Barclays is represented by the family of Barclay of Mathers and their des-cendants, a family renowned in more modern times for producing field-marshals, Quakers and bankers.[83] This line has not in fact been 'Barclay' by male descent since before the end of the twelfth century. Some charters of William the Lion prove that the Barclay estates in Laurencekirk and Fordoun were granted by the king to a certain Humphrey son of Theobald in right of his wife Agatha.[84] It was evidently Agatha who was a 'de Berkeley', and her husband and children adopted her surname. One of the charters luckily preserves the original surname of Humphrey, or at least that of his father Theobald, as 'de Adevil(l)e'.[85] I have

[80] *VCH, Somerset*, i, 496; Sanders, *English Baronies*, 72.

[81] *VCH, Somerset*, i, 495; and for the disposition of the Arundel and Douai estates, see the Domesday Map of Somerset contained in the *Proceedings of the Somersetshire Archaeological Society*, vol. xxxv.

[82] *RRS*, i, nos. 256, 292 and n.

[83] Michael, Prince Barclay de Tolly (1761–1818), Minister of War under Tsar Alexander I, 1810–13, Commander-in-Chief of the Russian army of the west, and in France; Robert Barclay of Urie (1648–90), author of the famous *Apology* for Quaker Christianity; and James, David and John Barclay, eighteenth-century founders of Barclay's Bank; all belonged to this line of the family.

[84] *RRS*, ii, nos. 344, 345.   [85] *RRS*, ii, no. 423.

searched thoroughly, but not exhaustively, for a place of this name in likely regions, and it seems that there is only one such place in the whole of Normandy. This is the hamlet and chapelry of Addeville in the commune of St. Côme-du-Mont, canton Carenton, arr. St. Lô, dép. Manche. Its chapel was in the patronage of the dukes of Normandy, and it had a minor proprietorial family, one of whom, Humphrey de Adeville, made grants to the abbeys of Montebourg and the Holy Trinity, Caen (both ducal foundations) in the early twelfth century.[86] It is a conjecture, but perhaps not a very wild one, that Humphrey son of Theobald de Adeville, given a rich heiress in marriage by William the Lion and enabled to found the ancient family of Barclay, was a grandson of Humphrey de Adeville who flourished in the time of Henry I.

Another beneficiary of King William was Roger de la Kernelle, who had a grant of Guthrie in Angus for knight-service, and was succeeded by his son Walter.[87] Their family, whose name in England became Carnail, had long been established on the Honour of Huntingdon.[88] The commune of La Carneille, from which they almost certainly derived their name, is in the arrondissement of Argentan, dép. Orne. In Scotland the name survives to this day, but, like Wingate and Vans, it has suffered from a misreading of 'n' for 'u' and become Carvel or Carville. I suspect that the family also survives under another guise. Black remarks that no one of the name of Guthrie is found in the first volume of the Arbroath abbey register.[89] The Guthries of that ilk have held Guthrie continuously only since 1465, but it was a Guthrie of Kincaldrum who then purchased the barony,[90] and his ancestors must at one time have been at Guthrie. I suggest that they were there in the twelfth and thirteenth centuries not as 'de Guthrie' but as 'de la Kernelle'.

The last cautionary tale concerns the family of de Quarrantilly. This name is not listed in Black's *Surnames of Scotland*, but before

---

[86] Delisle-Berger, *Recueil des actes de Henri II*, ii, 203; *RRAN*, ii, no. 1684.

[87] Above, p. 292.

[88] Farrer, *Honors and knights' fees*, ii, 360–2. It is probably significant of the link between the English and Scottish branches of the family that in 1216 Robert de la Carnaile was with the English king (John)'s enemies in Scotland (*Rot. Litt. Claus.* Record Comm., i, 374).

[89] Black, *Surnames*, 333.

[90] A. Jervise, *Memorials of Angus and the Mearns* (Edinburgh, 1861), 17.

giving up in despair we should look at his entries of CARMICHAEL and GRANTULLY. Under Carmichael we read 'The lands [of Carmichael] were long in possession of the family the first of whom in record appears to have been Robert de Garmitely (evidently an error in spelling).'[91] This is from the Dryburgh cartulary, and it was the indexer of the printed version who led Black into confusion.[92] Under Grantully Black says 'Perhaps from the lands of Grantully in the parish of Dull, Perthshire', and refers to Robert de Grantell' (*tempore* Alexander II), Adam de Quaranteley (*tempore* Alexander III) and Ellen de Quaranteley (around 1300).[93] We must start again from scratch. A late charter of William the Lion was witnessed by his chamberlain Philip de Valognes and by Robert Quarrantel'.[94] The Dryburgh charter cited by Black was given by Robert de Caramiceley, for which read Caraunteley, who refers to the soul of his lord Philip de Valognes.[95] We know that Philip was a younger son of the head of the family of Valognes,[96] which held a sizeable barony mainly located in Suffolk, Essex and Hertfordshire, and which took its name from Valognes in the department of La Manche, a little north of Morville. Philip de Valognes seems to have joined King William's service before 1171, and died in 1215.[97] Robert de Quarrantel' had evidently become his man, and held land at Cleghorn in Lanark. He is to be identified with Black's Robert de Grantell' of Alexander II's time, for the document reads Guarantell', for which we should certainly substitute Quarantell'.[98]

The commune of Carantilly, in the arrondissement of St. Lô and department of La Manche, lies about half way between Coutances and Soulles. In the thirteenth century the lords of Soulles held a sizeable fief at Carantilly, as well as the patronage of the parish church.[99] A lady named Emma de Carantilly (Karantilleio) figures on the Norman exchequer roll of 1198 for the bailiwick of Coutances, along with Ranulf de Soules.[100] This

[91] Black, *Surnames*, 135.   [92] *Dryburgh Liber*, p. 412.
[93] Black, *Surnames*, 325.   [94] *RRS*, ii, no. 469.
[95] *Dryburgh Liber*, no. 233.
[96] Above, p. 287; Sanders, *English Baronies*, 12–13.   [97] *Chron. Melrose*, 61.
[98] *Newbattle Registrum*, no. 122 (p. 92), Edinburgh, 24 June 1224.
[99] Bouquet, *Recueil*, xxiii, 500, 735.
[100] *Rotuli Scaccarii Normanniae*, ii, 295–7.

was presumably the younger Ranulf de Soules, lord of Liddesdale, who in 1207 was murdered in his own home by his own household servants. A few years ago the late Dr. R. C. Reid published a chirograph agreement between this Ranulf de Soules and Jedburgh Abbey, conveying land ˉin Liddesdale to the abbey.[101] Among the witnesses is Robert [de] Quarentilli, and this is probably his earliest occurrence in Scottish record. The conjunction of these names, Soules, Carantilly and Valognes, reminds us that the Normans were past masters in the operation of what is sometimes called a 'network'. The family of de Quarentilli, settled in Scotland presumably through the influence of Ranulf de Soules, prospered modestly in Lanarkshire until Robert Bruce's reign (1306–29), when Helen and Sibyl de Quaranteley seem to have been the last survivors of the senior line.[102]

This chapter has touched on few of the questions which will rightly be regarded as interesting and important. How many Normans came to Scotland, what was their impact upon Scottish life, did they really introduce feudalism, to what extent did their menfolk bring with them wives and children, how much did their womenfolk bring in the way of personal possessions and household goods, how far did they alter the character of Scottish trade, did they learn any language but French, how did they make the long journey north and who paid their fares? These are the questions whose answers would provide the very stuff of history. They are far more interesting and worthwhile than a pedestrian search for family origins in this commune, or canton, or arrondissement, or department, rather than another five, ten, fifty or a hundred kilometres distant. Yet before we try to answer the really interesting questions about the Norman families of Scotland, and before we make airy generalisations about what we have called, in compliment to them, the 'Norman age', we ought to find out exactly who our Normans were.

[101] *Dumfriesshire Trans.* (3rd Series), xxvi, 156.
[102] *Reg. Mag. Sig.*, i, 22, 463.

12 The earliest Stewarts and their lands

It is impossible to reconstruct in detail the organisation of any of the great fiefs brought into existence by the Scottish monarchy in the twelfth century, for the surviving evidence is too fragmentary. Unhappily, this is especially true of the earliest Stewart fief, the great feudal 'honour' or group of estates, created by royal gift, of which the first three hereditary Stewarts, Walter I, his son Alan and grandson Walter II, were the successive lords. But by piecing together what scattered evidence remains, a partial reconstruction is possible.

What follows is a survey of the lordship held by the first three Stewarts between about 1136, when Walter I seems to have entered the service of King David of Scotland, and 1241, when Walter II died. The survey is in two parts, (1) a list, by regions and parishes, of the subordinate fiefs of which the lordship was composed, with, where known, their holders' names and origins and the service rendered; (2) an index of some ninety-four major tenants and vassals of the early Stewarts.

In order to save space and to make the lists easy to use, references to authorities have not normally been given. Because of this, particular care has been taken to distinguish statements for which the evidence is trustworthy from those whose truth is merely probable or possible. All unqualified statements in the survey may be taken as belonging to the former class; the rest are given the appropriate reservations. All the historical information contained in the survey is drawn from the following authorities, unless otherwise noted: The cartularies and other records of Scottish cathedrals and religious houses published by the Abbotsford, Maitland, Bannatyne and Grampian Clubs, the Society of Antiquaries of Scotland and the Scottish History Society. Nearly all have been used, but the volumes laid under special contribution have been the records of the abbeys of Paisley, Melrose and Kelso. Among other sources which may be mentioned are R. W. Eyton, *History of Shropshire* (1854–60); G. Crawfurd, *History of the Shire of Renfrew* (1710); Fraser, *Lennox*; J. H. Round, *Peerage and Family History* (1901), and in *Genealogist*, New Series (1902); Scots *Peerage*; *Complete Peerage*; *Red Book of the Exchequer* (ed. Hall); *Reports* of the Hist. MSS. Commission; *Cal. Docs. Scot.*; G. Chalmers, *Caledonia* (2nd edn); *Origines Parochiales*; *Gilbertine Charters* (ed. F. M. Stenton); G. Neilson in *Hist. Berwickshire Nat. Club*, vol. xxiv; and the Ordnance Survey, 1-in., 2½-in., and 6-in. Maps.

Walter I, first of the hereditary Stewarts of Scotland, was the third son of Alan son of Flaald son of Alan son of Flaald. (All four ancestors were successively stewards of the lords of Dol in Brittany.) Walter was not a large landowner in England. He held North Stoke, near Arundel, by grant from his elder brother William Fitz Alan, lord of Oswestry, who in Sussex as in Shropshire had succeeded to land previously held by Roger, earl of Shrewsbury. He evidently held land at Manhood, south of Chichester. *Paisley Registrum*, 2–3, prints a document recording that the Prior of Wenlock surrendered property at Renfrew, which had been granted to Wenlock Priory by Walter I at the time when he was founding Paisley Priory with monks taken from Wenlock, about 1163. The surrender was made in exchange for property at 'Menewde'. Manhood was earlier called Manwuda, Menewode, Manewode (xii–xiv cents.) and in 1535 Wenlock Priory received a rent of 14s. yearly from the village of 'Monhode' in Sussex (*Valor Ecclesiasticus*, iii, 216). Walter I also held land at a place called 'Coneton' or 'Coueton', not identified, though Eyton (*Shropshire*, vi, 70) suggested Cound in Salop. In 1166, his holding on the Fitz Alan barony was assessed at two knights' fees.

Walter I seems to have entered the service of David I of Scotland in or before 1136, the probable date of the first 'foundation charter' to Melrose Abbey, to which he was a witness. It is difficult, if not impossible, to believe, with J. T. T. Brown (*SHR*, xxiv, 270–1), that Walter I joined King David as a result of the hostility between Stephen and the Empress Maud, for this did not become open in England until 1137 or later. Doubtless as a relatively poor younger son, Walter I saw a chance of bettering himself in the Scottish king's service. His brother William probably knew King David personally, and it is likely that the family of de Bidun, close neighbours of King David in the midland Honour of Huntingdon, came from the same region of Brittany as the stewards of Dol. One of the de Biduns, Walter, became King David's chancellor about 1150.

In addition to making Walter his steward, King David endowed him with a large part of the extensive estate surveyed below, and these grants were added to by King Malcolm IV (1153–65). Renfrew was given by David I, but it is not known whether north Kyle was the gift of David also or of his grandson Malcolm. The symmetry of the fiefs between Clyde and Doon— Renfrew (Steward), Cunningham (Constable), north Kyle (Steward) and south Kyle (Crown)—together with the enfeoffment under Malcolm IV of the king's sheriff of Clydesdale in Inverkip and Houston, suggests very strongly a deliberate and well worked out policy of defending a vulnerable coastline and doorway to Scotland against attacks from the Isles and Galloway.

1   A regional survey of the Stewart fief

t. Walter I means 'in the time of Walter I', *c.* 1136–77, more especially *c.* 1161–77.

t. Alan means 'in the time of Alan son of Walter I', 1177–1204.

t. Walter II means 'in the time of Walter II', son of Alan, 1204–41.

(i) *Renfrewshire and Lanarkshire (Strathgryfe)*

RENFREW

Held in demesne. Castle and burgh. Renfrew was the *caput* of the Strathgryfe group of estates held by the earliest Stewarts, and may have been regarded as the chief place of their whole fief.

WEST PARTICK. At the beginning of David I's reign the whole of Partick seems to have been in royal hands. The greater part of it was granted by King David to Glasgow Cathedral, but some remained in the king's possession at his death in 1153. This remaining section of Partick was granted to Walter I by King Malcolm, and may be identified with West Partick, the only part of Partick included in the parish of Renfrew.

WALKINSHAW. In some works, it is stated erroneously that these lands were held of Paisley Abbey by Dougal, son of Cristin judge of Lennox, in the thirteenth century. His holding was in fact described as 'in the island between Black Cart and Gryfe *beside* Walkinshaw'.

PAISLEY

A considerable part of this large parish was evidently held in demesne by Walter I; and even after the Cluniac monks from Wenlock, at first established at Renfrew, had been transferred to Paisley (1169), much of the parish continued to be held in demesne by Alan and Walter II and their successors. Included in this demesne were:

BLACKHALL, first mentioned in the thirteenth century, evidently a residence of the Stewarts, and part of the Stewarts' forest, south of Blackhall. The rest of this forest lay in what is now Neilston parish, q.v. This forest is sometimes known as the FOREST OF FERENEZE and the Fereneze Hills, in Neilston parish, are at its north-eastern corner. The editor of the Paisley Cartulary, the editor of the *Origines Parochiales*, and the local historians of Renfrewshire do not seem to have realised that 'Fereneze' is a 'ghost-name' which has apparently arisen through the misinterpretation of a term occurring in documents of the twelfth and thirteenth centuries. The misunderstanding had certainly taken place before 1504, since a document dated that year refers to the 'village of Ferrenes' in the parish of Paisley (*Registrum Episcopatus Glasguensis*, p. 511). Walter I granted the monks of Paisley the tenth of his venison, with skins, and in addition all the skins of the hinds taken by him 'in fermison' (*in Forineisun*, read *Formeisun*, Old French *fermeyson*, English *fermison*, the close season for stags and time for hunting hinds, 11 November–2 February). The word occurs in other early Stewart charters to Paisley, down to 1294. In the Paisley Cartulary, it is printed as Forineisun, Ferineisun, Forineisim, and Forineson. The correct reading would be Formeisun, Fermeisun, Formeson.

Cf. *Boldon Buke*, ed. W. Greenwell, Surtees Soc.,1852, pp. 28, 29, 32, where 'fonneson' [*rectius* formeson] is contrasted with 'the rut' (*ruyth*). There is no doubt that this is the technical term 'fermison' (related to French, *fermer*), meaning close season. Its context in the early documents shows that this was its meaning there, and that it was not the name of a geographical locality. The names Ferrenes (1504) and Fereneze (modern) have evidently arisen through an early misreading (doubtless by the monks of Paisley) of Fermeisun as Ferineisun, and an early failure to understand what this word meant. As such, it is surely one of the oddest examples of a 'ghost-name' in Scotland.

The Cluniac monks settled at Paisley at first held the parish church with two carucates of land, probably in the neighbourhood of the church and between the White and Black Cart rivers. Before the death of Walter II, they had obtained a substantial proportion of the parish.

INGLESTON. The lands of Ingleston lay between Ralston and the White Cart. They were held by ADAM OF KENT and his heirs, t. Walter II.

RALSTON. This name means 'Ralph's *tun* or manor'. Land was held in Hillington, in Paisley parish, t. Walter I, by a certain Ralph the chaplain; it is possible that this was Ralston. Alternatively, the name may derive from RALPH OF KENT, one of the knights of Walter I, and probably a predecessor of ADAM OF KENT, who held the adjacent land of Ingleston t. Walter II.

ARKLESTON. This formed a carucate of land and was held, probably in the twelfth century, by GRIMKETIL. Early in the thirteenth century this was already known as 'Arkylliston', i.e. 'Arnkell's *tun* or manor', and the reference shows that Arnkell succeeded Grimketil. Both these names are Scandinavian, and it may be noted that early in the reign of David I, when Partick was still royal demesne, his tenants there were Ailsi and Tocca, the former having an Old English name, the latter a Scandinavian one. The land of Arkleston was given to Paisley Priory by Walter I.

CROOKSTON. The fee of ROBERT CROC, a knight of Walter I and Alan. Robert Croc had a court and private chapel within Paisley parish, doubtless on the site of Crookston Castle, which together with the lands has taken its name from him. The name Croc is in origin Scandinavian, but Robert Croc himself was probably of Anglo-Norman stock. It is not a place-name, and the form 'Robert *de* Croc', found in some works, is incorrect. He is once called 'Robert *le* Croc, knight of Alan the Stewart', in a document of 1177–96. (See under Mearns, Eastwood, Neilston, Symington in Kyle, and Mow.)

An unlocated fee held by HENRY OF NES, t. Alan. It must have been a considerable fee, since Henry had a court and private chapel, and together with Robert Croc was described as the 'special friend' of the priory of Paisley. In view of the Croc holding in the east of the parish, and the demesne and monastic holding in the middle, it may be suggested tentatively that Henry of Nes's fee lay in the west of the parish.

The place from which Henry and his kinsmen took their name was probably either Little Ness, held by Walter I's brother William FitzAlan and his descendants in demesne, or else Great Ness, held from 1158 by the family of Lestrange, closely connected with the FitzAlans. Both these places are in north Shropshire.

POLLOK

Part formed the fee of PETER SON OF FULBERT, also called PETER OF POLLOK, t. Walter I and Alan. Fulbert occurs in record only as the father of three brothers, Peter, Robert and Elias. Pollok in Malcolm IV's charter to Walter I apparently meant both Upper and Nether Pollok, and the fee evidently included two parish churches, Nether Pollok (equivalent to the later Eastwood) and Mearns. Elias, Peter's brother, was incumbent of Mearns, and was a canon of Glasgow Cathedral, being usually styled, doubtless from the prebend which he held, as Elias of Partick.

Part of Pollok seems to have formed a fee for ROBERT SON OF FULBERT, Peter's brother, who was also known as ROBERT OF POLLOK and ROBERT OF STENTON. (For him, see under Stenton, below.)

'TALAHRET'

Dr. George Neilson (see bibliography above) identified this place with the modern Hurlet, in Paisley parish, noting that it appeared as Hulrett (but in fact more often as Hulzett) in the seventeenth-century *Retours*. The identification cannot be regarded as established. The order of names in Malcolm IV's charter seems to be roughly geographical, and if this is so we should expect to find Talahret between Pollok and Cathcart. But we are dealing with a late copy of the charter, and the name may well be corrupt or quite obsolete, in which case it is useless to hazard an identification.

CATHCART

The fee of REGINALD OF CATHCART, t. Alan. Reginald's origins are unknown. One charter of Alan is witnessed by Ranulf of Cathcart; this may be merely an error for Reginald, since the respective Old French forms Renouf and Renaud are not unlike in sound.

DRIPPS

The lands of Dripps were formerly in Cathcart, later in Carmunnock, and are now in East Kilbride parish. (The name appears as 'le Drep' in the earliest record, and means the 'bone of contention' or 'debateable land'. Mid. Eng. *threpen*, to dispute.) Held by WILLIAM, t. Walter I, who is probably the same as WILLIAM SON OF MAIDUS who held Dripps at rent from the Cluniacs of Paisley after the land had been granted to the priory by Walter I. Maidus occurs in record only as the father of William and George, and their origins are unknown. The personal name Maidus or Meidus is extremely rare, and I have not been able to discover what language it belongs to. It occurs in the *Liber Vitae Ecclesiae Dunelmensis* (Surtees Soc., 1841 and 1923).

MEARNS

Part formed the fee of PETER SON OF FULBERT, including Upper Pollok and the parish church of Mearns. (See above under Pollok.)

Part evidently formed the fee of ROLAND OF MEARNS, t. Alan. The only Roland otherwise known among the followers of the first two Stewarts is Roland, son-in-law of Nicholas of the Cotentin. (See below under Innerwick.)

FINGALTON. Robert Croc of 'Fingaldestone' (Fingalton) did homage to Edward I in 1296, but it is not known whether these lands formed part of the Croc fee as early as the time of Walter I and Alan.

EAGLESHAM

According to George Chalmers (*Caledonia*), Eaglesham was the fee of ROBERT OF MONTGOMERY, t. Walter I. The older historians were more cautious, and Chalmers seems merely to have made a guess from the known fact that the Montgomerys were lords of Eaglesham in the fourteenth century. Yet it is almost certain that Robert of Montgomery, one of the most prominent of Walter I's followers, did receive a fief from his lord, and this may well have been Eaglesham, not known to have been held by any other family.

Montgomery in Wales had been given this name by the Norman earls of Shrewsbury before 1086. At any time thereafter, a person born at Montgomery or having his origins in the Castellany or the Honour of Montgomery (then included in Shropshire) might well have been given the surname 'de Montgomery'. It is most unlikely that the Scottish family of Montgomery were related to the family which held the earldom of Shrewsbury until 1102, who took their name from Montgomery in Calvados. The Scottish Montgomerys probably came from the Castellany or Honour of Montgomery, which was close to the fief held in Shropshire by the FitzAlans. In the late twelfth or early thirteenth century, the abbot and convent of Haughmond, Shropshire (founded by the FitzAlans), granted a lease of a 'place' in Shrewsbury, in the lane by St. Werburgh's Chapel, to Robert, son of Robert of Montgomery (*de Mungomeri*), who was perhaps the son of Robert of Montgomery appearing in Scottish record, t. Walter I and Alan.

LOCHWINNOCH

The lands of MONIABROCK were granted to Paisley Priory t. Alan and the monks later acquired the land between Calder and Maich. If any other parts of the parish were subinfeudated to lay vassals before 1241, the vassals are unknown.

INCHINNAN

Granted to Walter I by Malcolm IV, and held in demesne. The church and some of the land of this parish had previously been granted to the Knights of the Temple, apparently by King David I.

NEILSTON

That part of the present parish lying west of the Levern Water and Loch Libo formed part of the Stewarts' forest, or FOREST OF 'FERENEZE', and was therefore held in demesne. (See under Paisley.)

The remainder of the parish was the fee of ROBERT CROC, who held it of Alan the Stewart for the service of one knight. The charter recording Alan's grant of this fee calls the land 'Kellebrid', which would be Kilbride if the name had survived. The description of the marches makes it clear that the land of 'Kellebrid' was the eastern part of what is now Neilston parish. It is possible that Robert Croc held this land from Walter I, and that Alan's charter was merely a confirmation.

The name Neilston presumably means 'Nigel's *tun* or manor', but who Nigel or Neil was is not known: he was probably sub-tenant under the Crocs. The only early follower of the Stewarts known to have had the name was Nigel of the Cotentin.

EASTWOOD

COWGLEN in Eastwood formed part of the fee of ROBERT CROC, t. Walter I and Alan. For the rest, see above under Pollok.

ERSKINE

Evidently the fee of a certain HENRY OF ERSKINE, t. Walter II (1225), whose successor John is called a knight in record of 1262. The earlier history of this fee is unknown.

HOUSTON

The fee of BALDWIN OF BIGGAR, sheriff of Lanark or Clydesdale, t. Walter I. The lands were then known as Kilpeter, evidently from the parish church. It is almost certain that Baldwin held them of Walter I and not of the crown in chief. Baldwin granted the estate as a fee to HUGH OF PETTINAIN, from whom it took its present name ('Hugh's *tun* or manor'). Pettinain is a parish between Biggar, which Baldwin held in chief of the crown, and Lanark, the royal castle which was Baldwin's headquarters for the administration of Clydesdale. Hugh of Pettinain and his son Reginald (who succeeded him in Houston), were tenants in Romanno, Peeblesshire, of Philip de Evermel (Vermelles in French Flanders). It is highly probable that like Philip de

Evermel, Baldwin of Biggar and Hugh of Pettinain were Flemish.

When Baldwin confirmed the fee of Houston to Hugh's son Reginald, it included the 'land which his (i.e. Reginald's) brothers, Boderic (Bodric) and Arkenbald held'. The uncommon Germanic personal name Boderic has survived today in the name BOTHER-ICKFIELD, west of Houston village; this was doubtless part of the land in question.

Houston continued to be held by the descendants of Hugh of Pettinain, the Houstons of that ilk, until 1740.

KILMACOLM

In the thirteenth century, this parish was divided between two chief baronies, DUCHAL on the south and DENNISTOUN on the north, both held of the Stewarts. Nothing is known for certain regarding the tenure of either barony in the period before 1241, but the following points may be noted.

The earliest recorded lord of DUCHAL was Ralph de Lyle (de insula, de l'ile, etc.), appearing in a document of *c.* 1270–83. It need not be doubted that this Ralph was related to RALPH DE LYLE (DE INSULA), a vassal of Walter I and Alan. It is probable therefore that Duchal was the fee of Ralph de Lyle t. Walter I. The surname is an exceedingly common and unspecific one, and the family's origins cannot be traced. It may be mentioned, however, that among the manors held by Walter I's brother, William FitzAlan, in Shropshire, was Up Ross Hall, near Shrewsbury, usually known, from its position in a bend of the River Severn, as 'The Isle'.

DENNISTOUN is called 'the land of Daniel' in a charter t. Walter I, but this does not mean, of course, that Daniel was then the tenant: he may have lived considerably earlier. The origins of the family who appear in the later thirteenth century as lords of Danielstoun or Dennistoun are unknown.

KILBARCHAN

Much of this parish was known as PENULD, t. Walter I, and formed the fee of HENRY OF ST. MARTIN. Henry gave the Cluniacs of Paisley two carucates out of this fee, an estate later known as FULTON. The name Penuld is now represented by Penneld and Penwold House, in Kilbarchan. Henry of St. Martin's origins are not known; there is no evidence to connect his family with the

St. Martins who held Bara in East Lothian. (See under Innerwick.)

INVERKIP

The fee of BALDWIN OF BIGGAR, for whom see above, under Houston. There is little doubt that he held as tenant of Walter I, since he granted the monks of Paisley the church of Inverkip 'beyond the moors' (*ultra mores*) to be held as the other churches of Strathgryfe were held, and Walter I had granted to Paisley Priory all the churches of Strathgryfe except Inchinnan. Inverkip included GREENOCK, but it is not certain that Baldwin's fee comprised the entire, twelfth-century parish.

(ii) *Ayrshire (Kyle, Walter's Kyle or Kyle Stewart)*

DUNDONALD

Demesne, with castle. The Stewart's bailiffs of Dundonald are mentioned, t. Walter II, and Walter II's son and successor Alexander was sometimes known as Alexander of Dundonald, perhaps because he was born there. This suggests that Dundonald may have been the *caput* or chief place of the Kyle group of estates, but the Stewarts' court was held at Prestwick in the time of Alexander the Stewart (1241–82).

Richard, parson of Dundonald, witnessed charters of Alan the Stewart probably *c.* 1177.

PRESTWICK

A demesne burgh of Walter I. The northern part of the parish was granted to the Cluniac monks of Paisley Priory by Walter I and became known as Monkton. The remainder of Prestwick was evidently held in demesne. The Stewart's court was held there between 1241 and 1282, and probably from the time of Walter I.

ST. QUIVOX (formerly Senechar or Sanquhar)

AUCHINCRUIVE was the fee of RICHARD WALLACE, t. Walter II. See Tarbolton, Mauchline and Riccarton.

A considerable estate in this parish was granted to a convent of Gilbertine canons and nuns, who were brought from Sixhills Priory in Lincolnshire, and settled at DALMELLING by Walter II (1208–14). The settlement was given up in 1238, and all the property passed to Paisley Abbey (see *Ayrshire Coll.*, iv, 50–67).

Much of this parish was evidently held in demesne as the FOREST OF SANQUHAR.

TARBOLTON

The fee of GILBERT SON OF RICHER, t. Walter I. Gilbert was a witness to Malcolm IV's charter granting the stewardship and the Renfrewshire lands to Walter I. He was almost certainly a tenant-in-chief of the king in his own right, and witnessed numerous royal charters in the earlier years of King William the Lion. His origins are not known for certain. He was clearly a man of some consequence, and in view of his personal names it may be surmised that he was possibly a member of the baronial family of De l'Aigle (De Aquila), whose main descent from 1084 to 1235 ran as follows: Richer, Gilbert, Richer, Richer, Gilbert, Gilbert. The second of these Richers succeeded about 1118 and died in 1176, having been lord of Pevensey for much of this period, and having been, in his younger days, a friend and patron of Thomas Becket—with whom the Scots kings Malcolm and William were on friendly terms. It is possible that the tenant of Tarbolton was a younger son of this Richer de l'Aigle; he would therefore have been a brother of Richer III de l'Aigle, who was lord of Pevensey 1176–c. 1186, and an uncle of Gilbert and Richer de l'Aigle, who flourished at the turn of the twelfth and thirteenth centuries. (The chief authorities here are Robert de Torigni (ed. Howlett, 270), Dugdale's *Monasticon*, vi, 912; Round, *Calendar of Documents in France*, nos. 622 and 643, and L. F. Salzman, *History of Hailsham*.) Gilbert de l'Aigle witnessed a charter of Earl Ranulf of Chester, 1144 × 1146 (*Early Medieval Miscellany for D. M. Stenton*, Pipe Roll Soc., 1962, 29).

When Walter I gave lands in Mauchline to Melrose Abbey, his charter referred to a permabulation between the land of Mauchline and the land of Gilbert, son of Richer, and it is evident that Gilbert's land lay west of Mauchline. Moreover, Alan the Stewart granted Tarbolton to ADAM SON OF GILBERT, to be held for one knight's service, and although Adam is not said to be the son of Gilbert, son of Richer, this is made very probable by the fact that Adam was tenant of Hutton in Dryfesdale under Adam, son of Adam, son of Richer.

In Alan's charter, the fee of Tarbolton was said to be bounded from between (?) Monkhead and the land of Ayr to the marches of 'Berenbouell' (Barnweill in Craigie), and by the marches of Mauchline to the River Ayr. It included Privick, Drumley, Enterkine, and (unidentified) 'Milnefinlen', 'Roderbren' and 'Brenego'.

BARMUIR in Tarbolton (formerly in Mauchline) was a fee of RICHARD WALLACE, granted by him to Melrose Abbey, t. Alan. In 1166, a Richard Wallace held of William II Fitz Alan in Salop the fee of one 'muntator', i.e. a man-at-arms serving on garrison duty.

MAUCHLINE

Largely held in demesne by Walter I, and granted by him to Melrose Abbey. Two fees within the present parish were also granted to Melrose by their respective subtenants. 'GOD'NEHC' or 'GODONEC' (unidentified, but probably the 'Galdunig' mentioned in the *Retours*, Ayrshire (xvii cent.), associated with Sornbeg in Galston), was held by RICHARD WALLACE, and granted by him to Melrose. DALSANGAN AND BARGOUR, evidently comprising the projecting northern end of Mauchline parish between the Garroch Burn and the Cessnock Water, were held by PETER DE CURRI, and likewise granted to Melrose (1205). A later Peter de Curry, doubtless a descendant, was slain at the battle of Largs in 1263, fighting under Alexander the Stewart. He was doubtless the Scots knight described in the Scandinavian accounts of the battle under the name 'Perus' ('Ferus'), i.e. Piers or Peter. According to these accounts, he was 'very powerful, both in race and dominions. (He) had a helmet all gilt and set with precious stones; and the rest of his armour to match. He rode boldly against the Norwegians and none of the others with him.' Again, 'There fell one young man of the Scots who was called Perus. He had come of the best families, and was the son of a powerful knight; and he rode boldly, unaccompanied by any other knight' (Anderson, *Early Sources*, ii, 632). The Scandinavian accounts tend to exaggerate the might of the Scottish force at Largs, since the Norwegians were repulsed.

CRAIGIE

The fee of WALTER HOSÉ, t. Walker I, and evidently the fee of Walter's father, whose name is not known, before him. The name

Hosé (*Hosatus*) means 'booted'. In England it became Hussey. It is presumably the original of the west-country Scots surname Hosie, not mentioned by Black in his *Surnames of Scotland*. Walter Hosé held Albright Hussy near Shrewsbury of William FitzAlan II in 1166 as one knight's fee. He witnessed a charter of William FitzAlan I (Walter I's brother), *c.* 1155–60, and made a grant to Lilleshall Priory. This Walter was very probably the tenant of Craigie, but the identification has not been proved. A slightly earlier contemporary of the Shropshire Walter Hosé was Hugh Hosé, connected with the FitzAlans and their tenant Richard of Marchamley, *c.* 1138–55. This Hugh may have been Walter's father, and the first tenant of Craigie under Walter I.

Symington

The fee of SIMON LOCCARD (LOCKHART), t. Walter I. The name Symington represents an original 'Simundestun' where the personal name is not the Biblical Simon but the Germanic Sigmund equated with it. Simon Loccard was not only a tenant of Walter I and Alan, since he held Symington in Clydesdale, probably in chief of the crown.

A fee was held here or in Craigie by ROBERT CROC, t. Walter II.

Riccarton

George Crawfurd in his *History of the Shire of Renfrew* (1710) says cautiously, 'from Richard, the proper name of their (i.e. the Wallaces') Predecessor, the Lands of Riccartoun, in Kyle, were probably called'. In the pages of Chalmers' *Caledonia* (ed. 1887, ii, 577) this had become certainty, and is now accepted without question. That the Richard of Riccarton ('Richard's *tun* or manor') was Richard Wallace, a contemporary of Walter I, or another Richard Wallace, a contemporary of Alan and Walter II, is, as Crawfurd said, probable; but it has not been satisfactorily proved.

The lands in Kyle known for certain to have been held, t. Walter I–Walter II, by Richard Wallace, have been mentioned under St. Quivox, Tarbolton and Mauchline. Riccarton may be included conjecturally among the Wallace fees.

Auchinleck

Little is known of this land before 1241. It was apparently held in demesne; the church was granted to Paisley Abbey, *c.* 1238, by Walter II.

(iii) *East Lothian, Berwickshire and Roxburghshire*

INNERWICK (E. Lothian)

This large parish was minutely subdivided even in Walter I's time. The known holders of fees before 1177 are RALPH OF KENT, HENRY OF ST. MARTIN, and NICHOLAS OF THE COTENTIN, and other knightly tenants probably contemporary with them were ROBERT AVENEL and possibly his nephew, GLAI (GLAY).

The Kent holding seems to have descended first to Ralph's son, ROBERT OF KENT, and then through HELEN (probably Robert's sister or daughter) to her husband JOHN, SON OF ALAN OF MONTGOMERY.

The St. Martin descent is unknown. Henry's successor in Penneld (see above, under Kilbarchan) was his son and heir Gilbert.

A family taking its name from the Cotentin peninsula of Normandy were prominent among the followers of the first two Stewarts (see index of vassals, below). They were very probably related to the family of the same name who were tenants of the FitzAlans in Shropshire. Kinship cannot be proved, however, and it must be noted that none of the Christian names found among the Scottish family seem to appear among the Shropshire family. In Shropshire, the name *de Costentin* became *Constantine*. Helias de Costentin held a fee of 1½ knights of William II FitzAlan in 1166, including Eaton Constantine for half a knight. His successors were Richard (dead by 1196) and Thomas, first of a line of Thomases. Geoffrey de Cotentin witnessed charters of the earls of Chester, 1162 × 1173; he held Stockport castle against Henry II in 1173 (*Early Medieval Misc. for D. M. Stenton*, 35–6; *Gesta Henrici*, ed. Stubbs (Rolls Ser.), i, 48).

The only member of the family in Scotland who is known to have held land of the Stewarts is Nicholas, tenant in Innerwick. But Robert of the Cotentin was such a prominent follower of Walter I, to judge from surviving record, that he can hardly have been landless. Nevertheless, the family seems to have come to an end early in Scotland, through failure of male heirs. The fee of

Nicholas of the Cotentin seems to have been divided between his daughter HELEWISA's husband ROLAND and his nephew, ROBERT HUNAUD. A family with the surname Hunaud (Hunald), derived from their eleventh-century ancestor of that name, were tenants under the FitzAlans in Losford, part of Marchamley, Salop.

Robert Avenel's share in Innerwick passed to his younger son Vincent. Robert Avenel was only incidentally a tenant of the Stewarts, being in his own right a baron of major importance, lord of Eskdale, to which his elder son Gervase succeeded.

Robert Avenel's nephew, a knight named Glai, may have held part of Innerwick, since his son Roger was a tenant there, t. Walter II.

For some of the vassals mentioned above, see under Paisley, Kilbarchan and Eaglesham.

A fee in Innerwick was also held, t. Walker II, by two brothers, William and Richard of 'Haucestertun' ('Hafkerrestun', 'Hauekeristun', 'Haukerestun'). I have not identified this place, whose name means 'the hawker's toun'. The FitzAlans had a Shropshire manor, part of Marchamley, called Hawkstone ('Hefkeston', 'Hauckestan'), but this is a name quite distinct from that found in the Innerwick documents, and means 'the hawk's stone'.

STENTON (E. Lothian)

Part at least was the fee of ROBERT SON OF FULBERT, t. Walter I, and he is sometimes called ROBERT OF STENTON. His rights in Stenton seem to have passed with his daughter ISABEL to her husband WILLIAM WALLACE (LE WALEIS, WALLENSIS, i.e. 'the Welshman'). William was probably kinsman to the other Wallaces found among the Stewarts' vassals, t. Walter I and Alan, namely Richard Wallace and Henry Wallace. The origin of the family is unknown. It seems likely that they came from Shropshire, where the name—a description or a nickname rather than a surname—was common in the twelfth century. But the name is too common generally to allow any certainty with regard to their origin. Here it may be suggested, extremely tentatively, that Adam Wallace (*flor.* t. Walter II) may have been the same person as Adam of Ness (*flor.* t. Alan and Walter II), and Henry Wallace (*flor.* late twelfth century) may have been the same as Henry of Ness (*flor.* t. Alan and Walter II). Adam of Ness and Henry of Ness were brothers. Adam of Ness and his heirs were granted land by Walter II which had formerly been held by Henry Wallace. Moreover—but this may be coincidence—the personal names of the Ness family are strikingly paralleled by those of the Wallaces (see below, index of vassals); and no surviving document is witnessed by both Adam Wallace and his contemporary Adam of Ness, or by Henry Wallace and his contemporary Henry of Ness, or by both contemporaries, Alan Wallace and Alan of Ness. In view of the interest attaching to the ancestry of William Wallace, these points are worth noting in case any evidence comes to light to confirm or disprove this suggestion.

HASSENDEAN (Roxburghshire)

Granted to Walter I by Malcolm IV, *c.* 1161, but evidently surrendered by him after 1172 or perhaps by his son, before 1189. It was apparently held in demesne.

LEGERWOOD (Berwickshire)

Legerwood and Birkenside were granted to Walter I by Malcolm IV, and together with Mow were to be held as one knight's fee. The lands of Legerwood and Birkenside probably made up the present parish of Legerwood. They seem to have been held in demesne by the first three Stewarts, and the church of Legerwood was given to Paisley Priory by Walter I. There may have been some subinfeudation, since Walter II confirmed to the Leper Hospital of MORRISTON, and subsequently to Melrose Abbey, a carucate and a half in the parish formerly held by the Lady Emma of Ednam.

Mow (Roxburghshire)

Now in Morebattle parish. In view of the hilly character of the old parish of Mow, and its present remoteness, it is surprising that a great many legal documents relating to its land have survived from the twelfth and thirteenth centuries. It must then have been relatively heavily populated and intensively cultivated. In the middle of the twelfth century Mow belonged to Uhtred, son of Liulf. About 1161, it was granted to Walter the Stewart by King Malcolm IV, along with Legerwood and Birkenside, the three estates forming one knight's fee.

According to Sir Archibald Lawrie, Walter I's wife, usually

called Eschina of Mow, was Uhtred's daughter. This would suggest that Mow passed into Walter I's possession as his wife's inheritance. But in one record, Eschina is called Eschina 'of London' (*de Londoniis*), which suggests that she was in fact related to the family of that name settled in southern Scotland in the reign of David I. This may be the family of the same name who can be traced in twelfth-century Somerset (like the Lovels and (?) Berkeleys). Eschina was perhaps Uhtred's granddaughter (see *RRS*, ii, no. 245, comment).

Mow was much subinfeudated, and the descents of the various fees are extremely difficult if not impossible to work out. It may be noted here that Eschina, Walter I's wife, enfeoffed ROBERT CROC in a small part of Mow, which came with his daughter ISABEL to her husband ROBERT OF POLLOK, doubtless son of Robert son of Fulbert (see above, under Stenton and Pollok).

2 Index of known and probable tenants and vassals of the first three Stewarts

After each name, the following information, where available, is given in this order:

(a) Whether known to have been a tenant, with name of property and tenure if known, thus: T. Neilston, knight-service.

(b) Number of occurrences as witness to a charter of one of the Stewarts or their vassals or in their company or connected with them, thus: W, 8.

(c) In brackets after this, the number of occurrences as witness to such charters, the date of which cannot be fixed more precisely than in either the period Walter I–Alan or Alan–Walter II, thus: W, 8 (1).

(d) Number of charters connected with the Stewart fief issued by the tenant or vassal himself, thus: Issued 2.

(e) Number of such charters issued to the tenant or vassal himself, thus: Received 1.

(f) Number of references in contemporary documents other than as witness, recipient or issuer of a charter, thus: Ref. 3.

(i) *Walter I* (c. *1161–77*)

1 BIGGAR, BALDWIN OF. (Otherwise Baldwin of Lanark, Baldwin, sheriff of Lanark.) T, Houston, Inverkip. W, 3. Issued 2. Ref. 1.

2 BIGGAR, WALTHEOF OF. (Son of No. 1.) T, Houston. W, 1. Ref. 1.

3 COTENTIN (COSTENTIN, CONSTANTIN), GEOFFREY OF THE. W, 1 (1).[1]

4 COTENTIN, NICHOLAS OF THE. T, Innerwick. W, 2. Issued 1. Ref. 1.

5 COTENTIN, NIGEL (NEIL) OF THE. (Brother of No. 7.) W, 4.

6 COTENTIN, ROBERT OF THE. W, 10 (1) (Consistently high up in witness lists).[2]

7 COTENTIN, WALTER OF THE. (Brother of No. 5.) W, 8 (1).

8 CROC, ROBERT (LE). (Father of Nos. 42, 43, 69; father-in-law of No. 63.) T. Cowglen; Crookston (probably), Neilston (possibly). W, 4 (4). Received 1. Ref. 1.

9 DONALD, EWEN SON OF. W, 2.

10 EWEN, DONALD SON OF. W, 2. Ref. 3. (Since Donald son of Ewen is mentioned as having perambulated an estate in a document of 1160–2, he was probably father of No. 9, not his son.)

11 FULBERT, ROBERT SON OF. (Otherwise Robert of Pollok, Robert of Stenton.) W, 5.

12 HESDIN, ALEXANDER OF. W, 1.

13 (?) HESDIN (HASTINGIS'), ROBERT OF. W, 1. (A family taking its surname from Hastings (or Hesdin?) was already established in Scotland in the later twelfth century. Robert may have belonged to it.)

14 HOSÉ (HUSÉ, HOSATUS), WALTER. T, Craigie. (Walter Hosé, who held Albright Hussy, Salop, of William FitzAlan, Walter I's brother, witnessed one of William's charters before 1160, and made a grant to Lilleshall Priory.)

15 JOHN THE DISPENSER. W, 1. (Perhaps dispenser of No. 33, q.v.)

16 KENT, RALPH OF. (Father of No. 53.) T, Innerwick. W, 2. Ref. 2.

---

[1] Above, under Innerwick. A Geoffrey de Costentin held $2\frac{1}{2}$ kts.' fees in Nottinghamshire in 1166 of the barony of Hubert FitzRalph.

[2] A Robert de Costantino held 1 kt.'s fee of the earl of Gloucester in 1166, perhaps in Wiltshire.

LANARK, BALDWIN OF. See BIGGAR.

17   LOCCARD (later LOCKHART), JORDAN. W, 1.

18   LOCCARD, SIMON. T, Symington. Ref. 1.

19   LYLE, RALPH DE (DE INSULA, DE L'ILE). W, 2.

20   MALAS (? same as Maidus, q.v.), ROBERT SON OF. W, 1.

21   MAIDUS (MEIDUS), WILLIAM SON OF. (Brother of No. 82.) T, Dripps. W, 1. Ref. 1.

22   MATTHEW, ROBERT SON OF. W, 2.

23   MEARNS, ROLAND OF. (Perhaps the same as Roland, son of Reginald, q.v. under Reginald.) T, Mearns (probably). W, 2 (1).

24   MONTGOMERY (MUNGOMERI, MONTEGOMERY, MUNDEGUMBRI, etc.), ROBERT OF. W, 9 (1). (Usually high up in witness lists.)

25   NES (NESSE), ROGER OF. W, 1.

26   NES, WILLIAM OF. W, 1.

26a PALGRAVE (PAGRAUA), ROGER OF. Clerk of Walter I. W, 1.[3]

27   PASSELET, WILLIAM OF (i.e. William of Paisley. Otherwise WILLIAM PASSELEWE). W, 1. (It appears that the Norman-French surname *Passelewe*, 'Pass the Water', has been assimilated to the place-name *Passelet*, Paisley.)

28   PETTINAIN, HUGH OF. (Father of No. 62.) T, Houston (under No. 1). W, 2. Received 1. Ref. 3.

     POLLOK. See FULBERT, ROBERT SON OF.

29   REGINALD, ROLAND SON OF. (Perhaps the same as No. 23.) W, 1.

30   RICHER, GILBERT SON OF. (Probably father of No. 47.) T, Tarbolton. W, 1.

31   ROBERT, WILLIAM SON OF. W, 3.

32   ST. MARTIN, GILBERT OF. (Son of No. 33.) W, 1.

33   ST. MARTIN, HENRY OF. (Father of No. 32.) T. Innerwick, Penuld (Kilbarchan). W, (1). Issued 1. Received 1. Ref. 2.

     STENTON. See FULBERT, ROBERT SON OF.

34   WALLACE (WALENSIS, LE WALEIS, etc.), RICHARD. W, 2. (A Richard Wallace held one garrison serjeant's fee in Salop in 1166 of William II FitzAlan.)

35   WALTER, CHAMBERLAIN of Walter I. W, 3.

---

[3] This name illustrates a family connexion. Palgrave in Norfolk belonged to the nearby manor of Sporle, which Henry I had granted to Walter I's father, Alan son of Flaald. (Raine, *N. Durham*, no. 170, *VCH, Norfolk*, ii.)

36 WILLIAM. T, Dripps. (Probably the same as No. 21, q.v.)

(ii) *Alan, 1177–1204*

37 ALAN, CHAMBERLAIN (? of Alan the Stewart). W, 1.
38 ANSELM, HENRY SON OF. (Otherwise HENRY OF CARMUNNOCK.)
   (Probably not tenant or vassal.) W, 3. Granted Carmunnock
   church to Paisley Priory. See *RRS*, ii, 40; possibly sheriff of
   Lanark.
1 BIGGAR, BALDWIN OF. T, Houston.
2 BIGGAR, WALTHEOF OF. (Son of No. 1.) T, Houston.
39 BIGGAR, ROBERT OF (otherwise ROBERT SON OF WALTHEOF).
   (Son of No. 2.) T, Houston. Issued 1. Ref. 1.
40 CATHCART, RANULF OF. (Probably the same as No. 41.) W, 1.
41 CATHCART, REGINALD OF. T, Cathcart, probably. W, 3.
3 COTENTIN, GEOFFREY OF THE. W, 1 (1).
4 COTENTIN, NICHOLAS OF THE. T, Innerwick. Issued 1.
5 COTENTIN, NIGEL (NEIL) OF THE. (Brother of No. 7.) W, 1.
6 COTENTIN, ROBERT OF THE. W, 3 (1).
7 COTENTIN, WALTER OF THE. (Brother of No. 5.) W, 4 (1).
42 CROC, ALAN. (Son of No. 8.) W, 2.
8 CROC, ROBERT. (Father of Nos. 42, 43, 69, father-in-law of
   No. 63.) T, Crookston, Neilston by knight-service, Cowglen
   in Eastwood, Mow. W, 13 (4). Received 1. Ref. 2.
43 CROC, WALTER. (Son of No. 8.) Ref. 1.
44 CURRI, PETER DE. T, Mauchline. W, 3.
45 FULBERT, PETER SON OF. (Otherwise PETER OF POLLOK.)
   (Brother of No. 11.) T, Pollok, Mearns. W, 3. Issued 3.
   (Landowner at Rothes and Dundurcas in Moray. Wife
   Helen; daughter and heir Muriel married Walter Murdac
   or Murthac.)
11 FULBERT, ROBERT SON OF. (Brother of No. 45, father of No.
   63.) T. Pollok, Stenton. W, 4. Issued 1. Ref. 3.
46 FULCO, CHAMBERLAIN (? of Alan the Stewart). W, 1.
47 GILBERT, ADAM SON OF. (Probably son of No. 30.) T, Tarbolton by knight-service. W, 2. Received 1. Ref. 5.
48 GLAI (GLAY, GLAIUS). T, Innerwick, probably. W, 4. Ref. 1.
   (Nephew of Robert Avenel, lord of Eskdale.)
49 HESDIN, REGINALD OF. W, 1. In Shropshire, t. Alan, he was a

tenant of the FitzAlans, and witnessed a number of charters connected with them. In 1212, he was constable of Oswestry. Probably not a tenant of the Stewarts in Scotland, but doubtless related to No. 12. He was almost certainly related to Ernulf de Hesdin, Walter I's maternal grandfather, since he named his son Ernulf (Eyton, *Shropshire*, ix, 274).

50   HOSÉ, JOHN. (Probably son of No. 14.) T, Craigie. W, 1.

51   HUNAUD, ROBERT. (Nephew of No. 4.) T, Innerwick. W, 1 Issued 2. Ref. 2.

52   KENT, HENRY OF. W, 1.

16   KENT, RALPH OF. T, Innerwick. W, 1.

53   KENT, ROBERT OF. (Son of No. 16.) T, Innerwick. W, 9 (1).

54   KINNERLEY (KINARDESLEIA, KINARDESLEC, i.e. Kinnerley, Salop.), STEPHEN OF. W, 2 (1). (One of these documents concerns Robert Croc and Henry of Nes, and the other two are witnessed in the company of Henry and Adam of Nes.)

55   LINDSAY, WILLIAM OF. W, 5.

56   LOCCARD, MALCOLM. T, Symington. W, 3.

18   LOCCARD, SIMON. T, Symington. W, 1.

19   LYLE, RALPH DE (DE L'ILE). W, 1.

21   MAIDUS (MEIDUS), WILLIAM SON OF. (Brother of No. 82.) T, Dripps. W, 3 (2).

23   MEARNS, ROLAND OF. T, Mearns, probably. W, 1 (and 1 simply as 'Roland', probably the same). (1).

57   MONTGOMERY, ALAN OF. (Father of No. 58.) W, 5 (2).

58   MONTGOMERY, JOHN OF. (Son of No. 57.) T, Innerwick. W, 1.

24   MONTGOMERY, ROBERT OF. W, 1 (2).

59   NES (NESSE), ADAM OF. (Brother of No. 61.) W, 2.

60   NES, ALAN OF. (Son of No. 61.) W, 2.

61   NES, HENRY OF. (Brother of No. 59, father of No. 60.) T, Paisley, W, 4. Ref. 2.

25   NES, ROGER OF. W, 1.

27   PASSELET, WILLIAM OF (i.e. William of Paisley; otherwise WILLIAM PASSELEWE). W, 9.

28   PETTINAIN, HUGH OF. (Father of No. 62.) T, Houston. W, 1. Ref. 2.

62   PETTINAIN, REGINALD SON OF HUGH OF. (Son of No. 28.) T, Houston. Received 1. Ref. 2.

63   POLLOK, ROBERT (otherwise ROBIN) OF. (Son of No. 11.) T,

Pollok, Mow. W, 2. Issued 1. Ref. 3. (Wife Isabel was daughter of Robert Croc, No. 8.)

64 ROLAND. (Son-in-law of No. 4.) T. Innerwick. Ref. 3.

32 ST. MARTIN, GILBERT OF. (Son of No. 33.) T, Penuld (Kilbarchan).

33 ST. MARTIN, HENRY OF. (Father of No. 32.) T, Penuld (Kilbarchan). W, 1 (1). Ref. 1.

65 WALLACE, HENRY. (Father of No. 90.) T, land unknown. Henry Wallace is mentioned in record, t. Walter II, (a) as the former tenant of land on the Stewart fief which Walter II granted hereditarily to Adam of Nes (No. 59); and (b) as the father of Richard Wallace (No. 90).

34 WALLACE, RICHARD. T, Mauchline. W, 3. Issued 1. Ref. 1. (It is possible that this Richard Wallace was the same person as the Richard Wallace listed separately as No. 90 below.)

66 WALLACE, WILLIAM. (Son-in-law of No. 11.) T, Stenton. Issued 1. (Wife Isabel was daughter of Robert, son of Fulbert, No. 11.)

(iii) *Walter II, 1204–41*

39 BIGGAR, ROBERT OF. (Son of No. 2.) T, Houston. Ref. 1.

67 CATHCART, ALAN OF. T, Cathcart, probably. W, 2.

68 CATHCART, GILBERT OF. T, Cathcart, probably. W, 5. See *RRS* ii, no. 476.

42 CROC, ALAN. (Son of No. 8.) W, 8.

8 CROC, ROBERT. T, Crookston, Neilston, Cowglen, land in Symington or Craigie, in Kyle. W, 7.

69 CROC, SIMON. (Son of No. 8.) W, 2. (A tenant of the earl of Lennox.)

70 CROC, THOMAS. W, 4 (1). (Described as a knight.)

44 CURRI, PETER DE. T, Mauchline. Issued 1.

71 ERSKINE, HENRY OF. T, Erskine, probably. W, 1.

47 GILBERT, ADAM SON OF. (Probably son of No. 30.) T, Tarbolton. W, 2. Ref. 2.

72 GLAI (GLAY), ROGER SON OF. (Son of No. 48.) T, Innerwick. W, 19.

72a 'HAWKERSTON' (HAUCESTERTUN, HAFKERRESTUN, HAUEKERISTUN, HAUKERESTUN), RICHARD OF. (Brother of No. 72b.) T, Innerwick. W, 1.

72b 'HAWKERSTON' (as above), WILLIAM OF. (Brother of No. 72a.) T, Innerwick. W, 3.

50 HOSÉ, JOHN. T, Craigie. W, 5. Ref. 1.

73 HOUSTON, HUGH OF (otherwise HUGH SON OF REGINALD). (Son of No. 62.) T, Houston. W, 4. Ref. 1.

74 KENT, ADAM OF. T, Ingleston in Paisley. Ref. 2.

54 KINNERLEY, STEPHEN OF. W, (1).

55 LINDSAY, WILLIAM OF. W, 5. Ref. 1. (Steward or seneschal of Walter II.)

56 LOCCARD, MALCOLM. (Father of No. 75.) T, Symington. W, 9. Issued 1.

75 LOCCARD, MALCOLM. (Son of No. 56.) W, 2.

76 LOCCARD, WILLIAM. W, 1.

77 LOGAN, ADAM OF. W, 1.

78 LOGAN, ROBERT OF. W, 3. Ref. 1.

79 LYLE, ALAN DE (DE INSULA, DE L'ILE). W, 1. (Also witnesses charters of Walter II's son, Alexander the Stewart.)

80 LYLE, RALPH DE. W, 1. (Almost certainly not the same as No. 19.)

81 LYLE, WILLIAM DE. W, 2.

82 MAIDUS (MEIDUS), GEORGE SON OF. (Brother of No. 21.) W, 1.

21 MAIDUS (MEIDUS), WILLIAM SON OF. (Brother of No. 82.) W, 3.

83 MEARNS, WILLIAM OF. T, Mearns, possibly. W, 2.

57 MONTGOMERY, ALAN OF. (Father of No. 58.) W, 11. (Described as a knight.)

84 MONTGOMERY, HENRY OF. (Brother of No. 85.) W, 1.

58 MONTGOMERY, JOHN OF. (Son of No. 57, brother of No. 85.) T, Innerwick. W, 9. (Described as a knight. Wife Helen was heir of Robert of Kent, No. 53.)

85 MONTGOMERY, ROBERT OF. (Brother of Nos. 58 and 84.) W, 6.

59 NES (NESSE), ADAM OF. (Brother of No. 61, father of No. 86.) T, land unknown. W, 2. Issued 1. Ref. 1.

60 NES, ALAN OF. (Son of No. 61.) W, 2. (Described as a knight.)

86 NES, DUNCAN OF. (Son of No. 59.) W, 1.

61 NES, HENRY OF. (Brother of No. 59, father of No. 60.) T, Paisley. W, 4. Received 1. Ref. 2.

62 PETTINAIN, REGINALD SON OF HUGH OF. (Son of No. 28, father of No. 73.) T, Houston. Received 1.

63 POLLOK, ROBERT OF. (Son of No. 11.) T, Pollok, Mow. Ref. 2.
REGINALD, HUGH SON OF. See Houston.
87 ROLAND, NICHOLAS SON OF. (Son of No. 64.) T, Innerwick. Ref. 2.
88 WALLACE, ADAM. W, 5. (Described as a knight.)
89 WALLACE, ALAN. (Brother of No. 91.) W. 2. (Given title *dominus*.)
65 WALLACE, HENRY. (Father of No. 90.) See above, in Section 2.
90 WALLACE, RICHARD. (Son of No. 65.) T, Auchincruive, Mauchline. W, 5. Issued 1. Ref. 2.
91 WALLACE, STEPHEN. (Brother of No. 89.) W, 1.

13 The Highlands in the lifetime of Robert the Bruce

To gang to the hielans wi' you, Sir?
I dinna ken how that may be.
For I ken na the land that ye live in.
Nor ken I the lad I'm gaun wi'.

Leezie lass, it is little that ye ken
If sae be that ye dinna ken me;
For my name 'tis Lord Ronald Macdonald,
A chieftain of high degree.

I suspect that Leezie Lindsay's caution, understandable as it might have seemed in the seventeenth or eighteenth centuries, would have struck with surprise a thirteenth-century native of the Lowlands of Scotland. Neither in the chronicle nor in the record of the twelfth and thirteenth centuries do we hear of anything equivalent to the 'Highland Line' of later times. Indeed, the very terms 'Highlands' and 'Lowlands' have no place in the considerable body of written evidence surviving from the period before 1300. 'Ye hielans and ye lawlans, oh whaur hae ye been?' The plain answer is that they do not seem to have been anywhere: in those terms, they had simply not entered the minds of men. We commonly think of this highland-lowland dichotomy as being rooted deep in the history of Scotland, as being, indeed, imposed upon that history by the mere facts of physical geography. Yet it seems to have left no trace in the reasonably plentiful record of two formative centuries. It is necessary to ask why this should have been so, and also, if thirteenth-century Scotland was not divided into Highlands and Lowlands, to ask how it was divided, what were the regions familiar in popular or official usage. Down to the beginning of the nineteenth century Gaelic was the ordinary vernacular of the counties of Sutherland, Ross and Cromarty, Inverness-shire (save for Inverness itself and its environs), Argyll and Arran. In the counties bordering the North Sea between the Moray Firth and the Firth of Forth, the use of Gaelic had become confined to the upland parishes from about the middle of the fourteenth century, and a parallel development had probably taken place in the sheriffdoms of Stirling and Dumbarton. In the sheriffdoms of Fife, Kinross and Clackmannan, where there was no big tract of mountainous country into which it could retreat, Gaelic was probably almost or quite extinct as a native vernacular after about 1350. Thus one great historic divide between Highland and Lowlands had established itself before the end of the middle ages. The Highlands and Islands were now synonymous, as they had not previously been, with the Gaidhealtachd, the Gaelic speakers and their culture, while the Lowlands, from Inverness round by Aberdeen and Perth to Dumbarton and everywhere south of that line, became the country of the Sasunnach, the people who (whatever their racial origins) spoke and wrote a variant of the English tongue. Lowlanders, for their part, recognised the same division, though they thought in significantly different terms. They were not Sasunnach either to themselves or to the English south of the Border. They were Scots, their speech came to be known as Scots, and to them the highlander was at most only a 'wild Scot', *Scotus silvester*. More commonly the highlanders were described as 'Irish', and it was the lowland Scots form for 'Irish', *erisch*, that begot the unlovely and unloved word 'erse' by which Dr. Johnson and his contemporaries meant the language nowadays called Scottish Gaelic.

After the Reformation large areas of the Highlands adhered to Catholicism, while much of the Lowlands, urban and rural alike, became strongly Protestant. At the same time, a slight but perceptible increase in the pace of commercialisation and industrialisation, together with a rapidly deepening educational gulf, drew the Lowlands and Highlands steadily apart. To Boswell of Auchinleck, born in Edinburgh in 1740 and brought up in Ayrshire, much more than to Robert Bruce, born at Turnberry in 1274, the Highlands were a foreign country, alien in language, in religion, in dress, in traditions, alien even in their own particular varieties of hospitality and of poverty. It was far otherwise in the thirteenth century. Between mountain and plain there was then no religious barrier, and the Gaelic language must have been perfectly familiar up and down the east coast from the Ord of Caithness to Queensferry. It must, moreover, still have been the ordinary working language of Carrick and the rest of Galloway. The social and agrarian pattern of Scotland may have had regional variations, but there was no significant variation between Highlands and Lowlands, as there came to be later. On the contrary, scattered townships and farmsteads, infield and outfield agriculture, and the use of summer shielings, were common features of peasant settlement everywhere from the Cheviot Hills as far north and west as record will allow us to go.

At the time of King Alexander III's death in 1286, the primary divisions of his kingdom were four in number. The largest was Scotland north of the Forth. Down to about 1250 it had been usual to call this region simply 'Scotia'. After 1250 it seemed increasingly inappropriate to apply to only a part what was rapidly becoming the name of the whole Scottish kingdom, but no effective substitute for Scotia, as applied to the northern region, was ever discovered. *Albania*, Albany, was tried for a time, but it never caught on, save in the somewhat rarefied world of peerages and heraldry. Scotland benorth Forth, Scotland this side Forth (or beyond Forth, according to one's point of view), *Scotia ultramarina*, 'Scotland beyond the Scottish Sea'—such were the rather unsatisfactory attempts to solve the problem of nomenclature which arose when the name Scotia, Ecosse, Scotland, was adopted for the whole kingdom. The counterpart of Scotland north of Forth was of course Scotland south of Forth, which had never been known by any single name, although in 1286 it was understood to comprise the larger Lothian, Clydesdale, Tweeddale and Teviotdale, and also—though their inclusion was more gradual—Cunningham, Kyle and Dumfriesshire. This left, also well to the south of the Forth, our third primary division, Galloway, with which we must include Carrick, together forming a region which was both geographically and culturally distinct from the rest of southern Scotland. Finally, there were the Isles, from the Calf of Man to Sula Sgeir and North Rona, fifty miles north-west of Cape Wrath, which when King Alexander died had been part of his kingdom for almost exactly twenty years. Since most of the western seaboard of Scotland from the Firth of Clyde northward is difficult to reach from the east except by certain well-defined routes, men of the late thirteenth century, when they thought of Kintyre, Argyll and the west coast generally, tended to associate these remote districts with the Isles rather than with Scotland north of Forth to which they strictly belonged. Matthew Paris's map of *c*. 1250 terms what appears to be Argyll 'a sea-coast inhabited by highlanders', *pars maritima et gens montana*. When John Barbour is describing the composition of the Scottish army at Bannockburn he says that the king's brigade or 'battle' included the men

> of Argile and of Kentyre,
> and of the Iles, quharoff wes syre
> Angus of Ile, and But and all tha'.

To distinguish thus the far west from the central and eastern parts of northern Scotland was a practice at least as old as Columba's time, for Adamnan in his life of the saint says explicitly that the 'spine of Britain', *druimm nAlban*, Drumalban, formed the boundary between the Picts and the Scots. Drumalban is nowadays restricted to the fine range of peaks running from Strath Fillan to the Moor of Rannoch, but presumably in earlier ages it referred generally to the high watershed parting the long rivers which flow into the North Sea from the short rivers which flow into the Atlantic. It is in this context that we can understand the old description given to the deep River Pattack, which, rising on Ben Alder, flows well to the east of this watershed before swinging suddenly into Loch Laggan and so heading for the Firth of Lorne: 'Black Pattack of the pools, which turns its back upon the rivers of Scotland'.

There were two other major subdivisions of Scotland north of Forth. Once again, they arose from a way of looking at the country which was at least as old as the Columban age, and still taken for granted in the time of the Edwardian occupation of Scotland. When Bede tells us of northern and southern Picts separated by *arduis atque horrentibus montium jugis*, and Edward I in his Ordinance of 1305 declares that for the lands beyond the

Forth there shall be two pairs of justices, one pair *entre la rivere de Forth et les montz*, the other *pur les terres de la les montz*, we cannot doubt that the same mountains are in question, or that they were what popular, and quite often official, usage knew as the Mounth, the mountainous tract stretching from Ben Alder to the coast at Stonehaven, to which in the past three centuries the curious ghost-name Grampians has been generally applied. But though it formed a recognised subdivision, Scotland north of the Mounth was certainly not what we should call the Highlands, any more than Scotland south of the Mounth was the Lowlands; both subdivisions included Highland and Lowland territory.

At the end of the thirteenth century, then, Scotland was not divided, officially or in common parlance, into Highlands and Lowlands. Not only had most of the reasons for this familiar dichotomy not yet made their appearance, but there were also other divisions which seemed to be more valid and useful. This point requires emphasis, but having been emphasised, it must, like all historical generalisations, be immediately qualified. It will not do to push too far the thesis that at the turn of the thirteenth and fourteenth centuries men did not see any difference between the Highlands and the rest of Scotland, or that there were then no differences to be seen. It is the geological rather than the simple orographical map of Scotland which tells us why there was one fundamental quality which marked out the Highlands as a distinct region. It was not the hilly nature of the country, for after all there is scarcely any part of Scotland which is not hilly. It was the poverty of the soil and its unsuitability for settled agriculture; and this was a consequence of the acid rocks of which the greater part of the Highlands are composed. Matthew Paris was aware of this difference in social and human terms when he wrote on his map across the central and northern Highlands 'a mountainous wooded region, breeding a wild pastoral people on account of its bogs and marshes', and across the north-western littoral, 'a marshy trackless country, suitable for cattle and herdsmen'. Admittedly, in the thirteenth century there was a large pastoral element in the rural economy of every region of Scotland, but throughout what came to be known as the Lowlands, with but few exceptions, agriculture already predominated. In the Highlands it was the other way round. Herds, flocks, hunting and fishing gave the highlander his subsistence. It must not be thought, of course, that he never put his hands to the plough. A charter issued in 1289 at the castle of Ruthven in Badenoch by John Comyn, lord of Badenoch, stipulated that his men of Invertilt (what we should now call Blair Atholl) might take enough material from the local woodland to make ploughs, harrows, carts and hurdles. There is, indeed, sufficient though hardly abundant evidence to show that in the thirteenth century ground would be cultivated wherever this was physically practicable. The bishops of Moray, e.g. referred in a matter of fact way to corn teinds from parishes in Strathspey or beside Loch Ness, and insisted that every landward parish in their largely highland diocese should be endowed with a toft and croft of at least one acre, over and above the sizeable quantity of arable which seems to have formed a typical glebe. It was, no doubt, a modest subsistence agriculture, carried on by primitive techniques, but nevertheless it was agriculture of a sort. As for the conservative tenurial customs which hindered its improvement, there is a depressing similarity between conditions described by two knowledgeable authors, the first writing in 1269, the second 500 years later. The agricultural lands of Scotland north of Forth, says the writer of the *Lanercost Chronicle*, referring to an estate in Angus or upper Aberdeenshire, 'are not let out, as elsewhere, on a perpetual tenancy. The leases are renewed annually, or else the rents are raised.' And he goes on to narrate the story of a great lord who each year threatened to evict a certain peasant tenant if he would not pay a higher rent, spurred on by an outsider who had offered him more for the holding. Lachlan Shaw, who was minister of Kingussie from 1716 to 1719, has this to say in his *History of Moray*, published in 1775: 'The severe exactions of Masters, and the poverty of Tenants, hinder all improvements; Tenants have neither ability nor encouragement to try experiments; some have no leases, and if they who have them shall improve their farms, strangers will reap the benefit of it; for at the expiration of the lease they must pay an additional rent, a high grassum or entry-money, which if they refuse, the farm will be put to the roup, and the improver will be removed.'

It is noteworthy, as evidence of highland agriculture, that the same unit of corn-growing capacity, the davoch, was employed

N<small>KS</small>

throughout northern and eastern Scotland, from Fife to the Isle of Lewis, in Highlands and low country alike. This unit was relevant to an economy in which agriculture was at least as important as pasture. But it is equally significant that in the Highlands the davoch seems to have been adapted to conditions where pastoralism prevailed. Boswell has preserved the poor opinion which James Macpherson, the author of Ossian, entertained of agriculturalists. Talking with the earl of Eglinton about Gray's *Elegy in a country churchyard*, Macpherson exclaimed: 'Hoot! To write panegyrics upon a parcel of damned rascals that did nothing but plough the land and saw corn!' One suspects that something of this attitude might be found in the Highlands in the thirteenth as well as in the eighteenth century.

Before we leave the question of whether the Highlands differed from the Lowlands in ways that mattered at the turn of the thirteenth and fourteenth centuries, there are two points to be considered, namely the size of population and the state of contemporary knowledge of highland geography. If it could be shown that the Highlands carried an appreciably sparser population than the Lowlands at the turn of the centuries, still more if it could be shown that the total population of the Highlands was appreciably smaller than the Lowland total, then one obviously relevant differential would be established.

The late Lord Cooper of Culross estimated the population of Scotland in 1300 as 400,000. For a number of reasons it may be thought that Lord Cooper's figure is an underestimate; but whether or not the total is too low, what matters for our enquiry is its probable distribution. Lord Cooper assigned 350,000 to the Lowlands and eastern Highlands, and only 50,000 to the central and west Highlands and Islands, believing that the bulk of the population must have lived 'on or near lands that can be farmed or coasts that can be fished'. But it must be objected that rivers and lochs may be fished as well as coasts, that the west coast offers fishing at least as good as the east, and that land that can be farmed must include hill ground capable of carrying cattle, sheep, goats and even deer, as well as level ground which can be brought under the plough. An illustration of highland resources here is given in an English Exchequer account of 1296. When Edward I invaded Scotland in March of that year, the Border nunnery of

Coldstream was partly devastated. In order to re-stock its lands, Hugh Cressingham, King Edward's treasurer, ordered 700 sheep and forty oxen to be sent from Atholl by the sheriff of Perth. Lord Cooper's argument is more convincing when he points to the eight parishes into which the whole of western Sutherland and Wester Ross were divided, and contrasts this 'empty quarter' with Fife and Dumfriesshire, each having some 'seventy parishes. Broadly speaking, of course, the contrast must be valid. But I doubt if the supply of parishes in the thirteenth century can be taken as more than a rough guide to the distribution of population. There was no standard or ideal size of parish, and the founding of new parishes and suppression of old ones were affected by factors quite unconnected with population. Moreover, the records of papal taxation on which Lord Cooper relied do not always do full justice to the facts. It would, e.g. be impossible to deduce merely from the text of Bagimond's Roll of the 1270s that the district of Badenoch was served not only by the parish churches of Laggan, Kingussie, Insh, Alvie, Rothiemurchus, Duthil, Kincardine and Abernethy, but also by the chapels of Banchor, Rait and Dunachton. Neither the church of Urquhart nor its dependent chapel of Glenmoriston is entered on the roll, so that Abriachan wrongly appears to be the only parish west of Loch Ness.

That Highlanders were scattered more thinly, square mile for square mile, than Lowlanders we may reasonably believe. But I doubt if we can be sure, from the sources available to us, that the total number of people in the Highlands was very much smaller than in the rest of Scotland.

The second point for consideration is the state of contemporary knowledge about Lowland and Highland geography. To what extent were the Highlands *terra incognita*? Here again, the evidence may be misleading. We are lucky to have two English maps, Matthew Paris's of *c.* 1250 and the famous Gough Map from the middle decades of the fourteenth century. Matthew Paris displays such a swingeing ignorance of Scottish geography as a whole that his relatively more extensive ignorance of the Highlands might pass unnoticed, were it not for his disarming trick of inserting brief prose essays in those spaces on his map which his lack of knowledge would otherwise leave totally blank. The Gough Map is altogether more businesslike. Its draughtsman surely had informants in or connected with the royal administration. On this map there is a marked contrast in quantity and quality between lowland and highland information. It was perhaps only by a slip that the map-maker turned the Moray Firth inside out. It is more serious that of northern royal burghs he knows only Aberdeen, Elgin, and Inverness, and of castles or other staging places only Cowie (Stonehaven), Kildrummy, Darnaway and Wick. In the west he makes Argyll an island lying off the inland district of Balquhidder. He knows of the districts of Lorne and Badenoch, and of Sutherland 'where wolves abound'. He knows of Bute and the Outer Isles (*lez outislez*). He inserts Loch Tay correctly in Atholl, and beside it he tells the story usually attributed to Loch Lomond: 'In this loch three wonders: a floating island, fish without intestines, and waves without wind.' He knows of only two passes through the Mounth, the one at Cowie in the east, and the Capel Mounth which links Glen Clova to Glen Muick. Somewhere in the centre or slightly west of centre, he has been told of a place called Colgarth, where the hunting is evidently exceptional: *Hic maxima venacio.* I do not know where Colgarth was, but recalling that Loch Mhor at the head of Stratherrick, above Loch Ness, was formerly known as Loch Garth, and that at its foot is Corriegarth, below the fine deer forest of Sronlairig, it is a possible guess that this was the locality in question.

To the Gough map-maker the Highlands, if not unknown, were very ill-known. But he probably, and Matthew Paris certainly, worked in the south of England. Other Englishmen—and there were many of them—who in the 1290s and early 1300s had to make weary journeys throughout Scotland seem to have had a better grasp of the country. Nowhere is this more impressive than in the confident, above all the methodical and tidy way, in which King Edward I carried out his two great expeditions from Berwick to Moray, the first in 1296, the second in 1303. It is true that he never used the Drumochter Pass, which today seems the obvious route from Perth to Inverness, and it is true that he never went beyond the Great Glen. But in 1296 he rode from Elgin to Kincardine O'Neil in five days. From Craigellachie he sent one detachment up the Spey to search the country of Badenoch and another under the bishop of Durham to come south probably by

Tomintoul and Braemar. The king himself went to Kildrummy by way of Cabrach, not an easy route even today, and stopped one night at Invercharach (at the head of the Deveron), where, as one of his entourage wrote, 'there are only three houses between two mountains'. In 1303, having stayed a while at Forres and Kinloss, King Edward headed southward over the moors to Lochindorb, and seems to have reached, and perhaps crossed, the Spey at Boat of Garten—his deepest penetration into highland territory. If he and his servants avoided Drumochter, it was from knowledge rather than ignorance. One of them described it as 'the worst of passes, without any fodder' (*pessimum passagium sine cibo*). Some of these royal servants took Highland and northern journeys in their stride. In 1290, Thomas Braytoft and Henry Rye travelled from Newcastle upon Tyne to Wick, by way of Nairn, Cromarty and Dornoch—430 miles—in nineteen days, and returned in twenty-three. In 1304 James Daliley and John Weston, with sixteen men-at-arms and occasional reinforcements, journeyed on the king's affairs from Aberdeen to Inverness and back, and there is no hint that the difficulties and dangers they encountered were due to the strangeness of the country; they were caused by the large numbers of Scots who had not yet come into the king's peace. In 1308, over two years after Bruce's accession, messengers could still get through from Edward II to John Macdougall, lord of Lorne, at his castle of Dunstaffnage near Oban, and to the earl of Ross at Balconie on the Black Isle.

As for Scottish kings and magnates, Highland journeys do not seem to have held any special terrors for them. Between his coronation in March 1306, and his defeat at Methven outside Perth three months later, Robert Bruce was active in the mountains north of Crieff trying to compel the earl of Strathearn to come into his allegiance. The earl took refuge in the 'Isle of Kenmore', presumably the peninsula on which the church stands or else the little Eilean nam Bannaomh, the island at the mouth of Loch Tay. After Methven, as is well known, Bruce retreated to Strathfillan, where a second defeat forced him to flee to the wilder parts of the Mounth. Surviving appalling hardships, he eventually escaped to Dunaverty at the south end of Kintyre, and from there crossed first to Ireland and thence probably to the southern Hebrides. By the end of 1307 he was ready to fight a campaign against the earl of Ross which must have carried him well west of

Inverness, and early in the following year he was back in the
Garioch at the edge of the Eastern Highlands. In the autumn he
had threatened John of Lorne at Dunstaffnage 'by land and sea',
and both that movement and the brilliant August campaign of
August 1308 culminating in the Battle of Brander which put an
end to Macdougall opposition, imply a sure grasp of highland
geography. In 1309 Bruce seems to have carried out a wide
circuit of the west, moving from Inverness to Loch Broom in the
early summer and turning up again at Dunstaffnage in the
autumn. In 1310 he was busy in the south-west Highlands or
Islands, and in May 1315 he had himself borne across the 'tarbert'
or isthmus dividing Knapdale from Kintyre in a galley with sails
set—a proof of his understanding of highland psychology as well
as geography.

> And quhen thai that in the Ilis war
> Herd tell how the gud kyng had thar
> Gert schippis with the salys ga
> Outour betuix the Tarbertis twa,
> Thai war abasit all utrely.
> For thai wist throu ald prophesy
> That he that suld get schippis swa
> Betuix the seis with salys ga
> Suld win the Ilis swa till hand
> That nane wyth strynth suld him withstand.

The king then remained in the west for some time:

> Still all that sesoune thar duelt he
> At huntyng and gammyne and gle.

John Barbour, from whose poem this passage is taken, displays
a reasonably wide knowledge of Highland topography. The
relationship between Bute, Arran, Kintyre, Islay and Argyll
seems to have been firmly fixed in his mind, and he is a reliable
guide in the Central Highlands. He describes vividly the Pass of
Brander, and with more accuracy than his latest editors and com-
mentators would allow. Indeed, the most interesting of all his
geographical touches comes in his account of the Battle of Brander,

which was fought on the southern slopes of Ben Cruachan. 'Crech-aneben hecht that montayne, I trow that nocht in all Bretayne ane higher hill may fundyn be.' Humourless critics have laboured the objection that at 3689 feet Cruachan stands only in the middle rank among the higher hills of Scotland. To my mind it is more rewarding to dwell on the proof this passage affords that educated men of the 1370s could speculate intelligently as to which might be the loftiest hilltop in the whole British island, and draw on their knowledge of the Highlands to produce an answer.

If lowland Scots could travel confidently throughout the Highlands, they could also settle there and acquire lands and offices. This process can be traced back to the late twelfth century, when there was still a considerable influx of new land-owning families into Scotland as a whole. It is worth noting that movement from the Lowlands to the Highlands continued, perhaps without very much abatement, at the turn of the thirteenth and fourteenth centuries. In part this seems to have been connected with the royal policy of annexing the Isles which culminated in the Treaty of Perth of 1266. It was, e.g. in the 1260s, that Walter Stewart, earl of Menteith, acquired in obscure circumstances a large part of Knapdale from Dugal Macsween. The earl still possessed Knapdale in 1293, and the Macsweens nursed a grievance. In 1301 Knapdale was being held on behalf of Earl Walter's younger son, Sir John Stewart, better known as Sir John Menteith, and John Macsween complained to Edward I that Menteith, one of King Edward's enemies, had deprived him of his inheritance. Nine years later, John Macsween was granted Knapdale by Edward II provided that he could recover it from Sir John Menteith. The Menteiths remained in possession, and the Macsweens were forced to find a home in Ireland. It seems probable that before the end of the thirteenth century the Isle of Arran had also come into the possession of the earls of Menteith.[1] In 1306 Sir John Hastings was given by Edward I the earldom of Menteith together with the islands forfeited by Earl Alan, a supporter of Bruce, and grandson of Earl Walter; at the turn of 1306 and 1307 Hastings had garrisoned the castle of Brodick. Sir John Menteith, Earl Alan's uncle, who had control of the earldom of Menteith

[1] Adam parson of Arran witnessed a charter of Walter Stewart earl of Menteith, *c.* 1275 (NLS, MS. Adv. 34.6.24, p. 377).

until about 1320, certainly held Knapdale and probably held Arran also, and we know that both territories were in the lordship of Sir John's son and heir. Knapdale and Arran were not the limit of Stewart penetration across the Firth of Clyde. Bruce gave Sir John Menteith the lands of Glenbreackerie, in the south of Kintyre, and an unidentified island called Aulisay or Eulisay which may perhaps have been the Ailsa Craig. The main line of the Stewarts had long been lords of Bute and the Cumbraes. We learn that in 1296 James the Stewart had in his hands the barony and castle of Glasrog, unidentified, but apparently in Kintyre. By the terms of the Ordinance of 1293, to be mentioned later, it was James the Stewart who was to be sheriff of a new sheriffdom of Kintyre, comprising Kintyre and Bute and almost certainly Arran. Although this Ordinance was not given effect, we are left in no doubt of the extension of Stewart property and power in this region.

Before 1293, a senior royal servant of King Alexander III, Master Ralph of Dundee, one of those secular clerks characteristic of the period, had acquired the barony of Glassarie in Lorne for half a knight's service, either as the successor or the supplanter of Gillespie MacGilchrist. This estate passed to Master Ralph's son and heir, John Glassary, after 1312, and in the time of his son, Gilbert of Glassary, was enlarged to include lands forfeited by the heirs of John Ewensson MacGilchrist, Gillespie's nephew. In Robert Bruce's reign the pattern of lordship and landholding in the south-west Highlands and Islands was chiefly determined by the aggrandisement of two local families, the Campbells of Lochawe and the Macdonalds of Islay. It is therefore as well to remark that land and power in this purely Gaelic area could be successfully sought and kept by lowlanders like Ralph of Dundee and the Stewarts and Menteiths.

In this same period there was penetration by lowlanders, at baronial and knightly level, into Atholl and Breadalbane. The family of de Meyners or Menzies, which already enjoyed a respectable position in Lothian and included among its members senior officials of the royal household, was evidently established at Fortingall, within the earldom of Atholl, by the middle of the thirteenth century, when Sir Robert Menzies was feuing out the lands of Culdair. In 1296 Sir Robert's son, Sir Alexander Menzies, was granted Weem and Aberfeldybeg in Strath Tay by John, earl of Atholl, and in 1312 or thereabout Earl John's son Earl David granted to Sir Alexander's son, the second Sir Robert Menzies, as 'his beloved and faithful confederate', the whole thanage of Crannach in Upper Glenlyon. Just as Ralph of Dundee's heirs profited by the disloyalty (presumably to Bruce) of John MacGilchrist's heirs, so this Robert Menzies, a steadfast supporter of Bruce, profited by the disaffection of the Macnabs, the hereditary lay abbots who held the lordship of Glendochart in the upper part of Breadalbane. King Robert first of all gave Menzies the lands of Finlarig by Killin, and afterwards granted him the whole barony of Glendochart. By the end of Bruce's reign, the head of the family of Menzies was in possession, either as a tenant-in-chief or as a vassal, of estates which stretched almost continuously from Aberfeldy in the east to the bottom end of Glenfalloch in the west, within a mile or two of Loch Lomond.

Other families comparable with Menzies gained a footing in Atholl during the years when John of Strathbogie and his son David held the earldom, 1284–1314. Prominent among them was a knightly family taking its name from the estate of Inchmartine in the Carse of Gowrie, which they held from the Crown in chief. Sir John of Inchmartin, who played a notable part in both phases of the war with England, was closely associated with Earl John of Atholl, and received from him a grant of Bonskeid and Borenich in Strath Tummel and Coille Bhrochain at the confluence of Tummel and Garry. He also held, by inheritance from his father, a considerable estate in upper Strathardle. One of his sons, also John of Inchmartin, appears in the early years of the fourteenth century as parson of Rannoch, a living which he must have owed to the earl of Atholl's favour. The Inchmartins were connected by marriage to another knightly family from the Carse of Gowrie, the Camerons, who were tenants-in-chief of the neighbouring fief of Baledgarno. Like the Inchmartins, the Camerons were also tenants of the earls of Atholl, and again like the Inchmartins the Camerons took their turn at serving as sheriff of Perth. Whether or not the fief which the Camerons held of the Strathbogies lay within the earldom of Atholl itself, the exercise of the sheriff's office undoubtedly meant that some members of these two Lowland families became familiar with administering a tract of

Highland territory stretching from Strathearn and Stormont in the east right across the mountains to the Firth of Lorne.

One might illustrate this Lowland readiness to take land and office along or beyond the highland line by other examples. Through the favour of Robert Bruce, the Burnards of Roxburghshire and the presumably south-country Irvines acquired hereditary lands and office in the old royal forest of Drum on Deeside, and were able to lay the foundations of the later gentry families of Burnett of Leys and Irvine of Drum respectively. A greater servant of King Robert I, Sir Robert Lauder, the justiciar of Lothian, was made constable of Castle Urquhart on Loch Ness. His direct descendants became a respectable family in Moray, and most notably his descendants by marriage brought the surname of Chisholm from the neighbourhood of Hawick to Strathglass, west of Glen Urquhart. It was presumably a coincidence, but if so an odd one, that a hundred years before Sir Robert Lauder came to Urquhart a man by the name of Thomas of Thirlestane appears in record as lord of Abertarff, some fifteen miles south-west of Urquhart on the opposite side of Loch Ness. How long he enjoyed his lordship is not clear, but we know that he had time to engage in litigation with the bishop of Moray and to build a timber castle in which he was taken by surprise and slain by a Highlander (probably a Hebridean) named Gillascop. Thomas of Thirlestane, who acquired Abertarff by grant from the Crown, was tenant of Thirlestane by knight service under the lords of Lauderdale. Subsequently Abertarff was surrendered to the Crown by Richard Maitland who was a successor to Thomas of Thirlestane, probably through the female line. In any case, we should not regard either Thomas of Thirlestane or Robert Lauder as specially exotic; they take their places in a steady flow of southron immigrants in the north, Fentons, Bissets, Barclays, Stirlings and others, who were still the backbone of the gentry in the region at the head of the Moray Firth as late as the first decades of the fourteenth century.

With this background in mind, let us look briefly at the political situation in the Highlands at the turn of the thirteenth and fourteenth centuries. If we take a broad view, we can see that the course of highland history in this period was chiefly determined by two events, the overt Norwegian retreat from the Hebrides in 1266 and the latent English retreat from a large part of Ireland in the first half of the fourteenth century. The first event brought the Isles directly under the Scottish Crown, and provided the kings of Scotland with a challenge to which they must respond if their monarchy was to survive. The second event opened up to Hebrideans and West Highlanders an almost limitless prospect of interference in Irish affairs and of lucrative employment in Irish wars. From the stand-point of the Scottish Crown the advantages gained from the Norwegian withdrawal were to a large extent offset by the disintegration of Anglo-Norman Ireland. From the point of view of highland history, these Irish developments, far from healing the old division between west and east, between the Isles and the mainland, in fact perpetuated it.

So much for the broad view. In detail, and at the level at which contemporaries could see the significance of events, the course of highland history in this period was dominated by the fall of two great families, the Comyns and the Macdougalls, and the rise of several families not quite so great, among whom the leading place was contested by the earls of Ross, the Campbells, the Macdonalds the Macruaries, and the Randolph earls of Moray. Between 1286 and 1306 the Comyns wielded formidable power in the Highlands and the north, all the more formidable because it was matched by comparable power in the Lowlands and the south. A younger branch of the family held the earldom of Buchan and the constableship of Scotland, and for long periods the earls of Buchan had exercised the office of justiciar north of Forth. Earl John of Buchan occupied this office in 1301. Three years later, his brother Sir Alexander Comyn, who had secured for himself the castles of Tarradale in the Black Isle and Urquhart on Loch Ness, and was petitioning for Aboyne Castle, was appointed sheriff of Aberdeen. A coastal earldom, Buchan was defended by coastal castles, Slains, Dundarg and perhaps others; the earl also possessed the strong and strategically-sited castle of Balvenie in Glen Fiddich. Balvenie was a sort of Comyn stepping-stone, for the senior line of the family took its title from the lordship of Badenoch, whose eastern boundary was only twenty miles up the Spey from Balvenie. The *caput* of Badenoch, Ruthven Castle near Kingussie, controls the northern end of two passes over the Mounth, Drumochter and the shorter and more direct Minigaig. It is possible, therefore, to see the logic if not the legality behind the action taken in 1269 by Comyn of Badenoch in starting to build the first recorded castle at Blair in Atholl, which controlled the southern end of these two passes. Despite protests by the earl of Atholl, the lords of Badenoch apparently still held Blair Atholl at the end of the century. Before that they had pushed further into Atholl by acquiring lands in Stormont and the custody of the Appin of Dull at the foot of Glen Lyon. In addition, they held a large estate in Kintyre.

It is not generally realised that along with the lordship of Badenoch went the lordship of Lochaber. As well as controlling the western passes through the Mounth, the Comyns thus controlled one of the two main east-west passages across northern Scotland, the one which makes use of the Spey and Spean valleys, while at the same time they occupied the southern outlet of the Great Glen, the other main east-west passage. The Comyn castles were splendidly sited and built in a manner to match their location. Mr. Stewart Cruden has drawn attention to the family likeness which links Lochindorb, Castle Roy in Abernethy, and Inverlochy in Lochaber. It is interesting to see that he also likens Inverlochy to Dunstaffnage, for the lordship of Lochaber made Comyn of Badenoch a neighbour of the Macdougalls of Lorne, and Alexander Macdougall married the sister of John Comyn of Badenoch, the Competitor, who died at Lochindorb about 1303. The Macdougalls were not as rich and powerful as the Comyns, but they held the leading position in the west during the twenty years which followed Alexander III's death in 1286. They were the senior line among the descendants of Somerled of Argyll in a period when descent from Somerled was virtually an essential qualification for Hebridean lordship. As with the Comyns, Macdougall power found its visible expression in superbly-sited castles, strongly built of the intractable local stone, some rising sheer out of the sea, such as Cairnburghmore in the Treshnish Isles and Dun Chonnell in the Garvelloch group, others, such as Dunstaffnage and Dunollie, using mainland positions of great natural strength. In alliance—and the Comyn-Macdougall alliance made a notable contribution to the Scottish resistance to Edward I down to 1304—the two families complemented each other, the Comyns chiefly a land-based power, disposing of considerable infantry forces and some knight-service, the Macdougalls sea-based with a sizeable fleet of 'birlings' or galleys. Together, their territories stretched almost from sea to sea, and they had the means if need be of blocking communication between north and south. As soon as Robert Bruce was able to break through the English cordon in the autumn of 1307 he devoted all his energies to annihilating the power of the Comyns and the Macdougalls. No one could have become effective king of Scotland without either their support or else their abolition, and for Bruce there was no choice.

Round the edges of the great chain of lordships and castles in Comyn and Macdougall hands were the nobles of second rank, well-placed when the time came to profit from the massive re-distribution of lands which followed the collapse of these two families. The earls of Ross, though their principal castles and interests lay in the east, were lords of Applecross and exercised lordship in Skye and probably also in Lewis. The Murrays of Petty, with lands scattered across Moray from near Inverness to Boharm in Banffshire, were the leading family in a province which had no earl until 1312. Andrew Murray, the father of Wallace's colleague and grandfather of Andrew Murray of Bothwell the Guardian, was a man of sufficient standing to hold the office of Justiciar of Scotland north of Forth in the 1280s and 1290s. Farther east, the earl of Atholl was established through paternal inheritance in Stratha'an and Strathbogie, and beyond that again the earls of Mar held a potentially strong position in Strathdon and Strathdee, with castles at Kildrummy and Brae-mar. This earldom, however, had suffered dismemberment in the middle of the thirteenth century, and between 1290 and 1320 it was still further weakened by the early death of one earl and the long minority of another. In the Highlands between Dee and Tay there was no single dominant lord, for although the earls of Angus possessed large Highland estates they had none of the monopoly of lordship in Angus enjoyed by John Comyn in Buchan or by John of Strathbogie in Atholl. Three half-Highland earldoms stretched south-westward from Angus to the Firth of Clyde: Strathearn, Menteith and Lennox. The earls of all three figured prominently in the Anglo-Scottish war. Of the Menteith interest in the south-west Highlands we have seen something already. The earl of Strathearn's hostility to Bruce after Comyn's murder was serious but not fatal. The earl of Lennox's consistent support, on the other hand, almost certainly meant the difference between success and defeat for Bruce, indeed between life and death.

It remains for us to notice three West Highland families who rivalled the Macdougalls, and were ready and willing to profit by their fall: the Campbells, the Macdonalds and the Macruaries. The rise of the Campbells is the great success-story of the period. In 1286 the head of the family, Sir Colin Campbell, was a respectable landowner on Lochaweside, a baron of Argyll but not one of the great magnates of the realm. By the middle of Robert Bruce's reign, the Campbells had acquired most of Lorne and Benderloch, the earldom of Atholl and extensive lands in Kintyre. They were well on their way to becoming the great dominant power on the Argyllshire mainland, and most of this advance had been achieved at the expense of the Macdougalls of Lorne. Unlike the Campbells, the Macdonalds and Macruaries, being descended from Somerled, already occupied a leading place in West Highland society at the end of the thirteenth century, and in 1284 Angus Mor of Islay and Alan Macruarie ranked with Alexander Macdougall as magnates of the realm in the solemn acknowledgment of the Maid of Norway as heir to the throne. Yet the Macdonalds had much improved their position by the end of Robert I's reign. Angus Mor's eldest son, Alexander Macdonald, adhered to Balliol and lost his inheritance, but his two brothers, Donald of Islay and Angus Og, supported Bruce. Donald disappears from history about 1309, but Angus and his heirs were confirmed in possession of Islay, Morvern, Ardnamurchan and lands in Kintyre, and were given in addition the Comyn lordship of Lochaber and the Macdougall lordships of Mull, Coll and Tiree.

The Macruaries' history is less well-known, perhaps because they bequeathed to later generations no famous surname or numerous clan of descendants. Moreover, Alan Macruarie, who died before 1296, seems to have left only one lawful child, Christina, who married Duncan, son of Earl Donald of Mar. Christina of Mar, or Christina Macruarie, survived until well into the fourteenth century. There is no doubt that she is to be identified with the lady called by John Fordun Christiana of the Isles, to whose succour and protection Robert Bruce owed his survival in the winter of 1306–7. But Christina Macruarie, the lady of Garmoran—that is to say, of Moidart, Knoydart, the Small Isles, Barra, Uist and Harris—clearly did not exercise sole dominion over these widely scattered territories. It is not at all likely that at that period in the west men would have tolerated legitimacy of birth as the sole test of succession to lordship and property, especially when the legitimate heir was female. Christina herself might be a patriot; the attitude of her two bastard brothers, Lachlan and Ruairi, was decidedly ambiguous. A small dossier might be compiled to cover twelve years of Lachlan Macruarie's career. In 1296, in common with most of the principal freeholders of Scotland, he did homage and swore fealty to King Edward I.[2] Within a year he and his brother, Ruairi, attacked and slew the men of Alexander Macdonald of Islay loyal to King Edward, ravaged the Crown lands of Skye and Lewis, slaying men, violating women and (what perhaps seemed worst in the eyes of Alexander of Islay) burning galleys assigned to the royal naval service which had been placed for safety in ecclesiastical sanctuaries. The brothers were arrested by Alexander of Islay, but Lachlan escaped and took refuge in Lochaber under the protection of Macdougall of Lorne and Comyn of Badenoch. At Inverlochy they fitted out for war the two largest galleys in the isles, but eventually burned them to prevent them being used on behalf of the English. In 1299, however, when Robert Bruce and John Comyn were fierce rivals for the leadership of the community of the realm, Lachlan Macruarie allied himself with Alexander Comyn, the earl of Buchan's brother, and was reported to be ravaging the north and attacking the people of Scotland. By 1301 the Macruaries were reinforcing the pro-English fleet commanded by Hugh Bissett of the Glens lying off Bute and Kintyre. On 12 August 1306, at Ebchester in Co. Durham, Lachlan

---

[2] *Cal. Docs. Scot.*, ii, 209–10, 'Rouland fiz Aleyn MacRotherik, del counte de Inuernys'. Clerks of this period writing Anglo-French documents often had difficulty with the name Lachlan, and rendered it by some form of the more familiar name Rothland or Roland. Thus, unnoticed by historians of Clan Lachlan, Gillespie MacLachlan figures on the Ragman Roll as 'Gilascope fiz Rouland, del counte de Perth' (ibid., 209). Lachlan Macruarie's true patronymic was 'son of Alan', his clan name Macruarie, after Alan's father Ruarie or Roderick, son of Reginald, son of Somerled of Argyll (who died in 1164).

Macruarie of the Isles ('Loughlan Mac Lochery des Illes') petitioned King Edward in person to have the lands of Sir Patrick Graham. Our last, characteristic news of him comes early in 1308, in a letter to Edward II from the earl of Ross.

> We took the lands of the isles from our lord the king your father, on whom God have mercy. We assigned them to Lachlan Macruarie to answer to us for their revenues. Since he refuses, may it please you, dear lord, to command him to answer to us as justice requires. For we have answered to your chamberlain for the revenues of these lands. But Lachlan is such a high and mighty lord, he'll not answer to anyone except under great force or through fear of you.

It would be unfair to judge even Lachlan Macruarie, still more the class to which he belonged, by this brief one-sided dossier. King Robert was compelled to recognise the power of such men and the force of West Highland custom when he persuaded Christina Macruarie to share her inheritance with her nephew Reginald, son of her half-brother Ruairi Macruarie. These Hebridean chiefs had grown up without a tradition of strong royal government, for the kings of their fathers had resided across the seat at Bergen and when King Haakon came in 1263 it was 150 years too late. Feudalism cannot have been absolutely strange to them, and they accepted it, without recorded protest, at the hands of Alexander III and Robert I. They had not absorbed the sub-French culture of eastern and southern lords and gentry, nor could they share the Scots culture of east-country gentry, burghers and peasantry. But their masons built remarkable castles and their clerks wrote letters in passable and vigorous Latin. In 1296 Alexander Macdonald of Islay politely reminded King Edward I (of all men!) of a rule of law first enunciated by Glanvill. 'Many people say', he wrote, 'that no one ought to lose his inheritance unless he be impleaded by writ and named in the writ by his own name.' Given a continuously strong monarchy, given an Ireland closed to foreign interference, there is little to suggest that the political future of west highland lords would have differed in any marked degree from that of lowland families—Stewarts and Douglases, Erskines, Boyds, Livingstones and the rest. Despite the long war with England, the Scottish Crown cannot be charged with neglecting the Highlands between the Treaty of Perth in 1266 and the death of Robert I in 1329. When Alexander III crushed the Manx revolt in 1275 Alexander Macdougall of Lorne and Alan Macruarie were among the leaders of his fleet of ninety ships. In 1284 they joined in recognising the Maid of Norway, and about this time Alexander Macdougall seems to have been entrusted by the king with a lieutenancy over most of the West Highlands and islands. In 1293 John Balliol's first parliament saw the promulgation of an Ordinance which resembled Edward I's Statute of Wales. If the war had not prevented its enforcement the Ordinance would have given the west three new sheriffdoms, (1) Skye under the earl of Ross, consisting of Wester Ross, Glenelg, Skye, Lewis, Uist, Barra, Eigg, Rum and the little isles; (2) Lorne under Alexander Macdougall, consisting of all the districts which are comprised in modern Argyllshire save for lower Cowal and Kintyre; and (3) Kintyre under the Stewart, consisting of Kintyre, lower Cowal, Arran and Bute. Out of the wreck of this sensible scheme something at least was salvaged by Robert I, but possibly at the expense of royal authority. Between 1315 and 1325 a new sheriffdom of Argyll was created, ending the absurdity of administering Mull or Loch Fyne from Perth. Tarbert became a burgh with a royal castle and enjoyed a remarkable prosperity. In the north, instead of sheriffdoms, King Robert deliberately built up the power of two trusted adherents. Thomas Randolph was made earl of Moray in 1312 and his earldom, with regalian powers, consisted of the sheriffdoms of Moray, Nairn and mainland Inverness-shire. The earl of Ross enjoyed almost as powerful a position in what until recently was Ross and Cromarty, and also in Skye. As long as King Robert was alive this scheme worked well, and was associated with a general policy of feudalising the West Highlands to bring this region into line with the rest of Scotland. In later times the history of Scotland was to take a course which both engendered and aggravated a schism between Highlands and Lowlands, but if we search for the beginnings of that schism as early as the turn of the thirteenth and fourteenth centuries, we search in vain.

Index

Abbotrule, Roxburghshire, 181
Abbotsford, Roxburghshire, 208
Abel, bishop of St. Andrews (formerly
   Mr. Abel of Gullane), 227–9
Aberchalder: *see* Cawdor
Aberchirder, Banffshire, 58
Abercorn, W. Lothian, 149
Aberdeen, 58, 59, 100, 113, 370
Aberdeenshire, 112
Aberdour, Aberdeenshire, 65–6
Aberdour, Fife, 302
Aberkarf (in Cromdale?), Moray, 58
Aberlady, E. Lothian, 154
Aberlemno, Angus, 58
Aberlosk, Dumfries-shire, 58n.
Aberlour (Skirdustan), Banffshire, 54,
   58
Aberluthnot (Marykirk), Mearns, 58
Abernaftathar, Angus, 77
Abernethy, Inverness-shire, 369
Abernethy, Perthshire, 37, 190, 307–8
Abernethy, Hugh of, 119
Abernethy, Laurence of, 302
Abertarff, Inverness-shire, 376
Abriachan, Inverness-shire, 365
Ada, countess of Northumberland, 302,
   308, 328
Adam (of Kilconquhar), earl of Carrick,
   98, 128
Adam, *judex* (Angus), 76
Adam, son of Abraham, *judex*
Adam, son of Gilbert, 348
Adam, steward of Arbroath Abbey, 82
Addeville, Manche, 334
Adeville, Humphrey de, 334
Adeville, Theobald de, 333–4; *see also*
   Berkeley, Humphrey of
Æbba, Saint, of Coldingham, 32
Aedan, Saint, 67
Æthelthryth, Queen, 32
Agnew, family of, 326

agrarian land units (ploughgate, davoch,
   arachor, acre, oxgang), 264–77
   passim
Aigneus, William des, 326
Ailred (Saint), of Rievaulx (d. 1169), 37,
   47, 180, 262–3, 280
Ailward (in Tottenham), 10
Airdrie, Fife, 263
Airthrey, Stirlingshire, 38n.
Alan, earl of Menteith, 373
Alan, son of Elsi, 297–9
Alan, son of Fla(h)ald, 326
Albany (Scotland north of Forth), 155,
   202, 364
Alberic, papal legate, 180, 182
Aldborough, Yorkshire, 25
Aldgate, London, priory of Holy Trinity
   of, 177
Aldred (in Tottenham), 10
Aldwin (in Tottenham), 10
Aldwin of Winchcombe, 166
Alexander I, king of Scots (1107–24), 38,
   72, 147–8, 169–72, 193–4, 196, 211,
   226, 280, 320
Alexander II, king of Scots (1214–49), 37,
   82, 90–1, 97, 106, 111, 112, 113, 118,
   127, 139, 217, 240n., 283, 301, 304,
   335
Alexander III, king of Scots (1249–86),
   91, 97, 107, 133, 134, 209, 217, 218,
   235, 301, 335, 364, 382, 383
Alexander III, pope (1159–81), 136n.,
   209
Alexander IV, pope, 217
Aleyn (Aleynson), Robert, 15
Alness, Ross-shire:
   davochs in, 269
Alnwick, Northumberland, 287, 288
Alvie (Skeir Alloway), Inverness-shire,
   54, 369
Alwin, abbot of Holyrood, 178–9